RICHER BY ASIA

RICHER
BY ASIA

EDMOND TAYLOR

SECOND EDITION

1964

HOUGHTON MIFFLIN COMPANY

BOSTON · The Riverside Press Cambridge

To my friends and colleagues of Nandana
with whom I shared the most basic and
important of all these adventures

Acknowledgments

I AM INDEBTED to Doctor James Alexander Hamilton of San Francisco for encouragement and advice in writing this book, for constructive criticism of the manuscript, and above all for clarifying from the psychiatric point of view the theory of institutional delusion which I have developed in it.

A less direct but no less great debt is owed to Doctors Gregory Bateson and Margaret Mead of New York, particularly the former, who was one of my wartime colleagues in Southeast Asia. Many, if not most, of the viewpoints on cultural problems expressed in the book were influenced in some way — when they were not suggested — by conversations with Bateson. Since, however, opportunity did not arise for me to discuss the Ms., or any part of it, with Doctors Bateson and Mead, whatever sociological and anthropological heresies the book contains must be considered — like the political and cultural ones — entirely my own. As I have pointed out at various points in the text, my book is a personal history and is not intended to be any kind of scientific work. For this reason it contains no bibliography, but because they contributed so greatly to clarifying my ideas and to supplying perspective on either the cultural or the political problems discussed, three books deserve special mention: *The Discovery of India*, by Jawaharlal Nehru (John Day, 1946); *The Psychological Frontiers of Society*, by Abram Kardiner and associates (Columbia University Press, 1945); *The Anatomy of Peace*, by Emery Reves (Harper and Brothers, 1945).

I owe a special debt for encouragement and constructive criticism, surpassing the normal editorial contribution in the making of a book, to Lovell Thompson and Paul Brooks of Houghton Mifflin Company. Most indirectly, yet most fundamentally, I owe a great debt to Major General William J. Donovan, who not only made possible the travels and adventures recorded in this book, but demonstrated to me, as to hundreds of others, how leadership can lead men to surpass themselves in the duties of war, thus suggesting that they are equally capable of surpassing themselves in solving the problems of peace.

Preface to the Second Edition

IT IS NEARLY TWENTY YEARS since I wrote the original edition of *Richer by Asia*. In these years numerous changes have occurred both in the world situation and in the writer's outlook on it. The area with which my book is primarily concerned — Southern and Southeastern Asia — is among those that have changed the most. The disappearance of European colonial rule in this region has solved some of the problems I wrote about — and given rise to others. The triumph of Communism in China has radically altered the strategic picture in much of Asia, while the power struggle between the Western democracies and the Communist bloc that was just starting as I was finishing my book has even more radically altered the political climate in the world at large. It has led, among other things, to the frustration of the United Nations, not to mention its blighting impact on the bolder — or dreamier — projects for world government that were current in the 1940's. Thus, many of the hopes — and perhaps certain of the fears — voiced in my book have since vanished, or at least have become for the time being irrelevant and unreal.

In a limited number of cases I have accordingly effected deletions or other modifications in the original text to bring it into harmony with the political and psychological realities of 1963–64. Occasionally I have allowed myself to be inhibited in making a seemingly logical revision by the thought: Suppose the reality of 1983 — or even that of 1970 — proves closer to that of 1946 than to that of 1963? (This is not, perhaps, a very serious hope but it certainly is not an absurd one in view of the slight but definite improvement in the international atmosphere that has taken place since Stalin's death.) My book, moreover, does not deal only with hopes, realized, or unrealized; it is, if anything, more concerned with the problems of international anarchy and of political delusion, and who can say these problems are less topical today than they were in 1946? The dream of world government seems a great deal wilder now than it did then, but the need for specified limitations or delegations of national sovereignty for such purposes as the international inspection of nuclear stockpiles and missile sites is so much more evident that it does not seem wildly unrealistic to hope that it may yet be met before it is too late.

No doubt if *Richer by Asia* had been primarily an objective study of Asian and world problems, I would have felt obliged to revise it far more drastically than I have. A large part of the book, however, is essentially subjective, even autobiographical. It is much less about Asia than about the impact of Asia on one Western mind, and therefore it is part, however humble a part, of Western social or cultural history; in many places it could not be altered without falsifying its testimony. In the same way, it is the story of the gradual awakening of one contemporary mind to consciousness of the greatest of all contemporary problems; thus it is part of the record, at the molecular level, of a generation's strivings to grow up. To preserve this aspect of the book — the most significant one, in my opinion — I have sometimes found it necessary to leave untouched what today may seem naïvetés of judgment or expression, without counting a few straightforward bad guesses. Counterbalancing these defects, at least to some extent, the reader will note for himself a certain number of findings or evaluations not generally accepted at the time the book first appeared that have since been upheld or pointed up by events. Of all these validated conclusions the most basic and perhaps still the most timely remains the one implicit in my title. Asia has much to offer us besides its problems, but even if it had nothing else, the growing Asian presence and participation in world affairs since the end of the colonial era would be an enrichment for the West. For in discovering the problems of Asia, as we have been forced to do, we have enlarged our awareness of the problems of man. This was true twenty years ago when I began the personal exploration of Asia's problems here recorded, and as the reader can verify from his own experience if he cares to, it is true today.

EDMOND TAYLOR

Contents

xv

PART I

Prelude to Discovery

I

Our Tribe is Man

THIS IS A BOOK of curious travels and discoveries and adventures in the mind.

The travels narrated in it took place in India and the countries of southeastern Asia during the war but they are less an exploration of Asia — or of war — than a use of them as catalysts of understanding. The discoveries and the mental adventures relate as much to the West as to the East, more to peace than to war. Primarily, they are discoveries and adventures in participation, participation in the unity of mankind, and, as such, they bear, though sometimes indirectly, upon the central problem of our time: The founding of a planetary commonwealth to achieve lasting peace upon our planet, Earth, before its inhabitants succeed in disintegrating it.

Many political solutions to this problem have been proposed, all tending to the ultimate goal of world government, but the psychological and cultural aspects of the problem as they concern the individual have so far received little attention. My book involves an informal, unsystematic, and highly personal exploration of this neglected field. It is the story of a rather casual attempt, during a wartime assignment which lasted twenty-eight months, to understand some of the problems of Asia and of how this attempt gradually, and at first unconsciously, turned into a pilgrimage in search of the psychological reality beneath the verbal formula: We are all members of the tribe of man.

3

It seems to me very important that we should be able to feel, as well as to say, that we are all members of the tribe of man, because unless we have this feeling there can be no effective government of man. No political institutions, however skillfully contrived, have ever proved lasting except when they became part of the cultural heritage of the people who adopted them or upon whom they were imposed. World government, to be lasting, to be effective, must become part of the cultural heritage of all the peoples of the earth, must become one of the tribal institutions of man.

This is very easy to say. The difficulty is that, since there are at present no tribal institutions of man, there is no tribal spirit. The tribe of man does not exist, except in our minds — and in biology. There is no psychological or cultural foundation for a world-commonwealth, except the belief, or hope, in our minds that man is potentially capable of unity, that the divisions between the present tribes of man are of a lesser order of divisiveness than those which render impossible the political union of whale and pheasant, of wolf and bear, and even of stag and stag.

Is the hope that man is at least potentially capable of unity an illusion or a reality? All those who believe in the feasibility of world government, all who reject the suicide of man, must consider it a reality, but if they are honest with themselves they will admit that it is only a subjective reality, unconfirmed by objective evidence. It is the kind of hypothesis which can be proved by putting it to the test, but, short of that, can only be supported by analogy. It is the direct analogy, the analogy of success, with which we usually seek to bolster our faith, and perhaps it is the most convincing. That some men, previously disunited, have achieved union certainly entitles us to advance the argument that man is capable of unity. That tribal wars have been banished from some parts of the earth suggests that they can be banished everywhere.

On the other hand the history of our species is strewn with examples of the triumph of violence over peace, of madness over reason, of disunity over unity, which at times appear to us as inexorable markers along the foredoomed path of planetary suicide. Even the great American commonwealth, the most power-ful single argument for the principle of world federation, is not a final argument. This union has split apart once in its history on the issues of states' rights and slavery who can say that it will never be sundered again, that the social hatreds and fears, the conflicting greeds and jealousies, which it contains, are forever held in check?

In refuting the determinism of doom, in the rebuttal of doubt, the indirect analogy, the analogy of failure, has its place. When-ever reason can be found at the roots of human irrationality, whenever delusion can be discovered in the causes of conflict; whenever the barriers which divide mankind can be proved ephemeral, the sources of aggression accidental, the factors of madness external; whenever human error and failure can be traced to anything less irremediable than an instinct of doom in human nature, then hope is strengthened or revived. Sometimes the most pathological manifestations of humanity are the most re-assuring because they reveal so clearly the inevitable effects of remediable causes. Where the documenting of man's hope is im-possible, a critique of the ideologies of despair can be useful. When the light fails there are lessons to be learned from darkness.

For this reason, if for no other, a close study of the problems of Asia is indispensable to an understanding of the problem of world-peace and world-unity. From a political and social point of view Asia — and above all, India — has long been the fatherland of darkness, of darkness superimposed upon darkness. It is the pathological museum of modern society where every form of human oppression, every aberration of human reason, every ideology of disunity is placed on exhibit. Whatever demonstra-tion of the seemingly incurable separatism of man the Asiatic mind has failed to produce, the Western mind has supplied in the institutions of imperialism. The Moslems and the Hindus of India did their best for many years to prove that a cow is a good enough reason to start a civil war. The British, French, and Dutch who ruled southern Asia for its own good for two hundred years have repeatedly demonstrated Kipling's dictum that, east of Suez, the best is like the worst. The Americans and British during the war in Asia established that the need for saving the world from certain slavery was not enough to prevent the two most like-minded great powers on earth from spending more energy in bickering among themselves than in fighting the common enemy.

A wartime pilgrimage in Asia in search of the spiritual unity of man was of necessity a journey to the end of night. Some of the stages of this pilgrimage which I have attempted to retrace in my book may have today a more direct relevancy to the central problem of man than I originally perceived, may supply a more striking *reductio ad absurdum* to the doctrines of despair than I ever imagined. Certain Asiatic problems which interested me precisely because it seemed possible to say of them that if they could be solved, then there is no problem of man which cannot be solved, may today be very near a solution.

For example, when I left Southeast Asia at the end of January, 1946, I was convinced that the ultimate independence of India was a foregone conclusion in the sense that it would be impossible for England to continue ruling India against the will of the Indian people. As far as I could discover, most of the British recognized this inevitability and were more or less resigned to it. I knew that certain British government services, in anticipation of the total Indianization of the Government of India, were beginning to burn their secret files, the more malodorous archives of imperialism. This meant that the imperialist mind had turned defeatist, not that it had reformed, and I was inclined to fear that the final British withdrawal from India would be a stubborn military and political delaying action.

Up to the time of my departure from India nothing that I had learned about the imperialist mentality suggested that it was capable of attaining the heights of constructive statesmanship reflected in the proposals for the solution of the Indian problem released by the special British cabinet committee in May, 1946. Anyone can read between the lines of this remarkable document the deep political wisdom, the lofty purpose, and the evident sincerity which make it one of the great state papers of our day. Only someone who has seen the workings of British imperialism at first hand could realize what a tremendous victory over the imperialist mentality it represented and how important that victory was likely to prove not only for India but for Britain and for the whole world.

Asia as a study in the psychopathology of social defeatism, Asia as the school of doubt in which one learns faith in man — that is the context of many of the travels and adventures related in this book.

Others have a context even more directly related to the central problem of one world because they involve the cultural implications of this concept. The idea of world government in its modern form is a product of Western, particularly American, culture. That we are capable of developing, even in the abstract, a conception of the political unity of man, suggests that our culture contains at least some of the elements of a universal culture, that it is based upon premises which are valid, not just for ourselves, but for all men.

Certain questions arise, however. Is Western culture a sufficiently broad basis for the one-world concept? Does it permit or encourage among its members attitudes toward power and violence which implicitly contradict its universalism? Can it provide an emotional as well as an intellectual understanding of the oneness of man? Is it capable of communicating enough of its universalist values to members of other tribal cultures — and of assimilating from them enough of their universalist values — to lay the psychological foundations of a world-community?

These are important questions because if the answers to some or all of them are negative, then we can understand why we are making such dishearteningly slow progress toward the ideal of world government which all the enlightened minds of the age recognize is the only thing that can save us from destruction If the Western mind which conceived the idea of world government is incapable, by itself, of implementing the idea, then we are only exhausting ourselves by tugging at our own bootstraps and we would do better to enlist the assistance of some other minds.

My travels in Asia did convince me that the Western mind is incapable, without outside aid, of implementing its own best ideals. Perhaps even more important than the cultural elements which Asia can contribute to the foundations of a world community is the understanding of ourselves, of our own weaknesses and self-betrayals, as well as our strengths, which the contrast between our culture and the cultures of Asia brings to light. This contrast is the central theme of certain chapters of my book and is implicit, to some degree, in all of them.

The thread which knits all these political, social, and cultural themes together is one of personal experience, or personal realization, for this book is primarily the story of the growth of a mind. The adventures it relates are all, in final analysis, adventures in self-understanding. Just as it is impossible to understand the world of politics without some knowledge of the laws of individual psychology, so is it impossible for the individual to understand himself without some knowledge of the political, economic, and social forces which mold our personal lives.

Whether we realize it or not we are all actors in the great drama of our day, the drama of the integration or the disintegration of man. This drama is being acted out not only upon the global stage but upon the private stages of our minds. The development of mass media of communication, the attendant intensification of propaganda, the preoccupation of the individual with public questions, his growing tendency to become involved in collective issues and to identify himself with collective causes — all these factors have revolutionized the emotional life of man. Individual psychology is no longer capable of providing a full explanation of man because the individual psyche is influenced by too many factors external to the individual.

Today the path of self-understanding which all the sages have taught was the way to inner peace, which the psychiatrists have discovered is the key to psychic health, does not end at the foot of the Boh tree nor at the analyst's couch. It winds through the battlefields, the propaganda services and the council-chambers of the world, it explores the group-antagonisms which poison our individual minds, which fill us with nightmares of personal insecurity, it leads into the prison camps of race and caste and cultural prejudice in which we segregate ourselves from our brothers.

As I found for myself in Asia, the study of the causes of man's disunity becomes an adventure of the mind and a discipline of self-knowledge when it is used to discover the roots of disunity in ourselves, to lay bare the resistances, the hesitations, and the contradictions hidden beneath our own verbalizations of the ideal of human unity.

Such discoveries are sometimes painful but they have a peculiar liberating effect and tend to make the discoverer feel at peace with the earth upon which he walks and with the other living creatures who walk with him, to feel that this planet upon which he dwells is his home, the home of man, and that he himself is at last a member of the tribe of man. This feeling is, of course, a purely personal acquisition, yet it is a useful feeling to have because if we have it strongly enough we may find the strength to solve the problems of realizing one world, while if we try to solve them without it, the result is very likely to be no world at all.

Because the adventures related in this book are adventures of the mind, they take the form that mental adventures always take — embarking upon quests after meaning, seeing new shores of thought, getting shipwrecked and discovering desert islands. Some of the desert islands turn out to be thoroughly charted and others may be mirages, or at best, speculations. The reader will have to decide for himself. He is less likely to be disappointed if he bears in mind that, because it is a personal narrative, this book cannot be the systematic development of an idea or the orderly exploration of a subject. It is a journey toward a goal, and that goal is not a formula for achieving one world but a formula for living in a world that has not yet made up its mind whether it will be one or none. It is not a philosophy of man but a philosophy of our participation in mankind.

Perhaps my whole aim could be expressed most simply by saying that the book records the stages of an attempt to realize one world in one mind, not merely a political and geographical one world, but a felt unity of human experience.

One óf the methods employed in this attempt is an elaboration of a technique I used freely in my earlier *Strategy of Terror*, that of self-analysis after exposure to public influence, of regarding one's own mind as an instrument from which one can take readings of other men's uncommunicated thought. This use of introspection as a tool of objective discovery is unscientific in the sense of being unreliable and would be antiscientific were it not for certain underlying similarities in the psychic processes of all men.

Thanks to the common denominator in human experience, it was possible for me in my earlier book not only to give a fairly complete and accurate description of modern psychological warfare methods, which are relatively accessible to direct observation, without always knowing how I knew them, but even to penetrate in some degree the minds of the modern witch-doctors who practice these methods, without having ever knowingly been intimate with one. Later in the war when I became a witch-doctor myself I was startled to discover how deep and nearly accurate had been my insight into this strange, closed world. The explanation was neither accident nor telepathy. It was simply that before becoming one hundred percent witch-doctor I had been perhaps five percent witch-doctor, as most humans are some percent witch-doctor, and all I needed to understand their minds was to know in which part of my own to look.

In a similar manner, when I was in Algiers in 1943, I 'discovered' the assassination of Admiral Darlan more than a week before it took place, and felt so confident of my discovery that I informed my superiors (no believers in psychology, among other things). I was neither in the confidence of the assassins nor did I read their minds, but I was in close personal contact with them and the assassin in my own mind recognized in the furtive steeliness which came into their eyes and their voices the tensing for a kill.

It is the principle of finding a strayed horse by thinking where you would go if you were a horse, and then going there. Whether or not there is enough of the horse in every man to render this technique generally valuable in animal husbandry, there is enough of the human in every man to make it a legitimate intellectual scouting-device when used circumspectly within the limits of a well-defined cultural group.

In this book I have sometimes deliberately exceeded the legitimate, as every adventurer must. I have tried to leap across barriers of race and time and circumstance. I have tried to think in the thought-channels of alien cultures and men long dead. I have assumed in reaching certain conclusions that my mind was some percent Asiatic as well as some percent witch-doctor and assassin, that it contained fractional Hinduisms and Buddhisms, as well as fractional fascisms and imperialisms, that one world necessitated using my fractional Hinduism to understand India as it necessitated using my fractional fascism to fight fascism.

These are bold assumptions, and in employing them as tools of thought I realized that I must expect more misses than hits. I have chosen to accept this risk because it seemed to me that if I scored any hits at all, this in itself would be a strong indication that the barriers of culture and history are less formidable than we think, that man does not communicate with man through spoken language alone, and that one world is a psychological reality whether it be a political one or not.

II

The Absence of Asia

BEFORE I WENT to the East I had wandered for many years upon this planet and I thought of myself as a man of the world, chiefly in the sense of being a man of one world. I did not like to call myself an internationalist because I believed so little in nations — united or otherwise — but I believed in a great community of peoples and felt that I was a very civilized man because I included all peoples in my community, great peoples and small peoples, white peoples and black or brown peoples, and wanted all of them to enjoy at least the four minimal freedoms.

I thought that I had no cultural prejudices and a rather praiseworthy eclecticism, befitting a man of the world, in my appreciation of the cultural contributions of other peoples. I liked Soviet art, Chinese cooking, African sculpture; I felt I would have been able to appreciate an Annamite mistress as well as would a Frenchman, and I believed firmly that the Indians should have a self-governing commonwealth — or even an independent republic if they felt that strongly about it.

This was in 1943. At the time the Japanese had the best Chinese cooks and the prettiest Annamite mistresses, and the Indians, I felt, were unreasonably obstructing the war effort of the United Nations. Not only were they refusing to co-operate with the British, but the 'Quit India' campaign launched by Gandhi a few months earlier was equally directed against the American forces stationed in India. It was the sort of thing one might expect from Gandhi but I felt really annoyed at Nehru, a reason-

12

able man, a thoroughly modern and westernized Indian, an anti-fascist who had understood that to fight fascism in India you had to fight it in Spain, too. Why could not Nehru see now that he was helping Hitler by hampering the Anglo-American military effort in Southeast Asia? It seemed clear enough to me. Of course, the war against Hitler was all that interested me and Asia was only important in so far as it had a bearing on that war.

Asia meant mostly China to me in those days and, except for the cooking, I felt that Lin Yutang and Pearl Buck were adequate to supply as much China as my system needed. Of the five hundred million humans who live in the lands to the south of China I thought very little, and when I did think of them and of their lands it was purely as geopolitical factors. Sometimes I had to write military papers about those lands so I had to know something of the factors, and I knew them well enough, considering that I was not supposed to be an expert. Gandhi, of course, was a factor, but I thought of him chiefly as a political *swami* who drank goat's milk.

On the political side, I knew something of the nationalist movements in India and the countries of Southeast Asia. They seemed to me matters which, in normal times, a liberal man, a man of the world, should study; not causes to be espoused but problems to be examined with sympathy on the principle that examining with sympathy makes for a better world.

Of the arts — from architecture to music — of southern Asia I knew only enough to know that I did not care for them. I could not see any relation to modern — i.e., Western — art.

The two great religions of Southern Asia — Hinduism and Buddhism — I knew had some relation to modern life. They were responsible for theosophy and Schopenhauer and many other horrors.

In regard to Asiatic history, I did not consider myself an authority but I felt I knew enough to assert positively that there was no such thing, certainly no ancient history and the only meaningful pattern I could detect in modern Asiatic history was that the nineteenth century seemed to be moving east.

This is what I, a man of the world, a very civilized man without prejudices, a journalist, and supposedly an expert on foreign af·fairs, felt about Asia and the war in Asia in 1943. I felt that way and most of my American friends at the time felt the same way. A few of them, it is true, took some intelligent interest in the af·fairs of Asia, especially of China, but as far as I was concerned they were incapable of communicating, or even justifying their, interest. With my strong European bias I was inclined to feel that an interest in the East was not only eccentric, but intel·lectually not quite respectable. It suggested a secret inclination toward theosophy or at best a puerile exoticism *à la* Loti.

When it finally was decided — late in, 1943 — that I myself was to go to the East, my wife and many of my friends were almost horrified, less, I suspected, at the apparent misemploy·ment of competences which might have been of value on one of the European fronts than at the sheer loss of face in allowing my·self to be shunted to a secondary and so unfashionable theater of war. I had no enthusiasm myself for wartime service in a theater that I knew to have only a slight bearing on the outcome of the war and in part of the world which had never interested me in peacetime, but I was desperately anxious to escape from Wash·ington and I feared that the political implications of some of my activities in North Africa in 1942 would disqualify me in the eyes of my superiors for another European assignment, at least in the immediate future. Consequently, when the opportunity pre·sented itself to accompany Lieutenant General (then Major General) Albert C. Wedemeyer to New Delhi as part of the Amer·ican contingent of the newly created Southeast Asia Command (SEAC) under Admiral Lord Louis Mountbatten, I seized it. Actually I was rather pleased at the prospect of this Asiatic exile — provided it did not last too long — not because of the oppor·tunities it offered for learning something about Asia but because I hoped to contribute at my modest level to reducing the inter·Allied frictions which had already assumed serious proportions in that area. In those days it appeared to me that Anglo-Ameri·can misunderstandings were the greatest threat to winning the

war and winning the peace that would follow victory, and it seemed intolerable that any petty Asiatic problems should be allowed to generate such misunderstandings.

That these petty problems of Asia had any importance in themselves, that chaos in Asia might be even more serious for the world than chaos in Anglo-American relationships, did not occur to me. It was not that I was emotionally an ardent Anglophile — I had lived too long in France for that — but Anglo-American co-operation seemed to me the cornerstone of the future world-republic and I hoped that out of the wartime partnership of the two English-speaking communities would grow a political union which in turn would prove to be the nucleus of a world-commonwealth. It was not quite clear to me just how Soviet Russia fitted into this dream, and as for Asia, if anyone had pointed out to me that more than half the human beings who inhabit this planet are Asiatics and that it is somewhat impractical to think of a world-commonwealth without taking them into account, I would doubtless have replied:

'The problem of achieving union among the democracies of the West is already complicated enough as it is; we cannot afford to pile a lot of Asiatic complications on top of those that exist in the West.'

The truth is that I, like most other Westerners, simply had no awareness of the East and was unconsciously steeped in an Occidental insularity as fantastic in its way as that of a British general I once encountered in Bangkok who was overcome at the discovery that 'hardly any of these Siamese blighters speak English.'

III

The Art of Awareness

THE FIRST MORNING I awoke in India was an awakening of mingled panic and enchantment. For a long time I could not remember where I was, or why I was anywhere. Had we finally gone to bed in Khartoum instead of getting back into the plane? Was I still back in Washington, waking from a long dream of flying? Wherever it was, there was something uneasy, something unpleasant . . . did I have to go somewhere? No, it was the other way around, I wanted to go somewhere, and I could not. I must stay here. But where was here?

I opened my eyes and saw that I was lying on some sort of a cot from which the mosquito-net had been pulled back, and that I had no blanket or sheet over me. I should feel cold, I thought, but I was not cold. I was more deliciously at ease than I had ever felt in my life and the cool air I was taking into my lungs was like no air that I had ever breathed before. It was at once soothing and tonic, bland and vigorous, an air that was like some noble nourishment, distilled to rarity.

I raised my head a little and saw a squatting, turbaned figure polishing some shoes; a few feet from his head, a medium-sized black bird like a raven was hopping about on a table. I studied the bird with calm wonder for awhile, thinking, in this country they have ravens of morning. Then the bird flapped out of the window on indolent wings, and the turbaned man said something I did not understand and went out of the room and I realized that I was waking in India.

Now I looked curiously about the room, which was immensely large with polished marble floors like a room in a palace. There were three other cots like mine in it, pieces of uniforms hanging here and there, three studio portraits of women, a few toilet articles, bottles, pipes, and other things that belong to men. On one table there was a disorderly heap of the little bright paper-backed books issued by the Army Special Services Branch.

In the great, bare room these personal belongings of men looked pathetically lost and impersonal. The littered tables and dressers, which would have seemed so human in another context, were depressingly sordid against the background of the shining floor and the whitewashed walls. In this room, I realized with a chilled, trapped feeling, men led lives of loneliness and squalor, equally remote from war and peace, equally lacking in privacy and companionship, in dignity and in homeliness. Neither the breezy fraternity-house atmosphere of junior officers' quarters nor the boarding-school solidarity of the enlisted men's barracks were reflected in this room. It was a place where staff officers of high rank could let themselves go to seed after working hours in the company of their peers.

I remembered now that I was in the Imperial Hotel of New Delhi, which had been taken over as the senior American officers' mess; I was trying to recall the impression that my room-mates had made on me when I met them the day before, when the bearer returned and placed alongside my bed a tray with tea, buttered bread, a banana, and some gaudy fruit I had never seen before.

'Eight o'clock, sahib,' he said.

It was a shock to hear myself called 'sahib.' I had always thought of sahibs as Englishmen in sun-helmets, and it made me a little uneasy somehow to think that I, too, was now a sahib, just as this splendid sordid palace in which I found myself billeted made me uneasy.

Indirectly, the Imperial Hotel played a big part in awakening my interest in Asia. Within a few days after my arrival, I began to keep a casual, disconnected diary, or rather collection of ob-

servations and comments on life in India, which filled up a good deal of my spare time. It was not that I had any idea of eventually writing a book about Asia, the subject seemed more tiresome to me than it had in Washington.

I was driven to these exercises of observation and analysis by a consideration of psychological hygiene, by loneliness and boredom and discouragement and the determination not to let myself become like the lonely, bored, and disoriented old men, the withering male spinsters whom I used to see in the early evening, sprawling flaccidly in their underwear with a gin sling in hand, snarling at their bearers, cursing the country, the war, the British, the Indians, their cronies and themselves in the bedrooms of the Imperial Hotel.

The Imperial Hotel was a wartime manifestation of the White Man's Asia which deserved study as a cultural curiosity, but it was a depressing introduction to the East and I was glad when after a few days I was moved to a tent-camp which had been set up near the Vice-Regal Lodge for both British and American officers of the Southeast Asia Command. There at least I could lie alone at night in my tent, on my *charpoy* of criss-crossed rope under the mosquito net which the chill nights would soon render unnecessary, listening to the mad cries of the jackals and thinking of how I might set about to create for myself a spiritual habitation in this human wilderness of Asia which was half-desert and half-prison.

Everything is unfamiliar and without meaning, I thought. All these British and all these Americans are exiles living in the past, living their real lives thousands of miles away. There is a wall between them and the natives thicker than the wall of any prison, they can't even whisper through it. What is there for them to say to each other? Surely there must be some solution, surely somewhere in this desert, if one only knows where to look, there must be hidden springs that can keep alive the spirit.

I think the first clue came to me the night my bearer finally took down the mosquito-net, saying, 'Winter now, sahib, mosquitoes all gone.'

I felt quite lost. I had liked sleeping under the net, I suddenly realized, and I wondered why. Partly it was a question of local color, but there was more than that. I had been carefully indoctrinated in tropical hygiene before my departure and out here in the theater there were posters enough, and booklets and even match-covers to remind me of the significance of the mosquitonet. More than once, tucking myself in at night, I had reflected upon the drama implicit in this humble routine, a drama with definite, even official, social significance, for malaria prophylaxis was a military duty as well as a personal precaution. At least theoretically, an officer who tucked himself into bed carelessly, without making sure that the folds of his net were tightly closed, was liable to court-martial. Moreover, the drama had a touch of irony in it, I thought, remembering other aspects of my medical indoctrination. The wayward GI, sprawled in drunken sleep beside a native prostitute in some off-limits alleyway of the Old Delhi, was hardly exposed to more drastic natural penalties for his forgetfulness than I in my chaste, but perhaps clumsily enclosed bed.

More than ever that night I realized how far the slender strands of my net reached, how intricately they were enmeshed both with the spirit and with the flesh. This gauzy fabric, woven by indifferent hands, this net, mosquito, one each, which the quartermaster had given me in exchange for my signature on a piece of paper, was a perpetual monument to Western thought, to the giants and the martyrs of Western science, to the marvelous chain of discovered causes and contrived effects which had surrounded us in the West with an armory of implements for living so numerous, so complex, so excessively admirable that they had gradually paralyzed our capacity to apprehend, and so turned our homes and our cities into a wilderness of gadgets, not really so different in its effect on the spirit from my wilderness of Asia.

Conversely, it came to me (in what I now recognized was a waking dream) that my net was also another kind of monument to the wilderness of Asia, and to all wildernesses, a *memento mori* (and a *memento vitae*) reminding man of his ambiguous niche in the hierarchy of living creatures: The nemesis of all large beasts — including himself — the prey of everything most small. Even at home, even in peace, life was not what it seemed to be — an effortless state of being, a smooth gliding over a firm surface, interrupted from time to time by physiological or other accidents. Rather, life was a kind of unconscious *tour de force*, a mastery of conflicting forces whose tensions support us as the hydraulic tensions support the swimmer who knows how to use them, even without knowing that he knows. Everywhere, at all times, in the jungles of the East and the cities of the West, man's world was a battle-field. Invisible hosts — of which the micro-organisms and viruses known to science were probably only one element — constantly assailed him; other invisible hosts, some known, many unknown, mobilized to defend him. Man himself joined hands with man for common defense, in the process multiplying his protections and his vulnerabilities. His cities — in the West — became hygienic fortresses, relatively impervious to external attack as long as the garrison remained vigilant, but terribly exposed to any break-down in the perfect functioning of their centralized food and water supply, their sewage systems, and their whole machinery of epidemic detection and control.

Here in the East the battle seemed fiercer and more dramatic because it was more evident and more a war of movement. The inoculations, the rigorous food and water discipline imposed on us, the daily atabrine in the heavily malarial areas, and the sleeping-nets and nocturnal repellant nearly everywhere, were all symbols reminding us that we were outside the fortress, living behind improvised field defenses in the midst of the enemy. Beyond the perimeters of our mosquito-nets, our camp latrines, and our policed kitchens lurked the malignant, invisible hosts of the plagues of Asia: Malaria, which the army in its health-propaganda constantly represented as more dangerous than the Jap; dysenteries which tore bloody holes in your intestines and went on tearing them for years; smallpox of medieval virulence; loathsome skin diseases, venereal infections capable of eating away the genitalia like acid in a few days, and the ultimate horror of cholera.

All of these terrors, we were told over and over again, were linked with the native. They lurked in the food from his kitchens, the water from his wells; in the bodies — and even on the bodies — of his women, in the lice from his clothes when he brushed against you, in the spittle-stained dust of his bazaars, in the clouds of mosquitoes that swarmed around his villages. Thus we were initiated from the moment of our arrival into an essential article of the white man's folklore of Asia. This nightmare of lurking menace, which white men in the East have always had, this fear, purely bacteriological at the beginning but gradually assuming an unconscious sexual connotation of contagion through contact with the native, strongly colors the intercultural attitudes of all Westerners toward the East and is probably an important ingredient in the almost pathological hatred of the East which so many Westerners, especially germ-conscious Americans, develop when they are forced to live there.

I had lived too long in France to be a germ-conscious American and the lethal potentialities of the microbian flora and fauna of Asia were, if anything, an attraction, one of the few charms of the East I could as yet discern. Awareness of these potentialities made me feel mildly adventurous — which is always pleasant — but above all it brought home the underlying drama of life itself — the greatest sovereign against boredom — and alleviated my loneliness by affirming my solidarity with the great and the humble, from Pasteur to the Mess Sergeant, who had fought or were fighting man's war against the enemies of man, and with the anonymous, unfamiliar Asiatic millions, the peasants, the merchants, and the maharajahs who were, with me, the common prey of the anopheles.

The longer I stayed in the Orient the more frequently I came across this leitmotif of death in the midst of life (or life in the midst of death). The most unlikely menaces to life were constantly developing not only in the jungle but among urban surroundings which in our culture carry a connotation of invulnerability, and everyone, even the exiles from the West, accepted them as natural and often diverting.

When one of my colleagues, sleeping on the verandah of the bungalow-headquarters we maintained in the heart of New Delhi, got out of bed in the middle of the night, stepped on a snake, and phoned the American hospital, a bored sergeant said to him, 'Come here if you have a car and can get here in eight minutes; otherwise don't bother.'

Another time I was a participant in a small drama which delighted me hugely. I had moved from my tent camp during the winter and was living in a maharajah's town-house with some American civilians, and we were having a dance. Sometime after dinner the butler came into the large room where we were dancing and diffidently hovered around the edge for several minutes until he caught my eye. I was afraid that we might have run out of gin, but it developed that it was only a mad dog in our compound. He had bitten one of the bearers, quite badly, and was frightening the women of the compound, and the butler, a Christian Goanese, wondered very apologetically if one of the sahibs could drive the injured bearer to the hospital for the needle treatment (Pasteur's great popular success) and perhaps, if it wasn't too much trouble, could someone shoot the dog? I drove the bearer to his needle treatment, someone shot the dog after a rather agitated *shikari* among the rose bushes, and the dance continued.

These anecdotes, however, are a digression from my mosquito-net reverie to which I want to return because it was a disproportionately significant milepost in my Asiatic evolution.

The removal of the net, reminding me of the precariousness of life in Asia, of life in general, of the vigilance, the tactical sense, and the co-operative effort necessary to safeguard life, had shattered the obliviousness to peril and struggle which our culture erroneously considers one of the conditions of happiness, or at least comfort of mind. The mental process set in motion by this household event had, instead, brought to full consciousness a far-reaching chain of associations, the central link of which was the metaphorical image of the swimmer sustained by his reconciliation of the conflicting forces in which he was immersed. A new war, a war whose battlefront extended to my bedside, had been added to the war which was already so much in my thoughts, and in the thoughts of all men, but the peace of my mind had been fortified. The mortal plagues of Asia had risen before me as in a nightmare, but the face of Asia which had seemed so stony had become almost friendly. The madness in the voice of the jackals had become the madness of court jesters, cavorting for my amusement.

I had made a discovery and the discovery had brought me peace and warmth of spirit. What had I discovered? That life is a struggle? That Asia is unhealthy, that microbes are dangerous and mosquito-nets useful? Surely a little more than that. But what?

It is like this, I said to myself: I have wasted several hours of the night and consumed thousands of psychowatts solving a childish problem — why I enjoyed sleeping under a mosquito-net. I have accomplished nothing except to endow with some meaning a hitherto meaningless piece of equipment, which I had looked at with unseeing eyes; in a broader sense, perhaps, I have enriched with an emotional and philosophical content a certain amount of practical lore I am obliged to carry in my mind, somewhat as one might put a handsome case on a dull piece of baggage. It is very little, yet I feel like one who has discovered something and accomplished something. I am like a man who has trotted several times around the block and comes home all aglow as if he had won a race. That is probably the answer. I am mentally aglow and at peace with myself because I have flexed my muscles of awareness, extended by a few millimeters the range of vision of the inner eye, stimulated by my exercise the torpid nerves which link the mind with the heart.

If that is so, my thought continued, why not attempt to apply this same gymnastic of awareness to the whole Asiatic milieu in which I am, for the time being, forced to live, to this Asia which seems to me such a desert of the mind and the heart because I have never tried to understand it? Surely Asia cannot be duller than a mosquito-net. Probably I shall never learn enough about Asia, no matter how far I stretch my powers of awareness, to

invent some magic formula for the solution of the colonial problem or discover some shining key to the cultural mysteries of the
East, but what does that matter if everything I do learn enriches
my understanding of my own world, as my little meditation on
a mosquito-net has done, and brings me the same inner peace?

Thus, without fully realizing it, I crossed a psychological
threshold which later I was to discover was also one of the
thresholds to the East.

PART II

The Pathology of Imperialism

I

Graduating from Kindergarten

IMPERIAL NEW DELHI, with its sunset-hued government buildings combining the ideals of the West and the East in an architectural potpourri that was offensive to the taste but pleasant to the eye, with its trim suburban bungalows in sun-wasted gardens, with its metropolitan boulevards and its nocturnal jackals, with its westernized Indians trying to marry a parody of Asia to a caricature of Europe, with its Englishmen so inveterate they had become exotic, twisting their culture into a mental sun-helmet to insulate them from the glare of Asia, with its Anglo-Indians, the biological synthesis of East and West, disowned by each and almost convincing themselves they came from old Spanish families; Delhi at its seventh incarnation, already ravaged by so many glories and fissured by so many contradictions, proved to be an ideal kindergarten of Asiatic studies — and a stimulating mental gymnasium for the practice of awareness.

Save for Delhi I doubt that I would have had the courage to learn anything about Asia, or even to try to study the impact of Asia on myself. Its contrasts were so facile that they tempted the mind like a childish toy — and like other childish toys they led very far.

As a political capital, as a wartime headquarters, Delhi offered a political approach to Asia, an intellectual flirtation which I did not feel too much beneath my dignity, in which there seemed little danger of the heart becoming involved. I could begin by concen-

27

trating my attention on sound, familiar, kindergarten subjects, things which all of us in this age know to be important and meaningful, with no unforeseen yogis popping up to distract me.

Later, when I knew my way a little better in the maze of wartime Asiatic politics, I might try to explore some of the deeper human factors which the abstractions of politics so often — and so conveniently — conceal. Already my first Sunday walks in the history-littered plain of Delhi, my first encounters with those victims of the neurosis of empire whom we used to think of as empire-builders, my first contacts with those domesticated Indians, the curious race of house-servants, especially the bearers, who have played such an astonishing historic role in shaping our mental image of Asia, had given me an exciting foretaste of what such advanced studies might reveal.

The headquarters of the Southeast Asia Command, to which I remained attached for nearly a year, provided an ideal intellectual base for my explorations of the political arcana of the East — and a marvelous laboratory for studying the bio-chemistry of military bureaucracies. Every morning I would walk — or bicycle — through the satin haze from which another crystalline North Indian winter day was unwrapping itself, skirt the huge government buildings, weighty with empire, into which the Anglo-Indian drudges of empire were scurrying like ants, then I would plow through the dust or mud of an uncouth military compound on the edge of the vice-regal park to my office in a temporary structure of brick and mud.

I would wait in the chilly passageway while one of the sweepers of the Raj, with the punctiliousness of a child accomplishing an important but uncomprehended rite, would beat the dust from the floors and furniture into an opaque fog, and then, when it had settled back again, I would sit down at my desk. A bewildered, barefoot Indian boy, looking like Kim after the first lesson, would shuffle into the room and thrust at me a tray of papers, the uppermost one usually being a top-secret, numbered copy of the latest plan for a great offensive against the Japanese. I would try to explain to him that the papers were meant for the Staff

Planners, in the main building, and he really shouldn't be carrying them at all, especially face up, and I would watch him drift off unhappily in the direction of the staff veterinarian, then I would settle back in my chair and wait for the daily crisis to arise.

I seldom had to wait long and it was nearly always the same crisis: Some friction, misunderstanding, or conflict arising out of the failure of the two greatest Western democracies to reconcile their wartime strategies, their national policies and ideals for the most effective joint prosecution of the war in Southeast Asia. More than once I saw such controversies, originating at my obscure level, soar rapidly to the politico-military stratosphere of the Combined Chiefs of Staff, or even to the two governments, only to come floating back a few weeks or months later with an attached decision in Anglo-American official double-talk that decided nothing.

At the bottom of all these inter-Allied disputes in the theater was a real and reasonable — and ostensibly resolvable — divergence of view between the American and the British Joint Chiefs of Staff. In the American strategic view Southeast Asia was a minor theater of war where no decisive result could be accomplished while China was relatively important. The Americans, therefore, wanted a limited and predominantly British effort in Southeast Asia, aimed at recovering with maximum speed enough of northern Burma to open a land-supply line to China over the Burma road in order to strengthen the armies of Chiang Kai-shek. The British discounted the Chinese army as a major factor and wanted the greatest possible amount of American help to strike a blow at the pivot of Japanese military power in the theater — Singapore — where they believed they could simultaneously recover the military prestige they had lost in the Malayan debacle of 1942 and acquire a base for subsequent operations in the South China Sea in direct support of the American Pacific campaign.

Somehow, at least in the theater, this reasonable argument over strategy led to endless confused, petty bickering over trivial issues and to some of the most curious inversions and contradictions in official thinking I have ever seen.

In no field did all these conflicts, contradictions, and cross-purposes show up so constantly and so glaringly as in my own, which involved the control of clandestine, and to some degree, of psychological warfare activities. Here everything was, almost by definition, political. Nominally a SEAC staff officer, my real, or at least my main, function was to obtain authorization for the American Office of Strategic Services to carry out its guerilla and intelligence activities against the Japanese in this British-controlled theater and to make sure that in the process of co-ordinating these activities with their own military plans the British did not divert them from their American and strictly military purpose.

These curious functions within a curious profession often provided me with fascinating glimpses of the more subterranean aspects of colonial and international politics, but they were rather exhausting to the spirit because they involved me in a perpetual two-front war: Against the relevant authorities of the Government and Army of India who, at the time I arrived in Delhi, had not yet relinquished control of military cloak-and-dagger activities to Admiral Mountbatten's new command; against the American China-Burma-India theater headquarters which retained a power of veto over the operations of OSS. The former consistently opposed all American clandestine activities — and many overt OWI activities — either because they feared we would rummage among the cupboards where the family skeletons of empire were concealed or because they feared that we might, perhaps innocently and accidentally, give undue encouragement to the aspirations to freedom of the subject peoples in Asia.

The American theater authorities had only one fear but it was strong enough for two: That OSS by operating in a British-controlled theater might be gradually 'integrated' with the corresponding British agencies and thereby be exposed to some subtle political contamination. The only sure way to avoid this contamination, according to some of the Americans with whom I had to deal, was not to operate. Neither British nor Americans appeared to give much thought to the relation of these controversial activities to the problem of defeating the Japanese.

During my first months in India I was reluctant to admit that there was any basic Anglo-American conflict back of the constant suspicion, the constant bickerings, and the daily crises in our military relationships. When I heard American officers say, 'Why don't we fight the British instead of the Japs? That would be a popular war'; when I heard British officers say, 'Why don't you damn Yanks stay home where you belong?' I dismissed it as a symptom of poor morale — and poor leadership. I had heard talk like that in Algiers, but Eisenhower had not allowed it to last long. I knew it could be stopped here, too.

The real trouble, I thought hopefully, was not so much Anglo-American friction as friction between the local British leadership — the Government of India and High Command of the Indian Army — and the local American leadership — our China-Burma-India Command headed by the late General (then Lieutenant General) Joseph W. Stillwell. It must be a jurisdictional clash, a clash of professional rivalries, a clash of personalities, a clash between the campaign hat and the stuffed bush-shirt.

By October, 1943, this clash had become a chronic and stubborn quarrel which was seriously impeding the Allied war effort. Washington and London were equally aware of the problem and though they were by no means in agreement on the basic strategy to be followed in Southeast Asia they agreed that something must be done to end the local bickering that was certain to nullify any strategy. The fruit of this agreement, finally consummated at the Quebec Conference, was the Southeast Asia Command, an integrated inter-Allied general staff, modeled after Eisenhower's but with the emphasis reversed — that is to say, with a British head and an American deputy at each staff level — to be superimposed upon the American forces — nearly all non-combat elements — under General Stillwell, the Indian army under General Sir Claude Auchinleck, and the Royal Navy and the Royal Air Force under God and their respective commanders.

In principle, the formula seemed a reasonable one. Though it did not imply a resolution of the conflicting policies of the two governments with regard to the war in Asia, it apparently set up organizational machinery through which the problem could be approached in an orderly and constructive manner. In fact, so many limitations, anomalies, and contradictions, expressing the basic divergencies, not only of the two governments but of conflicting group-interests in each of them, were incorporated into the formula that its virtue was quenched.

As an organizational structure the Southeast Asia Command was a monstrosity. The sinister whimsy of its morphology, the surrealism of its anatomy, reflected the widespread confusion between ends and means in our society, the deep-rooted tendency of democratic governments to implement their aims not by choosing executive personnel imbued with the democratic ideal but by creating executive machinery which caricatures the legislative machinery, by entrusting the execution of their decisions to bureaucratic oligarchs in striped pants or khaki.

I had seen enough of such organizational nightmares in wartime Washington to realize by now that they functioned as smoothly as any organism with five legs or a bifurcated spine functions, but I was willing to believe that the Southeast Asia Command might still fulfill a useful purpose in dampening the smoldering embers of Anglo-American hostility, if only by involving the disputants so closely in quarrels over the mechanics of collaboration that they would not often be tempted to question the principle of collaboration. There may be times when the next best thing to clarifying an issue is to befuddle it completely and SEAC seemed admirably adapted to this end.

At first it seemed that the new command was going to succeed in reducing inter-Allied friction. The instantaneous polarization of hostilities which it effected, the transference of the reciprocal hatreds of the original disputants to the intruder, was, on the whole, an encouraging symptom. (Only later did it become clear that the two Delhis, the American and the British, hated each other not the less that they hated Mountbatten more.) The Americans, that is, the aboriginal or CBI Americans, dubbed Lord Louis the 'Glamor-Boy of Southeast Asia' and the 'Chocolate Sailor.' In the presence of British brother-officers they crooned a parody of their own composing of a twentieth-century American folk-song: 'Million-dollar admiral, five-and-ten-cent war.' They proclaimed that the mere existence of the Southeast Asia Command was the greatest deceptive operation in military history because its constant fabrication of plans for offensives which would never take place, combined with its loose security, must create indescribable confusion in the mind of the enemy.

The aboriginal British, including some who had been transferred from the India Army to the new command, were more genteel in the expression of their hostility but no less deadly. They seemed to have even more contempt for Mountbatten than the uncouth Americans had. They did not sneer at him in words, they merely used refined British inflections. They deplored the difficulties he was having, they spread rumors about his discouragement, his desire to be relieved of his grotesque and futile command. Mostly they harassed the new command by methods of bureaucratic passive resistance and nonviolent sabotage.

The Americans were divided into two political camps, the CBI camp, the followers of Stillwell, and the SEAC camp, the followers of Wedemeyer and through him of Lord Louis. The British, however, did not merely seem two rival factions but two different races. Most of the officers on the British section of the SEAC staff came out from England with Mountbatten and many had never been in the East before. A number of them were politically reactionary; by British domestic standards, perhaps, their belief in the mission of the Empire might be no less than that of the professional colonials, but they had an entirely different outlook toward the war — they wanted to get on with it — and their central preoccupations seemed little different from those of most of the Americans.

Between the Americans and the British on the SEAC staff, relations were cordial, even comradely, at the beginning. The SEAC Americans apologized to their British colleagues for the really spectacular boorishness, mulishness, and obstructiveness of the CBI Americans. The British were equally apologetic over the bad faith, lethargy, lack of combative spirit, military backward-

ness, and medieval political attitudes of the colonial British. Most
of the SEAC Americans were, I think, sincerely attracted by the
personality of our glittering royal-blooded commander — a phenomenon which our CBI compatriots regarded with the derisive
suspicion of the *Chicago Tribune* regarding a Rhodes scholar —
while the British, in order to be agreeable, grimly set themselves
to discover some amiable qualities in the picturesque personality
of their Deputy Supreme Commander, General Stillwell, whom
both British and Americans attempted in their minds, or at least
their conversation, to dissociate from his staff.

There was, in fact, a great difference between Stillwell and his
staff and even between a handful of superior men, mostly rather
young, on that staff and the general level. Stillwell identified himself so completely with the mass of his troops that even as a
theater commander he retained a field-soldier's contempt for
headquarters. Delhi was his rear echelon and main headquarters, and he seemed to regard his Delhi staff as something between a necessary evil and a useless ornament of rank imposed on
him by regulation. His heart was always at his field headquarters
in Ledo, or up the line from it, and his body was there whenever
possible. He gave little thought to the selection of his staff
officers, tolerated gross incompetence if reinforced by habit and
loyalty and demoralized his few good men by taking them too
seldom into his confidence and refusing to delegate to them authority to act in his name. He was thus indirectly responsible for
fostering the attitudes of systematic suspicion, petty legalism,
professional peevishness, and general negativism which we came
to think of as the CBI spirit. (It was only the rear-echelon CBI
spirit, not the Ledo Road spirit, not the Hump spirit.)

Stillwell himself was too great a man to succumb to the CBI
spirit. He was a soldier-prophet, a militarized Moses, miscast as a
military bureaucrat. Also contrary to a widespread belief in the
theater there was no personal animosity between him and his
nominal chief, Lord Louis. Yet the characters and viewpoints
of these two men both expressed and determined to some degree
the pattern of Anglo-American misunderstanding in the theater,

and as I studied the contrast between them from the vantage-
point of a subordinate, whose duties imply·reconciling the irrecon-
ciliable positions of two superiors, my understanding of the significance of Asia in world politics deepened, and the problem of
Anglo-American co-operation, which had once seemed so simple
to me, appeared highly complex.

Outwardly as unlike any two humans can be, as unlike perhaps
as Churchill and Gandhi, Mountbatten and Stillwell had a number of things in common. They were both superior men, in my
opinion, and I had enough personal contact with both of them to
have a reasonable opinion. Both were great leaders of men,
Stillwell more than Mountbatten. As an old newspaperman I am
suspicious of the legends that grow up around public figures but
the legend that has grown up around Stillwell, the legend of
vinegar-faced, kindly hearted 'Uncle Joe' driving his troops to
almost superhuman hardships and yet beloved of them, even falls
short of the reality, the only case in my personal experience of a
man greater than his legend. Of Mountbatten's leadership — at
least of his ability to capture the imagination and hold the loyalty
of men — as shrewd a judge as Major General William J. Donovan, the creator and chief of our wartime Office of Strategic
Services, once said to me:

'If that man had been born Mr. Mountbatten he might be the
next prime minister of England.'

I would not be willing to go quite so far myself and Donovan's
judgment may have been influenced by the fact that he had just
concluded an almost incredibly advantageous agreement with
Lord Louis for the operations of OSS in Southeast Asia, but I
think that his acute perceptions had really detected the subtle
radiations of something approaching genius in the British aristocrat.

From my own contact with him, I thought Lord Louis's greatest gift was imagination — the intellectual counterpart of his
physical daring. Almost any novel, daring, or unorthodox strategy, tactical conception or lethal gadget that could be brought
to his notice was assured sympathetic consideration.

Stillwell had imagination, too, as he proved by his sponsorship of such unorthodox organizations as the OSS Kachin Rangers and Dr. Seagraves' medical unit, but his greatest military virtue was the steely quality of his will, as his greatest moral quality was his passion for integrity. Nothing endeared Uncle Joe so much to the American GI as his hatred for every variety of hypocrisy, cant, sham, and affectation — particularly the military varieties. Some of his enemies suspected that his aggressively homespun ways, the battered campaign-hat, the muddy boots, were themselves an affectation, but this was not so. Uncle Joe, as I used to see him later during his brief stay in Ceylon, clinging to his hat for dear life as he roared along in a mud-spattered jeep, with his four-starred Cadillac, packed with second lieutenants, following behind, was the symbol of an older, ruggeder, and more moral America, clinging stubbornly to the verities and the decencies in which the world had ceased to believe.

Stillwell's passion for integrity, his private and continuing revolution against accepted illusion, led him astray in other ways. When he came to Ceylon in the summer of 1944, replacing Mountbatten during the latter's absence in England, his behavior seemed almost childishly boorish to the British. He refused to install himself at the handsome desk, in the spacious, richly carpeted office of the Supreme Commander. While his youthful followers wrestled on the Supremo's carpet he sat hunched over a desk in a cramped cubbyhole with five members of his staff, blissfully directing the movement of patrols in north Burma and sending long telegrams of vituperative encouragement to the commander of the Kachin Rangers. He refused to attend the daily intelligence talks for the staff which were one of Mountbatten's favorite office rituals, not because he wanted to boycott the British but because he thought such gatherings were time-wasting nonsense.

It was his creed to boycott pretentious nonsense and he did it in Kandy as he did it in Washington — and in Chungking. When he fixed a beady eye on some high-ranking British staff officer and interrupted his suave verbal opening with terse, rasping comments, punctuated with less terse profanity, on the central core of the matter that the Britisher was leading up to, he was not trying to be insulting, he was merely exercising Joe Stillwell's God-given right to be himself, that is, to love truth and be impatient of any fumbling with or about the truth in all circumstances.

Stillwell's determination to be himself in all circumstances was an offense to many of the men with whom he had to deal and sometimes almost nullified his really great political gifts, but oddly enough I don't think that Mountbatten was offended by him. Lord Louis, in his own way, offended some people by a similar, if lesser, bent for being himself.

He had the reputation of a playboy and he was certainly intelligent enough to realize it was one of his most serious liabilities but he could not bring himself to take the steps to live it down. He worked hard and he was very serious-minded about his work, but he was a worldly, civilized, intelligent man with highly sophisticated tastes and he was not going to try to be dull in order to seem serious. He allowed himself very little relaxation but when he did relax it followed the Mayfair pattern, offending both those who liked their whisky without epigrams and those who liked their dialectics without soda.

He looked a little too well in uniform but he could not refuse himself a handsome man's pleasure in wearing a handsome uniform.

He had the graciousness and the simplicity, including the simple love of ceremony, of a great aristocrat who is almost without sense of caste because his own caste is so small. He also had the natural arrogance of a man born with more brains and more hormones than most of his fellows, and many mistook it for aristocratic arrogance and resented him for what they admired in more plebeian leaders.

Actually, Mountbatten was most effective as a leader on the occasions — for Stillwell there were never any other occasions — when he was arrogantly content to be himself. By nature he was imperious, impetuous, intuitive — frequently wrong but brilliantly right when he was not wrong. He was, perhaps, too prone to snap judgments but his snap judgments were amazingly good, and usually, his best. Unfortunately, lacking Stillwell's stubbornness, he usually allowed himself to be talked out of his first judgments by his staff advisors or his field commanders. To me this indicated both the strength of the man and the weakness of his position. His goal was to restore the white man's prestige in Asia, the foundation-stone of the empire and to achieve it he had to use the blunted and discredited tools of empire.

Stillwell's point of view was almost exactly the opposite. He did not believe in the goal of empire and he did not believe that the British military forces in Southeast Asia, impregnated with the toxins of a decaying imperialism, were capable of achieving the kind of spectacular military success which might restore the white man's prestige. I do not think he particularly desired the restoration of the white man's prestige; he was more concerned with avoiding the appearance of war between the white and the yellow races, with spreading to the lesser Asiatic peoples the concept of a war between a democratic and a fascist Asia in which the white democracies of the West were aiding the yellow democracy of the East — China. As for the principle of colonial rule, I think he did not hate it so much as he despised it. Burma had convinced him that colonialism was a dangerous sham because it created the illusion of power — above all, in the minds of the colonials — without the military reality of power.

At first, before I knew him, before I became well acquainted with the few men around him who knew his mind, I was inclined to think that Stillwell's hostile attitude toward Mountbatten's mission was due to personal prejudice and the general crotchetiness of his temperament. I still think today that he impeded the prosecution of the war in tolerating so much frivolous obstructionism on the part of his staff, but gradually I came to realize that Stillwell's attitude toward Anglo-American military co-operation was the natural consequence of a definite, carefully thought out and coherent policy — a policy, moreover, which differed from American government policy in Asia only in that he took no account of the other government policies which contradicted it. Also it was a policy firmly rooted on the one hand in a realistic interpretation of modern history, on the other in a personal and American philosophy of life — a belief in human dignity in the sense of believing that the human animal is capable of dignity and therefore entitled to it.

Stillwell expressed his philosophy by seeking to give military dignity, the kind that meant the most to him, to the Chinese, the Burmese, and other men, the pigmentation of whose skins, in the traditional colonial view, precluded them from the attainment of any kind of dignity. I doubt that any of his followers ever heard him talk about human dignity — to avoid suspicion he always talked of killing Japs — but he betrayed himself by the special enthusiasm he took in the business of killing Japs when it incidentally involved teaching some other Asiatics to respect themselves and be worthy of respect. This is what lay back of Stillwell's keen personal interest in the Kachin Rangers, in Seagrave's Burmese nursing unit and in the Ramgarh Chinese, whom he ferried across the Hump, nursed, fed, equipped and trained in India to prove his lifelong contention that the Chinese can be a good soldier.

I doubt that many Americans in the theater shared Stillwell's philosophy, or were even aware of it as a conscious philosophy, but nearly all of them unconsciously revealed the same basic distrust of the principle of empire, even those who were more intoxicated with the poison of race-superiority than any Britisher. In the same way nearly all the British, even those who most hated the abuses of empire and were fighting the hardest to correct them, were committed, consciously or unconsciously, to uphold the principle of empire. The most reactionary and cynical Americans held on to the idealistic bias against imperialism even when they repudiated all the ideals from which the bias was derived. The most liberal and realistic British retained the imperial approach to politics even when they resigned themselves to the liquidation of empire.

Against this deep-rooted conflict of traditional attitudes, all the charm, all the tact, and all the skill of Lord Louis, all the sincerity and good will of the American officers on his staff could not prevail. Ultimately all the Americans aligned themselves in one camp — even if they continued to quarrel among themselves within it — and the British from England formed an unhappy but united imperial front with the colonial sahibs and tuans.

The political reaction which began to develop in the United States after Roosevelt's death and the revolution in colonial policy which marked the advent of socialist leadership in Great Britain both reached Southeast Asia with too great a lag to have any discernible effect on Anglo-American relations in that theater up to the time of my return home in January, 1946.

The immediate effect of my SEAC experience was to expose me to the appealing Stillwell philosophy of Asia and to expose to me the shams, the betrayals, the futility of imperialism, thus awakening in my mind sympathy for those submerged millions whom I had previously regarded as mere geopolitical factors.

II

The Sickness of Being a Sahib

THE MAIN INGREDIENTS of my professional life in Delhi were
fairly familiar ones. SEAC headquarters was very like Washington and at times it even reminded me of Geneva — the mechanics of producing a good war out of the co-operation of two
sovereign nations was very similar to the mechanics which had
failed so disastrously to preserve peace by the co-operation of
fifty-two.

The colonial mind was a new thing to me but certain of its
aspects were strongly reminiscent of the French mind as I had
known it in 1940 and, in North Africa, in 1942. A joke, popular in
Delhi both among Americans and newly arrived British, would
have applied as aptly to the French General Staff in 1940 as it did
to GHQ India in 1943. A visitor is trying to find his way to
headquarters and he asks an officer emerging from a double
entrance to one of the government buildings, 'Which side is
GHQ on?'

'We aren't quite sure,' the officer replies, 'but we hope it's on
ours.'

Another joke of the period could likewise have applied to
France, an explanation of the India Army shoulder patch, a gold
star against a red-black background: 'The star of India sinking
into a sea of ink against a sunset glow of red tape.'

The Japanese Malaya-Burma campaign of 1942 had been
similar in its psychological impact to the German blitzkrieg of

41

1940. From the accounts of reliable eye-witnesses, it appeared to me that human deficiencies, therefore ultimately moral deficiencies, had played an even greater role in the British colonial collapse than in the fall of France.

The psychological factors which had produced defeat in 1942 were clearly reflected in 1943 in the uniformly negative approach of many colonial soldiers to all problems, in the impairment of their military reflexes by political inhibitions. What was not yet clear to me was the relationship between their professional mentality and their personal way of life.

I set myself to study this relationship as I had tried to study it in Europe. As a temporary sahib, surrounded by authentic sahibs and leading physically the same kind of life, I should feel in myself some slight trace of the malady of the spirit which made them what they were. I did feel traces of this malady, or of some malady. At first I thought it was merely not being adjusted to India, but after a couple of months I realized that it was something deeper. Just living in India seemed a malady and I began to observe my malady the way a laboratory rat, if he were capable of thought, might try to understand the experiments that were being performed upon him by relating them to his own symptoms.

As I studied myself and the rats in the neighboring cages I thought: Rat, you are not a glossy rat, a brisk rat; you are not the rat you were. What has happened to you? What principle of sterility has entered, or principle of maximum vitality departed? What is this sickness of being a sahib?

It was a hard malady to define, or even to describe, for the symptoms were slight and difficult to distinguish from the loneliness and the boredom of all men in armies away from their homes, from the frustration which hangs like a fog over every military headquarters. Some called their malady homesickness, some called it sex-starvation, others just said it was this damn country, this India. All of us said, apropos of almost anything or nothing at all, 'We (I, or you) have been in the East too long.'

It was a fashionable piece of local slang and everyone who had been in India more than three days was constantly proclaiming

that he had been in the East too long. (When he stopped saying
it he probably had.) What it meant was that we were mocking
ourselves for being something a little less than we had been before,
confessing by a joke, not only that something was lacking to us,
but that we were also slightly lacking, that our spiritual metabolism was lowered, bringing us an almost imperceptible but certain
step closer to those tragic and ludicrous tropical wrecks, those
ossified old soldiers and broken-down planters who have become
conventional figures in our folklore of the East.

All the Americans I met in India showed traces of this subtle
psychic deterioration and I felt it in myself. After awhile the
Army began to take official notice of the poor state of morale
throughout the theater and made numerous well-intentioned,
sometimes intelligent, attempts to improve morale. The Army
was chiefly concerned over the morale of the men in the ranks and
rightly diagnosed a deficiency in leadership among the officers;
what it failed to perceive was that the morale of the officers,
especially the senior officers, was more in need of attention than
that of their men, and that this deficiency in officer morale was
responsible for the poor quality of their leadership.   In the
muddy, leech-ridden jungles of Assam through which the Ledo
Road was being cut, on the front-line airfields in China, morale
was much higher than it was in the comparative luxury of Indian
bases, and it was lowest at New Delhi, the theater headquarters,
lowest among the lieutenant-colonels and the colonels of the military peerage who by day dispensed wisdom, power, and splendor
from their desks, and at night relaxed — as I had seen them so
grimly relaxing — in the spacious comfort of the Imperial Hotel.

Part of the morale-problem among the Americans in Delhi was
fairly easy to diagnose because it had political roots. In a sense
the Americans were victims of their own psychological warfare.
The arguments used against the British in official controversies
became rationalizations for private defeatism: Where Washington
told London that no more troops or supplies could be spared for
Southeast Asia because the theater was not important strategically, individual American officers told their gin-glasses that

nothing in the theater mattered a damn. Where official Washington wanted the British to show more combativeness, American Delhi assured itself that the British would never fight. The more the Americans quarreled with their Allies the more they sneered at the Allied effort of which they were a part, failing to realize that in so doing they were belittling their own importance, condemning themselves to a sense of futility and wasted effort and supplying one more demonstration — among many that I had seen — that man is essentially a self-defeating animal.

Beneath this relatively superficial political neurosis, however, besides this continual cutting off of the American nose to spite the British face, I felt sure that there lay deeper and more subtle factors of discontent, unconscious mechanisms of self-defeat in the American soldier's relationship to India as well as in his relationship to his Allies.

I noticed, moreover, that my English friends on the SEAC staff, those whom Admiral Mountbatten had brought out from England with him, seemed as depressed by Delhi as the Americans. Some of them were much more violent about it than any American, were so consistently apologetic that they seemed to feel it as a personal disgrace, and were completely blind to the scattered beauties that one can find anywhere if one looks for them — even in the stony soil of Anglo-India.

The real natives of New Delhi, the British civil servants and army officers and other Old India hands, at first glance seemed relatively content with their environment, but I suspected it was because most of them had been in the East so long they were no longer aware that they had been in the East too long. Later, when I came to meet some representatives of this class, I discovered both that they were less content than they looked and that they often had political and social reasons for their discontent far more specific than the indefinable *Weltschmerz* from which I suffered. From some of them, though, from certain really old Old India hands, who admitted wryly and proudly that India was in their blood, who loved India the way some men love a cruel mistress, who remembered the good old Kiplingesque days when the sahibs had no political or social worries, I learned that they, too, and all white men in the East, suffered from the same *Welt-schmerz*.

'It's something in the soil,' one of these Old Hands said to me, 'or rather something that isn't in the soil. Like these vitamins you Yanks are always talking about.'

He went on to explain that the impoverished soil of India is actually lacking in vitamins and minerals so that those who stay for long in the East tend to become demineralized and to suffer from mild vitamin deficiencies without realizing it. He was about to develop a theory of an analogous spiritual avitaminosis, but, like a good Englishman, caught himself in time and concluded the conversation by advising me to drink two fingers of Scotch — if I could find any Scotch — every night before turning in, to make up for the deficiencies — material and spiritual — of my diet and to ward off malaria. .

This conversation stuck in my mind because the metaphor of a spiritual vitamin deficiency expressed so perfectly my feeling about life in India, at least in the capital of the White Man's India. A few days later it was Sunday and I was still thinking about spiritual vitamins as I sat on a high cornice of Humayan's tomb, a grandiose Moghul ruin set in a little park, looking out across the sun-drenched plain of Delhi. It was an airy and philosophic perch, high enough to make the groups of women strolling in their Sunday *sarees* on the grass below look like clumps of exotic flowers, high enough to measure the goverment buildings of the new city for ruins and imagine how massive and right they would look when the sham had worn off. High enough, too, to cut a metaphor loose from its moorings and go sailing off on it toward new horizons of the mind.

Suppose, I asked myself, that there are spiritual vitamins, that this figure of speech is not a metaphor but an exact analogy?

Surely the principle of deficiency which even the least sensitive Occidentals detected in their Eastern life suggests the existence of psychic factors in social relationships which are as quantitatively insignificant in the consciousness of the individual as vitamins are in his food, as significant to his emotional life as vitamins are to his bodily functions. These factors must be present in a healthy and fruitful society, influencing the minute daily relationships of the individual to his society, without his being aware of them, just as vitamins are present in the husks of the rice which the Asiatic peasant enjoys in blissful ignorance that he is eating anything but rice. They could not be things unknown but must be things unnoticed, or noticed in the wrong contexts, perhaps certain abstractions recognized as being important to the understanding of history or to the control of men in the mass, but not usually considered as important to the personal life of the common man.

No man ever really understands that he is a patriot until his country is endangered and we normally think of patriotism as a duty or a virtue or at most a privilege — not as an emotional possession. Yet I have seen some European refugees, untouched in their personal possessions by the war, mourn for their lost country the way one mourns for a lost child, mourn and be emotionally impoverished, as one is impoverished by such a loss. If the patriot's loss can afflict him like a private neurosis, is it not possible that his patriotism in normal times is one of the elements of his private health, as well as of his public behavior?

As I climbed down from my perch in the warm twilight with clouds of green parakeets wheeling and diving around me on wings hardly less swift than those of my liberated metaphor, I felt sure of one thing: The key to the kind of understanding I was seeking in Asia lay in this notion of the importance of the most slight. Whether metaphorical or not, it was in terms of spiritual vitamins, instead of spiritual starches and proteins, that I must learn to reorient my thinking. My tower-top speculations might or might not offer a clue to the always-sought Northwest Passage between the political continent and the continent of individual psychology but they did constitute a bridge, valid in terms of my personal experience, between the political world of the Southeast Asia Command and the human world of the sahib in which I found myself living. I did not want to attempt a complete analysis either of the sahib's mind or of the politics of empire. I wanted to have some understanding of the relationship between the emotional aridity of the sahib as a human being and the politico-military sterility of SEAC. Hitherto I had been baffled by the appearance of slight causes and great effects.

Leading an uneventful life in India, I felt like the survivor of some social catastrophe — but there were no ruins. The other sahibs who surrounded me seemed the victims of some chronic famine and I felt a victim myself — but there was no observable famine, except the chronic, material, and very observable near-famine of the Indian people. The psychological conditions of my life in India seemed only slightly different from anything I had known before, but the psychological effects of life in India were tremendously different. The sahibs seemed to differ only slightly from other men, yet their mental world was the world of another race. Was I spiritually hungry because I was living among people who were physically starving? Was the slight pity, the slight indignation, the slight feeling of wanting to escape if I could not help, which I felt in my conscious mind only the reflection of a much greater unconscious reaction?

I did not know. I wondered. And I resumed my study of the sahib's way of life to see what other slight things I might discover which would explain the enormous difference between it and my normal world, the American way of life, and the enormous difference between the sahib's approach to war and politics and the American approach.

For the visiting American sahib the spiritual vitamin most conspicuously deficient in the soil of Asia is the vitamin of progress. This is the principle which is responsible for some of the most striking American manifestations, such as the prose of Sinclair Lewis and a number of things associated with it, for example, small communities introducing themselves to approaching motorists with the slogan 'Watch Us Grow,' or advertisers trying to convince the public that it is essentially American — in the sense of conforming to the noblest American traditions — to want a better can-opener than the one to which it is accustomed. Oddly enough, the advertisers are right. It is an American, and even a noble craving, to want a better can-opener once you have allowed yourself to be convinced that a better can-opener is a real symbol of technological progress and if technological progress is equated with the progression of man. There is an evident danger that we may come by this path to worshiping can-openers instead of progress, if we have not done so already, but we are right to worship progress as long as it means to us what it does.

Myth or reality, our belief in progress, in evolution toward a better world, is an essential ingredient of our psychological as well as of our social well-being. It is more than a personal and collective hope: It is an incentive to co-operative effort, for the belief in a bettering world lays upon the individual the duty to contribute to it, to want the best thing for oneself, perhaps, but better things for all. In the capitalist societies it is probably the chief antibody to the toxins of exploitation, the chief factor which prevents, or at least retards, the realization of the dark Marxian prophecies, for it is one of the rare bonds that unite the exploiter and the exploited.

Until I went to India I had never realized that the legend of Progress, of which I have long been consciously skeptical, was unconsciously one of the vital factors in my own morale. Most of my adult life before the war was lived in Europe, and Europe is not so fanatically devoted to the cult of progress as is America. I thought that progress was just one of the quaint superstitions of Sinclair Lewis's characters and that it did not exist in Europe and that I could get along very well without it. I was not distressed by the knowledge that in twenty years the ruins of Les Baux would be no bigger and better than they were twenty years ago, or that Avallon would not have a new sewage system.

Actually, the myth of progress is the common heritage of all Western societies. It exists even in the most backward countries of Europe, and in Soviet Russia it is probably more fanatically worshiped than in the United States.

Only in Asia, above all in India, does progress seem totally absent. There are no Asiatic communities which ask you to watch them grow. Population growth, which in American communities is one of the most popular indices of progress, is a manifestation of decay in a land already too poor to support the millions it spawns. The 1943 bullock cart was no improvement over the 1942 model, or even the 1429 model, and if it had been, there were fewer Indians who could afford to buy one, proportionately far fewer than in 1429. The plow with which the Asiatic peasant turns the soil of his fields is usually no great technological advance over the crooked sticks of the ancestral Aryans. To Western eyes almost the whole of Asia wears the face of a land fettered by a changeless tradition, including the tradition of misery, where man is content to use the tools that his fathers used, to be what his fathers were, except possibly in India where he is lucky if he can be what his fathers were or have any tools at all.

What shocks Americans most in the East is the seeming technological backwardness of the European communities, the enclaves of Occidental urbanism which the white masters of the East have built for themselves at the geographical key-points of their economic and political control. Not only do these fractional metropolises reveal curious lapses from Occidental standards of municipal life — such as the legal immunity enjoyed by jackals in New Delhi in recognition of their indispensable services as scavengers — not only does their dependence on native labor involve picturesque anachronisms like charcoal-burning kitchens and female bricklayers whose hods are their heads, but their mechanical equipment, while it is authentically Occidental, reflects the Occident with a technological lag of a generation. One encounters this lag for the first time in the bathroom. The toilets not only look old-fashioned because, unlike American ones, they are starkly utilitarian, but they flush on a still more primitive version of the pull-and-let-go principle which baffles so many American visitors in London.

To many Americans it seemed inevitable that men who in 1943 tolerated 1913 toilets in their bathrooms would accept 1930 tanks for equipping their armies. It fitted in with the prevalent American cliché of an Immemorial East, timeless and changeless, and of a race of white colonials gone slightly tropical, nodding just a little from the torpor which holds their subjects in millenary slumber. This was my own mental image of the East before I went there but I discovered it was an oversimplification. The East is not so static as it seems. The illusion of changelessness, at least in India, is the fine balance struck between revolution and cancerously swift decay. The slumber of Asia is constantly stirred by dreams of the future and nightmares of the past. The sahibs are not so much unprogressive as deprived of progress. The sahib is what he is — among other things, a man who clings to 1913 toilets and sometimes to 1930 tanks in 1943 — not because of Asia but because of himself in Asia, to a large extent because of the safeguards he sets up against Asia in his mind.

For example, the logic of the sahib's political position forces him to deny his own works, to belittle his own contribution to the progress of Asia. His greatest contribution has been a cultural one: He has brought the ideals of democracy to the East. Now the peoples of the East want to implement the ideals of the white man by getting rid of his rule, and they mean to do it. Sometimes the sahib takes a kind of ironical pride in this. We taught them all this, he says. We showed them how. They owe it to us. It is a true boast, but the sahib cannot quite sublimate his hunger for progress to the point of deriving real satisfaction from admiring the skill with which his own weapons are used against him. Every sahib is a little like one I met in Delhi, a formidable lover of dead crocodiles and live brown women who boasted to me that he had killed more than one hundred crocodiles and begotten fifteen illegitimate children by native mistresses.

'How many more children do you expect to have?' I asked him.

'None, since my oldest son turned into a Gandhi-*wallah*. I'm not going to breed any more little bastards to help kick us out of India.'

(He had also lost interest in killing crocodiles.)

Democracy is the fruit of the sahib's spirit and he has lost his zest for propagating it in the East, along with his zest for slaying crocodiles or other dragons, because it has turned against him. He cannot repudiate democracy without repudiating his own society so he tells himself that the democracy he has begotten in the East is a bastard democracy, that it can never grow into anything strong, progress toward anything more perfect, because of the curse of the East in the mother's blood — his seed has been wasted.

These people are quite hopeless, the sahib says. They just can't understand our concept of public morality. They recite all the phrases so glibly you think they understand, then the minute you let them alone they get themselves into a mess. They howl for their freedom and the minute you give them a little bit they use it to oppress one another. You can't change the East.

Those are almost exact quotes from a young, very intelligent, very conscientious member of the Indian Civil Service whom I met toward the middle part of my stay in Delhi. He was no ruthless imperialist but an earnest man who looked upon the British Empire as a British trusteeship over backward peoples and conceived his mission as helping to create the transition from Empire to self-government in India. In conformity with his ideals he had once in his early days in the service worked under an Indian chief and he had several times turned over his job upon promotion to an Indian he had trained — only to see them get themselves into a mess and undo what he had tried to build up.

Nearly every servant of empire that I met in the East held the same view, told the same story in different accents. Sometimes the accent was one of bitterness. Sometimes it was one of self-justification. Sometimes it was one of cynical, even humorous resignation.

Whatever the individual approach might be, there seemed to me complete unanimity among all the sahibs in regard to the native's unfitness to rule himself and the mess India would get into when she finally attained freedom. There was no doubting their sincerity. On the other hand, there was no doubting that this view echoed the current themes of British government propaganda and that it served very handily to answer those critics of empire, both in England and in the other democracies, who kept making pointed references to the Atlantic Charter and asking,

'Why doesn't the British government give India her freedom?'

Looking back on it today, it seems clear that the colonial servants I met in India in 1943 and 1944 were ideological laggards
compared even with the Churchill government, which itself was
lagging badly behind British public opinion in regard to the Indian
problem.

What interested me most at the time — and still interests me
today, for its application is not confined to the imperialist context
— was the effect on the individual sahib's morale of his colonial
ideology, the analogy between the self-defeating mechanisms in
his mind and those which inter-Allied friction set in motion in the
minds of the New Delhi Americans.

In the golden age of empire the sahibs took the native's incapacity for granted but they wasted relatively little energy talking
about it. They were too busy bringing progress and enlightenment to the East to expatiate at any great length upon Eastern
backwardness. Both in official propaganda and in their private
mythologies of the white man's burden, the sahibs placed the main
emphasis upon their own superiority rather than upon the native's
inferiority. They despised the native — but not too much to
dedicate their lives to helping him. Save in rare moments of discouragement, they did not proclaim that the native was utterly
hopeless, for the justification of their own mission was that they
were bringing hope to him.

With the rise of the Indian nationalist movement after World
War I, a subtle change took place in the ideology and propaganda
of empire. A defensive, recriminating note crept in, corresponding to the tactical requirement of rebuttal to the Indian nationalist propaganda.

Gradually, in trying to convince themselves and the world that
India was not yet ready for self-government, the sahibs convinced
themselves that it was useless to try to fit Indians for self-government, that the idealism of empire was a mockery. As the twilight
of empire deepened, as the certainty of ultimate withdrawal became steadily more certain, the sahibs, in order to score a last
point in their argument with Gandhi, implicitly repudiated their

own accomplishments and denied their own historic mission. By proclaiming the hopelessness of India, they avowed the futility of empire.

In the end the sahibs were reduced to boasting of their failures, as a neurotic boasts of his illness. They demoted themselves from pioneers of progress to rearguards in a delaying action with history. Their whole professional character became hinged on a negative goal, on the cultivation of frustration. Their record as soldiers was exactly what one would expect of a soldier who cultivates the ideology of defeat.

Unlike the decadent democrats of Western Europe, the sahibs were not the target of enemy propaganda, before they were attacked by arms. Their will-to-resist was undermined neither by preliminary psychological bombardment nor by social divisions. There were no fifth columnists among the sahibs themselves and it was only in the last stages of the Allied collapse in Burma that native fifth-columnism played any significant military role.

They were not overwhelmed by superior numbers and awesome machines of war like the French, the Dutch, and the Norwegians. They failed, from conscious political motives, to mobilize the psychological resources of Malaya, Burma, and India; the last thing they wanted was a people's war in Asia, but their native mercenary armies, reasonably well trained and equipped, fought as hard as they were asked to fight.

Like the French, the sahibs had a Maginot-legend — the belief in the impregnability of Singapore, the impassibility of the jungle and the superior fighting ability of the white man — and they had to suffer the psychological shock of seeing this legend shattered, but they had thousands of miles and many months in which to recover from the shock.

Nowhere along the whole route of the British withdrawal from Southeast Asia (the less said about the corresponding Dutch withdrawal the better, and, of course, the Vichy French did not withdraw at all, they stayed and learned to hiss through their teeth) was there a Wake or a Bataan. Nowhere was the earth scorched.

Nowhere were men and equipment and space that had to be given up anyway sold to the enemy for the highest price in time they could fetch. The men whose lives were dedicated to a delaying-action with history fought one of the poorest delaying-actions in history.

Why? Because of a character deficiency in a substantial number of the individuals who constituted the directive machinery of British power in Asia. Because the successors of the men who built the greatest empire in modern history had come, by a process of autopsychological warfare, to found their philosophy of life upon a negative proposition: It cannot be done; it cannot be done by the enemy and it cannot be done by us.

Despite the long history of achievement behind him the sahib of 1942 lacked, because he had lost, the Western tradition of achievement, closely associated with our myth of progress, which Rotarian-minded Americans — except in New Delhi — expressed — sometimes to save themselves the trouble of expressing in any other way — by keeping on their desks the printed slogan: 'The difficult we do immediately. The impossible takes a little longer.'

In reaching these conclusions, I felt reasonably confident that I had isolated at least one of the principles of defeat which had played a decisive role in the military failures of 1942, which was delaying the organization of victory in 1943. The making of this discovery had been for me an intellectual adventure as well as an intellectual exercise. As in France before 1940 I had seen once more how the incessant psychological warfare between nations and groups which is inseparable from modern power-politics becomes a war in the mind within individuals.

India, however, rendered me more aware than I had previously been of the importance in maintaining our psychic health of those minute social idealisms, those spiritual vitamins, present in the rinds and pips of our conscious cynicisms. The sickness of being a sahib, for both American staff officers and British colonial officials in India, was a self-induced deficiency in social achievement, a relinquishment of the emotional rewards of contributing to progress. It was caused in each case by getting so involved in a political quarrel that one was willing to belittle one's own social mission in order to belittle the adversary, by trying to use defeatist propaganda as a poison-spray against the enemy and having it blow back in one's face.

It was a very common ailment, I reflected. One did not have to wear a sun-helmet to catch the sahib-sickness. For instance, the American businessman, trying to make himself believe he had never worked for anything but money, saying, 'What's the use of trying to make money when the government takes it all away from you? I'm going to retire and live in Florida.' He had the sahib-sickness. For instance, the soldier and the diplomat, thinking that they had never believed in all this one-world nonsense, saying, 'Let's face facts, there have always been wars and there will always be wars.' They had the sahib-sickness.

In its Indian form, as I experienced it myself, the malady was more complex. It was a multiple deficiency. Other elements, besides the vitamin, progress, were lacking, but I suspected most of these lacks were due to some mechanism of self-defeat in the minds of the permanent or temporary sahibs.

For example, the same mechanism that deprived Americans of the sense of making a useful contribution to the war also deprived them of the special, Western, obscure, but probably quite important, little vitamin, Anglo-American brotherhood. Similarly the mechanism which rendered the British deficient in achievement also deprived them of the more homely and important elements in the brotherhood complex — the elements which enable one to obtain spiritual nourishment out of the humblest human contacts, from the bootblack who wants your opinion about the outcome of the sixth race, from the washwoman whose corns are rendered painful by the dampness. There was too great a distance in India between ruler and ruled for such contacts to be significant, and Americans suffered from the same isolation, for the fear of germs usually filled any breaches in the wall of race-prejudice which separated them from the most current local manifestation of man. Such isolation can be very depressing, for man is a sensitive brute, most sensitive, perhaps, at his most brutal level.

There is some kind of Early Christian vitamin surviving in the Western cultures of today which is too slight to be detected by the most delicate instruments, but a deficiency in this principle, caused by the necessity of using violence against believers in non-violence, seemed to me to play quite a role in the decay of the sahib's morale, and noticing this made me wonder, for the first time, whether Gandhi was really as big a fool as he seemed.

A far-reaching horizon of unsuspected relevancies was beginning to open in front of me, an exciting glimpse of new unities in old diversity, of wide meanings in small, familiar things. Nothing could be wholly neglected, not even the trivial, not even the ludicrous: A *Weltschmerz* might be a military factor, a generation might lose itself if the industrialists of America abandoned the dream of a better can-opener.

This vision of newly perceived relevancies among ideas suggested an analogous multiplication of relevancies among the lives of men, a more symbiotic conception of the relationship between personal and social life, between politics and man, than I had yet developed.

Is it not possible, I asked myself, that, without being less selfish than we believe, we are more social, perhaps even more socialist, than we realize? That our lives are happy and full — when they are — because they are filled, and perpetually refilled, with imperceptible fractions of the lives of our neighbors? That we feel free not only because we are not enslaved but because we see that our fellows are free? That our pursuit of happiness is a fruitful one precisely because so many are in the chase? That the mechanism of all these fulfillments and exchanges lies in the institutionalized contacts between man and man, depending for its effectiveness both upon the technical adequacy and smooth co-ordination of the institutions themselves and upon the ideology of the individual, his acceptance of the abstractions — liberty, brotherhood of man, civic progress — in the name of which the institutions are founded? That a deficiency in such an institution — for example, an institution for fostering brotherhood which only verbalizes brotherhood — begets a deficiency in the individual, and that a conflict between two institutions — such as the conflict between democracy and imperialism — inevitably produces a neurosis in the individual?

May it not be that much of the conflict and confusion in our minds arises from a deficiency in the basic institution of language, from the failure of self-knowledge which occurs when we try to express modern experience in medieval syntax, when we use the idiom of rugged individualism in discussing the problems of a co-operative society, the idiom of sovereign nationalism in discussing the problems of what is really one world?

III

The Mirror of Nature

THE SAHIB-SICKNESS with me was like a recurrent fever of gradually diminishing intensity. From the first there were intervals of buoyant mood between the fits of depression and these intervals began to lengthen as my mind, like a patient spider, spun out new filaments of human participation to replace those which had snapped when I left the familiar Western world behind me.

It was some time before I realized there was a connection between my subjective moods and my rediscovery of humanity in its Oriental aspect, before I learned to use the Brown Man's Asia as an antidote to the conflicts and aridities of the wartime White Man's Asia. My first attempts to reach through the bars of sahibdom to establish a contact with the Indian people were largely on a nonverbal and presocial level, so much so that our intercourse was through the medium of climate and landscape and pictorial image rather than by word or gesture.

The letters I wrote home during my first months in India reflected both my steadily developing adaptation to the contact of Indian culture and the sense of paradox or mirage which arose from my unawareness of the processes of adaptation. In a letter I wrote to my wife in December, 1943, I projected upon the Indian' climate my feeling of paradox at the strangeness and familiarness, the attractiveness and repulsiveness, of Indian society. Starting with a description of a winter evening in North India, I wrote:

> The sky is pale and clear, the air is filled with the flight and
> twitter of birds, including some small, vivid green parakeets and

other strange and tufted sorts.   This is the tepid twilight hour that I love here, the most Indian time of day.   Soon the shadows will deepen and the smoke of many small cow-dung fires will float in motionless blue layers between sky and earth.   It is the most vesperal sort of evening, the most propitious to meditation that you can find, and the one which expresses the aspiration of short southern winter days toward long northern summer twilights.   It is typical of this country that it should choose the abrupt, semi-tropical sunset to express lingering charm.   Winter evenings are the June moments of India, the time of the mild, the tepid, and the bland, because they represent a brief truce in the seasonal warfare of man against the elements.

The soft light is like a lotion to the eyes after the glare of the sun.   The air is neither hot nor cold but a delicious repose to nerves and capillaries which have been trying all day to adjust themselves to brusque alternations of heat and cold.

The climate here is very unsettling for anyone raised in Europe or America.   It tends to break down fixed associations and to rearrange their components in ambivalent patterns.   The promise of morning carries the threat of noonday heat; the blessed surcease of evening is a threshold to the Nirvana of night.   Winter is the comfortable season because it is the longest release from summer, but is also the season of shortened light and long chill darknesses. Spring is the inferno of the dry season, and the monsoon months which follow it bring fertility to the earth, but prickly torture to the skins of men.   Thus, the spirit of man is driven to seek refuge in the quarter notes of the daily and annual cycle, in the last breath of morning and the first flower of evening, in the false spring of February and the Indian summer of November.

These moments being so tragic in their brevity, the mind falls into the perversity of opposites which seems to me characteristic of Indian art: The sweetness of sour things, the brightness of dark things, the coolness of hot things.   This is India, land of large apples and large worms, of filth and loveliness, of transcendent benevolence and transcendent cruelties.

There is doubtless a lot of literature in all this but at least it reflects the mixture of hostility and charm which seems to me to emanate from everything in this country.

Apart from the climate, there are certain basically alien rhythms of India which I suspect have important repercussions on the mind. I cannot discern all of them clearly as yet, but there are two movement-patterns which it is impossible not to notice. One is the slow, regular rumbling tread of ox-carts in the streets and roads; the other, just as ubiquitous, though perhaps less noticed, is the endless, deliberate, wheeling of kites in the sky. In our culture fast motion is associated with hurry, and hurry with so many things, that it seems to me the constant repetition below the level of consciousness of these slow Indian rhythms must have far-reaching effects upon one.

A short time later, in another letter home, I turned again, and again unconsciously, to meteorological symbolism as a means of describing the invisible impacts of Indian culture, but now some animal and human figures were beginning to appear in my mental image of India.

A lot of imperceptible impressions accumulate and build up a mood, [I wrote] and you can't put your finger on anything that explains the mood.

It was like that last night at the Uday Shan-Kar ballet. (The dance-forms created by this gifted artist seem very westernized ones to Indians, but to Westerners they seem unmistakably Eastern.) I was completely charmed. I don't know by what, but somehow graceful movement and gracious sound built up in me a mood that had something magical in it. Magical, because it gave me a feeling of limits rolled back, of outlines becoming blurred and transfigurations possible — anything into anything else.

This is the peculiar magic of the ballet but it is also the magic of India, and there is a special quietness, a release from anxiety, at the core of it. India is truly the land of transfigurations, and the legends she weaves are sometimes breathtaking in their vividness — and in the audacity of the imagination which conceives them.

For example, I bicycled a short distance out into the country the other day to look at some Moghul tombs and found myself strolling amid the picturesque antiquities of eighteenth-century Rome, as the old engravings depict it. There was not the slightest objective reason for such a mirage, but nothing could shake the reality of the impression.

There is one extraordinary mirage which occurs every morning for about an hour after sunrise. You step out of your tent into a morning light which elsewhere can only be found in a high mountain meadow in June. The air is crystalline, the light falls like a cascade upon a fresh and dewy world, and for that one hour of the day India is everything that India is not.

The evenings are less startling, but they are the true Indian hour. The light falls, the fields become velvet, the horizon a mirage, and a magical hush descends upon the world, like a sorcerer falling into meditation before a trance. This is the threshold hour, bringing excitement in the knowledge that anything may happen, and serenity in the certainty that everything will happen.

Another potent factor of magic in this land is the promiscuous association of men and beasts. There seems to be no sharp dividing line between the human and the animal kingdoms here. Cows and dogs and many other creatures are simply animal members of the Indian community. In the morning, when I walk from my tent to the mess-tent, the birds — large black things like crows — hop along with me and barely move a few inches one way or the other to avoid being stepped on.

I have almost learned to get along with the wasps who work in my office. There is a little balcony coffee-house downtown where I sometimes drop in when I have been seeing someone at the American headquarters and it is always full of sparrows. They walk about on the marble-top tables and perch on the backs of the chairs. I have almost been tumbled off my bicycle by packs of pariah dogs gamboling in the road, utterly oblivious of my existence, and the jackals, as far as I can make out, are not wild creatures at all but an animal scavenging-caste with nocturnal duties.

After a while you cease to notice these city-dwelling animals but I am sure these continual assaults upon your sense of where things belong beget a tolerance of the irrational and an expectation of the unlikely which are propitious to magical thinking. If the beasts of the field live like men, perhaps they are gods in disguise or, as the Indians sometimes believe, members of the human family who have come down in the world through animal reincarnation. Whatever they are, they are like something else, and likely at any time to turn into the other thing.

The evolution toward the establishment of a conscious relationship with India by means of cultural translations and exchanges
is marked in a letter I wrote at the end of February, 1944.
Though the letter reflects some naïvely subjective interpretations
of Indian culture, though it emphasizes the secondary and puts
the first last, it reflects a growing realization of the connection
between magic mood and the simple magic of participating in the
marvelous variety of human experience. This is what I wrote:

> I set out just before noon on my bicycle with some sandwiches
> and fruit and a thermos bottle in my pack and took a road which
> leads out of town some ten miles across the plain to a loathsome
> phallic ruin called the Qutab Minar. I did not want to visit the
> Qutab again, but I love this road which is dusty and lined with
> shade trees on both sides and runs straight across the plain littered
> with the ruins of ruins. It is a perfect road for pilgrims and ad-
> venturers, a road that sweeps them along like a river, each to his
> appointed destination, each at the pace his destiny allots: The
> pace of the quiet ox, the pace of the disdainful camel, always hur-
> rying away from something unpleasant toward something equally
> unpleasant, the pace of the nervous pony, the unhurried peasant,
> bicycle, and the motorcar.
>
> The freemasonry of the highroad which gave so much flavor to
> the old travelers' tales in the West has never ceased to exist in
> India, and you cannot take to a road here without having very
> clearly the feeling that you are entering into a brotherhood. As
> long as you are moving from somewhere to somewhere else along
> such a highway you are the accomplice and the equal of every
> other moving creature; no camel will despise you because you have
> not his loftiness, no ox will hate you for going fast when he must go
> slowly. Nowhere more than on the road are you conscious of the
> attitude which is perhaps the most basic of all Indian attitudes:
> Their total, magnificent, slightly inhuman toleration of all des-
> tinies. You are what you were meant to be, you go where you
> must go, I do not know you, but I accept you, because I also am
> what I was meant to be, and I, too, go where I must go.
>
> There was a great bustle on the road this morning, it was never
> so Whitmanesque, and the slightly spinsterish, but still charming,

Indian spring with its withered ardor had produced a budding proliferation in the roadside villages which I passed. It is one of my regrets that I have not yet learned to see an Indian village or bazaar; my eyes just aren't trained, and I could not describe one to save my life. I love them and am endlessly fascinated; but all I can make out is a wild surrealist confusion of men and animals and many kinds of inanimate objects, arranged in completely implausible patterns, probably because the Indians do not make the same clear-cut distinctions between these categories that we do. In fact, it is doubtful to me whether they have any sense of categories, or if they have, they must be based on entirely different principles from ours. For example, we put beds in bedrooms because the two ideas have an obvious kinship in our minds, whereas the Indian takes his charpoy of criss-crossed ropes out of the house and sets it up in the street and lies in the sun, because he wants to lie down, and a bed is a thing to lie on, not a part of a room that you lie in. Quite possibly he is right and our esthetic sense is still bound to a medieval theology which our reason has long since rejected.

In some of these Indian villages and along the road I noticed something I had never observed before, a type of peasant woman, very tall and a little gaunt, with a kind of ghastly beauty, like some Byzantine Madonnas.

I did not know where I wanted to go, but I thought I would just pedal along until I saw something promising, and finally, about twelve miles out of town, I found a little dirt road, hardly more than a path, which seemed practicable, more or less, and ran through fields of flowering mustard to a village plastered against some ruins in a grove of shade trees.

I rode along for quite awhile, and very merrily, over that dirt path, feeling adventurous and well-satisfied with myself because it was something almost unheard-of in this part of India, not that there was any danger in it, but it was just something people don't do, almost like walking into one of the cages at the zoo, so I was glad to be doing it. I passed the first little village and went on some miles through still others, and several small adventures happened to me. In one village two huge pariah dogs attacked me but I put them to rout with psychological warfare, and in another a black water buffalo with strong nationalist sentiments lumbered to his feet and made at me, but I was too fleet. Also I must have raped two rather pretty peasant girls, or they would not have screamed so shrilly as I came upon them around a sharp turn and passed them — Indian women are always haunted by the fear of rape, with them this fear is the basis of modesty.

At last, and quite by chance, not knowing where I was, I came upon a vast jumble of walls and terraces overgrown with vegetation, much larger than most of the Moghul tombs upon the plain, a palace by its appearance, and seemingly of an earlier time. I had a wonderful time exploring it, peering into dim, ruined vaults, crawling through archways, climbing up winding stone stairs and clambering out on high terraces with a magnificent view over the plain to the distant city, all the time keeping a sharp eye out for snakes, because there were creepers and underbrush everywhere, and the place reminded me of the ruined palace in the *Jungle Book* where Mowgli had the adventure with the blind cobra.

I was looking for the perfect place to have lunch and finally I found it: A little walled Moslem graveyard where the sky came through great breaches in the crumbling walls, and small trees, something like wild olives, had thrust up between the tombs. While I sat there in the shade under a tree, three ragged little village boys appeared from nowhere and then a young Indian soldier, very slim and beautiful, who apparently considered himself responsible for my safety in this wild place. They all sat at my feet, staring at me with wild surmise, while I ate four beef sandwiches, two oranges and two bananas, drank lemonade out of a thermos bottle, lit a pipe, then, for no particular reason, took out a pad and proceeded to put John Donne's celebrated sermon on the bells into a somewhat Taylorized version of seventeenth-century English verse.

At first I was somewhat uneasy under the steady gaze of my retinue and thought feebly of trying to bribe or frighten them into going away, but after awhile I came to like their attitude. The little boys were quite good and when they did occasionally utter an awed whisper the soldier silenced them with a frown, lest they disburb my improbable, but obviously lordly, occupations.

They took their role so seriously that when a vivid green parakeet with a scarlet beak, like an actress' toenail, perched on the cornice of the broken wall and began to chitter and cackle, one of the little boys picked up a stone and looked inquiringly at the soldier. The soldier held him suspended with a cautionary gesture then looked inquiringly at me. I thought carefully for some time, then said in a clear voice, 'Let the bird live,' whereupon the soldier whispered in Hindustani to the boy and he dropped the stone.

I got back to town somewhat leg-weary after a twenty-five-mile ride and with a near-sunstroke, but it was well worth it. Then, to complete the day, we had four Indian couples to dinner, all the women lovely and very cultivated, and had much pleasant talk with them.

When I wrote this letter I was on the road to convalescence from the sahib-sickness. From the reader's point of view it is perhaps an anticipation to cite it here, but, as he will discover in the chapters which follow, my dissection of the colonial mind did not by any means exhaust the discoveries of man's self-defeating and self-impoverishing mechanisms which Asia held in store for me, no more than the description of the mellow mood, which arises from even superficial and fragmentary participation in the lives of one's fellow-men, exhausts the possibilities of human enrichment.

IV

The School of Delusion

THE CONTRAST between certain aspects of the Asiatic cultures to whose influence I was exposed and my own wartime professional activity as a member of a clandestine organization led me to the most far-reaching personal discovery that I made in the East, the one which unlocked the greatest number of sealed doors and tore down the most significant mental partitions that had prevented me from attaining one world in my own mind.

This discovery concerned the problem of delusion, as applied to mankind in general, and to myself in particular. It can be summarized in the following conclusions:

1. That delusion, in the literal psychiatric sense, attacks the mind of man almost as universally and frequently as the common cold attacks his nasal passages, but with much graver consequences.

2. That we are largely unaware of this prevalence of delusion in our lives because it is institutional rather than personal, and while we are trained to recognize private delusion, we tend to assume that everything which is public must be real.

Before relating the experiences and reasonings which led me to develop this point of view, it may be well to clarify the distinction I have drawn between private and public, or institutional, delusion.

By private or personal delusions I mean delusions which primarily concern the individual, false or distorted perceptions of reality in interpersonal relationships or in the relationship of the individual to society as a whole. When a man, without objective evidence of homicidal intent, concludes that his wife means to put arsenic in his coffee, he is suffering from a private delusion. When a murderer says he was fully justified in murdering because he is a genius and the victim was an inferior being somehow standing in his way, he is suffering from a delusion. The two examples are clearly recognizable as illustrating the delusion of persecution and the delusion of grandeur which, when they become deeply imbedded in the personality, characterize the dangerous disease, paranoia.

Individuals who suffer occasionally from mild forms of delusion without allowing their whole lives to be dominated by delusion are often classified by psychiatrists as paranoid types and most of us behave at times as if there were something of the paranoid in us, for we harbor suspicions about our neighbors' attitudes toward us and/or exaggerated ideas of our own importance which seem to reflect in miniature the paranoid view of the world. Usually we recognize such imaginings as delusions — if not at once, then a little later — are ashamed of them and try to repress, instead of developing them, which is why most of us can get married without hiring a taster and why we are rarely arrested for murder.

By public or institutional delusions I mean applying the I-am-Napoleon principle and the Wifey-Has-Arsenic-in-Her-Eye principle to the relationships between organized social groups of which we are members and other groups, or between our group and human society as a whole. I mean behaving in our public capacities as members of racial, social, or political groups, or of official institutions, in the way that the private paranoid behaves toward other individuals.

Sometimes we are able to recognize the more extreme public delusions in the same way we recognize our mild private delusions and to spot the manifestations of mass-paranoia which correspond to strait-jacket cases on the level of the individual. The Nazi delusions that the Germans were a master-race and that the Jews were conspiring against them were recognized by quite a few people outside Germany — even by some inside — and the lynch-mentality which exists in some parts of the United States is widely accepted as a pathological state of mind.

We are even capable of recognizing slightly more subtle forms of institutional delusion — when they arise in the minds of men belonging to a group which is not our own. When the ideology or propaganda of our own group contains delusion an iron curtain of the mind shuts down on us and makes it nearly impossible to discover the truth.

'It's no delusion when you actually find arsenic in the cup,' we say. 'Wives don't normally poison husbands but nations really do put arsenic in other nations' coffee.'

The possibility that much of our thinking about public affairs, even in normal times, even in civilized countries like America, might be twisted by delusion, first occurred to me during a trip I made to one of the OSS jungle-bases at the end of December, 1943. In the plane flying there I read a little Indian booklet on Gandhi's doctrine of nonviolence which I had picked up in a bookstore before leaving Delhi, and though the Mahatma did not make a convert on this occasion, the contrast between the inner serenity of Gandhi's world and the murkiness of the wartime cloak-and-dagger world in which I lived stood out vividly in my mind.

With two exceptions, I thought, all the classic symptoms of paranoia are embodied in the folkways and folklore of this cloak-and-dagger culture in which I have been immersed for the last two years. Our obsession with security, the constant feeling of lurking menace, of invisible hostilities, of enemy minds plotting against us — where outside of an insane asylum could one find a better example of a persecution-complex?

Very few of my colleagues in clandestine activity went about proclaiming they were Napoleons but some of them, especially the nationals of countries which possessed a well-ripened secret-service tradition, frequently behaved as if they thought they were Fouché, Napoleon's minister of police. The feeling of secret power which comes from possessing secrets that ordinary mortals may not know, from pulling invisible strings of intrigue, from committing with impunity acts for which the ordinary citizen is jailed and the ordinary soldier court-martialed, can be a dangerous mental intoxicant, leading to a sense of self-importance so inflated that it resembles certain classic manifestations of paranoia. The tradition of ruthlessness in the long-established secret services, the almost debonair cynicism with which normal scruples and repugnances of feeling are brushed aside in the interests of operational results, are akin to the criminal paranoid's contempt for the wormlike humanity which must be crushed under heel in the interests of his godlike self.

Living and working in this atmosphere, I said to myself, is like attending a school for paranoia, like training oneself to become insane, in the way that professional beggars sometimes train themselves to become cripples. What progress am I making in the art of being paranoid?

In some ways, none, I decided. There can be no paranoia without delusion, and though the cloak-and-dagger cosmos is like a paranoid's delusion, it is not one. There are real enemy spies and subversive agents plotting against us. The systematic suspicion with which we are trained to look upon everyone is not a groundless suspicion. When we caution staff officers against exposing themselves to the risk of being captured alive, lest they be broken down by enemy tortures and forced to reveal our secrets, we are not filling them with nightmares, we are giving them a sober statement of reality. In this world it is almost a symptom of mental derangement not to look under the bed at night.

There is another important difference between the private paranoid and the cloak-and-dagger man, my thought continued. In the orthodox psychiatric view, paranoia is a personal maladjustment to social reality. What might be called, in terms of the one-world concept, the antisocial orientation of the clandestine mind, is an impersonal, or extra-personal thing. Most of the Allied cloak-and-dagger men I have encountered are not antisocial types as far as their attitudes toward their own societies are concerned. They are usually high-minded patriots willing to sacrifice themselves for their countries and relatively indifferent to the normal rewards of military merit; some of these professional paranoids are even one-world idealists. Our ruthlessness and lack of scruple do not reflect an overevaluation of self but a fanatical loyalty to a cause beyond self.

Yet, I told myself in rebuttal, there is something wrong about this correct evaluation of the cloak-and-dagger man's social role, something right in the inaccurate metaphor of the professional paranoid. There is some subjective relation between the delusive world of the paranoid and the world of clandestine realities which is so like a delusion. There is a special feeling that comes when one has lived for a long time in such a world, something which appears as a kind of personal fascism, a dictatorship of the ego over the more generous elements of the soul. Like all dictatorships, this is dedicated to the cult of power and prestige, perhaps not one's own, but the power and prestige of something with which one identifies oneself.

The tyranny of this soul-fascism weighs most heavily upon the function of conscience, transforming it at times into something much more terrifying and ugly than a being without conscience. Conscience becomes a weapon in the hands of the central dictatorship, serving as a cowed or purchased magistrate serves a tyrant, to legalize crime, converting murders into executions, robberies into expropriations, attacks on others, into preventive wars or misunderstood crusades.

Like other dictatorships this personal one rules by terror and in terror. The tyrant ego is forever haunted by a lurking sense of insecurity which no triumphs and no purges of enemies can ever quite set at rest. Being a professional or institutional paranoid feels amazingly like being any other kind, like being a paranoid, period. It was all very puzzling.

The puzzle began to sort itself out in my mind when I arrived at the OSS camp and found an extraordinary psychological situation, which was not a morale-problem in the ordinary sense of the word, but a psychiatric one. There were no serious internal frictions, *esprit de corps* was strong and discipline excellent, there was no discouragement, begot of professional frustration — for this group had been accomplishing prodigious things and dozens of exciting new opportunities were developing for them; unlike most other Americans in the theater, they even maintained cordial relations with their British colleagues in the neighborhood.

Yet there was an atmosphere of tension and strain in the place, a thick fog of delusion hanging over it, and a number of the men I met were obviously very near to collapse. In psychiatric terms the prevailing atmosphere in the camp was created by a mixture of paranoid and schizoid symptoms in the behavior of the men within it, the latter being particularly alarming because the type of work they were doing required men who were cool as well as brave, and suicidal heroes were a menace.

The commanding officer was well aware of the problem and, as subsequent events proved, capable of solving it, but when I arrived, he had been in command too short a time for his leadership to take full effect. His predecessor had been an extraordinary individual, a man of tremendous courage, energy, and resourcefulness, but one so possessed with the melodrama of his cloak-and-dagger role that he filled his whole detachment with nightmares of brutality and menace. All of his talk was about killing Japs in devious or spectacular ways, and being killed by them in still more hair-raising circumstances. In more relaxed moods he would invite friends to hold lighted cigarettes to his bare arm, in order to test his ability to withstand torture, should he ever be taken alive by the enemy, or urge them to jump on his belly from a considerable height in order to demonstrate his toughness.

He was willing to run any risk himself, including some unjustifiable ones, and equally willing to expose his subordinates to extreme peril. He drove himself and others beyond the limits of normal endurance and punished the most trivial failures or inefficiencies with such disproportionate severity that he became a legend of mingled dread and admiration in the minds of his men, something between a military Caligula and a jungle Ahab in their imaginations.

It is a considerable understatement to say that a multiple sense of insecurity prevailed among the members of this group.

The influence of the former commanding officer's personality upon the group had been re-enforced by the recent arrival of a number of men from the United States who had received an overly strenuous indoctrination in the OSS training schools at home, building up in their minds exaggerated ideas of the sinister, ruthless, and dangerous elements in their mission. The emphasis on secrecy and on violence, I knew, was often excessive in these training courses (an error arising out of the frantic improvisation which had to be done in the early days of the organization and perhaps stemming in part from a reaction to the still more dangerous underemphasis on the peril of enemy clandestine warfare in the orthodox military mind). Instructors in the OSS training schools had been known to make statements to their pupils like, 'Gentlemen, this is a course in murder,' and such statements, coupled with the fantastic rigmarole intended to impress the students with the importance of secrecy, often overstimulated their imagination.

Though I had often heard General Donovan fulminate against those of his subordinates who encouraged this cloak-and-dagger mythology, it had always seemed to me more grotesque than harmful — until I observed its effects, in this Asiatic base, upon men suddenly thrown into a particularly tense form of jungle warfare. The real cloak-and-dagger world was sinister enough, and enough of a strain on one's sanity, but these poor devils had brought with them from America a collection of delusions about the reality which was itself so like a delusion.

There is a delusion, after all, in the cloak-and-dagger picture of the world, I decided. It is hard to detect because it is an exaggeration rather than an invention, a generalization of the occasional or even of the frequent rather than of the exceptional, a systematization of the merely possible rather than of the unlikely. On the other hand, this relatively subtle distortion of institutional reality easily passes into the extreme form of delusion found in the private paranoid. Looking under the bed at night may be a salutary routine precaution in certain situations but when one is forced to live for a long time in such a situation there is a danger of falling into the state of mind where one looks, sees no enemy agent, yet remains convinced that an invisible one is hiding there.

Public, or institutional, delusion arises when one accepts, or is forced into, a social situation which mirrors one of the usual personal delusions, I concluded. One inevitably develops delusions when reality casts one's social attitudes in the same pattern that delusions cast the paranoid's. The difference between the professional paranoid and the clinical one is simply that the former's social behavior ends by distorting his thinking, whereas the latter's distorted thinking is the source of his social, or antisocial, behavior.

Graduate from a school for murder, believe that your mission is to murder other men called the enemy, and you will come to be haunted by the idea that the enemy is plotting to murder you. This supposition of hostile intent will not, in itself, be a delusion. On the other hand, there seems to be something about the human mind which makes it impossible for you to think of yourself as a potential murder-victim without distorting a grim reality into a delusion, without somehow falsifying and exaggerating it, as for instance by believing that some friend is the enemy in disguise, come to murder you.

You begin with a perfectly conscious and rational assumption that what you seek to do to the enemy, he will seek to do to you. (Or, perhaps more commonly, by seeking to do to the enemy what you think, perhaps mistakenly, he is seeking to do to you.) Even if there is no mistake in your assumption, even if it does not begin with a delusion, it always ends with a delusion. The rational assumption of identity in attitude between yourself and the enemy operates like the paranoid's unconscious projection of his own aggressive feelings toward others upon others; hating with cause leads to the same mental results as the causeless feeling of being hated.

There is another point at which the metaphorical paranoia of public life converges with the paranoia which is treated as a private disease, another reason why violence, or any kind of social conflict, tends to breed delusion, as well as to feed upon it. In the foregoing paragraph I have used the rhetorical you. When the rhetorical 'you' merges with the personal 'you' — with you, Jones, or Smith, or Taylor — when you identify your personal fate with the fate of your organization or cause, when you worry about having your private throat cut in the course of your official duties, or when you worship the god you yourself have become through possessing Aryan blood — then your delusions are no longer wholly institutional ones and to the degree that you found your life upon them you are no longer merely a professional paranoid, but a plain old-fashioned one, the kind any psychiatrist will be glad to write up.

When the professional paranoid becomes a paranoid, period, when personal fascisms begin to fill the members of an aggressive group which has hitherto functioned on a basis of close comradeship within and aggressiveness without, then group-morale disintegrates and its members begin to develop delusions about one another, leading to the historic phenomenon of revolution devouring its children. Actually it is the children of revolution who devour each other. My contact as a newspaperman with the mass-paranoias of German and Spanish fascism provided me with some striking examples of this process, and I have seen the same thing begin to happen within clandestine organizations which seemed to have an excessive *esprit de corps*.

More than once I saw my colleagues in OSS or the clandestine services of the other United Nations led through delusive thinking, to propose operations which not only were contrary to the ideals for which we were all consciously fighting, but self-defeating in terms of strategic results. The problem was not whether it was permissible in some circumstances to fight fire with fire and poison with poison but it was to know how to fight fire with fire when it was really necessary without becoming so addicted to the habit that one attempted to do it even when it was positively harmful.

The incurable paranoid cannot resist fighting fire with fire. He is apt to make a cult of ruthlessness and cunning. His lack of scruple is frequently a tactical advantage in war but the delusive mentality associated with it inevitably falsifies his strategic judgment. The paranoid mind is clearer than the nonparanoid mind in some respects but it almost invariably goes astray in gauging the psychological reactions of the adversary and in the determination of relative risks. Germany lost the war because of Hitler's paranoid strategy, because Hitler could not understand the Anglo-Saxon mind and because his psychic insecurity drove him to the mad attack upon Russia. Like Napoleon, that other great paranoid, he had a superstitious contempt for real dangers, a superstitious dread of imaginary or potential ones.

Once my attention had been called to the problem of institutional delusion and I began to recognize the delusive elements in my cloak-and-dagger view of the world I became increasingly aware of the tendency of delusion to overflow its strictly professional channels and poison other social relationships, besides our relationship with the enemy.

More than a trace of our delusive attitudes toward the enemy was apparent in the relationships between OSS and other Allied cloak-and-dagger agencies in Southeast Asia. Since the Anglo-American relationship in general was bad in this theater, one could hardly expect that relations between American and British clandestine organizations represented in it would be good, but they were actually even worse than one might have expected and they were marked by the pathological suspicion, the persecutory sense of conspiracy, which characterize the cloak-and-dagger mind.

After a year on the SEAC staff where as an assistant umpire in the OSS-British squabbles I frequently found myself equally unpopular with both sides, I found this paranoid atmosphere rather oppressive and was pleased when I succeeded in getting myself transferred to the OSS headquarters as a co-ordinator of intelligence activities. Within a short time, however, I discovered a curious thing: Though pitched to a lower key of violence, the controversies within OSS had the same delusive character as the ones between OSS and the British clandestine organizations.

The atmosphere of our headquarters at times was the atmosphere of a Byzantine court. A constant struggle for power was going on between individuals and groups. Plots and persecutions, suspicions of plots and persecutions, flourished endlessly, but somehow without destroying the bond of comradeship among us.

Learning to control this psychic infection was both a strenuous and fruitful inner experience. The secret, I discovered, lay not so much in trying to uncover the logical fallacy which lies at the bottom of all delusions, public or private, as in trying to envisage the consequences of my behavior if I assumed the delusion to be true and acted in accordance with it. If I believed that a colleague, X, was plotting against me or taking some unfair advantage of me, my impulse was to take some kind of hostile action against X or at least have nothing more to do with the fellow, but when I paused to examine the implications of such behavior I would realize that by following this course of action I would betray my own ideal of duty and therefore be false to myself. X might be a plotter, I would decide, but I had no choice but to work with him. Attempting to foil his plots would, in the long run, do me more harm than the plots themselves. Whenever I could bring myself to that conclusion my perspective on the plots would change as if by magic. Either I would discover the plot was a delusion developed out of a misunderstanding in my mind, or I would realize that it was a real plot developed from a misunderstanding of me in X's mind. In the latter case I might have to oppose X but I no longer hated him because I understood so well from my own experience how a delusion about me could lead him to plot against me. When X finally realized that my opposition was not a systematic one, based on hatred, his delusion about me would vanish.

Consciously or unconsciously, this process, I believe, was going on in the minds of most of us and it is the reason why, though we sometimes sounded as if we had just escaped from the dangerous ward of some asylum, we worked together as well as most groups. We would have worked together better if certain organizational flaws had not bred internal insecurity in our detachment and if our professional indoctrination had not filled our minds with nightmares, but the very things which made OSS a school for delusion helped to develop a discipline for overcoming delusion. Our familiarity with the techniques of subversive and psychological warfare made us realize better than most men the undesirability of using these techniques in personal relationships. The delusive temptations to which we were constantly exposed made us realize how much our sanity depended upon the social and ideological mechanisms that held us together.

The closer delusion came to putting on mufti and developing on the level of personal relationships, the more successful we were in recognizing and dispelling it. We did not shake off personal delusion entirely, because humans almost never do, but we maintained, and possibly even surpassed, the normal level of civilized human relations in our culture.

On the semi-institutional level of office-politics it was much harder to recognize delusion, but the fact that our struggles for power took place among members of a group knit by close ties of fellowship turned all our fraternal daggers into rubber ones, our poison-cups into merely bad-tasting potions, and consequently our delusions into delusions of rubber daggers and harmlessly disagreeable powders slipped into our coffee.

On the true institutional level of professional relationships with Allies and enemies, we were usually unable to recognize delusion at all, we called everything that we believed reality. Yet even on this level certain civilized restraints — like our inhibition against torturing the enemy — certain social or cultural ties — like the dim, occasional realization that the British, after all, were allies — certain vestiges of civic conscience reminding us that we were servants of a democratic nation and not a power unto ourselves, helped to keep our world from turning completely into a paranoid nightmare and checked the tendency of delusion to seep into every compartment of our minds.

As far as I could make out from personal observation of other official, but not clandestine, Americans and British in the theater, delusion was not a monopoly of the cloak-and-dagger world. There was certainly as much delusion in Anglo-American relations on the respectable levels as on our clandestine levels. Only the form was different. At the higher brass levels, one did not worry about bribed servants and Mata Haris; one had delusions about the minutes of conferences being dishonestly written-up by the party which was taking them, one scented plots to foil national policy in the wording of a communiqué. One did not think in terms of preventive or punitive assassinations, but one thought in terms of preventive or punitive dishonesties — and one was filled with a deep sense of persecution to discover that the adversary was thinking in the same terms.

The only difference between cloak-and-dagger delusions and other official ones, it became more and more clear to me, was that the institutional delusions of the cloak-and-dagger world were relatively easy to recognize because they resembled fairly closely the unsanctified delusions of private life — doubtless because our operations so often required the personal touch — whereas those of respectable officialdom were hallowed by convention, they were officially considered reality.

Thus when the instructors in our training schools talked about courses in murder they dramatized the kinship between our war-time operations and common crime, causing us to develop delusions of criminal persecution. Of course, it was murder to kill the guard of a Gestapo headquarters in order to rifle the safe, but it was also murder for Allied aviators to drop bombs on sleeping women and children. Failure to call murder by its right name in all circumstances does not protect one from developing delusions when one is a murderer or the accomplice of murderers. The man who thinks in terms of killing individual enemies to rifle safes is haunted by delusions of lurking assassins and attacks on his own safe. This delusion is technically termed being security-minded. The man who drops bombs on women and children, and his accomplices, are haunted by delusions of bombs dropping out of the sky on their own wives and children. This delusion is called thinking of national security.

Calling war by its right name, mass-murder, will not end it, but it helps us to recognize the institutional delusions which arise in our minds when war breaks out or seems near at hand.

This view of institutional delusion which, if pushed to its logical conclusion, might cause most of the political activity of nations to seem delusive to us, may seem too extreme to the reader. If so, he is free to reject it or to modify it to conform to his own sense of institutional reality. It can hardly be denied, however, that there is a great deal of delusion in the world, the only possible argument is over the exact tracing of its limits, and nothing is lost by asking oneself whether a given institutional assumption is, or is not, a delusion.*

For this reason, I believe that in the chapters which follow the reader will find this viewpoint toward the problem of delusion a useful aid to understanding, as I found it one in my personal problem of trying to understand Asia. If nothing else, it helps to overcome the cultural prejudices, themselves usually founded on delusion, which make the study of any alien experience a difficult one for us, which make emotional participation in the mental life of men who do not belong to our culture an arduous achievement.

---

* Observation and study of world affairs since 1947 has only strengthened my feeling that the concept of institutional or group delusion outlined in the foregoing pages is a useful one. As the reader will note in later chapters, however, I was not far from believing at the time I wrote *Richer by Asia* that any power-struggle, in fact almost any kind of group-conflict, is delusive in essence. This, of course, is the Buddhist view and philosophically it is a tenable one. Perhaps because I have not been again exposed to the direct influence of Asia in the intervening years, I have largely abandoned it. Moreover, it seems to me today that on the practical level there is a sound objection to any such quasi-metaphysical extensions of the concept of delusion. They risk diminishing its usefulness by distracting attention from the numerous cases where governments or other political organizations involved in a power struggle, do quite literally reason and behave like clinical paranoiacs. For similar reasons, I am no longer sure that anything is gained by considering the doctrines of national sovereignty and national defense as being in themselves "delusive," even though history has demonstrated — and continues to demonstrate — that they engender a great deal of unquestionably deluded thinking. Another modification of my earlier views that post-war experience has forced on me, concerns the types of delusion that are politically relevant. Some passages in my book might

give the impression that only the typically paranoid delusions of hostility or of self-aggrandizement are significant in public affairs. Alas, as we have seen at times in recent years, there can also be delusions of harmlessness or safety no less systematic and institutionalized than any other kind, and in certain contexts, just as dangerous. In other words, there are pacifist and internationalist as well as nationalist delusions; in fact, there are almost innumerable kinds. In general, I feel that I should have drawn a sharper distinction than I did between two related but separate problems. One problem, which my book quite properly stresses, concerns the tendency of groups in conflict to develop and perpetuate characteristically paranoid distortions of judgment. The other, with which I hope to deal more adequately someday, involves the broader role of social influences in determining how close we come to perceiving reality in any context.

V

How Irony was Lost

ONE OF MY pleasant experiences in the East — and one which enriched my understanding of institutional delusion as a major element in Western culture — was meeting the Kachins.

This meeting took place during the winter 1943–1944 in the course of one of my tours of the OSS establishments in the theater, this time to the camp on the Assam-Burma borderline at the foot of the Naga Hills, where, under the brilliant leadership of Major (later Colonel) Ray Peers, an OSS team was training the first cadres of the most remarkable guerilla force of the war, which under the name Kachin Rangers eventually won great glory for all concerned.

Peers was proud of his Kachins, and evidently much taken with them as a people. So were most of the other Americans at the camp. Even the British liaison officers attached to our group, and the neighboring tea-planters, liked the Kachins and, from the way they talked about them, it was clear that the Anglo-Kachin relationship was one of the few happy ones which the colonial system in Asia had produced.

After Peers had shown me around his camp and I had exchanged jokes or greetings with the Kachins who knew a little English, and watched them training, or relaxing between lessons, I could easily understand the general liking for these cheerful, agile, courageous, wiry, sympathetically ugly little yellow men. My curiosity about the Kachins was awakened by these superficial contacts and I began systematically pumping my hosts with questions as we sat around at night after dinner on the verandah of the small tea-planter's bungalow where Peers lived, watching an incredibly red, savage moon rise behind the forbidding mass of the Naga Hills, or, if it was too chilly, sitting in front of the fire in the big room decorated with various trophies of jungle-life — the tiger-skin, the elephant-tusk, the Naga warrior's spear, the captured Jap pilot's cap — while outside the jackals and the greater beasts of the jungle commented freely upon the biological delusion of survival.

What the Kachins like best, on the whole, is to be let alone, but if they cannot have that, they like to be interfered with in a polite and kindly way. The British had treated them kindly — and by Kachin standards politely — almost from the first, whereas they have been pushed around for centuries by their powerful southern neighbors, the Burmese, who consider them an inferior race and treat them with contempt.

For a persecuted minority, they are remarkably free from persecutory deformations of the character. This reflects both their native virtue and the fact that the Burmese are not excessively efficient in anything, especially persecution; also the fact that most of the Kachins live in country where it is very hard to get at them. Nonetheless, the Kachins do not love the Burmese and they do — because of the Burmese — value British protection. Consequently when the Japanese — bringing Burmese administrators along with them— arrived in their hills, the reception was chilly, and it was easy for us to recruit Kachins from behind the Japanese lines to train as guerillas.

In the remote jungles the Kachins do a bit of squabbling and feuding among themselves, but not in any concentrated way. Though courageous, they are not a real warrior people and unless they are thoroughly trained and well led, they will run when a mortar-shell explodes near them. Being great hunters, they know their way about the jungle, but often no better than white men who have bothered to learn it.

Their great military virtues lay, I was told, in a combination of social and cultural attitudes. Though in their own culture they carry an almost unbearable load of superstition, having extremely active imaginations, they have a remarkably well-balanced, rational, down-to-earth approach to the practical problems of life. They are sociable by nature but are also proud and independent, so that they adjust easily to elementary military discipline, take pride in looking after their own equipment, and possess some initiative in the field.

The Kachin attitude toward their white instructors and officers was a basically healthy one, as I could see myself. They were impressed but not awed. They lacked the doglike loyalty of some Asiatic peoples toward their white superiors, but evidently liked them and were anxious to be liked and respected by them, so they worked hard at learning what they were supposed to learn.

They learned easily, having quick minds. Though their own culture is so backward technologically that the Burmese and the Siamese, in comparison with them, seem to possess advanced industrial civilizations; so backward that at first they were not able to use even a modern military rifle and we had to send in old muzzle-loading buffalo guns to them, they seemed to grasp immediately the basic concept of the machine — that it is something to use, something you have to learn to use.

Racially, I learned, the Kachins were a Mongoloid people akin to the neighboring Shans, Burmese, Karens, and Siamese, and there were many common denominators, both of temperament and formal institution, among all these peoples. They all have sunny dispositions and a strain of frivolity, though the Kachins can be serious-minded when they need to be. Many Kachins had been converted to Christianity, I was told, the rest remained primitive animists. Buddhist influence, seemingly, had not touched them, but they possessed the courtesy and kindliness of a Buddhist people.

Flirtation is a great pastime among young people in all these cultures and the Kachins seemed outstanding in this respect. Though anything but severe in their morals, they have an elegant and poetic amorous tradition which is so highly respected in

Kachin society that many jungle villages, as a communal facility, maintain so-called 'love-huts' in propitious, isolated nooks, where young lovers can concentrate, sometimes for weeks, on the matters that seem most important to them, without fear of distraction or interference.

Of course, I was told, the Kachins have their faults, too. They are greatly addicted to opium and syphilis, are unthrifty, inclined to be lazy, are not overly clean in their personal habits, have little desire to get ahead in the world, and are plunged to the eyebrows in superstition. They are almost totally illiterate, and not particularly distressed by this condition, though they recognize the advantages of education.

It is certainly no exaggeration to say that Kachin culture lacks completely the tools for overcoming delusion which Western psychiatry has perfected, yet it seemed to me that the Kachins suffered less from group-delusion than any people I had ever encountered and that this freedom from delusion was a good part of their charm. It was closely associated with their sense of humor, a special kind of self-irony, which I found their most endearing trait.

Poking fun at oneself in a gentle, yet ego-deflating, way seemed the great Kachin specialty. It was by no means incompatible with a highly developed sense of self-respect and sometimes contained a touch of boastful understatement. Thus, in the favorite Kachin game — which is played by a group of men standing in a circle and trying to keep a small wicker ball in the air by hitting it with their knees — the object of the play seemed to be to miss or fumble the ball, for whenever this happened there were shouts of joyous laughter and the player who had committed the error seemed more delighted than anyone else. It is difficult to imagine any other people putting up with a game in which the certainty of frustration is so great — in baseball terms, a batting average of .125 would be sensational in this game — and by continuing to play it, the Kachins appeared to be using sport as a means for passing ironic comment on the attempts of all men, especially Kachins, to amount to something in life. When watched by a foreigner, the expressions of the players constituted a group-apology for their clumsiness — but any unwary Americans who allowed themselves to be lured into the game quickly discovered that Kachin clumsiness is an agility beyond the white man's attainment.

I heard innumerable stories illustrating the Kachin knack of laughing at oneself and at the same time boasting of superior achievement. One of my favorites was about a Kachin hunter who walked three weeks through the jungle from a village behind the enemy lines to a British military camp and presented the commander with two pairs of Japanese ears, an abject apology, and a request for more ammunition. The Kachin was an ex-soldier and should have done much better, he confessed, but he had only three bullets to start with and he had to save the third one to kill some game because the Japanese had taken all the meat in his village and the people were starving. In view of that he thought perhaps the sahib would forgive his poor performance, and maybe let him have four cartridges, which he promised to use exclusively on Japs.

The finest flower of Kachin irony, the one in which they surpassed their own cultural requirements and developed a message valid for all men, was a legend explaining the poverty, illiteracy, and superstitiousness of the Kachin people, which I memorized because it delighted me so greatly, while I was at the camp. The legend — in my own version — runs as follows:

In the dawn of humanity, the gods, who are kindly at heart, noticed that this new experiment of man was not getting off to a very good start, so they developed a three-year plan for the improvement of human happiness. They sent messengers to the Kachins, the Shans, the Karens, the Burmese, the Chinese, and the Manipur Strangers (Indians), inviting them to send representatives to a conference at the capital of the gods, in the high mountains.

When all the delegates had assembled, the president-god made a short address, outlining the plan. Then the delegates were presented with handsome parchments containing the secret of the art of reading and writing and much other useful information, including the agenda of the forthcoming celestial conferences, which would take place for the next two successive years on the same date. After that there was a question-period, then some light entertainment, and the conference adjourned until next year.

All the other delegates got home safely, but the Kachins, being naturally improvident and having a long way to go, ran out of food, so to avoid starving they boiled and ate the parchment of the gods — which explains why the Kachins have remained illiterate to this day.

When the Kachin delegates got home they explained what they had done and apologized for depriving their people of the valuable secret of reading and writing, but nobody really felt badly about it and all the Kachins agreed that the delegates would be able to catch up with *belles-lettres* at the next conference.

When the time came, the Kachins were the first delegation to arrive at the capital of the gods and the delegates this time had an ample supply of food for the return journey, but they had no other baggage, whereas the representatives of the Shans, the Karens, the Burmese, the Chinese, and the Manipur Strangers, all arrived with enormous empty hampers and sacks.

The agenda of the conference turned out to be Distribution of Gold and Silver to Representatives of the Human Races, and whereas the other delegates hauled home great loads of treasure, the poor Kachins could take only what they could hold in their hands, which explains why the Kachin people have remained poverty-stricken to this day.

'At least,' the delegates explained to their constituents, 'we won't be caught napping next year. Let every Kachin set to work at once building the greatest baskets ever seen, and we will bring them home, spilling with treasure, even if it breaks our backs.'

The Kachins worked so hard making huge baskets that it almost broke the delegates' backs just hauling them empty to the capital of the gods for the third conference. The delegates therefore were surprised — and inclined to be a little smug at first —

when they noticed that in lieu of baggage the delegates of the Shans, the Burmese, the Karens, the Chinese, and the Manipur Strangers, carried nothing but a single flower in their hands.

'Ho,' said the Kachins to a friendly Shan delegate, 'you don't expect to take home much gold and silver in the cup of that flower, do you, friend?'

'Gold and silver?' replied the Shan. 'Haven't you fellows read the agenda?'

The Kachins were forced to admit that they had eaten the agenda instead of reading it, whereupon the Shan delegate smiled and said, politely, though somewhat obscurely:

'No doubt spiritual treasures are the most valuable.'

The Kachins discovered what he meant when the meeting was called to order and the gods began to distribute *Nats* (spirits) to the human representatives. Each delegate stepped up to the platform and held up his flower, which was just big enough to seat one Nat comfortably. By providing their delegates with flowers as a means of transporting the Nats, the other races manifested their respect for these superior spiritual beings and at the same time assured themselves against any exaggeration of the unworldly in their cultures.

The Kachins, of course, had to smile and look grateful while the gods filled their baskets with left-over Nats. They spilled quite a few on the way home, which explains why the Kachins have remained the most spirit-ridden of all the peoples of the East, so much so that a Kachin today cannot make a trip without stopping every few miles to propitiate the Nats which his ancestors spilled all over the countryside, coming home from the capital of the gods.

This legend seemed to me such a delicious and profound commentary, not only on the weaknesses in Kachin character, but upon all tribal delusions of grandeur in the world, that I was inspired to add a new ending to it as I was flying back to Delhi. The gods, I decided, held a fourth conference at their capital. This time they sent invitations to the Tall White Ones in the West, as well as to the Shans, the Karens, the Burmese, the

Chinese, and the Manipur Strangers. Remembering all the
trouble the Kachins had been having with conferences since they
ate the parchment, the gods sent a special messenger to them to
explain the purpose of the forthcoming meeting, but to the other
more literate nations, they merely enclosed the printed agenda
which read: Instruction by the Gods to the Human Delegates
on the Uses of Irony as a Tool of Self-Knowledge.

At this conference the Kachins surprised everybody, including
themselves, by turning out to be the most brilliant pupils. The
other Asiatics did pretty well, too, all except the Manipur Strangers who were so busy writing the *Upanishads* at that time that
they asked to be excused from the conference.

The Tall White Ones did not even bother to reply — although
the invitations were plainly marked R.S.V.P. Sec'y of the Gods —
and the head Tall White One remarked contemptuously to his
secretary, as he tossed the card into his waste-basket:

'Those Eastern gods are appallingly backward. They can't
even spell. Look — "iron" with a "y" on the end of it.'

'You're right, boss,' the secretary replied. 'Maybe it's time we
went out there and started giving a few lessons to those wogs.'
('Wog' was a contemptuous GI term for native. Some authorities believe that it derived from Kipling's Wily Oriental Gentle-
men; others, that it originated in South Africa. It was used much
more by Americans than by British soldiers in the theater and
may have been a telescoping of wop and dog. In any case it was
used by most American GI's as if this were its derivation.)

VI

The Virus of Race

ONE AFTERNOON when I came back to my office from lunch I found a message on my desk asking me to call on the security officer in a certain wing of the India Army Headquarters. I was puzzled. I had never had any dealings with this particular section and I wondered what they wanted with me.

It developed they wanted to give me a leather wallet with three hundred rupees in it. The wallet was mine. I had left it in my tent when I went to the office and had failed to notice the loss all morning. Not a rupee was missing.

'How did you get hold of this?' I asked the security officer.

'Your bearer brought it here.'

When I got back to my tent that night I found my bearer, a sad and sentimental Indian Christian named George, looking like a man who has been through a harrowing emotional experience. I gave him a substantial reward for his honesty. George timidly presented a bill, running to about thirty-five American cents, for incidental expenses in connection with the restoration of the wallet — fare for a pony-cart ride, which no bearer would ever take if he could walk, and a telephone call, although I knew he would rather pick up a cobra than the receiver of a telephone. Having maneuvered myself into a hopeless tactical position by tipping him before he presented his bill, I paid up. Then I started to ask some questions.

'George, why didn't you just keep the wallet for me until I got back?'

That question made George very unhappy. He was embarrassed to tell me the reason because it was associated with a great fear and a still greater shame. When it dawned on me what the shame was, I felt embarrassed, too. There are some things in Asia, particularly things about the relations between white and brown men, that are not very nice. This was one of them, one of those slight lesions on the surface of human dignity which reveal a horrid shame beneath.

George had been afraid that I might miss the wallet and return and not believe that he was keeping it for me and think I had caught him stealing. He had been afraid some other servant would see him with the wallet and denounce him before he could find me. He had been afraid that the British sergeant of MP's who kept an eye on the camp while the officers were at work might stroll by the tent and see him with the wallet in his hand and arrest him as a thief caught red-handed. He had been afraid that his pocket might be picked on the way home to lunch. No doubt, he had been afraid of himself, of the temptation of eight months' wages in his hand, of the evil which his faith taught him was born into man.

George's terrors, like his shames, had shot off endlessly in all directions, each one begetting a new one in a chain-reaction of fear. He was terrified even to touch the wallet. He was more terrified to leave it, because then some other bearer might steal it, and he would be blamed. He was terrified to speak to the MP because he was a white man and a soldier, and because he might take some of the money himself and frame George.

Poor George must have felt like an innocent burgher who comes home and finds a murdered woman in his bed. In his desperate panic he had apparently done quite wild things, perhaps even hired a pony cart. I did not want to look any farther into the paranoid abyss George was causing to yawn in front of me so I tried to get him onto less painful ground by another question.

'But, George, why did you go to the security officer at GHQ when you know my office is at SEAC?'

George's explanations remained a little incoherent, but the

ellipses and *non sequiturs* which made them hard for me to follow were those of delicacy rather than naked shame. As far as I could make out, he had made a half-hearted attempt to find me at SEAC Headquarters but the guard at the door had refused to admit him. In his despair he remembered he knew someone who knew a police sahib (so George had official connections, like so many of us) and he consulted his friend and the friend consulted his sahib and George was advised to go to the security officer.

'What a filthy place Asia is,' I wrote to my wife that night, 'I feel as if I needed a carbolic bath after something that happened today.'

'A curious little story, don't you think?' I was concluding. 'At least it gives you some idea of the half-infuriating, half-pathetic charm of these people (the Indians) and the fantastic, roundabout way in which their minds work.'

Suddenly I stopped writing. A thought had struck me with the impact of Newton's apple.

What am I doing? I asked myself. Here I am making sweeping generalizations about the Indian mind because of my observation of one man, a Christian at that, and a bearer, a highly specialized caste which is probably as different from other Indian castes as fox-terriers are from timber-wolves. Unconsciously I have been creating a picture of the Indian people in the image of my bearer — he is the only Indian I know. I have been assuming that the culture of the servant class — the special section of the servant class which hereditarily serves the white man — is the culture of India. I have been viewing race relationships through the eyes of my bearer. We are all of us doing that, all the Americans here. We spend half our time telling stories about our bearers, making fun of their queer, exasperating, on the whole lovable ways. We are always saying to each other: Look how backassward these Indians are, why, yesterday my bearer ——

What about the British? Did they, too, unconsciously think of Indians as a race of bearers? Did they look upon their political relations with the three-hundred-ninety millions of Indians in terms of the intimate tyrannies, the domestic loyalties, and the housekeeping betrayals of their relations with their bearers?

Did the British conviction of the incurable dishonesty of the Indian civil servant and politician arise from his own acceptance of the conventionalized, therefore legitimate, household grafts of his bearers — the squeeze on purchases and on the pay of lesser or part-time servants, the graceful padding of expense accounts, the inconsistent, but by no means loose, financial morals, so similar to those of American newspaper reporters, which caused masters to pay for the pony-carts of bearers who walked on their errands? Did the British conviction of the hopeless fumbling of the native, his ineptitude to manage himself, arise, like the American soldier's conviction of his technological 'backasswardness,' from watching Indian bearers pull something that it was easier to push; in final analysis, therefore, from our own failure to realize the immense cultural context of our technological achievements, our muscular awareness of the laws of Western science?

The bias we all have in favor of imposing and faraway, instead of humble and near-by, causes, made me reluctant to believe that the British, like the American, view of India could be falsified by such a plebeian factor of distortion as daily contact with a servant. Surely, I argued with myself, the British had too many other contacts with different classes of Indians to be unduly influenced by that one.

Gradually, however, I discovered that the British in India did not have many significant native contacts. Most Britishers had none, except their bearers. They worked with Indians as colleagues — usually very humble colleagues — in their offices and their regiments, but such contacts in the East are not channels of cultural exchange, they are not emotionally fruitful contacts, except some of the military ones. The relationships are too formalized, the roles of the participants too conventionalized. Mask meets mask instead of man meeting man.

Out of office hours there are no contacts. Even formal social contacts, where the masks are more highly conventionalized than in the business contacts, were almost nonexistent in Delhi in 1943. Indians seldom went to British parties and British even more rarely to Indian ones. Few Britishers had any Indian friends.

Once it had been common throughout the East for white men to take native mistresses. This practice had ceased to be respectable — and therefore has virtually disappeared in most places — after white women started coming to the East to live, bringing with them a host of psychological evils and impediments to interracial understanding in addition to the tabu on the native mistress.

Only the bearer remained as a really significant link between the mind of East and the mind of the West. I could easily see why it was an important, if unreliable, one.

For one thing, the bearer, whose principal function is that of a valet, is the most intimate of house servants. His domestic role is more intimate than that of any male servant in the West; he comes close to being a male ladies' maid, the kind who combs her mistress's hair. As a man, he will not try to comb your hair for you, but he will put on your pants for you, if you let him, and he will be positively unhappy if you don't let him take off your shoes and put your slippers on your feet when you come home.

Being such an intimate servant, almost as intimate as a dog, his relationship with you is an intimate one. Seemingly trivial but certainly intimate — the kind of relationship which makes it both difficult and unnecessary to keep up the play of masks. It is very hard indeed to keep your mask on when you take your pants off.

In addition to its intimacy, the relation between bearer and master is a special one, an archaic and therefore emotionally significant one. Unlike the Western servant, the bearer is not a household worker. He is a slave. He gets paid and he is free to leave you if he wishes, but emotionally his relationship to you is that of a slave. That is the convention of his profession and the white man accepts it — because it is flattering to the ego to be the master of a slave.

How can it be surprising, therefore, that the master becomes aware of the human soul of his bearer, little as he may be aware of interest in the soul of any native, and that since this is the only native soul he knows, he unconsciously assumes it is the soul of India?

Of course the white man knows that the politics, the educational level, the intellectual or artistic interests of his bearer are not those of all Indians. Since he knows no Indian soul except his bearer's, however, he is apt to think the emotional and moral character of his bearer is the character of all Indians, and it is precisely the bearer's character, his tradition of voluntary servitude, which sets him apart from nearly all other Indians.

Once I was willing to admit that the experienced British sahib habitually makes the same elementary, natural — and tragic — error that the naïve Americans do, many things became clear to me. I could begin to understand the witches' cauldron of British-Indian political relations without having to postulate hypocrisy on one side or sheer perversity on the other and without having to call in the Devil to explain the inexplicable. My hypothesis did not explain either why the British wanted to rule India, or why the Indians wanted to get rid of their rule, but it did explain certain irrational and sometimes self-defeating behaviors on the part of both participants in this dispute.

It explained why the British never say 'please' when they give orders to India or 'thank you' when India obeys. They say 'thank you' and 'please' to their own servants at home, but they are convinced, not only that Indian bearers do not expect it, but that it makes them uneasy. Perhaps they are right.

It explained some of the curious and unpleasant British behaviors that are considered necessary to keep up face, behaviors which often seemed grotesque to Americans and deliberately insulting to Asiatics. Bearers are said, probably correctly, to attach much importance to their masters' 'face,' and to suffer in their dignity when the master does something that makes him 'lose face.' The sahib accepts a servant's conception of human dignity and tries to live up to it; even worse, he makes a servant's jeers of another servant (for having an undignified master) his criterion of correct social demeanor. We use that theme on our stage in comedies but it is a bitter kind of satire to the cultivated Asiatic who sees that he is expected to be impressed by the splendor of his servant's symbol of splendor, by the graciousness of his servant's symbol of gentility.

How great a role did this tendency to identify the soul of one's bearer with the soul of a people play as a concrete factor in Asiatic politics? There was no way to be sure but it seemed to me at the very least a singularly illuminating metaphor, one which accurately described, even if it did not wholly elucidate, the psychological character of race relationships in Asia.

I had been puzzled — and before I went to the East I had been irritated — by what seemed to me the hypersensitiveness of Asiatic intellectuals in regard to the race question, by a certain hysterical quality in their hatred of the imperialism they were fighting. I had been alarmed — as many Americans were — by the specter of the antiwhite counterracism which Japanese propaganda was striving so vigorously to fan up in Asia, and I had been impressed by the parallels which British propaganda drew so skillfully between Asiatic — particularly Indian — nationalism and German Nazism. I had been appalled by what had seemed to me the frivolous motivation of the Indian National Congress leaders in rejecting the Cripps proposals in 1942.

The element of the sick and the irrational in the psychology of these Asiatic revolutionaries seemed to stem not so much from an abstract love of freedom or even from a passionate brooding on the injustices and oppressions their people suffered, as from personal humiliations which they, as men of color, had suffered at the hands of the white man. The biographies of most Indian revolutionaries, including Nehru, including even Gandhi, contained specific references to such experiences. What was puzzling about them was that the humiliations seemed very slight to leave such great scars.

If these Indians had been born Negroes in America, I reflected grimly, their bitterness would seem understandable. Here in India the color line seems much more flexible, the British color-prejudice much less violent than our own. In America, even in the North, there are restaurants and hotels which no Negro may enter, whereas in India all but a handful of the British clubs are open to Indians — at least to very wealthy Indians. Even some of the most liberal Americans would not like to see their wives or daughters dancing with Negroes, but these reactionary British sahibs think nothing of seeing theirs dance with Indians. Why then should the Indians resent so bitterly the relatively slight social discrimination practiced against them, particularly since such really great progress toward eliminating discrimination has been made in the last thirty or forty years?

The answer is simple if you accept my bearer-hypothesis, my theory that the white man in the East unconsciously attributes to all natives the soul-characteristics of native servants, that his politeness to them — when he is polite — is like one's politeness to a temperamental cook, that when he admits them to his clubs and restaurants it is with the air of treating a servant democratically, of asking the maid into the living room for a drink on New Year's Eve — in a word, that the individual white man behaves at all times to the individual Asiatic not like a member of a superior race to an inferior race but like a member of a superior social class to a member of a lower social class.

When an Asiatic who is behaved to that way is an Indian of a low class there is not a deep wound. Perhaps he does not feel happy about it but he feels natural about it.

The trouble is, the Britisher, even without meaning to, treats all Indians as if they were of the same class — the servant class.

The Brahmins are the farthest in India from the servant class — the farthest up, because you can also go a long way down, to about the dog-class. They feel holy about being Brahmins, more holy than any high class in any other culture feels about being so high. When a Brahmin feels that a Britisher, especially a Britisher who is not a Brahmin in English society, is treating him as if he were a servant, he is not just humiliated. His sense of holiness is humiliated, his sense of security in being a Brahmin is wounded, he is filled with shame and he becomes sick. When he gets a little well he starts hating. If he is a strong man he has a strong hate. If he is a good man he has a good hate, but even when the hate is strong and good there is a trace of sickness in it and that sickness is reflected in his revolutionary action.

All of the leaders of the Indian revolution are not Brahmins but nearly all of them belong to classes much higher than the servant class and I think they have all been through this sickness. Following them are the masses of simple men who are not sick, who simply do not like being pushed about even when it feels natural.

Now I come to a very curious thing: I discovered in India that there is the same kind of sickness and irrationality in the way the white man feels about the native. The floor-rules about color are like a liberal nightclub where Negroes who are artists are treated as humans, but the feeling in the atmosphere is like a town in the South where a lynching could happen.

I could not account for this paradox until one day, in the extreme south of India, I went into a railroad station to try to get the jeep, which I had driven some eighteen hundred miles down from Delhi, put on a flatcar so that it could be ferried across to Ceylon. A greasy, fat, hateful *babu* — the sahib's word for a greasy, fat, hateful, native clerk — was in charge of the office and he was insolent to me. He sneered at me and he gloated over there being no flatcars and over me being a white man stranded in the south of India.

My ears began to buzz and I could not see clearly for a few seconds and everything seemed to be in a brownish light and if I had said what I felt like saying I would have said, 'Listen, you bloody bastard Nigger ——'

When I pulled myself together again I thought I understood at last why there is something sick in the sahib's feeling about the native.

The sahib is accustomed to being obeyed, to being feared, to being surrounded with deference and servility. He belongs to the British middle-class himself but in the East his life is filled with the symbols of domination and grandeur. He may not be enjoying fantastic luxury but deference is a more deeply rooted symbol of power than luxury, and on the scale of deference, as far as his relations with the natives go, he lives like a prerevolutionary grand duke in Russia. I think it must be a law of psychology that when a bourgeois suddenly starts living the life of a grand duke he does not feel like a grand duke but like a god.

The sahib feels like a god as long as he is with his bearer and as long as he is dealing with humble and servile people. Until a few years ago he hardly saw anything but humble and servile Indians. Now increasingly he encounters Indians who feel themselves his equals, who insist on being recognized as equals, who turn nasty and insolent, like my babu station-master, when they are not treated as equals, or even when they fear that they might not be so treated.

When that happens the sahib feels, as I felt, almost as if his bearer had suddenly slapped his face, because he is so used to thinking of all Indians as being like bearers. He flies into a rage, as I did, but he does not come out of it, because with him it is not just a case of breaking a pleasant habit. He has received a wound — and above all a threat — to his self-esteem and his self-esteem is dangerously swollen from living like a god. He is getting a dose of the Brahmin's medicine, just as the Brahmin gets a dose of the Untouchable's medicine from the Englishman. After a certain number of these affronts to his self-worship his personality begins to take a very sinister orientation.

He starts looking for insolences the way the color-conscious Indian looks for insults. Even when the Indian is polite, even when he is servile, the sahib suspects that he is sneering mentally, sneering behind his back. The more he feels he is being sneered at behind his back, the more furious he gets. Also the more frightened, because he knows his rule depends much more on awe than on force. The sneers become plots in his mind. The Indian sneers at him today because he is planning to cut his throat tomorrow. Not planning to cut his throat metaphorically, but actually; not planning to cut Britain's throat abstractly, but the sahib's own throat personally. Maybe his own bearer is planning to cut his throat, because if all Indians are like bearers, then bearers are like all Indians. It is a public delusion with strong personal implications.

I had expected to find something paranoid in the attitudes of Asiatics toward whites. What surprised me was to discover that the white man had even more strongly paranoid attitudes toward the native. I knew he suffered from race-prejudice. I had not known that he also suffered from race-hatred. There were certainly traces in the East of the antiwhite ideology which Americans feared, but its manifestations were psychologically rather localized and childishly easy to break down — if one wanted to break them down. Asiatics responded to the white man who respected their dignity with a warmth that melted away purely political barriers.

'General Auchinleck is a fine man,' a young and ardently nationalist Indian army officer once said to me with an expression of almost comical wistfulness. 'If only we could persuade him to head our revolution . . .'

I never heard an Englishman wish that he could persuade Nehru to be the prime minister of the British Commonwealth. The antinative ideology of the white man, that is, of the white man who habitually lived in the East, was more of a political reality than the native's antiwhite ideology, white racism more widespread, tainting more individuals, and more intricately entwined with all the individual's attitudes than was yellow or brown racism.

The native resented certain manifestations of the white man. The sahib often hated and feared and despised everything native in all natives.

A cultivated and intelligent young Englishwoman I knew in Delhi could not talk about natives without getting hysterical.

'They're just like animals, looking at you all the time with those blank inhuman faces. They look at you as if you were another animal. There's nothing human about them. They're beasts, they're worse than beasts.'

Another young woman said:

'It used to be so pleasant to live in India and now it's so horrid. Everyone has turned against us. The shopkeepers, the servants, everyone. They owe everything to us and they treat us like dirt. They have no sense of decency.'

An old woman who lived in a high, remote mountain jungle in Ceylon, alone except for her husband and her hunting-dogs, had such a phobia of natives that she did all her own housework rather than have a native servant around the place. When I went up with some friends to hunt over a weekend she received us with gracious hospitality but she would not allow our Sinhalese chauffeur to sleep on the place, not even in her stable.

Everywhere I found the white memsahibs more violently intoxicated with the race-poison than their men. The virulence of the disease also varied according to regions and occupations as well as individual temperaments. It was lower in Ceylon, a crown colony which enjoyed virtual home-rule, than in India, but lower still in Burma where political tensions were high. It was naturally high in Indonesia and French Indo-China when armed race-war marked by frightful atrocities on both sides broke out after the Japanese surrender, but it was very low on the Northwest frontier of India where guerilla warfare was chronic. It was lowest in independent Siam. It was lower, on the whole, among soldiers than among civil servants, and much higher among businessmen and planters. A few rare superior men, including some in high places, such as Lieutenant General Sir Philip Christison, commander of the admirable XV Corps, General Auchinleck, and possibly Lord Wavell, seem to have escaped or outgrown the disease altogether.

It still remained for the white man a potent, perhaps decisive, factor in Asiatic power-politics. It impeded the prosecution of the war directly and materially and it was one of the main reasons for the anarchy and bloodshed in Southeast Asia when war officially came to an end.

On the native side it was an even greater factor, I discovered, particularly after I came to know something of Indonesian and Annamese nationalisms. The revolutions of Asia, like all revolutions, were economic and political. They were struggles for bread and power, but more than any revolutions which have ever occurred in the West they were struggles for human dignity. They were struggles to win for the peoples of Asia the Four Freedoms we promised them and a fifth freedom we have failed to realize was just as basic — Freedom from Contempt.

Until I went to the East, the ideal of human dignity which is one of the most essential elements of our cultural heritage had seemed to me the loftiest, but at the same time the most abstract, if not the most vague, of all democratic ideals. I used to feel slightly guilty, slightly romantic and sentimental, attaching so much importance to such a vague thing when there were so many specific, concrete, measurable, human problems and evils in the world to trouble a liberal conscience. I tried to reconcile my attachment to the ideal of human dignity with the ideological climate of modern liberalism by telling myself that after all a minimum economic standard was an essential condition of human dignity, as was the protection by law of civil liberties.

The East did not change my belief that it is meaningless to talk of dignity to a man who is starving to death, or to one who lives in constant dread of aggression and persecution, but it did convince me that freedom from want and freedom from fear are not enough to safeguard human dignity, even if you add freedom of conscience and freedom of speech. Confronted constantly as I was by the grievances of Asiatics and the sneers or apprehensions of Europeans, I came to realize that back of the abstraction, human dignity, there is a concrete reality, which is each man's appreciation of his own dignity.

The colonial system in Asia perhaps violated the democratic ideal of human dignity by denying to the native political, economic, and sometimes legal, rights which it gave to the white sahib. It violated the ideal much more grievously and much more directly by using as political and economic overseers in colonial lands a class of men who believed in and practiced systematic rudeness to most of the natives with whom they had any personal contact. It was the sahib's rudeness which did the native the most harm because it deprived him of his most valuable possession — his personal dignity. No reform of colonial rule would represent any victory for the Occidental ideal of human dignity unless it included a reform of the sahib's character, for the sahib, in terms of the Occident's noblest ideal, was a cultural renegade. Perhaps the peoples of the West do not realize that they are fre-

quently represented in the East by cultural renegades, I told myself — and perhaps the culture which the sahibs have betrayed no
longer exists in the West, perhaps we have ceased to believe in
human dignity without realizing that we no longer believe.

These conclusions, germinating in New Delhi and slowly ma-
turing over many months, led me to more than a new view of current Asiatic history. They led me to a new view of America.
They made me realize for the first time that the relations between
the thirteen million Negro citizens of America and the one hundred and twenty million white citizens was the most serious, the
most difficult, and the most disgraceful colonial problem in the
world.

Before I went to Asia I had never paid much attention to the
race problem in America. When I thought of it at all I thought
of it in terms of the historic struggle between prejudice and
progress, with progress, as usual, winning.

When I started looking back on America from Asia it did not
seem possible any longer to think that progress was winning. The
economic position of the Negro might be slowly improving, his
educational level might be gradually rising, the legalistic or terror-
istic devices which in some states made a farce of the Fifteenth
Amendment, might be more discredited, but all this did not
necessarily mean that the Negro as a human being was getting
happier. It might mean that he was becoming more miserable.

I suspected, from Asia, that the Negro was in fact getting more
miserable. If the parallel between India and America held true,
if most Americans unconsciously thought of all Negroes in terms
of Negro servants — of old-fashioned Negro servants — then the
Negro was certain to be getting more miserable. The very fact
that his economic and cultural status was rising meant that his
capacity for being hurt, his emotional vulnerability, was increasing. If the recognition of his human dignity was not increasing at
the same rate, he was getting more hurt than happiness from his
progress. The higher he rose from the servant or slave state the
more bitterly he would feel the gap between the place he had
earned in American society by his own efforts and the recognition

accorded him by white Americans. He might be a skilled technician, a great doctor, a renowned artist, an army officer, or a
member of Congress, but if he was expected to say 'sir' to a white
farmhand, if he could not eat in a restaurant open to any white
American who could afford a decent suit and a haircut, then the
very scale of his achievement would be the measure of his humiliation.

I did not feel any more confident that racial tensions were diminishing in America than I did that the Negro was making real
progress toward the fifth freedom. It seemed likely that the
people who never had much race-prejudice now disapproved of
race-prejudice more strongly then ever. This was no progress if
those who always had race-prejudice were beginning to develop
race-hatred. That was what I saw happening in Asia where the
white man was unwilling to recognize the social implications of the
political and economic concessions he made to the native. There
were many signs that it was happening in America, in fact, that
the paranoid character of race relations, particularly the paranoid
attitudes of white Americans toward race relations, was a great
deal more pronounced than it was in Asia. In many parts of the
South it had been more pronounced than in Asia ever since the
carpetbag era.

This thought disturbed me considerably. After seeing what
could happen to the British sahib in the East, knowing that the
Englishman at home is one of the least, if not the least, paranoid
of all Westerners, the precariousness of the American way of life,
the psychological fragility of American society, seemed much
greater than I had ever realized.

America, I concluded, is not an evil state because it tolerates
this evil of race-prejudice — what state does not tolerate some
evil within it? It is only a frail state because the evil that it tolerates is one which will not stand still.

PART III

City of Dreadful Night

I

The Fable of Darkness

A CURIOUS ADVENTURE which befell me during a visit to Calcutta, a few months after my arrival in India, proved to be the turning-point in my Asiatic education, focusing my attention upon Indian life itself, rather than upon the sahib's world, in which I had until then been engrossed. A colleague whose devious duties led him so often to Calcutta's Chinatown that he was looked upon by many American officers — and some Chinese — as the unofficial mayor of that strange community, had invited me to dinner at the best Chinese restaurant in the city. It was still early when we finished our meal and my friend, who had a permanent authorization from the provost marshal to wear civilian clothes and to circulate at discretion in off-limits areas, asked me if I would care to see the Calcutta night life, meaning the brothels. These were a standard tourist attraction at all times, doubly attractive in wartime, for not only were the entire brothel areas off-limits to Allied military personnel, but the houses themselves had been theoretically closed, and there is always a special fascination in the spectacle of vice, crushed to earth, rising again.

We entered the brothel-area with the dramatic, through-the-looking-glass suddenness characteristic of Indian transformations. One moment we were on a broad, bustling, modern, lighted avenue. The next moment we were twisting through a world of silence and brooding shadow, a nocturnal jungle of tortuous alleys, gaunt eyeless walls, and tile roofs gleaming pallidly from a

107

moon unseen behind a range of high tenements. There were no human sounds, no animal sounds, except the unhealthy scurrying of cats and once a dog pawing at a garbage can. Like a jungle, this city wilderness seemed to be closing behind us as we penetrated deeper into it.

The halo-effect, which projects upon neutral objects the aura of an emotionally significant object associated with them in our minds, made these streets seem inexpressibly sinister to me. The familiar stench of an Indian slum here seemed to carry an underscent of some more infamous corruption, some necrophile emulsion of sexual and carrion reeks. There was something hypnotic about our own uncertain and fumbling progress; whereas in reality my friend was lost in the sense that he could not find the brothel he was looking for, I felt that we were lost in the sense that one is lost in the depths of a swamp; instead of our looking for a brothel, somewhere in this morass a brothel was magically drawing us toward it. When a stunted Indian suddenly stepped out of the shadow and began capering and gibbering obscenely at us, it was like an evil wish materializing.

We followed the evil wish under a portico, into the black pit of a hallway, and up a winding unlit stairway. At the top he pulled aside a greasy curtain and we stepped into a bare room lit by a single flickering mustard-oil lamp. This was the brothel.

There were four Indian girls, two in short European-style skirts and blouses, two in sarees. Two dirty male Indians with bad teeth were inexplicably lolling on mats on the floor. The madam was an Anglo-Indian who looked like a black, droopy-chinned vulture.

'You want some good jig-jig, gentlemen?' she asked in a brassy voice.

One of the girls repeated in a more throaty, native voice, 'Jig-jig, sahibs,' and tried to look rapturous. Another girl smirked. The third looked frightened and ashamed without any pretense, and the fourth simply stared blankly.

They were neither young nor old, horrible nor attractive. They did not look particularly depraved and the brothel itself had none of the glamor of degradation which surrounds the more infamous brothels of Marseilles. It was trite, colorless, not a chapel of vice or an abattoir of virtue, just a room where you bought jig-jig for five rupees. In Europe you see sailors go into places like that, stay five minutes, and come out buttoning their pants and whistling.

Yet this was not that kind of place either. It was perfectly dull but its very dullness had a quality of horror. It was not an ante-room of the tomb but the tomb itself, with the coldness and the dullness of the tomb. The girl who had tried to look rapturous was not caricaturing love like a European prostitute, but caricaturing life. The one who smirked was smirking at an indecency of the worm. The two natives on the floor were the most sinister of all, they were so obviously there for no reason except that they had been buried there.

Even my matter-of-fact friend was affected by the ghastly chill of the place. Normally a cocksure and rather blustering man, he was strangely subdued. He told the madam we didn't want any Bengali jig-jig, we were looking for Chinese girls, and she did not have any, so we would now leave.

Everyone seemed to find this statement perfectly absurd. The girl who had been smirking laughed. The blank one looked aston-ished. The madam just smiled a sinister smile and said nothing, waiting for us to come to our senses, to remember where we were. Nobody tried to stop us but we had a panic feeling that we were trapped. We could simply have turned on our heels, pulled back the greasy curtain and walked down the stairs and no one would have moved — but we could not move either.

Suddenly, incredibly, ludicrously, the spell was broken, the nightmare shattered. My friend used an old Chinatown trick for breaking away from a too insistent prostitute to break away from these, who were not insisting at all, who were just smiling at us for our naïveté in thinking anyone could break away from such a place. He deliberately offended their modesty by pretending to make an indecent proposal to them. For a couple of seconds the madam looked stunned. Then she roared like a fiend:

'Get out, you bastards, you pigs! Get out, you dirty men! What you think — this is a French house?'

Followed by an avalanche of shrill, feminine imprecations, of cries of outraged womanhood, deserted, disowned by our pimp, we stumbled down the stairway laughing until the tears ran.

As we walked back to our car through the maze of twisting alleys, no longer sinister now, but magically restored to their true shape, to the sordid, but not nightmarish, aspect of an Indian nocturnal slum, it seemed to me that some subtle and philosophic god of the Hindu pantheon, some friend of mortal wisdom among the immortals, must have contrived this bawdy jest to illustrate the Buddhist-Hindu doctrine of Illusion for our enlightenment. The lesson in any case was as profound as it was Rabelaisian.

The halo-effect which in my mind had converted a nocturnal street scene into a stage décor for a Beaudelairian ballet of vice was itself the projection of the idea of death upon the idea of vice. Dalliance in an Asiatic brothel is not a healthy sport, but back of the rational and well-founded fear of venereal infections is the superstitious dread of the infection of sin itself, the unconscious conviction that the wages of sin is death. It was this linking of the ideas of death and sin which in my mind had transformed the brothel into the likeness of a tomb, which had converted my sight-seeing tour quite literally into a waking nightmare, that gradually waxed in vividness and horror up to the moment when my friend broke the spell with his magic formula.

Back of my feeling that we were being drawn to this tomb by an invisible will-o'-the-wisp, that when we reached it we were trapped and could not escape, there must have been, I realized, a strong temptation. Merely looking upon the trappings of sin — which was all we consciously planned to do — would hardly have justified so strong a feeling of hypnotic compulsion. There had unquestionably been the desire to sin as well as to see sin.

The flaccid and tainted meat we had been offered could not appeal to any healthy lust. Whatever-the lure of the brothel was, it was not the lure of sensuality. I tried to imagine myself embracing one of those drab creatures and found it almost unimaginable — almost but not quite, for one of them was imaginable, the one who looked frightened and ashamed. Here, then, was another linkage and overlapping of ideas, the ideas of sensuality and aggression. The Indian version of the House of Illusion could not furnish the illusions of passion or of tenderness to the sophisticated Westerner but it could furnish better than any other the illusion of slavery. Even in the brothels of the West this illusion is one of the most popular in the whole stock and it is what the client from the higher social classes goes to the low-class brothel to purchase — what he buys is not so much sensual pleasure as the right to commit a social and psychological aggression against a woman of lower caste, to become a temporary slave-owner. The more wretched and degraded the prostitute is, the more marked the social gap between her and her client, the more real becomes his fantasy of slavery. Even the sordid atmosphere of a cheap brothel can be a sexual attraction because it suggests the atmosphere of a slave-hovel.

This taint of slavery is inseparable from organized prostitution in our culture, and our reluctance to abolish this sinister institution, to enforce the laws we make against it, is the measure of how deeply rooted in the hearts of men is the desire to return to old and evil ways that we imagine we have put behind us forever. This was the real temptation upon which my nightmare was founded, the illusion behind all the other illusions.

The cream of the jest, of course, and the kernel of the lesson, lay in the cross-cultural misunderstanding that had arisen in the brothel. Because Western prostitutes have very little self-respect, I had expected the girls in the brothel, since they were Eastern prostitutes, to have none at all. I had assumed that they would be degraded below the lowest level of human degradation known in the West and this assumption had created in my mind the temptation of sexual slavery. It was the horror aroused by this temptation which had transformed our prosaically wretched prostitutes into ghoulish figures in a nightmare, into female monsters of degradation.

I had been filled with panic at the thought these monsters of degradation would never let us escape from their clutches, that we were trapped in a tomb. Instead, we had been ejected from an unexpectedly straitlaced brothel by four indignant young women and one outraged madam who considered us monsters of depravity. The suggestion my friend had put to them would not have shocked any Western prostitute, and any well-run house of prostitution in England, France, or America, would have maintained on the staff at least one specialist to deal with such requests. In the slums of Calcutta, however, it was an unspeakable perversion, and merely to make the suggestion to a respectable bawd was to offer the gravest offense to her modesty, the most intolerable insult to her dignity.

I thought of the Hindu *swami* who had startled his disciples by saluting with deep reverence a prostitute encountered one day in the streets of Calcutta. In reply to the disciples' timid questions the swami had said:

'I was venerating the principle of feminine purity which is embodied in all women, even in this poor prostitute.'

Some Englishman had told me that anecdote as an illustration of the grotesqueness of Hindu religious thought and I had accepted it as such. Now it seemed to me to have a different meaning. All things have very different meanings, depending upon the meaning you want to put upon them.

I wondered what meaning the girls in the bordello had put upon our visit, what Occidental nightmares it had generated in their minds, what generalizations about Western culture they had construed from it.

I thought about some of the weird generalizations which Occidentals make about Eastern cultures, about the strange Oriental nightmares which certain aspects of Indian life generate in our minds, about the curious halo-effects which distort certain Indian scenes when we look upon them.

It was this train of thought which caused my brothel-adventure to be a turning point in my Asiatic education. All the time I had been living in Delhi I had been meeting Indians, reading Indian newspapers and books printed in English, going to Indian movies and ballets, absorbing through my pores thousands of unnoticed or half-noticed impressions of Indian life, but I had not made a real attempt to understand India. It had seemed hopeless. I was not prepared to accept the sahib's favorite dictum that you only began to understand India after you had lived there for twenty years, but for me, not speaking any of the languages, having no previous background of book-knowledge about the East, with strictly limited opportunities for observation, it had seemed preposterous even to think of learning anything worthwhile about India in the few months I would remain there.

Certainly I could not expect to acquire any deep and comprehensive understanding of India, but now it seemed to me there was one thing I might do: I might be able to discover what Western impressions of India were simply nightmares, comparable to my brothel-nightmare, and dispel them in my own mind by uncovering the realities beneath them. If I could not study India I could at least clear away the debris of myth and prejudice which obstructs such study. This I decided was a feasible effort of awareness.

Actually, I discovered, the problem of clearing away the debris of myth and prejudice is the greatest problem in studying India. The conditions of life in this land are often so terrible that the mind is almost forced to invent nightmares about them in order to disguise the grimness of the reality.

Normal living in India is like living in times of catastrophe in the West. When food is plentiful tens of millions of Indians eat less than Europeans in the midst of famine. In times of prosperity the Indian worker earns less than the dole given by most Western societies to the unemployed in times of economic crisis — before the wartime inflation set in, fifteen dollars a month was very good pay for an industrial worker. Not only do epidemics of infectious diseases break out much more frequently than in the West but when there are no epidemics death ravages the families of India the way the casualty lists of a modern war ravage ours. In certain slum districts in the great cities one infant out of every two may die in the first twenty-four months of life and when only one out of five dies, that is very good. When there is a day in which only a few thousand Indians die of cholera, smallpox, typhoid, malaria, tuberculosis, and malnutrition, in addition to accidents and the diseases of old age, then that is a quiet day on the Eastern front.

It is impossible to live amidst so much human misery without one's feelings becoming blunted to some degree. The emotional shock which produces this blunting also tends to distort one's thinking, to beget curious mythologies of horror. One forgets that poverty and starvation and disease are the social effects of definite material causes and one tends to think of them as character traits of the Indian. It begins to appear something typically Indian to die of hunger or cholera, almost a willful perversion. Dying of cholera seems an Indian way of life, instead of just being an Indian form of death, and one begins to feel something of the same horror of this way of life that one has of the disease itself.

Unconsciously one is looking for an excuse for thinking that Indians are inhuman because their lives are less happy than human lives should be, and it is not difficult to find excuses. The early Portuguese and English adventurers, not excessively sensitive souls, were genuinely shocked by the Hindu custom of *suttee* — widows following their husbands in death, usually by throwing themselves upon the funeral pyre. Originally *suttee* was a highly romantic act reserved for romantic occasions and practiced mainly by literary ladies whose royal husbands had perished in battle, but by the seventeenth century it had become quite an ugly thing, deserving condemnation. It had gradually become fashionable, probably because it was once so closely associated with royalty, an extreme and sinister method of keeping up with the Joneses, which annually caused a number of high-born and not necessarily inconsolable widows to burn themselves alive, for no better reason than that failure to do so would have let down their families and their friends. The early visitors from the West recognized the inhumanity of the practice but failed to discern that what was most inhuman in it was an imbecile snobbishness by no means unknown in the West.

Later visitors were appalled, and rightly, at the inhumanity of the Hindu caste-system — 'Jim Crowism on a fantastic scale.' Missionaries and sociologists with a background of professional Christianity were even more appalled at certain Hindu religious or social institutions such as child-marriage and the employment of temple-prostitutes, usually children. Their moral indignation, however, was based less, I suspect, on a realistic appreciation of the evils of formalizing the sex-life of children by precocious marriage or of associating it with the sex-life of adults, than on our quaint myth of the purity of childhood. In our culture a man who had intercourse with an eight-year-old girl would be considered a sex-pervert, and the outrage would only be increased if it took place in an ecclesiastical building, for we try to keep sexuality and religion in different compartments of our minds, just as we dislike admitting that there can be any sexuality in childhood. No matter how sophisticated we may be it is hard not to think of Hindus as sex-perverts, therefore monsters.

In fact, we do think of India as a monstrous land, perhaps even of Indians as monsters. Everything, including the climate, contributes to this impression of monstrousness which India always produces on the Western mind. India in our minds is the land of the fabulous, the terrible, and the grotesque — the land of transposed emotions, where suffering is uncleanness; sensuality, ghoulishness; muddle, horror; and horror, nothingness. Three centuries of literary nightmares, converted into political propaganda, have distorted our vision before our eyes ever look upon India. We go to India expecting to see nightmares and when we see an Indian reality that is like a Western nightmare we are convinced that we have seen an Indian nightmare; India seems to us the land of dark fable, and when we have exhausted all other accusations, we blame India for our own tendency to twist her dark realities in our minds into dark fables; we accuse her of spawning nightmares.

The Indian has enough fables and nightmares of his own, but no more than the white man in India. When we go to India we are all a little like two American friends I had in Delhi who knew perfectly well that it is impossible for a man to climb up a rope thrown into the air, but they believed some Indians had the power to make a sane man think he was seeing someone climb up a rope thrown into the air, so for two years they doggedly kept on looking for a fakir who could perform the Indian rope-trick for them

The darkness and the muddle of India are not myths like the Indian rope-trick. They exist, and the only problem in verifying their existence is to convince yourself that your eyes have not deceived you. They become delusions in the Western mind only because we refuse to accept them as part of the human heritage of darkness and muddle, because we are unwilling to admit that men like ourselves can become like that, or even that such things can happen to man, because we prefer to explain them as the deeds of monsters, or the destiny of monsters living in a monstrous land.

The studies which my Calcutta adventure inspired had as their final goal the discovery of what is human in the monstrousness of India. They proved singularly fruitful studies, not because I learned very much about India but because I learned some new things about man, because I developed a clearer and deeper realization than I had ever had before of what happens to men when they, through weakness or through error, betray the human mission. Such learning is always a discipline of the spirit as well as an enrichment of the mind, a discovery of self as well as a discovery of the world; for, as my brothel-visit taught me, every man is a monster partially redeemed from darkness, every mind is a small clearing in a wilderness of muddle.

II

The Key to Paradox

ONE OF THE MOST DEPRESSING Indian nightmares arises from the
Westerner's contemplation of the racial, political, and social
diversity of India. It is not simply that there is conflict between
group and group and that the conflict is bitter; it is even more,
that the conflict appears to be aimless. The passions that are
generated by the clash of group rivalries and interests seem the
exasperation of frustration and cross-purpose rather than the
clear flame of rational enmity. The confused and angry mutter
of the bazaars is to Western ears the gibberish voice of an Eastern
babel — the age-old symbol of man doomed to strife and futility
through his inability to be understood by man.

This impression of unmeaningful strife, this seeming chaos of
clash, is heightened in the Western mind by our inability to trans-
late exactly even the cleavages of Indian society in terms of the
factors which divide man from man in the West.

To begin with, the main Indian social groups, usually called
communities, whose conflicts with one another fill the Indian
forum with sound and fury, are so unlike any Western group-
categories that it is impossible to define them exactly in Western
terms. The Sikhs are a good example. Originally a religious sect
which developed in the western Punjab, they have become some
kind of a cultural unit, though not a race as we understand the
term, nor a people like the peoples of the West, for historically
they passed from being a persecuted religious minority to being

117

the ruling military caste of a small empire, without ever quite becoming a nation. Today their aspirations to become a nation —
inevitably confused in their minds with memories of having been
an empire — bring them into conflict with the Moslems, for they
live as an ethnic or cultural enclave in a broader geographical
division of India which is predominantly Moslem.

The Moslems themselves are an ambiguous category. Rulers
of India before they became Indians, the Moslems of today are
partly a church, partly a dispossessed aristocracy, partly a racial
minority. In northwest India, where they constitute an over-
whelming majority of the population — save in the Sikh enclave
— they form an homogeneous society, closely related, both by
blood-heritage and culture, to the Afghans and other neighboring
Middle-Eastern or Central-Asian tribes. Yet the tie which is
strongest in their minds — the bond of Islam — links them also
with the other Moslems scattered all over India, with Indians
who are not the descendants of western invaders but the descendants of Hindu Indians converted to Islam by the invaders.

Finally the Hindus, who constitute some three-fourths of the
Indian people, are, like the Moslems, simultaneously a religious,
a social, and a political category. They unquestionably constitute a people but the ethnic and cultural framework of the nation
which used to be theirs has been so broadened by nearly a thousand years of Moslem domination that they can no longer be considered as constituting the Indian people.

As if the status of the Hindus with relation to the other ethnic-
cultural groups of India were not complicated enough, it is further
complicated by a division within the ranks of Hindu society itself
— the division between caste Hindus and the so-called Untouchables or Depressed Classes. For political purposes the British considered the Untouchables as a separate community, like the Sikhs
or the Moslems or Parsees or Anglo-Indians, and though the
Indian nationalist leaders bitterly attacked this classification, it
had some justification, since most orthodox caste Hindus regard
the Untouchables as being completely outside Hindu society —
for Hinduism is a society and not just a body of believers. Yet,

though they are rejected by Hindu society, the Untouchables are bound to it by many ties. Without being indisputably Hindus they are believers in Hinduism as a religion, just as the pariah dogs of Indian villages are domestic animals disowned by their masters. Their discontent when it assumes a political expression is half a secession from Hindu society, half a plea to be reunited with it.

These Indian forms of social cleavage and grouping are bewildering, but in themselves are no more illogical or irreconcilable than any in the West. The great danger for a Westerner studying them — as I often noticed myself — is that because we sometimes despair of understanding Indian politics we are tempted to conclude that they are desperate; because we are forced to define Indian political forms and institutions in terms of Western negatives, India is very apt in our minds to seem a series of negations — the likeness of nothingness since it is like nothing in the West. This, it seems to me, is the error of the India-is-hopeless school of thought, chiefly represented by British writers like Beverley Nichols.

There is an opposite error, I discovered, which consists in applying Western political terminologies to the very different Indian context, overlooking the important differences between any Indian social categories or institutions and their nearest Western analogues. This is chiefly the error of passionate friends of India, and even of Indians, themselves.

Unquestionably, the Indian himself is confused by his political terminology, and there is every reason why he should be, because it is a terminology borrowed from a language not his own. His political culture is not Indian but British, for since he was under British rule he had to utilize the embryonic forms of British parliamentarianism which the Raj fostered in India. Above all, in order to take advantage of the freedom of expression which British liberalism tolerated throughout the Empire he had to employ British political terminology in the propaganda he aimed at his rulers. He was obliged to fight the enemy with the enemy's own weapons and since these were unfamiliar to him it is not surprising that sometimes he picked the wrong one for his purpose. Neither the Moslem League's conception of the Indian Moslems as a racial minority entitled to self-determination, nor the Congress conception of India as a unitarian national state, quite corresponded to Indian reality, but the Indian himself could hardly be aware that he was using them in a false context.

It is useless, however, to try to dispel entirely the nightmare of Indian political life by explaining it away as a problem in semantics, an accumulation of errors in translation. Undoubtedly confusion is caused in the Indian mind by the use of borrowed terminologies and alien forms of political expression, and this confusion becomes worse confounded in the mind of the Western observer who fails to note their misapplication, but this is not the whole story. There seems something nightmarish about the quality as well as the forms of Indian political life, an emotional muddle as well as an intellectual muddle. It is not so much the violence of Indian politics that is distressing as the sickly pattern of the violence.

For one thing, there is an instability in Indian political alignments, a flickering of political hates and loyalties which resembles the fickle passions of a street-mob. The burning issue of one week is forgotten the next. The hero of a season is the arch-enemy of the next season. Coalitions of previously mortal enemies are born overnight, hold together for a little span, then split apart in a deflagration of deadly hatred. Only conflict seems to remain constant.

During the winter I spent in Delhi the bitterest political quarrel was that between the Indian National Congress and the Moslem League. The second most bitter quarrel was between the Congress and the Communists. Yet Congress and the Moslem League had co-operated during most of the twenty years from 1916 to 1936 and during the first part of that period Hindu-Moslem brotherhood had flowered as it had during the Great Mutiny of 1857 and during the reign of the Moghul emperor Akbar, in the sixteenth century. Congress and the Communists had usually collaborated, despite some Communist sneering at the Congress followers as lukewarm revolutionaries, until Russia's entry into the war had caused a sudden shift in the party line. Then the Communists became public allies of the British Raj — to help Russia — and therefore lackeys of imperialism in the eyes of Congress.

Such fluctuations are by no means unknown in the West but they seemed to me more frequent and more extreme in India. In no Western country could I have seen what I saw in Calcutta in January, 1946, as I was awaiting transportation home — the posthumous apotheosis of Subhas Chandra Bose, leader of the Japanese-controlled Indian National Army. It was not because Bose had been a Japanese quisling that I was amazed by the frenzy of ecstatic eulogies to his memory in the Congress press, by the mushroom growth of portraits of Bose in Calcutta shop windows, by the Bose memorial funds, the Bose parades. It was because Bose, who had been cast out of the Congress as a fascist before the war, had been as bitterly hated by the same Congress leaders, who were now launching a veritable Bose cult, as Trotsky was hated by Russian Stalinists.

Even within the larger and relatively stable political formations, like the Congress, factional schisms were constantly opening, healing, reopening. Outside the approximately disciplined ranks of the big parties public opinion — such public opinion as there is in India — rolled about like a tumbleweed. The fissiparous tendency of organized groups was reflected in the fractionalization of individual opinion. Most of the Indians I met seemed to have some 'but' in their opinions. They revered Gandhi but they thought his economic philosophy was ridiculous. They admired Nehru but they thought he was too Western and too socialist. They disapproved of Mohamed Ali Jinnah, leader of the Moslem League and the father of the Pakistan scheme for partitioning India, but they deprecated the Hindu attacks upon him. When they argued about politics they seemed half the time to be arguing against themselves, but they only argued the more passionately for that. The more likely they were to change sides within a month, the more intensely they felt about the issue of the moment, the more uncertain their own allegiance to a particular political cause, the more heatedly they denounced the treason of the renegades to that cause.

At times I came very close to the widespread British view that there was some fissiparous or centrifugal principle in Indian society, perhaps even some principle of instability in Indian character, which made it impossible to hope that Indians could manage their own affairs without lapsing into chaos when Britain withdrew.

Not only in the instability of political hatreds and loyalties does Indian politics resemble the movements of a street mob. There is a stridency in the pitch of propaganda and polemics, a shrill emotionalism, a strategic animism which is characteristic of invertebrate social organisms. Political controversies in India may be no more irrational than those of the West but their irrationality appears of a lower order: The participants seem unreasonable not only in terms of their principles but in terms of their objectives, their tactics irrelevant to the decision as well as to the issue.

In fact, a political controversy in India resembles a sublimated bazaar riot and the bazaar riot, itself, one of the most striking manifestations of Indian public life, is less a clash of organized hostilities than a sympathetic detonation. Men fight because they hear that men are fighting; by the time they hear it the cause has become legend and they do not know themselves why they have joined the fight. At the peak of the great Calcutta riots of November, 1945, which resulted in the death of scores of Indians and of one American soldier, most of the public services workers of the municipality of Calcutta suddenly went on strike, giving the disorders the aspect of a general revolution and terrifying the local Congress leaders no less than the British authorities. This municipal strike, which very nearly turned a local riot into a general uprising of the Indian people, did not express any revolutionary intent but neither was it entirely accidental. The workers disapproved of the action of the police in firing on a crowd of protesting students — the spark which set off the riots. They did not, however, feel strongly enough about this question to base their strike upon indignation. They just mentioned the moral issue in passing and then went on to say they wanted higher salaries, without stressing the economic motive very strongly either. Without quite knowing why, they seemingly just felt it was a good time to strike.

Underneath all these incoherent conflicts and random explosions there are some meaningful patterns, though they are not wholly rational ones. When a minor street riot in Calcutta or Bombay flares into localized rebellion or civil war that may last for days, or sometimes weeks, there is always a reason for it. A British policeman has killed an Indian, or a British judge has imprisoned one. A Moslem has kicked a sacred cow or a Hindu has beat a drum in front of a mosque while Moslems are at prayer. An Untouchable has drawn water from a forbidden well, thus polluting it, or a well reserved for Untouchables has been fenced off so they cannot get at it.

The reason why such trivial incidents have such tragic and far-reaching consequences is that in the minds of Indians they symbolize tragic and deep-reaching antagonisms, the result of major cleavages in Indian society. When a Moslem kicks a cow, the Hindu suspects that it is not an accidental, or even an isolated act, but only the most recent evidence of a Moslem conspiracy to humiliate him by insulting his religion. All Moslems are in this conspiracy, he feels, at least to the extent of fostering among their members the attitude of contempt toward Hindus which expresses itself in such gestures as kicking a cow.

Consequently he is not furious merely at the Moslem who actually kicked the cow, but at any Moslem, at all Moslems. Even if you prove to him that the particular incident which has enraged him is only a bazaar rumor and has not actually occurred, he does not calm down. He can remember enough authentic incidents in the past, and he knows there will be others in the future. The incident in question is only a reminder — a reminder of the hateful attitude of Moslems toward Hindus — and that is enough to make his own hatred blaze. In a sense, it is not unreasonable of him to feel like starting a religious war because a cow has been kicked. The unreasonable thing is the assumption that the whole Moslem community approves and encourages the cow-kicker, that all the Moslems of India are hatching plots night and day to humiliate the Hindus by kicking cows.

The Moslem, of course, assumes a similar Hindu conspiracy against his religion and this same assumption of organized hostility, of permanent conspiracy, on thé part of some other group is characteristic to a greater or lesser degree of most group-relationships in India.

Every significant socio-economic conflict in India — the Hindu-Moslem conflict, the Sikh-Moslem conflict, the Caste-Hindu–Untouchable conflict, the Indian–Anglo–Indian conflict and all the lesser ones — seems to follow the same twisted, delusive pattern that characterizes the fundamental conflict between British ruler and Indian ruled.

Just as the Indians as a whole interpret every British slight, rudeness, injustice, or even mistake, as a calculated act in a program of persecution, so do the Hindus interpret every manifestation of individual violence, boorishness, or intolerance on the part of any member of another Indian community as the launching of a pogrom against them.

Just as the British can never understand how their own rudeness provokes the insolence of the native, so the members of one Indian group can never understand that their own insults, threats, or oppressions can have anything to do with the hostile attitude of another group.

Pathological suspicion poisons the atmosphere of intra-Indian relations as it poisons the atmosphere of British-Indian relationships. When one group expresses an aspiration which conflicts with the interests of another group, members of the threatened group suspect that their adversaries are motivated not so much by selfishness as by hatred, by the intent to 'get' someone else, rather than by the desire to better themselves. Back of all this suspicion is always the delusive assumption of boundless hostility toward oneself on the part of others, the feeling that the casual adversary, who might become a partner tomorrow is really a mortal enemy bent on humiliating or destroying one at all costs, the conviction that anything unpleasant which occurs must be the result of some unseen enemy's plotting.

Like my own cloak-and-dagger world, I found Indian politics a school of delusion. From my personal point of view, a finishing course in this school was very valuable, for it was utterly impossible — providing one were not an Indian — to mistake the Indian form of institutional delusion for any reality. I was not always able to distinguish delusion from reality in my own professional viewpoints or even in my attitudes toward domestic and international political issues, but when I heard of men committing massmurder over the treatment of a cow, I had no doubts, I did not have to ask myself which side was right in such a dispute or who was the aggressor in such a war. Seeing such grotesque forms of delusion flourishing almost under my eyes made me ready to look for less evident and more plausible delusions in all situations where men usually consider it would be a betrayal of truth not to commit murder, or at least to call names.

My trouble was that in analyzing India's political delusions I was not doing much to break down my nightmarish first impression of Indian political life, to dispel my own delusion about India. The more I studied Indian politics the more monstrous Indian political attitudes seemed and the more difficult it became to understand the Indian in so far as he is a political animal. Not only the extremes of Indian character, but the contradictions between different phases of that character, made the Indian seem to me implausible as a human being. As the reader will discover in a later chapter, there is an almost indescribable charm and serenity about certain aspects of Indian life, a wisdom and humanity about certain Indian ways of looking upon the world, which simply do not fit in with the picture I have sketched of Indian politics.

For that matter, Indian political behavior is not always as irresponsible, irrational, and delusive as it usually appears to be. Although instability is one of the most striking traits of Indian political behavior, the careers of few Western politicians show such steadfast and unwavering devotion to an ideal as Nehru's. Although the paranoid complex of suspicion, self-righteousness, persecution, 'preventive' aggression, and unreasoning hatred is almost the leitmotif of Indian politics, no statesman of the West has ever matched Gandhi in his willingness to sit down with his bitterest enemies and talk reason at the height of a passionate political controversy. Although the Congress party always seems about to fall apart, it never does, and it holds together individual members of all the most irreconcilable groups in India. Although Hindu-Moslem relationships frequently resemble a race-war fought on the level of teen-age hoodlums, politically conscious Moslems and Hindus have worked together at times more closely than Democrats and Republicans in the United States have ever worked together.

In politics, as in everything else, I found that India was never gray but always dark or bright, usually more dark than bright, but dazzlingly bright when so at all. The contrasts, even more than the high incidence of darkness, were always pushing me back toward the classic and sterile Western view of India as a land of gods and demons rather than a land of men. I was not interested in gods or demons, only in men, but I expected men to have some kind of fixed character, bad or good, and the Indian character, especially in its political aspects, seemed an accumulation of paradoxes. There are certain abnormal and neurotic individuals whose characters, like my impression of the Indian character, do consist of a series of paradoxes, but I was loath to believe that a whole people could be so neurotic.

The alternative to considering Indian culture as a collective neurosis was to explore the possibility that the major delusions in Indian thinking, the contradictions in Indian feeling or behavior, might be the result of an external situation in which the Indians were placed, that the Indian people might be suffering from the paranoia of empire, the neurosis of modern history. I was never able to agree with myself how far this viewpoint could be legitimately carried, for the traumatisms of history with time certainly become imbedded in the culture of a people and ultimately in personalities of the individuals who compose it. No doubt the Indian people, like all others in the world, has its own special heritage of darkness. I did finally convince myself, however, that at least part of the darkness of India is a shadow cast on it by the West.

The delusions of Indian politics, for instance, seemed to me to be partly echo-delusions — the contagious influence of a delusive relationship upon other relationships, illustrated in my cloak-and-dagger life by the Anglo-American delusions which reflected our stronger delusions about the enemy. The great delusive relationship for all Indians was their relationship with their British rulers. It was the master-delusion not because the furthest removed from reality but because the most charged with emotion and the most sharply patterned. The echo-delusions of intra-Indian politics contained less reality but were less rigid, they had shallower roots but more luxuriant foliage. I suspected that this might be one of the laws of institutional delusion — that our most dangerous ones are often the least grotesque, the closest to reality, and therefore, the most stable.

In any case, I thought that Indian politics perfectly illustrated — if it did not actually confirm — what seemed to me the greatest law of delusion: That when two groups are placed in what I have termed, by analogy, a paranoid relationship with each other, the members of both groups begin to think in a paranoid manner, their minds become filled with delusion.

This is not the lesson of India alone. The nightmares of Balkan and Polish — to say nothing of Irish — politics follow the same pattern as those of Indian politics, and these lands, like India, lay for a long time under oppressive foreign rule. Wherever in the world there has been the reality of persecution there has usually arisen a delusion of persecution, which persisted long after the cause was removed. Wherever men are persecuted by other men, wherever men feel that they have a holy right to persecute other men, delusion tends to develop. Great power and great misery alike produce this condition; it is the occupational disease of prisons and of palaces, flourishing wherever men are raised up above their merits or cast down below their deserts.

It is because ours is a relatively happy and just society that we think extreme delusion a disease. In truth it is a disease but it is much more a disease of society than a disease of the individual. It is the twisted pattern which develops in the attitudes of nearly all men when social conditions place them in an unwholesome relationship with other men. It is the distorted thinking into which nearly all human minds fall under certain circumstances when they deal with ideas of personal or group status and survival.

This is, of course, a view that is difficult to establish scientifically, and my book, being the record of the adventures of a mind rather than a scientific treatise, does not attempt to do so, but it is a view which has the great merit, of explaining something otherwise very difficult to explain: The amount of paranoid behavior in the world. If anyone doubts the amount of paranoid behavior in the world, after reading the newspapers, there is a very easy way to dispel doubt: Read the newspapers of a party, nation, or other social group in conflict with your own.

Back of the question as to the significance of institutional or mass-delusion there lies, it seems to me, one of the deepest and most important intellectual issues of our day.

In the last fifty years our psychiatrists, psychoanalysts, and a small group of social scientists impregnated with the disciplines of the psychology of the unconscious, have forged weapons for the understanding of man and the control of human behavior that the world has never known before. These weapons have as yet been put to pitifully inadequate use and some of them are actually rusting away and may be lost forever. Although the vocabulary and the concepts of psychiatry are now familiar to an immense public, especially in America, our statesmen, administrators, preachers, magistrates, and even our political scientists, physicians, and educators frequently behave as if they had never heard of them. The number of neurotics in the world does not appear to be decreasing and as every practicing psychiatrist knows, the fact that increasingly large numbers of people are able to describe

their own behavior — and, above all, the behavior of their neighbors — in psychiatric terms does not mean that human behavior
is becoming less neurotic. The tragic reality is that the intellectual disciplines which, more than any other, should have led to a
fundamental re-education and perfectionment of human character have so far contributed very little to the betterment of the
world.

Psychiatry has become just as popular as magic was during the
Middle Ages but in spite of that has remained almost as hermetic
to the layman, partly because psychiatrists, like magicians, tend
to think of themselves as a priestly class. Since even the non-
clinical psychological disciplines of today have, historically, a
medical ancestry, their practitioners have retained something of
the Hippocratically ordained physician's attitude. More serious
than that, many of our psychological concepts reflect the basic
medical concept of disease, which subtly falsifies them when they
are applied to social and political philosophy, where they are
needed as badly as in medicine.

The whole modern concept of neurosis, which should be so
fruitful, has done even less to solve the problems of mankind than
the earlier concept of error and sin, because the psychiatrists who
invented it were led by their medical training and the nature of
the cases they studied to consider neurosis as an abnormality.
Anthropological research has proved that the abnormalities of
our society are frequently the norms of other societies, and even
within our society the psychiatrists have discovered that there is
no sharp dividing line between normality and neurosis — as well
as no general agreement among themselves on what constitutes
either.

Yet not only does psychiatry continue to limit itself largely to
the study of clinical abnormalities, but all of the psychological
and social disciplines which are nourished by psychiatric research
consciously or unconsciously apply to the study of individual or
collective behavior patterns the psychiatric criterion of clinical
normality. The result is that the men who should be the best
equipped to understand, and therefore to correct, the darkness of

the world are completely unable to make those who control the destinies of the world understand what are the principles of darkness.

In reality, it is not the neurotic — i.e., badly disintegrated — personality which is important to the world but the fragments of neurosis or delusion in normal men (including psychiatrists). It is not the technique of salvaging disintegrated personalities which most urgently needs development but a discipline whereby the normal man can train himself to become something healthier than a normal man, to become an athlete of reality. The world cannot be saved from destruction by eliminating clinical neurosis among individuals and groups. It can only be saved by eliminating the neurosis in normal men, which necessitates not only a doctrine for the psychic re-education of the human race, but the creation of political institutions that encourage the maximum integration of the average man.

Peace, justice, social co-operation and freedom are psychiatric tools for the cure of neurosis, just as the concept of neurosis and the doctrine of the unconscious are the true foundations of political science. Psychiatry and political science should be subsidiary disciplines of a single science of human survival, but before they can be there is a concept of the unity of human experience lacking in our culture, which we must borrow from the East. At present, the myth of the individual as an indivisible social atom stalemates the science of man, as the atomic theory of nineteenth-century chemistry, before Einstein and Curie, stalemated for some time the physical sciences.

These conclusions, doubtless, rest upon premises which have not yet been clearly presented to the reader, for this book, being the log of my mental life in the East, reflects the disorderly pattern of life itself, in which realization constantly anticipates future experience, just as it sometimes lags behind acquired experience.

If this lack of systematic presentation greatly distresses the reader, let him instruct the jury of his mind to disregard — as introduced without proper foundation — the nuclear social philosophy roughly outlined in the foregoing paragraphs, and to retain as a working hypothesis the simple view that Indian politics is largely a shadow-play of delusion, not because Indian minds are basically more deluded than ours, but because Indians share our inability to recognize delusion in its institutional form — and because our own Western delusions have helped to place the Indian people in an objective situation which makes straight thinking almost impossible.

If he accepts this view as applied to India, the reader will probably discover, as I discovered, that it tends to lessen his feeling of paradox in viewing many other situations, including Western ones, where human beings seem to behave in an inhuman way.

III

The Delusion of Rightness

ONE OF THE THINGS — besides those already touched upon — which makes the study of Indian politics a bewilderment for the Western mind is the relative absence of transition and climax in Indian political life. This seems particularly true of political conflicts in India.

Several times within the past quarter-century, British-Indian or Hindu-Moslem relations, after a deceptively brief period of mounting tension, have gathered into crisis, with all-out revolution or civil war apparently inevitable, and then the storm has blown over, leaving at worst only minor wreckage.

This pattern of averted clash and aborted agreement is apparent in the dramatic sequence of events in 1942. The mission of Sir Stafford Cripps to negotiate a compromise with the Indian nationalist leaders on the basis of full Indian co-operation without constitutional change during the war and full independence afterwards came very near to succeeding. It finally collapsed over a question of detail which seemed of vital importance to the Indians — all the more vital because they thought that the British had first accepted their demands and then changed their minds — namely, the powers and jurisdiction in defense matters of the Indians who were to be given ministerial portfolios under the viceroy.

Following the breaking off of negotiations and the departure of Cripps, the Indians sputtered for a while and then under Gandhi's leadership adopted the 'Quit India' resolution which the British interpreted as an open declaration of war on the Raj, a call to all-out insurrection. Accustomed as they were to the inconsistencies of Indian political behavior, they yet expected a nation-wide upheaval of formidable violence, and for months afterwards could hardly bring themselves to believe that the insurrection had really fizzled out in a few riots, a few acts of sabotage, a few assassinations, some executions, and thousands of arrests, leaving the millions of India in their normal sullen quiescence.

A few fools believed that this fiasco marked the collapse of the Indian revolution, but events soon revealed that it was merely one more example of the theme of anticlimax in Indian politics, which makes the recent history of that old land seem a series of political premature ejaculations. The Freudian mind might be tempted to take this metaphor too literally, especially since the theme of false climax and fading seems to run through many aspects of Indian life — notably Indian music — and deficient virility is evidently a prominent masculine preoccupation, to judge from the content of the medical advertising one sees in the papers and on the streets.

It is not necessary, however, to invoke whatever patterns of interruption may exist in the Indian soul to explain the inconclusiveness of Indian political conflicts. The immediate explanation, I discovered, is that Indians have an attitude toward conflict which is different from our own. There is not in their minds the same razor-sharp distinction between war and peace that there is in ours, there is not the same intense feeling of the incompatibility of conflict and negotiation.

With us, when men try to reconcile their differences and fail, there always comes a point when the last word is spoken and no arbitration is left save that of force — not necessarily the force of violence, but economic force, as in labor disputes, the force of public opinion as in political contests, legal force as in lawsuits. With Indians there never is a last word and the onset of conflict, the showdown, does not mean the end of reconciliation. Unconditional surrender and total war are both un-Indian concepts.

Gandhi has repeatedly negotiated with successive viceroys while engaged in launching 'all-out' campaigns of civil disobedience against them, or when sitting in jail. When communal warfare, marked by savage atrocities, breaks out between Hindus and Moslems in a large city, the leaders of the two communities may meet to settle the dispute while the rioting is at its peak, and I have been told by British friends that it is not unknown for some of these leaders to alternate sessions at the conference table with sessions of inciting the mob to further violence. If true civil war ever breaks out between the Moslems and the Hindus, no matter how bloody it may be, one can be sure that active peace-negotiations will be going on concurrently with the fighting.

Like the Chinese, the Indians find it emotionally possible to fight and negotiate at the same time, and, conversely, they are not as shocked as we are when negotiation is interrupted by violence. They differ from the Chinese in the relative absence of conscious cynicism about mixing combat and negotiation, in greater intensity of political passion which causes them to negotiate only by fits and starts, in attaching less importance to mere 'face' and in an almost paradoxical gift of being able to compromise without compromising principle.

To some extent this attitude results from conscious practice of the Gandhian discipline of nonviolence, which forbids hating — as well as physically harming — the adversary one opposes, but it seemed to me that it had much deeper roots and stemmed — among other things — from a peculiar Hindu feeling about truth, truth in the sense of being 'right' in a controversy.

An extraordinary, semipolitical, social gathering which I once attended in New Delhi brought out in sharp relief the difference between some of these Indian political attitudes and our own. It was a rather large but casual buffet supper at the leading Indian club, organized, as far as I could gather, by a group of women in order to give some of the wartime Americans in Delhi a favorable view of Indian life.

There were about a dozen other Americans, mostly from the house on Man Singh road where I lived myself, two elderly, civilian Britishers, and an almost incredibly heterogeneous collection of Indians. The dominant note was Congress and Hindu, but there was a good sprinkling of Moslems, several Communists or socialist revolutionaries, one or two Parsees, and a quite large representation of 'official' Indians — those who continued to hold office under the British and were consequently denounced as traitors or collaborationists by the extreme nationalists.

Such politically mixed company can be seen at large gatherings in Washington or any Western capital and mayhem seldom results, even in times of political tension, but they are not quite the same kind of gathering this one was. Though it was fairly large, it was not a rigidly social function, and an air of informality was carefully maintained. Furthermore, it had a definite cultural, if not political, intent; it was in a sense deliberate propaganda.

The hostesses had evidently contrived this buffet in order to show their foreign guests that, however much Indians might disagree among themselves on political questions, they were members of a united nation. This underlying purpose must have been explained in advance to the Indian guests and they had not only accepted but were playing the roles expected of them.

If some isolationist hostess in Washington in the days of bitter controversy before Pearl Harbor had tried to assemble a group of representative isolationists and interventionists of various sects in a social gathering of this sort in order to show a group of visiting Latin Americans that we were basically united despite our differences, she would have encountered considerable difficulty. If she had invited me I would have refused, on the ground that I did not want to give any foreigners the impression that I was basically united with isolationists.

Knowing the bitterness of partisan feeling that divided many of these Indians — the basic Hindu-Moslem antagonism, the venomous feud between the Congress members and the Communists, who were at that time vociferously supporting the British war effort, the contempt of all the revolutionaries for the 'officials' — it seemed to me remarkable that they were there at all. Far more remarkable was the way they behaved toward one another.

There was no constraint, very little merely social chitchat and apparently no effort to avoid conversational thin ice. The talk was largely political throughout the evening. Courteously but emphatically the Indians, both among themselves and in front of the foreigners, expressed their contradictory opinions about the issues of the day. Perhaps the most amazing thing about them was that they seemed to listen to Indians of conflicting belief, actually listen to the arguments of adversaries, not just keep silent in order to give the adversary his inning.

Most of these Indians seemed to be old friends, which explained the lack of constraint or rancor in their intercourse, but what was not explained was how they had happened to remain friends despite their differences. It is true that the most extreme shades of Congress opinion were represented by women, the men being in jail at that time, but the female of the species is seldom less fanatical than the male, and we had with us as the main attraction of the evening one of the leading political firebrands of India, Mrs. Sarojini Naidu, distinguished poetess, one-time president of the All-India Congress, also one-time jailbird.

Mrs. Naidu, a rich exuberant personality, a deep-bosomed and deep-minded Indian version of the clubwoman type, was then at large on probation, being forbidden to make speeches or to carry on any political activity. At a signal from one of the hostesses she rose and made us a little speech, a witty, barbed, and yet good-humored one, explaining that she was not making a speech because she was forbidden to make them. Her remarks, with evident self-enjoyment, were directed mainly at the two Britishers. Then she read us one of her poems, a melodious and effective bit of verse expressing the age-old pan-religious ideal of India by subtly blending and orchestrating the street-noises of world's religions, the bells of Christendom, the muezzin's cry from Islam's minaret, the chants of Jewish rabbi and Buddhist monk, the religious songs of Hinduism.

It was an apt and convincing pointing of the evening's lesson, I thought. The courtesy, the broad tolerance, the respect for sincerely opposed opinion, which these Indians of conflicting political faiths manifested in their behavior toward one another, had ancient cultural and religious roots. Throughout the ages the 'thousand waving arms' of Hindu pantheism had welcomed adherents of the most diverse belief and observance. From a theological point of view it seemed difficult to consider the Kali-worshipers, who sacrifice living animals to the Goddess of Death and eat meat, the Vaishnavites, whose worship of Vishnu as a personal and ethical deity is closely akin to Christianity, and the Brahma-worshipers whose God is an abstract, impersonal, all-embracing, theistic principle, as members of the same religion. Yet to the Hindus these three cults are not even different sects but specialized branches of Hinduism in the sense that the various monastic orders are specialized branches of Catholicism.

Even those outside the pale of Hinduism had never seemed wholly creatures of the outer darkness to the Indian mind. Since the Moslem invasions, and despite the secular strife they engendered, the theological liberalism of Hinduism had actually increased, there had been a reaching-out toward Islam, a definite effort to appreciate the values of Islam, and this had tempered the fierce Moslem intolerance, created at least the beginnings of an Indian, not just a Hindu, tolerance. This tolerance, in its purest Hindu form, was not mere passive toleration of alien belief; far more remarkable than the fact that Hinduism has never persecuted heretics or unbelievers, is the fact that the most devout Hindus have always considered it a duty of the mind to listen respectfully to their arguments.

How far this tolerance applies to the modern political religions was illustrated by the next item on the evening's program. A clamor arose for another poetess to be heard from, and when the poetess, Miss Mumtaz Shanawas, a young woman with the vivid, black-eyed Persian type of beauty, seemed reluctant to be heard after greatness, Mrs. Naidu took the lead in urging her, with many expressions of familiar endearment.

The younger woman, I gathered, was both a close personal friend and a literary disciple of Mrs. Naidu. Under the latter's indulgent but not patronizing eye, while across the room her wealthy, conservative Moslem parents beamed with tender pride, Miss Shanawas recited several vigorously talented verses filled with the woes and battle-cries of the Indian proletariat, for poetry happened to be only her hobby — she was an ardent and active member of the Indian Communist party. When she had finished, Mrs. Naidu led the warm burst of applause from the whole room and then embraced her.

Considering that Miss Shanawas' poetry, despite its literary merits, was straight Marxist propaganda, that her political comrades were supporting the alien government which kept Mrs. Naidu's in jail — and not just supporting the British but viciously attacking Congress as well — this seemed to me quite an interesting performance. If, in the black autumn of 1939, I had been called upon to hear a young Communist poet recite verses denouncing the imperialist war which the Soviet-Nazi nonaggression pact had done so much to make inevitable, I doubt very much that I could have achieved the mellowness of Mrs. Naidu's attitude. Yet she was no confused liberal, no compromiser, no appeaser, as the British had long since learned.

Indians — at least the Hindus — I decided, were more successful than we are at dissociating their feelings about a human being from their feelings about his ideas. More than that, they had a different feeling about ideas, about political truth. Again, it seemed, to me this attitude stemmed from their religious traditions.

Hinduism, unlike Christianity (or Marxism) is not a religion of revealed truth but of truths — truths which by their very plurality are suggestive guideposts to the discovery of God rather than unbreakable rules for salvation. Men are pilgrims and each man in his own age must find his own way to God. An individual pilgrim may feel that his path is the best for himself — or even for all men — but, if he is a Hindu, he is not disturbed when others take different paths, because what is important to him is not the path but the ultimate goal. Faith, to the Hindu, seems to mean an intense longing and constant striving for religious fulfillment rather than any kind of systematic belief; there is a definite feeling that the intensity of the longing is a much greater factor in religious success than the rightness of the belief.

Carried over into politics this attitude makes for mutual tolerance among followers of different political creeds having roughly similar goals, and even for a measure of understanding among those who pursue antithetical goals — doubtless the Hindu has a vague feeling that, just as all religious paths lead to God, so do all political paths lead to some goal of human betterment.

With us truth, faith, right belief are absolutes, finally and immutably revealed. Right belief is salvation and error is damnation. Because error is damnation it is damnable — and infectious. It is not just a personal misfortune but a community menace. One man's error may cause other men to lose their souls. The misguided individual is the agent of Satan as well as his victim. Hence he must be purged from the community — or at least shunned as if he had the plague. A young soldier in Franco's armies during the Spanish Civil War once explained it to me this way:

'We don't hate the Communists or want to punish them. It's just that Communism is an incurable disease they are spreading around so we have to put them out of the way. We have to rid Spain of this disease and there is no other way of doing it.'

Because all truth proceeds from God and all error from Satan, we contrive family trees for every fragment of truth or error that we think we discover. Every error is the child of more basic error, every truth the child of shining truth and destined to beget hosts of little truths. In our zeal to exalt or safeguard the pedigrees of truth and error we develop rigidly systematic ideologies which often come perilously close to those that flourish among the paranoid cases in our insane asylums — so close sometimes as to be indistinguishable. That clumsy adjective on page 59 of Comrade X's new novel is the cryptic footprint of a latent Trotskysm, the League of Nations failed because it did not insist on conducting its business in Esperanto, and the weather is less bracing than it used to be because the New Deal has undermined free enterprise.

The spread of science has not purged us of this theological attitude toward truth and heresy. Perhaps it has aggravated it, for the relative certainty of some scientific results has created the impression in our minds that the application of the scientific method — or even of scientific terminology — to such confused fields of human activity as politics automatically produces truths of scientific validity.

The cultural humus in which a great number of our specific delusions grow is a threefold delusion of rightness, which apparently the Indians do not have, or have less of: Our sense of rightness is apt to be excessively authoritative, our being right confers a quite disproportionate merit on us — and makes disagreement heinous as well as wrong — and the principle about which we are right has transcendent consequences.

Hence the frequency in Western history with which heretics get burned and deviationists get purged, hence the reason that psychoanalysts fill their journals with mixed personal and professional abuse of heretical colleagues, hence the tactical dissensions which barely permit the protagonists of the various schools of thought about achieving world unity through world government to remain on speaking terms with one another.

I was, perhaps, saved from confirming my own theory by applying it next to the movements of heavenly bodies, when a young Hindu woman approached me — we are still at the party — and said she understood I had formerly been a newspaper correspondent, and therefore did I know Herbert Matthews of the *New York Times?* When I said that I did, her look said, 'I thought so,' and with a sneer of bitter venom she said:

'We used to think when he was in India that Mr. Matthews was our friend, but now we see he has gone over to the other side.'

'I haven't seen any of Matthews' recent articles about India,' I said, 'but I know the man; he is a very honest and conscientious correspondent and he does not go over to one side or the other, he just writes the truth as he sees it.'

'Well, if you are right, then he should consult an oculist,' retorted the young woman, and flounced off, still hating Matthews for seeing truth the wrong way, and inclined to be a little suspicious of me for siding with the enemy.

Thus I was reminded that despite the extraordinary exhibition of Indian tolerance I had witnessed during the evening, delusion and intolerance were not Western monopolies, just as my studies of the repercussion of imperialism on the Indian mind had satisfied me they were not Eastern ones. Many Indian delusions sprang straight from their emotional roots without complication, like the delusion of enmity which the young woman at the party had said about Matthews, but some were as rationalized and systematized as any of our own. There were many Indians, I knew, who believed that poverty and disease and illiteracy were solely the results of British rule. There were also scores of millions who still believed that one was born a Brahmin or an Untouchable because of one's worthy or unworthy behavior in a previous life.

One big difference between Indian institutional delusions and ours, I concluded, is that the Indian ones are neither tempered nor reinforced by our master-delusion of rightness. No Hindu Pope has ever claimed infallibility, and no Hindu Mussolini would ever scrawl 'Mussolini is Always Right' on the walls of his cities, not so much because he would not be believed, as because it would not matter.

What is most important to the Indians in social relations is not truth, but harmony. They try to dispel their group-delusions by seeking to eliminate the element of hate from group relationships rather than by seeking to eliminate the element of unreality. Western thought denounces this method of combating delusion as a dangerous, damnable, sentimental heresy, yet I found from personal experience that, when I could succeed in applying it, the element of unreality in a delusive relationship often evaporated by itself, whereas, if I concerned myself only with the reality or nonreality of my belief, I frequently re-enforced the delusion.

When Indians try to apply this technique and fail, it sometimes makes them very irresponsibly wrong, but it is one of the things which makes it possible for them to negotiate with political ad-

versaries long after we have abandoned every thought except
cracking skulls. The passions generated among them by conflicts
of interest tend less than ours to crystallize into ideologies of hate.

Conversely, they can compromise without betraying their
ideals, whereas with us there is no middle way: It must always be
appeasement or unconditional surrender, defeatism or counterfascism, witch-hunting or burying our heads in the sand, the delusion of rightness or the rejection of all belief.

This contrast in Indian and Western attitudes toward the
problem of delusion — in so far as anyone recognizes it as a
problem — suggested to me another contrast between Indian delusions and ours, which helps create the nightmarish impression
of Indian politics in our minds. Most of the Western peoples
have lived for some time as nations and have developed a little —
though only a very little — of the ability to recognize delusion in
the relationships of near neighbors that we manifest in our private
lives.

India is still struggling with the problem of attaining nationhood, and the fraternal delusions which with us produced the
American Civil War are current ones in Indian society. Consequently, to find the Western equivalents to Indian political delusions we should not look to our domestic political arenas but to
our foreign relations, where our efforts to achieve one world approximate — though they have not yet quite caught up with —
Indian efforts to achieve one India.

IV

There May be Hope

IN TRYING to analyze the political nightmares of India, I found
that I was not merely learning something about Indian politics
but that I was fundamentally revising my whole outlook on the
world. I was learning that every time one discovers the factors
of unreason in another man's nightmare one dispels some nightmare of one's own; every time one dissipates a slight nightmare
one frees oneself to some degree from a greater one. The reason
for this is that all the nightmares of the world have at least two
things in common — the element of horror and the element of
unreality — and that most of them are related in some way to the
great collective nightmare of our day: The feeling, which haunts
all of us, that some irrational but irresistible force is driving mankind to the destruction of another and still more nearly total war.

I had already come to believe that the delusive atmosphere of
Indian politics was not caused by any fundamental deformation
of Indian culture but was, to a considerable degree, the natural
consequence of a vicious and delusive political doctrine of the
West — the doctrine that it is legitimate and even beneficent for
one human race to impose its rule on another by force. If my
diagnosis was correct, then both the Indian delusion begot by
oppression, and the Western delusion expressed in the doctrine of
legitimate oppression that we call imperialism, were curable — in
fact, the cure seemed assured, for the people of Britain had, even
by 1944, agreed in principle to renounce imperialism, at least as
applied to India. Since Indian character was not an incurable

143

neurosis, despite the evidence of Indian politics, then perhaps human nature was not an incurable neurosis, despite the evidence of history. Perhaps the worst of the world's muddle arose simply from our failure to recognize recognizable delusion.

In order to test the validity of this view, I decided to concentrate my attention upon one particularly significant Indian political conflict and to try to trace back to their ultimate origins the chains of delusive logic which bound the participants to conflict.

The most significant Indian conflict seemed to be the one, raging during the winter I lived in New Delhi, over the issue of Pakistan — the demand of the Moslem League for a separate Moslem state to be established by detaching from the rest of India those areas where the population was predominantly Moslem.

The main argument for Pakistan advanced by its greatest champion, Mohamed Ali Jinnah, president of the Moslem League, was simply that the Moslems of India are a distinct people with a culture of their own, entirely different from that of the Hindus. Jinnah did not contend that all the Moslems had a common and distinct blood heritage, yet he insisted that Islam was not merely a religion, but a way of life, a culture and a tradition of such strength that those who belong to it automatically constituted a nation. Because the Moslems of India were a separate nation Jinnah demanded that they be allowed to form a separate state.

He opposed the unity of India because he contended that it meant domination, and perhaps persecution, of the Moslem minority by the Hindu majority.

The Congress adherents usually denied Jinnah's main premises. They declared that there was no difference between Moslems and Hindus in race, culture, or language. They maintained that the rights of the Moslems as a religious minority community could be safeguarded within the framework of a unitarian India. Above all, they argued that Pakistan was unfeasible for economic, geographic, and ethnographic reasons since the Moslems of India were not all concentrated on the northwest frontier — Bengal on the other side of the subcontinent has a Moslem majority, and there are important Moslem enclaves elsewhere.

Superimposed upon these more or less rational arguments was a welter of polemic, of name-calling, of plotting and plot-exposing, of blind, unreasoning hatred, which laid bare the roots of the controversy, revealing its ancestry in the communal bazaar-riot.

Congress supporters denounced Jinnah as a traitor to the cause of Indian independence, as a hired tool of British imperialism, or at least as an unscrupulous demagogue, a would-be Mussolini, who was willing to sacrifice the cause of Indian freedom and unity to personal ambition. In the same breath they declared that Jinnah's Pakistan movement was of no importance because Jinnah spoke for an insignificant fragment of Moslem opinion, and even that Jinnah himself did not really believe in Pakistan, that he was only using Pakistan as a blackmail device to make Congress accept him as the true leader of Islam in India.

Communal-minded Hindu elements both within and outside the Congress party took a graver view of Jinnah. They accused him of being the spokesman of Moslem religious fanaticism and publicly voiced their suspicion that the real Moslem goal was the resurrection of the Moghul empire and the re-enslavement of the Hindus.

Such accusations were gleefully taken up by the supporters of Jinnah and woven into an elaborate argument seeking to prove the existence of a Hindu conspiracy to establish a Hindu dictatorship which would trample upon the religious as well as the civic rights of the Moslems. In developing this argument the Moslem League polemists usually identified Hinduism with the Congress party, totally overlooking the Congress claim to be an all-India, nonsectarian political organization and the undisputed fact that it contained in its ranks Untouchables, Sikhs, Indian Christians, and Moslems, including its 1943 president, Maulana Abul Kalam Azad, a noted Moslem scholar and divine.

The ravings of V. D. Savarkar, president of the retrograde communal organization called the Hindu Mahasabha, bitter enemy of the 'atheistic' Congress leaders and principal champion of recreating the ancient Aryavarta — Land of the Aryan Hindus — were constantly being dragged out by the Moslem League as substantiation of the alleged Congress plot to impose Hindu dominion over Moslems in the name of Indian unity.

The element of delusion in the Congress goal of a united, democratic India was much more subtle. If one thought of Indian communities as being analogous to Western religious communities, there seemed to be no delusion in it at all. Obviously, the Hindus, being in the majority, would dominate the central government. But why should non-Hindu Indians worry about that any more than American Catholics worried about the certain Protestant majority in our congress? This argument, often used by Hindus and Hindu sympathizers, overlooked one vital difference between India and America: American congressmen (whatever else they may do) do not legislate as Protestants or Catholics, whereas Indian politicians (though they refuse to admit it) would inevitably, in certain circumstances, legislate as Hindus or Moslems. They might grow out of this habit in time, but the other communities would not have a pleasant life while the Hindu majority was learning to think in Indian, instead of communal, terms.

Thus it seemed clear to me that neither the Moslem formula of Pakistan, nor the Congress panacea of a unitary Indian national state, could solve the problem of Hindu-Moslem relationships in India. Both formulas were expressions of the Western concept of nationhood, which became delusion when applied, out of its historic context, to the peculiar Indian muddle in which Moslems and Hindus had grown up. It was not the first time, of course, that delusion had twisted the relationship of these two groups.

From the eleventh century until roughly the close of the eighteenth century the Moslems were the ruling class of India. At first they were foreign invaders — an aristocracy of blood. Gradually, through interbreeding and forced conversion, there developed an Indian Moslem society superimposed upon Hindu society. The higher economic brackets of this Moslem society functioned as a superaristocracy, occupying the posts of command in the state and sharing among themselves the greater part of the national income. The lower elements in Moslem society, because their religion was a guarantee of loyalty to the rulers of the state, benefited from various economic or political favors above those accorded to Indians occupying a similar position in Hindu society.

In order to have peace in their lands, the Moslem rulers of India bit by bit abandoned the persecution of their Hindu subjects. In the reign of the Moghul Emperor Akbar — the contemporary of Elizabeth of England and Henry IV of France — almost complete economic and political equality between Moslems and Hindus was achieved and a realignment of Indian society along class, rather than racial or communal, lines began to take shape.

This trend was abruptly reversed in the reign of Aurangzeb (1659–1707), who resumed the religious persecution of the Hindus and with it their political and economic oppression. This anti-Hindu policy of Aurangzeb led to a series of Hindu and Sikh revolts against the Moghul throne — revolts which necessarily had something of the character of a revolutionary class-struggle because, although they were led by Hindu rajahs and nobles, they were struggles for political and economic power, as well as struggles for religious freedom.

The upheavals produced by Aurangzeb's palace counterrevolution, by the Moghuls' imperial and religious fascism, greatly facilitated the British conquest of India and explained the willingness of many Hindus to collaborate with the invaders from the West. Because they were the collaborationists of the epoch, the Hindus received such crumbs as the British were willing to leave to their new subjects, while the Moslems, smarting under the usurpation of the Moghuls' Peacock Throne by the infidels from the West, would have no truck with them, refusing government posts and land tenures even when they were offered. Thus, unwittingly, the British fostered a counter-counterrevolution in Indian society and established the Hindus as the most favored class of the nation — except for the British themselves.

The substitution in the nineteenth century of English for Persian as the official language not only destroyed an important cultural link between Moslem and Hindu Indians, but helped

complete the curious transformation of the Moslems into a depressed social class. For a long time the Moslems refused to learn
the language of the infidel and by their refusal they both deprived
themselves of possibilities for official employment and closed the
door on the modern learning, which in India, as everywhere else,
became one of the keys to social advancement. Without losing
their traditional sense of superiority toward the Hindus and their
memories of past grandeur, the Moslems by the end of the nineteenth century had become the hill-billies and the poor whites of
India. A Moslem intellectual renascence, based upon reconciliation with Western science, together with a stirring of Moslem
political consciousness, developed in the last quarter of the century, but the Hindu head start in economic competition could not
be overcome.

This is the background of Hindu-Moslem communal rivalry in
modern times and it is therefore the ultimate background of the
political controversy over Pakistan. Though the Moslem League
was founded in 1906, it was not until 1940 that the League under
Jinnah's energetic leadership launched an all-out campaign for
Pakistan. The Pakistan scheme, itself, had first been propounded
in 1933.

The events leading up to the separatist campaign of 1940 are
interesting. In the elections of 1936 Jinnah's party, which represented the more communal-minded Moslem elements, did poorly.
This was interpreted by the Congress leaders as a repudiation of
communalism by the Moslem electorate and an endorsement of
the advanced section of Moslem opinion which supported Congress. Jinnah had hoped to organize Moslem League-Congress
coalition governments in the provinces, but the Congress leaders,
rendered overconfident, and possibly arrogant, by Jinnah's electoral defeat, rejected his proposals. In doing so they apparently
aroused the suspicions of even those Moslem elements who had
voted against Jinnah's candidates. For four years Jinnah successfully exploited the theme of Hindu intransigeance in refusing to
make any concessions to legitimate Moslem aspirations. Thus, a
dispute over the division of power within the Indian state led

Jinnah and his followers to discover that they were members of a national minority which should form a state of its own.

From this brief and oversimplified summary of Hindu-Moslem relations in Indian history, it is clear that the present dispute between the two groups has a long history of delusion behind it. Not counting the full-dress wars between Hindu kings and princelings and the early invaders, there must have been thousands of bloody clashes between Moslems and Hindus in the last four hundred years.

Yet, the two groups have often stood side by side, as well as face to face, and, as late as 1936, there was some political partnership between them.

Why did the partnership break down? I asked myself. Why did delusion spring up just when the historic causes of delusion seemed to be dying away? Why did Moslem leadership pass from men like Azad to men like Jinnah? Why did Pakistan seem the most dangerous issue which had divided the Indian people since the days of Aurangzeb?

The answer to the last question, I decided, answered the others. Pakistan was a deadly issue because, while it stood for a delusive goal, it seemed to have an almost irresistible appeal for the Moslems of India. It was not a mere gesture of communal hatred, like kicking a cow. It was — in appearance — a positive, constructive program, one which corresponded to the modern, democratic principle of self-determination. It looked like progress — unless one stopped to realize that it could not work. It seemed perfectly pacific — but it implied war between the Hindus and the Moslems. It was obviously grotesque the moment one started asking oneself questions about it, but it seemed completely reasonable if one did not.

It was because — in Moslem eyes — it was such an attractive delusion that leaders like Jinnah, who made it seem real and realizable, won out over those who had nothing to offer except the tiresome reality of learning to get along with the Hindus.

It was because Jinnah had changed the Hindu-Moslem dispute from one about cows to one about Pakistan that fresh delusion

sprang up in Hindu-Moslem relations, just as the older ones, like
the cow-delusion, were dying out.

It was because Pakistan repudiated the basis of Hindu-Moslem
political partnership that the partnership had broken down.

As far as they went, I thought those answers were satisfactory.
They left one great question unanswered: What influences had so
shaped the minds of Indian Moslems that Pakistan was an irresistible delusion to a great many of them?

Here, again, it seemed to me that my long interest in psychological warfare, and my wartime familiarity with its more subterranean aspects, supplied a clue. Psychological warfare, in its blacker
forms, consists essentially in filling the minds of enemies with
delusions which will cause them to fight among themselves, or fall
into some other self-defeating activity. From what I knew of the
British, they did not quite consider the people of India as their
enemies, and they certainly did not think of their policy in India
as a psychological warfare campaign against the Indian people,
but it seemed to me that, both in its methods and its results, it
amounted to that.

While I was in India, the British were obviously supporting
Jinnah's Pakistan campaign. Jinnah professed to be as anti-
British as Gandhi, but it is one of the tenets of secret psychological war that you try, whenever possible, to have your enemies
spread your propaganda for you. (On the same principle the
British supported the Indian Communists during the war.)
Whether any British funds actually helped to finance the Pakistan campaign, I do not know. The mere fact that the British
press in India, officially-sponsored British writers, and even some
responsible British officials in their unofficial moments, all spoke
well of Jinnah and let it be known throughout India that they
thought well of him, helped him to attract a wealthy and influential Moslem clientele, even if it aroused suspicion among the
nationalists.

When the British White Paper on India came out, it was clear
that a change of policy had occurred and that Jinnah was no
longer being supported. That was only in 1946, however. Jinnah

had been carefully nursing his delusion since 1940 with British encouragement in some form, and it had grown quite large by then.

Looking back over British history in India, I thought I could see how British psychological warfare, illustrated by their support of the Pakistan campaign, had built up among Indian Moslems the delusive mentality which made this campaign so successful — also the mentality among Hindus and other Indian groups which fostered their own peculiar delusions.

In the early days of the East India Company, the need for conquering and ruling cheaply, so as provide the greatest possible profit to the stockholders of the Company, forced the British to practice intensively what we call today black psychological warfare. Fifth-columnists and crude methods of underground propaganda paved the way for the Company's troops, native quislings set up as puppet rulers lightened the burden of the Company's administrators in the conquered territory.

The British consciously and deliberately maneuvered so as to keep the native political forces opposed to them weak and divided. Unconsciously and without deliberate attempt they rendered the Indian character weak and divided, they filled the Indian mind with nightmares. For example, it was essential for the Indian government to have intelligence of underground political intrigues and conspiracies, to recognize the currents of public opinion before they became tidal waves. To do this it was necessary to employ spies. The Indian government employed very large numbers of spies — one Indian estimate I saw placed at thirty thousand the number of native police spies maintained by the Raj.

In employing thousands of Indians to spy on other Indians it never occurred to the British that they were waging psychological warfare against the people of India, yet they were doing just that, for it is impossible for a large body of spies to operate in a country without betraying their activity to some degree, and wherever spies are known to be operating there is spy-phobia.

The battle of Plassey, by which Clive won the immense province of Bengal for the stockholders of the East India Company, was the culmination of one of the most picturesque fifth-column operations in history. The circumstances are familiar to most American and British school-children but have been forgotten by many adults. Before attacking the armies of the Nawab of Bengal, Clive had entered into contact through a Hindu agent with Mir J'afar, one of the Nawab's principal commanders, and had concluded a secret agreement whereby in return for sabotaging his ruler's military plans and otherwise aiding the British to defeat him, Mir J'afar would become Nawab in his place and rule Bengal as a British puppet.

There is some question as to how great a role Mir J'afar's treachery played in the rout of Plassey but as quisling ruler of Bengal he rendered invaluable services to the Company for many years. When, in his old age, he became unco-operative in helping the British to strip his province of its wealth, he was deposed — on the grounds that he was implicated in a political murder — but upon his successor's turning unreasonable, was reinstated by British arms for the modest fee of some five million dollars divided between the Company and its individual servants.

Nearly a century later, in the First Sikh War (1848), the pattern of Plassey was repeated — as it had been many times in the intervening period — when a small British force was saved from annihilation, and ultimately handed victory, by the treachery of two Sikh field commanders, one of whom deserted his troops after destroying a bridge which was their only avenue of retreat. Thanks to this treachery the British became masters of the Punjab.

Three years later, when the Sikhs rose up against British domination, a young British officer, Lieutenant Edwardes, won fame, according to an authoritative British source,[1] 'by availing himself of the hostility which he knew to exist between the different races of the Punjab' to raise against the Sikhs a levy of Moslem Pathans in the same way that the British during the Great Mutiny of 1857 'afterwards armed the Sikhs against the Mussulmans and

[1] *Life of Lord Lawrence*, cited in *The Rise and Fulfilment of British Rule in India*, by Edward J. Thompson and G. T. Garratt, The Macmillan Company, 1934.

Hindus of Delhi.'

This British assault on the Indian psyche has sometimes escaped the notice of Western historians — except when they have
taken at their face value the hysterical exaggerations of Indian
political propaganda — not because it was committed in secret
but because it was committed too openly. British agents did not
— at least as a systematic policy — circulate divisive propaganda
tracts or employ *agents provocateurs* to stir up the races and classes
of India against one another. On the contrary, local British officials throughout the country spent a large part of their time in
strenuous and sincere efforts to keep the peace, to promote a minimum of civic co-operation among the warring social groups.
What these officials failed to understand — just as the world at
large has failed to understand it — was that the flames of civil
strife which they struggled so valiantly to quench were constantly being renewed by the incendiary results of British state
policy.

If the United States Army had the policy of balancing every
white regiment with a Negro regiment, if it systematically employed Negro troops to quell riots or uprisings among the white
population and white troops to suppress Negro disturbances, then
race-relations in America would be a good deal worse than they
are. A more effective program of psychological warfare against
the American people could hardly be devised. Yet for fifty years
after the Great Mutiny, according to Garratt and Thompson, this
policy of racial 'counterpoise and division' governed the recruitment and employment of the Indian Army.

It seemed to me that there was a very direct connection between the British practice of subverting Indians to spy on other
Indians and the paranoid suspiciousness which was so characteristic of Indian politics. When a political group fears that it has
been penetrated by spies it is forced to adopt semiconspiratorial
security precautions. This gives it an air of secretiveness which
inevitably appears sinister to other groups and makes them suspect they are being plotted against. Also spy-phobia renders
more difficult the reasonable settlement of political differences;

for example, the stubborn refusal of Congress for a long time to treat with Jinnah as a responsible Moslem spokesman arose in part from the widespread suspicion among Hindus that he was a British agent.

Apart from the conspiratorial delusions of persecution fostered in the Indian mind by this plague of spies, the more or less avowed divisiveness of British policy toward Indian political parties was a psychological assault on the Indian people. It was very natural and not particularly Machiavellian on the part of the British to give honor, power, and often money, to those Indians who were willing to co-operate with the Raj, to give political support or at least special indulgence to those groups whose loyalty to the empire seemed most sure. It was not even sinister in terms of Western domestic politics to give underhand encouragement — as the British have often done — to politicians or parties which were opposed to British rule but at odds with other anti-British factions.

The evil of the system lay in the special character of the Indian groups which British policy pitted against one another. When the British stirred up Moslems against Hindus to prevent them from uniting against the Raj, it was not the same thing as when Republican politicians in America maneuver to set Northern Democrats against Southern Democrats. Domestic politics in the democracies of the West is a kind of social cowpox, which sometimes induces a slight fever but protects us from more deadly ills. It is only a benign malady, however, because the plots, the conspiracies, and the persecutions which are its symptoms are harmless ones — kept harmless by an allegiance above all factional allegiances, reinforced by the police-power of the state.

In injecting the virus of Western politics into the Indian social system, the British unwittingly infected the Indian soul with a mortal disease. Indians had no common state allegiance and the British Raj was too unpopular to provide one. India was a nation because its citizens were linked by multiple ties of common residence, economic relationships, administration, and the habit of living side by side. It was not a nation like any of the West, however, and the different groups which composed it were not political factions, not even social classes, but self-contained societies, embryonic states. The rudimentary forms of political democracy which the British introduced could have served to break down the barrier between different classes of Indians, to hasten the unification of India into a real nation. If, for instance, the British had established an electoral law which would have obliged every candidate for office to seek support from the members of two or more racial or religious communities, the communal issue would soon have disappeared from Indian political life.

Instead, the British did just the opposite. They founded the electoral law upon the representation of communities, allotting to each a set number of seats in the central and provincial legislatures, thus requiring Hindus to vote for Hindu candidates, Moslems for Moslem candidates, and so on. This system inevitably produced the politicalization of communal tensions, which the British aggravated by supporting personalities or parties as it suited the tactical needs of the moment.

Politics in all lands is the struggle for power, and, by putting the racial-religious communities of India into politics, the British converted cultural groups into rival power-blocs. As far as Moslem-Hindu relations were concerned, Aurangzeb had already started the process by trying to combine the roles of secular ruler and religious zealot. Just as India was beginning to recover from Aurangzeb's heritage of hate, the British, turning their backs upon the lesson of modern European history, reanimated the flames of communalism and of religious fanaticism by inviting the deputies of God to sit in the parliament of Caesar, by transplanting the theological disputes of the temple to the modern forum, where worldly issues of power, wealth, and even group-survival hinge on the outcome of the debate.

Indian communities are not quite ecclesiastical communities like those of the West, as has already been noted, but they have this in common with them: A strong attachment to a group ideal higher and more sacred than any worldly interest, a holy allegiance. As long as no worldly forces interfere with this allegiance it should, in theory, have no worldly implications, but human nature being what it is, it always has. The spiritual interests of Islam, to the service of which the devout Moslem is pledged, inevitably tend to become slightly confused in his mind with the temporal interests of the Moslem community. The Hindu suffers from the same confusion, as do, for that matter, the members of other Indian communities, and it is not unknown in the West.

Because of this confusion, when the temporal interests of religious communities are allowed to become political issues they seem holy issues to those involved in them. Temporal — i.e., power — interests become sacred interests which cannot be sacrificed, or even submitted to arbitration, without betraying the faith. The political party defending the interests of a religious community becomes an arm of the church; in the eyes of its members its cause is always just, because the faith is always true, and its adversaries are always in the wrong because they seem adversaries of the church. To defend the faith against these adversaries all means are lawful, because the faith itself is the law.

In this tendency of communal groups, once they are involved in politics, to identify power-interests with moral principles, emotional with political sovereignties, might with right, there is a striking resemblance to the paranoid mentality. The resemblance is not accidental, for the mentalities are both delusive. Described in political terms, paranoia is the madness which makes individuals behave like states, which makes them self-patriots, self-chauvinists and self-racists. It is the self-sovereignty which makes the aggressions of others always seem persecutions, while sanctifying one's own persecution of others. It is the condition of being perpetually worried about one's status, perpetually suspicious of the designs of others. It is the feeling that murder to defend or even to enhance one's sovereignty is somehow not murder but a necessary sacrifice for a great cause. It is the habit of being one's own espionage service, of turning speech into political propaganda for the furtherance of self.

Described in psychological terms the ideology of the political group which considers itself a sovereignty above the law is a collective delusion of moral superiority.

Delusive ideologies and paranoid authorities are born of the marriage of holiness and rule, of group selfishness and self-abnegation, of peace within and aggression without. Every such ideology and every such authority rests upon a pathological premise which differs from the basic delusion of every clinical paranoid by only one word: My group, right or wrong, instead of Myself, right or wrong.

Thus, in playing the divide-and-rule game with the communal groups of India the British produced something much more sinister than the political disunity of India. They converted these groups into delusive political sovereignties unable to reconcile their conflicting interests except where reconciliation could be imposed by force, impervious to any logic but the logic of power. The British might have used their power to impose solutions which would ultimately have removed communal issues from the political field. Instead they used their power to foster the transformation of religious or racial minorities into tribal or religious fanaticisms, disguised as modern political parties.

For two and a half years I watched Pakistan grow like an evil weed under British protection and encouragement. It grew in two ways. It gathered more adherents among the Moslems of India, and the ambitions of its proponents swelled, making it more and more unlikely that they could ever reach an agreement with the other factions.

The delusive elements which Pakistan derived from its roots in Moslem religious fanaticism became reinforced by a Western political concept which is itself a delusion — the concept of absolute state sovereignty. Having decided that the Moslems of India should have a separate state, it seemed natural to Jinnah and his followers that this state should be like all others — an absolute sovereignty. It was a logical conclusion from their premise.

Shortly before my return to America I picked up in Ceylon a copy of one of the Muslim League propaganda organs and read a strident editorial claiming for Pakistan (when it should come into being) the right to manufacture atomic bombs for its defense.

To withhold the secret of the atomic bomb from Pakistan, the editorial implied, would be an intolerable menace to the security, and an intolerable affront to the dignity, of that state-to-be. I had already read in the papers from home similar demands put forward on behalf of various sovereign states of the West but this had made little impression on me. Somehow, when Pakistan likewise claimed the bomb as if it were an inalienable attribute of her sovereignty, that seemed to make everything clear. I understood at last why, if paranoia is the disease which makes men behave like states, absolute sovereignty is the principle which makes governments behave like paranoids.

Normally we are too deeply imbedded in the nightmare of our own history to perceive this intimate relationship between an abnormality of the individual psyche and the normal pattern of the world. We are unduly impressed by the rational motives for aggression or suspicion which characterize the behavior of governments, at least of the governments of great powers. We accept the patient's explanation of his own behavior and fail to remind ourselves that, since in every age the world has had the appearance of a madhouse, it is reasonable to suspect that some principle of madness may be abroad. We may recognize the need for a law above nations to control the madness of the world, but unconsciously we consider that such a law is needed to curb the mad, bad nations, to protect the sober and peaceful ones, as domestic law protects the good citizen by locking up the burglars. We forget that, without the law, we would all be burglars.

The pedagogic value of Pakistan to me was that it was a government yet unborn of a nation which existed only in propaganda, yet as it stirred in its paper womb, this innocent embryo of a government revealed the attributes which make all national governments mad and bad. It was committed to no oppressions or aggressions but it reserved to itself the right to judge what was oppression or aggression, and as sanction of its sovereignty, it claimed the right to possess the weapon of final destruction.

As its notion of its own sovereignty, its own self-importance, grew, its boundaries tended not only to become more holy, but to expand. As it became more conscious of its rights as a state, all these rights tended to seem more inalienable. As its will to exist increased, the need of survival came to seem more primordial and the criterion of survival tended to become the possibility or impossibility for other states to menace its existence, implying, almost of necessity, the ability of Pakistan to menace theirs. Hence, Pakistan, before it possessed a foreign office, began to develop a foreign policy oriented toward strategic alliances with the Moslem states of the Middle East. Before it possessed an army, it began to develop strategic doctrines of national survival. Eventually it would have, or want to have, some kind of a strategic Monroe Doctrine. Its real frontiers might be on the Indus but its strategic frontiers would extend to the Irrawaddy and the Euphrates.

Pakistan, unless the very extravagance of its gestation shocked its adherents into realization of its absurdity, would be born into the world as a paranoid state and its relations with other states would be those of a paranoid toward his fellows. Its people might be the sanest and most peace-loving in the world (although they were not likely to be), but its officials, those who guided its foreign and defense policies, would inevitably guide Pakistan's foreign relations into a delusive pattern.

They would do so because their ideology of state service would place Pakistan above the law of nations, as the paranoid's ideology places him above the laws of society. To be above the law is to be outside the law, it is to deprive oneself of the protections of the law, as well as to free oneself from its restrictions.

If you arrogate to yourself the right of belligerency it is natural and inevitable to fear that others will attack you, and to plan how you can forestall them, thus causing them to attack, to forestall you. The only thing mad about the paranoid's view of the World is his assumption that, because he has placed himself above the law and granted a right of unlimited belligerency to himself, everyone else is living in accordance with the same ideology. If the paranoid were right, if the world were composed exclusively of other paranoids his nightmares of plotting and persecutions would be perfectly justified, and paranoia would be a disease only in the extreme cases where it involved a secession from the laws of Nature, leading to plots of winds and persecutions of stones.

The future statesmen of Pakistan would not be madmen, they would merely be statesmen in a world of statesmen, and they would wonder, like everyone else, why the world is mad, and perhaps try sincerely to bring sanity into it, never realizing that the principle of madness in the world lay as much as anything else in the concept of statehood to which they had given their allegiance.*

---

* This chapter, like the rest of the book, was written before the partition of the Indian Sub-Continent into two sovereign nations, Pakistan and India; it reflects the hope I felt at the time — a delusive hope as events have turned out — that this disaster could be avoided by some compromise along federal or confederal lines between Moslem and Hindu nationalists. No doubt I underestimated the depth and authenticity of Moslem nationalist sentiment and thus was somewhat unfair to the founders of Pakistan. While therefore out-dated in certain respects, and unquestionably over-simplified in its explanation of the Hindu-Moslem rift, much of the material in the chapter appears to me to retain its essential relevance, not only in regard to Indian-Pakistani relations today, but even in the broader context of conflicts within or between former colonial areas everywhere. The explosive mixture of nationalist and tribal or communal delusions that it comments upon, has proved its deadliness in the Middle East and in Africa. As for India, the ghastly inter-communal massacres that accompanied partition, the Kashmir conflict and the continuing tension between the two states retrospectively justify the apprehensions that my book reflected about the Pakistan formula as a practical solution to the Hindu-Moslem problem. Bad as the solution turned out to be, however, it has not proved quite as catastrophic as I feared. "Pakistan," I wrote in the original text of this chapter, "would have added a geographical nightmare to all the other Indian ones, and started endless wars." East Pakistan, at least, is a kind of geographic nightmare, but no full-fledged war has as yet broken out between India and Pakistan. Although the gravest issue between the two countries — the Kashmir question — remains unresolved (as of December 1963), the leaders and the political elites of both have so far displayed a high degree of political maturity in containing the destructive passions it tends to generate. Thus, the conditional optimism expressed in the chapter's title still seems justified, despite the numerous changes that have occurred since it was written.

V

What Indian Politics is All About

AFTER I HAD STUDIED Indian politics for several months, I sat down one day and tried to summarize on paper what I had learned from this study. Somewhat to my disappointment, the results seemed largely negative. The main thing I had learned was to distrust my own first judgments — and the judgments of most Westerners — about Indian political phenomena. I wanted — by this time — to say that the Indian people were politically adult, that they were no more subject to group-delusion than the peoples of the West, that they were capable of attaining the degree of social co-operation necessary in a modern state, that they not only were entitled to self-government but were capable of making an important contribution to the political activity of a world of interdependent states.

Unfortunately, the facts which my limited opportunities for observation and research furnished did not justify any such sweeping generalizations. The most I could say was that the contrary generalizations would be equally unjustified on the basis of my facts.

Much of the confusion of Indian politics was really in the minds of Western observers and did not necessarily indicate that the Indians were confused.

Much of the conflict in Indian politics — including the inner conflicts of Indians which sometimes made them so ineffectual — was the direct or secondary effect of the British divisive policy.

Presumably it would diminish rapidly if the British either quit India or adopted more enlightened policies of rule.

Much of the irrationality in Indian politics — for example, the irrational mob-hatred which flared up periodically in communal riots, the ugliest features of modern Indian society — was a poisonous by-product of the frustration engendered by British rule.

The most alarming element in Indian politics — the clash between Moslem nationalism and the All-Indian nationalism of the Congress party — might be serious enough to discredit on grounds of public order the Indian claim to self-government, but it could not be imputed to a defect in Indian culture. The gravity of clash, in my opinion, was not due to a historic inability to get along between two peoples, but to the importation from the West of a political concept — nationalism — which had proved itself murderous in nearly any context. It was this Western malady which had caused the Moslems to imagine they were a nation and many Hindus to feel that they had a divine right to govern all Indians in the name of All-India. It certainly was not an expression of political backwardness — unless one considers the West as politically backward.

All this, I thought, added up to a fairly effective rebuttal of the more common arguments (at that time) against Indian independence but, when put down starkly on paper, seemed wholly inadequate to explain the enthusiasm for India, the belief in the importance of Indians as human beings, which I felt. Recently, my wife had written me, saying:

'I will admit that your letters make India sound like an interesting place, which I never would have believed possible, but what is it all about? And why does it matter?'

I could sympathize with her criticism, because whenever I try to sum up to myself my impressions of India I raised the same questions. Fifteen years of professional practice as a seer — i.e., foreign correspondent, lecturer, and writer — had developed in me the belief that I could go anywhere, discover what anything was about, and explain to the American reader why it mattered. It had seemed easy enough to go to Hungary or Yugoslavia or any unlikely place and in a couple of weeks discover that 'it' — a cabinet crisis, a *coup d'état*, or almost any political development — was about the struggle between fascism and freedom, or about a struggle to break the goulash monopoly, and that it mattered because it strengthened or weakened America's strategic position, or because it meant that ultimately the American goulash-eater would pay more or less for his favorite dish. When I wanted restful scenes and a little skiing I could always go to Switzerland and report on how the oldest democracy in Europe was coping.

As such things go, my seer-reports were usually pretty sound, that is, if I said a crisis was a goulash-crisis the reader could be reasonably sure that goulash was involved in it somehow, and the relevancies I pointed out were nearly always conceivable ones. Barring occasional out-and-out mistakes, few articles that I had written could be termed misleading, yet looking back on all this activity with a little Oriental perspective, I realized that the total effect of my work as a journalist had been to complement the efforts of other correspondents, of the exponents of the higher columnizing, the professors of political science and the diplomats, in building up a mythical picture of the world.

The world we, the political experts, have built up in the mind of the public is a mythical one for at least three reasons. (In addition to the semantic reason, propounded by Stuart Chase, that most of the words we use have no meanings.) The first is the impression we have created that the world — the political world — is composed of questions and themes instead of human beings. India to many observers was the Pakistan question and/or the independence theme. To others India — as a question or theme — was about yoga or backwardness or East *versus* West. In any case it was rarely 'about' four hundred million Indians.

The second reason for myth is that by concentrating their attention on those developments in foreign countries which are likely to have repercussions on American life, writers about foreign affairs, like the writers on popular science and on nature-lore, have produced a Ptolemaic distortion in the American view of the rest of the world. We seem to be the center of the political

universe because, by what we read in our papers or books, foreigners are always doing things for or against our interests, just as
science goes to bed at night wondering what it can do for our
home of tomorrow, and beneficent Mother Nature alternates her
suns and her showers so that our crops may grow. We seem to be
the goal or target of the world's endeavor, and since it is target
more often than goal, the door is opened in our minds to delusion.
Thus, to the orthodox American isolationist, the intrigues, the
quarrels, and even the disasters of the Old Continent seemed almost a European conspiracy against American peace of mind.
Thus to most Americans, including myself, the Indian refusal to
co-operate in the Allied war-effort on British terms had seemed
almost a betrayal of America — how could those Indians honestly
think that anything was more important than helping America
to win the war?

The third reason why the political experts (but not they alone,
nor in America alone) have converted the real world into a myth,
is a very subtle one. It is so subtle that it can be conveyed effectively only by metaphor: The experts have created in the public
mind a belief in a kind of elixir of certainty, not a single panacea
or cause-all, but an opinion-hormone which confers upon the
individual who takes it the faculty of being right in regard to any
specific matter which he studies. We, the experts, are obviously
not always or all right because we so often disagree, but we always
sound so certain that the public is convinced of the certitude of
certainty, has come to believe that the melee of conflicting human
passions and wills called politics is reducible to simple truths,
simply stated, that the corridor of political decision leads always
to two exits, one plainly marked Right Policy, the other marked
Wrong Policy.

Just as chiropractors occasionally relieve their patients by
thumping or massaging their spines, so the political seers and our
disciples among the public occasionally plucked from the nettle,
confusion, a flower of significant certainty; so the statesmen were
sometimes confronted with an unequivocal choice between right
and wrong policy, but our total view of the political world was as
false as the chiropractic view of the world of disease.

In my days as a correspondent in Europe the idea had often occurred to me — as it has occurred to a number of social scientists — that politics should really be considered not as the rational working-out of men's real, if conflicting, needs and greeds, but as an expression of the psychic life of man in which the emotional, the irrational, the unconscious, elements naturally were predominant. Politics was the dream-life of the masses. One adopted a certain political opinion, not because it fitted logically with the facts, not merely because it promised to further one's economic or social welfare, but because it symbolized one's deepest, most secret emotional loyalties and goals, because it resolved some conflict of unconscious fears and hates and loves. Political conversion, like religious conversion, was much like falling in love; the ideals one loved, like the human objects of love, were often forgotten echoes of things one had loved in the past, the political objects of hate were often things harmless in themselves, related by a grotesque and illogical chain of associations with something which once, perhaps, had justified hatred.

Applied to a context of blind partisan fury dividing individuals who were united in interest, this was sometimes a fruitful and saving view. I had found it so in 1940, when, returning to America from the wreckage of France, almost as a refugee seeking asylum in a foreign land, I had stepped into the midst of the bitter electoral campaign between the late President Roosevelt and the late Wendell Willkie, a campaign in which it seemed to me the only real issue was the technical qualifications of two superior and rather like-minded men.

I had never adopted this view as a coherent and comprehensive philosophy of politics because it seemed so close to cynicism that it must lead inevitably to inaction, to moral irresponsibility, and to withdrawal from the real world of which the chimera of politics is such an essential element in our day. Since the facts of political life did not permit me to reject this philosophy completely, there lay at the base of all my certainties a wider stratum of misgiving than it is comfortable to have.

Indian politics, I found, required a new approach, and in seeking it, both certainty and misgiving seemed to melt away. I had once been irritated by what had seemed to me a puerile, defeatist point of view among writers on India. They were always proclaiming, India is the land of paradox and exception, you can't generalize about India, the truth is never simple in this country, etc.

It's just because these people have never learned to cope with a goulash-crisis that they talked this way, I had thought. Forget all this nonsense, and cut through the propaganda and literature, and find out what it is all about.

As my wife's letter had revealed to me, several months of studying Indian politics had not made clear to me what it was all about, and I realized that even several years would not greatly change the results. I was the wrong kind of seer for India.

But why try to be a seer at all, especially since I am on military leave from the profession? I asked myself. Why strive for certainty when it is clearly unattainable? And what good would it do me if I did know all the answers? Why not accept the tentativeness and contradictoriness of India, learn to practice the noble disciplines of bewilderment and irrelevancy? Why worry about being right when I could be president of a republic of new experience?

Was not the special virtue of India, its greatest mattering for the Western mind, precisely that it defied our categories, routed our certainties, broke down by its contradictions the tendency to systematize reality into delusion which had enabled some of our most certifiable paranoids — e.g., Trotsky, Nietzsche, Torquemada — to become leaders of Western thought. Was not the real importance — for us — of Indian political delusions that they provided such grotesque and yet illuminating caricatures of our own?

What could be more real than the Indian hunger for independence? But how much unreality and childishness there was in it at times, how easily some of these fighters against oppression tend to think themselves like oppressors.

What could be more unreal, more grotesque, more delusive,

than the dream of fanatical Moslems of carving India into a crazy-quilt of states, or the dream of some Hindu fanatics of freeing India from these intruders who had been there for a thousand years? What, indeed, except for a foreigner to say that Pakistan was the solution to India's troubles, or that the quarrel between Moslems and Hindus did not exist, or that it was such a quarrel there was no solution and no hope for India at all?

How could one fail to admit that India was a nation when a vast majority of Indians, including some from all races and communities, felt themselves as belonging to a single nation? But how could one deny that many millions of Indians did not feel themselves as belonging to that nation?

How silly Western nationalism seemed in its Indian setting. But had it been any less silly in the West?

What better example of murderous delusion, of irrationality, of incapacity for self-government than the Indian communal riot? None better, but why was a lynching in Georgia not just as good?

What hypocrisy for the caste Hindu to cry out against British oppression while he himself oppressed the Untouchable. What hypocrisy for America to fight for democracy abroad while denying it to the Negro, our Untouchable, at home.

What liberalism in the Indian mind, what magnanimity and tolerance — and what pettiness, what fanaticism.

Paradox? Neurosis? Yes, the human paradox, the human neurosis, always different, but the same the wide world over. Indians are not paradoxical because they are Indians but, because they are human. They are not different from the men of the West, they merely break out in different places.

The lesson of India, of the Indian form of political paradox, I have it at last, I thought. It is this: I am unhappy about Indian politics because it is so full of myth and delusion and contradiction that I can't make it mean anything. I am always looking for a theory that will explain why everything I like about the Indians is important and everything I don't like unimportant. It is not really Indian politics that is confused but my relation to it. I am trying to escape from bewilderment into delusion, but have

not yet succeeded. As long as I remain bewildered there is hope
for me. If ever I discover the truth about India, I won't be good
for anything except getting into arguments with people who have
discovered contrary truths.

What I haven't seen up to now is that Western politics is just
as confused, contradictory, and deluded as the Indian variety,
and I have really been bewildered for years, while pretending to
myself that I was not. There is no shame in being bewildered by
politics, for by its nature it is a bewildering thing. Politics is not
just another expression of man's unconscious mind, but it involves
his unconscious mind, the roots of its emotional dynamism are
there, hence it must inevitably contain irrational and contradictory elements. Instead of admitting this to ourselves, we invent
ideologies and theories which rationalize our beliefs into neat,
orderly systems that are capable of explaining anything, because
they omit everything which their premise cannot explain. Such
ideologies usually end by becoming systematic delusions, and
many of them begin that way.

The basic fallacy which makes all these delusions possible is the
feeling that a political opinion or position should be 'sound,' that
is, founded on truth. The Indian knows better, at least he is less
ashamed to admit that his political convictions are founded on
emotion. The truth is, ours are, too. We are Rightists or Left-
ists by temperament and social background, just as we are believers or atheists, Catholics or Protestants, and there is no harm
in this, because different temperaments require different political
ideals to express their emotional needs.

Our refusal to recognize the subjective, the irrational, element
in political belief leads us inevitably to falsify the facts to conform
with our beliefs.

I had come to India with a delusion in my mind, the delusion
that all those who did not share my enthusiasm for fighting the
Axis brand of fascism were, at best, the victims of some principle
of error, some political form of original sin, something you could
point to and say, see, there it is again. Somehow, without any
soul-searching or questing, this delusion had evaporated under

the Indian sun; I realized that the leaders of the Indian revolution were in jail precisely because they were antifascists, and that the worst one could say of them was that they suffered from one of those distortions of strategic perspective, common to all men in the heat of battle, which had caused them to become hypnotized by the immediate menace, the menace of British imperialism, and had made them blind to the deadlier one in the distance, the menace of Axis hegemony.

My first contacts with the cold, beefy arrogance, the unutterable sterility, of British imperialism in India, and my growing sympathy for the Indian national revolution, created the constant temptation of a new delusion, that to which so many Indians had completely succumbed, the delusion that everything bad in India was the result of British imperialism. Every time the imperialist explanation of India would start to get nicely organized in my mind, some reminder would pop up that the British, after all, had not invented the caste system, they had not invented the Moslem invasions, they had not invented ignorance and superstition. Then I would be plunged back into uncertainty and bewilderment, but gradually I noticed a strange thing, the more I was willing to let my view remain confused, the less blurred my feelings became; the more contradiction I admitted in my ideas, the fewer contradictions in my sentiments.

We put the cart before the horse. We try to make sense out of politics, instead of using politics to try to make sense out of ourselves. We ask ourselves whether we should be Rightist or Leftist, pro or anti on a particular issue. Instead we should begin by admitting to ourselves how we can be whatever we are without myth and without delusion, in other words, how we can adjust subjective to objective reality.

Because the myths and delusions of politics, while rooted deep in our emotions, are less deeply rooted than our purely personal myths and delusions, politics, which fills the world with confusion, can actually be a means of liberating the individual from confusion. We have only to cease asking ourselves whether our opinions are right or wrong and start asking: What is the element of

myth in my opinions, what is the element of delusion? Or, better
still, what is the element of hate, the element of fear?

Unconsciously my own ignorance and bewilderment at the unfamiliar Indian forms of confusion had led me to discover and
practice a simple mental discipline I should have learned years
ago in Europe, one I could have developed just as well sitting
home and reading the newspapers. As far as I was concerned
that was what Indian politics was all about, and why it mattered.

PART IV

New Wine and Old Bottles

I

Akbar's Hilltop

IN MOST LANDS where men have lived for a long time and become complex there is usually some great thing to see, something to see and die. In India this is Fatehpur Sikri, but it is better to see it, as I did, and not die, to be filled instead with sober wonder at the power of man to exceed and multiply himself, and with many questions about the problems of men working together to produce greatness.

Fatehpur Sikri is one of those rare, removed spots which continue to fill the present with meanings of the past, transforming the casual tourist into a pilgrim. It is one of the great things of the world to see, but it is almost impossible to describe, except to say that it is a small sixteenth-century Moghul city or large ceremonial fort, built mostly of a sandstone usually called rose-red, which is really the color of anything old and warm when one looks at it thinking of red, and that it stands on a hilltop fringing the plains of the Ganges valley, near Agra. The landscape hereabouts — a mongrel pattern of inconclusive cultivation and spoiled desert, of flatness disordered by rises and gullies without either symmetry or feeling of movement — has only one clear-cut quality, that of meagerness, and the first miracle of Fatehpur Sikri is that, by concentrating all this meagerness into plain massive walls and then contrasting it with the richness of dome and terrace and battlement, it transforms it into grandeur.

Fatehpur Sikri has the organic relationship to its setting of

the best modern architecture. It ennobles the landscape by supplying what the human eye needs to discover grandeur in meagerness: The mountainous potentialities of the plains, the shady
groves implicit in desert. It is an elevated oasis in stone. Having thus ennobled the surrounding space, its terraces and towers
then exploit it, deriving their meaning from looking out upon
ennobled space. Not merely what we call view is framed by these
structures; not only the different varieties of space-perception are
built into this citadel. Every excellence of man's environment
has its specialized setting in stone, the place is a visual organ and
not a visual one alone, for there are latticed tower-chambers
tuned to the wind, cloisters of silence, halls of redundant echo,
fountain courts for the enjoyment of splash and murmur as well
as of light and shade upon dancing water; there are marble solari-
ums for the enjoyment of reverberant heat and vaults of coolness;
there are even very precise architectural expressions of the less
remote abstractions, of peace as repose, of dignity as balance, of
introspection as enclosure, incompletely veiling visual infinity.
As in most masterpieces of Islamic art, space, light, shadow, wind
temperature, and water are structural elements of the edifice, this
art being really a kind of landscaping in stone, but unlike even
the very great Moslem masterpieces such as the Alhambra, the
Red Fort of Delhi or the Taj Mahal (the most magnificent post
office in the world, whose only faults are that it was intended as a
monument to a loved woman, and that it was an attempt at perfection which had the bad taste to succeed), Fatehpur Sikri has
the further merit that it is pictorial from any angle.

All this is a great wonder of the capital which the Emperor
Akbar built out of a great weariness with the past centers of
Moghul rule and the limited greeds of his predecessors, out of a
great impatience for the future, out of an active man's need to
keep himself busy planning for repose, out of an imperious and
conscientious man's nostalgia for more worthy, splendid sensuali-
ties than his impersonal harem could provide, and (as we shall
see) in order to make propaganda for the greatest of all human
dreams.

There are two other wonders of Fatehpur Sikri. One is, strictly speaking, an illusion, unless we can credit the master-architect of the palace-city with a sense of creation for the future akin to prophecy, but it is an illusion which must owe something to intent even if more to accident. This illusion is that time, as well as space, is one of the structural elements of the buildings, that Fatehpur Sikri has been deliberately shaped to provide in the future a frame for the past, that it is constructed around a vista in time. Carcassonne and Pompeii evoke a like feeling, but only by metaphor; Fatehpur Sikri is itself the metaphor, an eastern Pompeii disinterred from layers of sun, a dry Atlantis raised from the deep of years, unmarred, unrestored, communicating rather than evoking antiquity. Not the spell of the past, the spell of pastness. By being old yet unchanged, hardly tarnished, certainly not mummified, Fatehpur Sikri appears divorced from physiological time, from geological time, from any concretion of time expressed in evidence of change. It seems a terribly literal metaphor for timelessness until the symbol of one's own echoing footfalls, returning to the self as referent, reminds one with a sudden shock that time is the metaphor.

This strange place, this accumulation of shocks and wonders, filled me with an intense yet sober excitement, a sudden fierce thirst for clairvoyance without the illusion of possessing it. My mind went racing after meaning and even emptiness seemed an exhilarating prey. Fatehpur Sikri emptied its own symbols of meaning but this meaninglessness was itself a possession.

Even its history was a subtle denial of metaphor. Fatehpur Sikri was unmarred because nothing had ever happened to it. It was enduring because it had nothing to endure. Historians are not quite sure why, after having been the capital and court of the Moghul empire for about thirty years, Fatehpur Sikri was abandoned and became a ghost-citadel without ever becoming a ruin. They are sure that it was not ravaged by war, earthquake, or pestilence. One theory is that the water-supply finally proved inadequate. In any case it was one of the splendors of the world and men lived there for a while and finally turned away from it for no grave or terrible reason, bequeathing to posterity a monument to the enigma of splendor — or, possibly, to the enigma of plumbing.

The final wonder of Fatehpur Sikri is that it is a unity created out of a hodge-podge of architectural styles. The minarets, the domes, and the arches which in the Western mind characterize Islamic art here reveal at least two distinct Islamic traditions, the Persian and the Moorish. The steep tiled roofs of many of the buildings with their upturned — or seemingly upturned — eaves reflect some Central Asian influence. The Florentine touch is unmistakable in some of the finer stonework and the mosaics. As in nearly all Indo-Islamic architecture, the fact that Hindu craftsmen have executed the plans of Moslem architects lends to the whole creation a diffuse, underlying Hinduism, but in Fatehpur Sikri this is re-enforced by conscious, explicit Hinduisms such as the elaborate brackets which support the cornice of the great mosque. Perhaps Akbar himself ordered this sacrilegious graft; unquestionably it must have pleased him, for the reconciliation of the Hindu and Moslem elements of his empire was his constant preoccupation and in his later years it became an obsession, leading him to seek a cultural, as well as a political rapprochement.

With exemplary impartiality, Akbar stocked his harem with Moslem and Hindu princesses, executed Moslem and Hindu political rebels or religious fanatics, employed Moslem and Hindu ministers and generals, made his court a rendezvous of the two Indian aristocracies and ultimately tried to found a synthetic state religion, the Din-ilahi, combining what he believed to be the best elements of Hinduism and Islam, in a new creed which he apparently thought of as the cultural framework for the unification of mankind. One is tempted at first to see Fatehpur Sikri as the architectural realization of Akbar's dream. In a very abstract sense it is, for it is a case of unity achieved by the use of diversity, but the unity of Fatehpur Sikri is not an abstraction when one looks at it, it is something which one has, not something which one understands, or if understanding is necessary, something that one understands in the way that a young horse understands meadow-grass — by rolling in it. It is not a syncretism of Hindu and Moslem esthetic concepts. It is a syncretism of plain and mountain and light and shade and stars and wind. The only real relation it has to Akbar's political and cultural dream is that the great Moghul's eclecticism helped to free the architects and craftsmen from the tyranny of esthetic universals, from the delusions of beauty which every culture develops. The need to defy the infidel with dome and arch and minaret, which disfigures much Islamic architecture, did not press heavily on Akbar's Moslem architects. The opportunity to preserve the identity of submerged Hinduism by torturing stone beyond the limits of any other people's tolerance was denied his Hindu masons. Both worked in a liberal and empirical atmosphere which made it easy to relax belief in the geometrical, mathematical, or pigmentary animisms which make us feel that certain shapes or colors are holy and therefore beautiful — always most holy and most beautiful when mentally contrasted with the aberrant symbols of some infidel art.

If Fatehpur Sikri is the expression of any philosophy it is doubtless Persian Sufism, but it owes as much to Sufi agnosticism as it does to the Sufi rapture, a more ardent and directed rapture than the diffuse all-lovingness of Hindu pantheism. It owes most to the master-art of all the Islamic aristocracies: The gift of ennobled sensuality, the Moslem concept of good living which lies somewhere between the Greek ideal of beauty and the modern ideal of comfort. With or without Akbar, whenever the Moslems built for living they built in beauty. They achieved universality because their architecture for living — as distinguished from any other type — had a physiological foundation, recognized the primacy of sense over symbol. Fatehpur Sikri ignores abstraction and seeks to give comfort to the eye — and to the other senses. It is universal in the sense that it will comfort any eye — any unprejudiced eye — within the needs and limits of its topographical and climatic context. It does not seek to make any statements valid in a Tuscan, a Norman, or a Virginian context. Its greatness is that its builders rejected esthetic imperialism and subjugation and sought no perfection except the one kind which was peculiar to a certain hilltop near Agra in the sixteenth century, as the builders of the Parthenon sought only the perfection of a certain hilltop in Athens, suggesting that the true cultural common denominator of all great art is apostasy, known, though not always practiced, by the Christians as humility.

In the heady atmosphere of rarefied meaning which surrounded Fatehpur Sikri, in this noble emptiness which was like mountain air to the imagination, in the heightened lucidity of consciousness sinking toward the Nirvana of the nonverbal, the age-old problem of Babel seemed to me to take on a new significance. The problem of getting men of different faiths to work together was not reconciling their beliefs, it was getting them to recognize that no two hilltops are ever the same, that every new problem of man requires a new faith to solve it, that every new task is a new world.

Akbar, as patron of the arts, had clearly understood this principle. In Fatehpur Sikri he had achieved his dream of human unity in so far as the limitations of the locale permitted. He had founded a new nation in stone, he had formed his court into a new culture, neither Moslem nor Hindu, but Moghul, or possibly Akbarian; he had promulgated a new faith — the faith in hilltops where the meagernesses of the world can be gathered into grandeur.

Whether as emperor and prophet he had done as well was hard to say. His empire had long since passed into other hands, and the creed of the Din-ilahi expired when he did. Yet his dream of a united Indian people and his larger dream of united man had both passed into many minds since his turned to dust. Neither man nor India was yet united, but both might be some day. In India, as in the world at large, the last word had not yet been spoken. Akbar's influence unquestionably still lived in India, but so did the influence of his successor, Aurangzeb, the apostate from apostasy, and other Akbars, other Aurangzebs, still disputed spheres of influence in the mind of Western man.

As to which influence would finally prevail, Fatehpur Sikri

maintained an enigmatic silence. It taught me nothing on this point, possibly because it had nothing to teach, but by its beauty, its removedness, and its enigmatic relevance to the great problem of man, it powerfully stimulated my imagination and turned my attention toward the deeper cultural problems of the East and of Eastern-Western relationships, to which I had so far given little thought.

II

The Esperanto of Illogic

OUT OF THE NIGHT and the watery fury of a premonsoon thunder-storm on the Delhi plain there once emerged a strange figure from India's past who provided me with a key to many puzzling aspects of Indian culture and to some of the problems of culture-change in general. It was a Sunday in early March, and I had bicycled out to the ruined Moghul fortress of Tughilakbad, about fifteen miles from New Delhi, with a young British girl who thought that she liked adventure. We had a picnic supper among those am-biguous ruins, more suggestive of feudal Europe than of India, set in a treeless, boulder-strewn landscape that was like a melancholy Provence, and started back in the early evening under leaden clouds.

Before we had gone two miles, the storm broke, and we took refuge in a peasant's hut. There, for nearly three hours, we squatted on the mud and cowdung floor, squeezed among warm, unseen Indian bodies, wordlessly ministered to by a felt Indian tenderness of solicitude that became almost stifling, while a wind of nearly hurricane force smashed lateral walls of water against our shelter and the whole plain came alive with malevolent, danc-ing balls of blue fire.

Shaken by the violence of the storm, unnerved by the inexora-ble lovingness of our hosts, in which the egocentric Western soul feels some subtle, gluey menace, my companion insisted on de-parting at the first lull. Warnings and protests that had the

Delphic quality of a cryptic tongue rose from the steaming hut as we mounted our bicycles, and by the time we reached the bottom of the first irretraceable hill, the second wave of the storm struck us upon the open plain.

Now there began a grotesque struggle that was half-farce and half-nightmare with the alien dissonances of the Indian sky. The wind was strong enough to make us stand on our pedals and pump laboriously even on the level stretches, but not strong enough to lift us off the road; the rain, we discovered, would not drown us if we kept our heads down, and though the lightning may have been dangerous upon that treeless waste, it was concentrating its fires with the precision of an artillery barrage on a low ridge some half-mile away. We were not cold or even very tired.

Nevertheless, within a few minutes after we had left the hut, the girl dismounted, sat down in the mud at the edge of the road and said:

'I can't go any farther.'

'We've got to go on,' I said, 'or else go back to the hut.'

'No, you go on and leave me.'

This conversation, suggesting the pathetic dialogue of two explorers trapped in an Arctic blizzard or dying of thirst in the Sahara, would have been completely ludicrous except for the authentic atmosphere of desperation which surrounded it. Not going on meant, in the girl's mind, lying down by the road to die. There was nothing likely to cause her death if we simply stayed there in the warmish rain until the storm was over, but there was such a real and total collapse of the will-to-live in her voice, such a primitive surrender to the alien magic of the Indian weather gods, such a doomed feeling that the white man's day had ended in the stormy night of Asia, that I began to believe intensely she would die unless she were kept moving, so I forced her on with a counter-desperation perhaps as irrational as her own.

We were still nearly ten miles from New Delhi, still entrapped in the illusion of a warm blizzard or sandstorm of wetness, when, as surprisingly as if it had really been northeastern Greenland or the Great Erg, the lights of a car showed behind us. The car, in addition to salvation, contained three Indians: A chauffeur, a beautiful painted child of about thirteen in a silk saree who was unmistakably neither a sister nor a wife, and a small, bright-eyed young man in expensive English tweeds, who spoke stage English, introduced himself (for the purposes of this book) as Mr. Ram Lal, and insisted on drenching his tweeds by getting out in the rain to help fasten our bicycles — which we had proposed abandoning as one might abandon a broken sled or a lame camel at the hour of rescue — to the back of his shiny American car.

This was the extraordinary setting of what was to prove one of my most curious mental adventures in India, and although the setting has no direct connection with the adventure, which was simply the discovery of the mind of Ram Lal, the two, with the passage of time, have merged in my mind into a single adventure, half-meteorological, half-psychological, proving that weather is, in a certain sense, a cultural phenomenon.

The adventure proper occurred a few nights later when Ram Lal, in response to my invitation, showed up for dinner at the Maharajah's town-house on Man Singh road which I was then sharing with a group of American civilians. Wearing an impeccable dinner-jacket, displaying just enough rubies, Ram Lal did not look like a figure out of India's past. In response to a tactful question from the senior member of the household, he said he would be delighted to join us in a cocktail, adding:

'Have no fear, I eat and drink everything, I am completely modern in all these things.'

The thought that we might have some doubts as to his complete modernity seemed to be preying on his mind. He praised the cocktail extravagantly and asked for the recipe, saying he wanted to give it to the barman of his club, so the blighter could learn to mix a decent drink.

'You Americans understand cocktails much better than the English,' he said with an air of worldly condescension. 'As for our Indian members — of course we have a rather conservative policy and do not accept many Indians — they don't understand the first thing about drinks. I am afraid my countrymen are still appallingly unprogressive in many ways.'

As an example of the appalling unprogressiveness of India he cited his own failure to emancipate the womenfolk of his own household from their incurable Hindu orthodoxy in regard to dietary and similar taboos.

'I have to keep a complete set of kitchen utensils and table-ware for my own use, so that their things won't get polluted by my foreign dishes. Quaint, isn't it?'

We felt that Ram Lal himself was rather quaint. We were accustomed to Indians of many faiths, castes, and political opinions but we had never entertained one quite like this before. Many of our guests refused cocktails, and some even had to be greeted in the Indian manner, without shaking hands, but in some indefinable way they seemed more modern and westernized than this strange little man in his perfectly tailored dinner jacket. This talk of English clubs and boasting about how Western one was in one's tastes was more than a generation out of date. Even the maharajahs hardly talked like that any more. The really modern Indians flouted caste taboos by encouraging their children to marry outside their own caste and by doing social work among the Untouchables, but in matters of dress and social convention many of them were traditionalists — or neotraditionalists — who proclaimed almost aggressively their attachment to their own culture.

Our curiosity was aroused and we began gently to pump our guest about his own background. He pumped very easily. In a few minutes we learned that he was a wealthy landlord, that he belonged to an ancient Hindu family which had been established in Delhi before the Moghuls were, that he had been educated in English private schools and an English college in India, that he owned some valuable real estate in Old Delhi but made his living mostly by collecting from his overseers the rent collected by them from his peasant tenants in the countryside around Delhi, that he had two American cars, a country-house and a town-house in Old Delhi, liked golf and thought the war was a bore, although he hoped the Allies would win because the Japanese were nothing but vulgar little upstarts.

In the course of his autobiographical sketch he mentioned that many of his tenants were Moslems and was about to dilate about their undesirable qualities when he checked himself, glanced around apprehensively and said:

'Your bearer is a Moslem, isn't he? — I thought so. I will tell you later about the Moslem question but your bearer is probably just outside the room listening to everything we say. They are all such spies, you know.'

My American companions looked rather startled at this, and I began to realize that I was in for a trying, though perhaps instructive, evening. This premonition was confirmed at table, between the soup and the fish-course, when the conversation, at the instigation of my guest, veered around to Indian politics. Ram Lal was anxious to set us straight on the Indian question and even more anxious to get his own position on the record.

'Gandhi is one of the greatest men in India,' he announced, apropos of nothing at all. 'All Indians revere him, but that does not mean his political ideas are always sound. If Indians were better educated that wouldn't matter, but sometimes our ignorant peasants are misled by agitators who distort Gandhi's thoughts and then a lot of harm is done.'

'What kind of harm do you mean?' asked our legal member, a liberal-minded lawyer attached to one of the civilian American agencies. 'Do you mean for instance that the peasants withhold rent from their landlords?'

Ram Lal accepted the challenge bravely.

'Yes, I mean that — that and demonstrating against the British and American forces in India — all this Quit India business.'

'Mr. Lal, don't you believe India should have her independence?'

'Frankly, sir, I do not. The masses of this country are too backward, too ignorant, too superstitious to be capable of ruling themselves. As an Indian it makes me very sad to say that, but it is the truth.'

As he said this, Ram Lal stared so mournfully at his fish, that with the possible exception of the fiery little lawyer, all of us, all the fanatical Indian nationalists from Manhattan and points west who sat around that table, forgave him his treason and felt a genuine pity for him.

One kindly spirit, hoping to comfort our guest and at the same time stimulate his patriotism, launched into an enthusiastic account of a recent visit to the Firestone Tire factory at Bombay, relating the pride one of the American officials of the factory took in the fact that his Indian workmen produced more tires per man hour of labor than were produced in any of the American plants of the company. Someone else remarked that the production record of the Tata steel mills, which are entirely under Indian management, was superior to that of most American steel mills, and a visiting aviation expert had high praise for the efficiency of the Indian workers in the American-managed aircraft factory at Bangalore. Surely, we argued, if Indians after very brief training are capable of equaling or even surpassing the production records of American workers born into a highly industrialized society, then they cannot be completely hopeless.

'Oh, no,' said our guest, 'I know Indians are not hopeless. You must remember that we were a great and civilized people when all the nations of the West were wearing skins and wandering around in forests. What you say about the Indian workers at the aircraft factory in Bangalore is not really surprising if you are familiar with Indian history. We were already making airplanes thirty thousand years ago.'

One of my companions, who was a little deaf, leaned forward in good faith and asked:

'How many years ago did you say?'

'Thirty thousand,' Ram Lal replied.

'What is the evidence for that?' snapped the lawyer.

'Oh, it's all in our *Vedas*, you know. We had radios in those days, too — radios so powerful they could talk directly from Ceylon to America.'

This stumped us. None of us felt sufficiently strong in Vedic scholarship to contradict Ram Lal's statement and I recalled having heard somewhere that among the retrograde and lunatic fringe of Hindu nationalism, the would-be restorers of the ancient Aryavarta, there was a myth based upon the interpretation of some obscure passage in the *Vedas*, that a great technological civilization had flourished in India in pre-historic times. For centuries Indians had consoled themselves with the memory of their ancient glories but this myth of a golden past was a relatively reasonable one, supported by considerable historic evidence. Then they had started going to English schools, and had acquired knowledge necessary to give their myth a demential twist by inserting airplanes and radios among the glories of a civilization which was glorious precisely because it renounced technology and made the cultivation of the soul its highest value.

Not all Indians, by any means, had followed this regressive path but neither was our guest of the evening as unique as one might imagine. For all his Western affectations Ram Lal was an authentic representative of a cultural counterrevolution which had swept Hindu society in the latter part of the nineteenth century, leaving deep scars upon the minds of even those enlightened Hindus like Gandhi who fought the most desperately to stem it. According to the sober and authoritative British historians, Thompson and Garratt, in their *Rise and Fulfilment of British Rule in India*, this counterrevolution was an outgrowth of the Indian defeat in the Great Mutiny of 1857, and above all, of the savage British repression of the Mutiny which led to such paranoid atrocities as the indiscriminate massacre of rebels — including women and children — and British sympathizers by Crown troops in Delhi and the hanging of Brahmins in Cawnpore after they had been forced to submit to ritual defilement.

In the bitterness of frustration and despair following the Mutiny, Hindu society turned away from Western culture which, in the previous half century, had made rapid progress among the Hindu upper classes. Western education could not be completely rejected because it was the key to worldly success, but the influence of Western thought upon Hindu religious and social life was renounced. The Brahmo Samaj, organizational spearhead of progressive Hinduism founded by the eighteenth-century Bengal social reformer Ram Mohun Roy — heir to a long line of moral geniuses which the subcontinent of India has produced and fore-runner of a school of practical idealists exemplified in our day by Gandhi — fell into a disrepute that lasted for several decades, and was supplanted by the Arya Samaj and the Hindu Maha-sabha, the former half-political, half-cultural, the latter mili-tantly religious, both dedicated to the cult of darkness, both preaching the doctrine of 'Back to the *Vedas*.'

Like all cultural regressions and counterrevolutions, the back-to-the-*Vedas* movement in India — as Ram Lal's amazing state-ment revealed — was not a return to the ancient values of Hindu culture but the formation of a new Hindu anticulture. To be-lieve that an Indian civilization of thirty thousand years ago possessed radio and airplanes was not merely to repudiate West-ern rationalism but it was also to repudiate Vedic idealism — it was as much a heresy to the teachings of the legendary Rishis as it was to the teachings of Descartes, Newton, and Darwin. It reflected unconsciously the delusive Western anticulture which the tensions of the Great Mutiny had so mercilessly brought to light. This Hindu regression was clearly a cultural revenge upon the West for the tortures and humiliations which the British regression from Western culture during and after the Mutiny had brought upon the Indian people. The basic premise of the whole Mahasabha-Arya Samaj ideology was the delusion that whatever the British despised in Hindu culture was admirable because Hindu, whatever seemed hateful to the British must be lovable because the British were the enemies of Hinduism.

Thus suttee, which the British — and progressive Hindu ideal-ists like Roy — had denounced and finally abolished by law, was defended by the neo-Vedists as a fine old Hindu custom. The caste system which the leaders of Hindu thought had been trying for half a century to liberalize, was not only restored with all its ancient horrors but was aggravated by restrictions and complica-tions unknown in Vedic times. Ayurvedic medicine — the an-cient Hindu version of the science — which was withering in the strong light of Western science, took a new lease on life, developed a luxuriant monstrous growth still flourishing in this day, and in the process almost certainly accumulated a lot of mumbo-jumbo which even the physicians of the Vedic Age would have denounced as quackery.

Child marriage, which rarely occurred and even more rarely was consummated in the great ages of India's past, became fashionable in the dominant regressive elements of Hindu society, and by many was looked upon as a kind of religious duty, a way of acquiring merit. Idol worship — any form of worship of any idol — which Roy and the other Hindu reformers had denounced as base superstition, disgracing and concealing the noble truths of Hindu philosophy, again became the ceremonial religion of upper-class Hindus.

In short, the retrograde leaders of Hindu society went out of their way to emphasize everything that was unsavory, irrational and degrading in Hindu culture, precisely because these cultural elements were the most antithetical to the West. For many years this was the only form of protest against Western rule that Indians felt they could make. Too cowed by the British repression of the Mutiny — and above all too discouraged by the revelation of the ineptitude of their revolutionary leaders for political organization or military action — the Indian nationalists of the post-Mutiny period expressed their patriotism by re-embracing the dark beliefs their minds had been taught to reject, by reverting to regressive mores their consciences had learned to abhor.

One of the last dying waves of this vast regression, which had once influenced almost an entire nation, had washed up to our dining room the implausible figure of Ram Lal. Before we had quite recovered from the shock of his prehistoric airplanes and radios, he launched into a new and still more astonishing flight from reality. The daughter of one of his tenants, he related, a girl of twelve, had, until her death a few months ago, the unusual gift of being able to remember a previous incarnation. In this earlier incarnation she had been the daughter of another of his tenants, and had died at the age of eight. Hardly any time had elapsed between her death as the daughter of tenant No. 1 and her rebirth

as the daughter of tenant No. 2. Both her fathers were still alive
and it was therefore easy to verify the extraordinary tale. Ram
Lal himself had interviewed the girl and her two fathers and satisfied himself beyond any shadow of doubt that this was an authentic case of the memory of one existence being continued into the
next one.

Such legends crop up frequently in all the Hindu and Buddhist
lands but learned Brahmin pundits and the higher Buddhist
clergy consider them as fanciful as we do. To hear my cocktail-
drinking guest, with his theory that Indians were too superstitious to be entrusted with self-government, guarantee from personal observation the authenticity of this bit of Asiatic folk-lore
gave us all a start, and some of my house-mates gave me a grim
look, which promised many compliments upon the fine lunatic I
had brought to the house.

Ram Lal's conversation did, in fact, have a pronounced psy-
chotic flavor, but there was method in his madness. I did not
question the sincerity of his belief in the extraordinary tale he
had just told us, but in the context of our table-talk its real significance was clear. Unlike the ghost-stories and similar fantasies
which I have heard highly educated and seemingly well-balanced
Westerners tell, simply because they believed them and enjoyed
telling them, Ram Lal's story had a politico-cultural-personal
moral. It was intended to prove that the doctrine of transmigration is true, therefore Hinduism is superior to the religions of the
West, therefore Ram Lal, being a Hindu, was superior to any
Western barbarian.

Instead of conflicting with his cocktails, his dinner jacket, and
his American cars, Ram Lal's superstitions about Vedic airplanes
and peasant girls who remembered earlier incarnations fitted into
the same pattern. It was not the ancient creeds of Hinduism that
warped his mind, but the politico-economic conflicts of modern
Indian life and the unfulfilled *karma* of Indian history, with the
personal insecurity and tensions they engendered. Ram Lal accepted from Western culture whatever it could contribute to
bolster his self-esteem. His 'modernism' and everything that

went with it — the cars, the club, the golf, the cocktails — made
him feel superior to other Indians, but left him with a gnawing
sense of inferiority with regard to the Western masters whose
customs he aped just successfully enough to get into the second-
best club in Delhi.

To overcome this inferiority in his mind he drew upon Hindu
culture, upon the darkest and most ancient superstitions of
Hinduism, reactivated and remodeled by other Indian minds like
his own to fit the same social and psychological need. In both
Western and Indian culture he rejected what was irrelevant and
what was detrimental to his objective. He rejected Western
rationalism because it conflicted with the fantasies of Hindu
superiority which he found so reassuring. He rejected the higher
Hindu idealism for the same reason that he gave his political
loyalty to the British and disapproved of the Congress program:
Because the doctrines of humanitarianism and renunciation of
worldly goals which it contained conflicted with his economic
interests as a landlord.

Over the coffee — and with the living-room doors closed against
spying ears — Ram Lal contributed some family history which to
my mind further resolved the implicit paradox in his position and
also laid bare the roots of his anti-Moslem fanaticism. Under the
Moghuls, he explained, his family had been stripped of much of
their wealth; the British had restored them to their former
grandeur. Privately, I suspected this was a much expurgated
and gilded account, but the kernel of truth it undoubtedly contained was sufficient to explain why Ram Lal's delusions of Vedic
grandeur, which rendered many Indians of his class violently if
ineffectually anti-British, extended up to the political foundations of his bank-account but no farther. The Moslems, in Ram
Lal's private mythology of history, served as scapegoats for all
the humiliations which went along with the British-protected
bank-account. The British could be excused for treating the
Hindus — a much superior people — with contempt because it
was really the Moslems who were responsible for the backwardness, poverty, and superstition which characterized the Hindus
in this age. Islam was to blame for all the evils of India.

When we asked Ram Lal just how the Moslems were responsible, he embarked upon a long and utterly incomprehensible historical lecture from which we were able to isolate only one definite accusation: A well had been poisoned by the Moslems. Whether this atrocity had happened last week or a thousand years ago, whether it was a personal grievance of his family or a historic atrocity against the Hindu nation, we were never able to discover.

Ram Lal's well-poisoning anecdote reminded me of a very cultivated officer in Franco's armies whom I had known in Spain, who believed that the ultimate cause of the Spanish Civil War was the invention of sewers (on the theory that without sewage all the Moors in Spain would have died of pestilences and their descendants therefore would not have been available to introduce Bolshevism into Spain). It reminded me also of some of the fantastic anti-Semitic mythologies I had heard in Nazi Germany, and for that matter, of the ravings of the lunatic fringe of American fascists. Delusion has no national boundaries, and between the incomprehensible gibberish of a deluded Indian, raised on the Vedas, and the hard-minded Western realism of the Protocols of Zion — or even of some upper-class American anti-Semitic mythologies — there is only the difference of a literary convention, a special cultural pattern in the form but not in the substance of delusion.

Ram Lal, however, brought home to me more vividly than any of his Western counterparts the historical significance of such aberrations of human thought. I began to study him with the fascination that the zoologist finds in certain rare creatures, which, because they constitute a link between existing species and those of earlier geological periods, offer living testimony in regard to the mechanisms of evolution. By himself, Ram Lal did not prove anything, he was far too special a case, but he suggested a great deal, and it seemed to me that he illustrated beautifully the hypothesis that had been forming itself for some time in my mind to explain the origin of a Hindu anticulture which, I suspected, had grossly distorted the face of Hinduism over the centuries.

The grotesque horrors of modern Hindu society, which have

provided such easy sport for a long line of Western writers, from the Abbé Dubois to Katherine Mayo and Beverley Nichols — incidentally leading them to exhibit in their most horrid light the traits of spiritual arrogance, cultural myopia, intellectual prurience, animistic materialism, and base racist superstition, which are some of the components of the Western anticulture — became more understandable if one postulated a series of cultural counter-revolutions in Indian history, like the one from which Ram Lal derived his neo-Vedic nonsense. I suspected that these counter-revolutions in a grim parody of Natural Selection had preserved exactly those mutations of Hindu culture that represented historic regressions.

There is some direct and more indirect evidence to support the view that Hindu culture as we know it today has been profoundly influenced by a series of such regressions brought about by the accidents of Indian history. Thus Garratt and Thompson, who have already been cited as authorities for the statement that the Great Mutiny brought about the cultural regression of the late nineteenth century, further note that Clive's sack of Bengal in the eighteenth century was followed by a striking recrudescence of the cult of Kali, the black-faced, many-armed goddess of death, in its most delusive forms.

One phase of this wave of Kali-worship was the proliferation of *thuggee* — the Thugs were a sect of Kali-devotees whose ritual was assassination; it is probably not accidental that Bengal, where thuggee was once widespread, has been in modern times the main center of political terrorism in India. Another phase of the regression was a fresh outbreak of the schizoid frenzy of self-immolation which had produced for the first European travelers in Bengal such extraordinary spectacles as mobs of Kali-pilgrims wading out into the sea to be eaten by waiting sharks, or the famous Tree of Death whose base was piled high with the bones of pilgrims who had cast themselves from its highest branches in honor of the goddess.[1]

[1] These particular examples are taken from Maurice Collis's admirable *Land of the Great Image* and appear well-authenticated.

It is difficult to determine how great a role was played in such regressive movements by the element of conscious or unconscious protest against foreign domination. Modern Indian literature suggests that the reacceptance of archaic customs or beliefs as a patriotic gesture is a fairly common occurrence in present-day India and it seems plausible that this has sometimes been a significant cultural factor in the past.

Similarly, it is difficult not to see some element of cultural protest against foreign domination in such social phenomena as the rise of the Ku Klux Klan after the carpetbag era in the American South, the rise of Hitlerism in Germany after the Treaty of Versailles, and the renascence of Shintoism in Japan after Western civilization had been forced on her at the point of a gun.

Those Western liberals who wring their hands over the incorrigible backwardness of India, over her seeming rejection of the blessings of Western culture, forget the manner in which these blessings have been spread, the imperialist purposes they have served, and in their forgetfulness lies the secret of an incorrigible Western backwardness.

Some modern Hindu writers insist that child marriage as a widespread practice dates from the eleventh century when the main wave of Moslem invasion began, giving as the reason that it was necessary to have girls married very young to protect them from the lust of the invaders. This sounds like a typical Hindu rationalization of an unpleasant fact, but there is much evidence that prior to the eleventh century child marriage was less common than afterwards. Dr. Santosh Kumar Mukherji, editor of the famous Hindu treatise on the art of love, the *Kama Sutra*, and author of a curious little booklet called *Indian Sex-Life and Prostitution*, cites a Hindu surgeon of the sixth century B.C. as recommending — on eugenic grounds — fifteen as the earliest marriage-age for a girl, and declares that in the reign of the Emperor Chandragupta (fourth century B.C.) the state laws for the control of prostitution even made it an offense for a man to have intercourse with an under-age prostitute. (Other features of this relatively enlightened legislation included the right of prostitutes to refuse diseased clients, and a ban on prostitutes' turning over their earnings or property to anyone but their mothers.)

Judging by the examples of modern times, it seems likely that the growth of child marriage in Hindu society after the Moslem invasion was again a cultural protest against foreign rule, a patriotic back-to-the-*Vedas* movement and, like all human attempts to recapture the past, an unconscious disfiguration of the past.

The case is even stronger for thinking that many of the rigid, irrational, and fantastically complex rules of caste, which sometimes make Hindu culture appear to the Western observer like a mass obsessional-neurosis, are partly the result of a communal nonfraternization policy laid down during the period of Moslem rule to combat political collaboration — in the form of religious conversion — with the invaders. Unquestionably the sinister power of the Brahmin caste was strengthened by the Moslem invasions, for the Brahmins as the highest class of Hindu society and the guardians of Vedic culture were the leaders of Hindu resistance to Moslem penetration.

Not all the vices of Hinduism, however, nor all the ascendancy of the Brahmins in Hindu society, can be explained by the struggle to preserve Hindu culture under foreign rule. Ramlalism is not wholly the by-product of invasion. The caste system, which is the social cornerstone of Hindu culture, goes back to Vedic times, and was either brought to India by the first Aryans or adopted by them from the conquered Dravidians. Like Hitler's Aryans, the conquerors of the Dravidians believed in a hierarchy of blood and founded a nation upon this principle. At the top were the three 'twice-born' castes — the Brahmins, the Kshatriyas (warriors), and the Vaisyas (merchants or cultivators). A great social gap — as great as the gap between officers and enlisted men in modern armies — separated them from the Sudras, the serf or menial class, who because they were of Dravidian stock and had dark skins, were entitled only to the privileges of one birth — the natural one — and were denied the privilege of initiation into Hindu society, which was considered a second birth.

In the sixth century B.C., there began a cultural and social revolution comparable in its historic significance to the Protestant Reformation in the West. Two Indian princelings — both significantly members of the Kshatriya caste, suggesting a revolt against Brahmin rule within the family of the twice-born castes — began preaching the doctrine of a society without hereditary classes and a religion without superstition. The first of these was Vardhamana Mahavira, the founder of the Jain sect. The second and more famous of the two reformers was Siddhartha Gautama, called Buddha, who challenged the foundations of the Hindu state even more openly than Jesus Christ challenged the Roman imperium, by declaring that no one became either a Brahmin or a pariah except through his own deeds.

Unlike the Graeco-Judean social democrats of the West in the times of the Caesars, the early followers of Buddha appear to have escaped persecution, although their subversive doctrines contained implicitly the democratic principle that all men are created free and equal. In the third century B.C., the greatest emperor of the Maurya dynasty, Asoka, the Constantine of Buddhism, made this faith the state creed of India and gave political implementation to its principles by renouncing war as an instrument of national policy, by establishing religious toleration as the law of the land, and by cultivating the social and economic welfare of his subjects, thereby lending considerable weight to the claims of some modern Buddhist propagandists that apostolic Buddhism was a religion of social reform rather than of personal withdrawal from the world. The only known records of Asoka's time, wall- and pillar-writings, must be considered as official propaganda and naturally present an unshadowed picture of tranquillity and happiness throughout the great emperor's realm — which included nearly all of modern India — but hardly anyone who has lived through the revolutionary upheavals of modern times will doubt that behind the untroubled façade of this Asiatic New Deal there must have developed violent political and social tensions.

At some time during the dynasty of the Gupta emperors (320 A.D. to 647 A.D.) these tensions exploded in a triumphant Hindu counterreformation and a Brahmin counterrevolution which in the course of the next few centuries completely banished Buddhism from its homeland and converted Jainism into a picturesque anomaly in Indian society. The first recorded instance of the struggle between social progress and social regression, which is the underlying pattern of Indian history and the mechanism which has produced the ambivalent Indian culture that we know today, had far-reaching results.

Hindu religious thought was profoundly influenced by Buddhist teaching and developed a noble ethical tradition, associated with a tendency toward monotheism and social reform which never died out, which throughout the ages has repeatedly flowered and reflowered in new reformist movements.

On the other hand, the Hindu counterreformation, illustrating the law of cultural regression which operates in all societies, including our own, substituted for Buddhist egalitarianism an aggravation of the Vedic rules of caste. Whereas, in pre-Buddhist times, marriage between members of the twice-born castes, including Brahmins, and the non-Aryan Sudras, had been permissible, the children taking the caste of the father, such marriages are sternly prohibited in the Laws of Manu which are attributed to the Gupta period. The elastic race-prejudice which inspired part of Buddha's protest was replaced by a rigidly drawn color line like that which slavery developed in the United States some twelve or fifteen centuries later. A good deal of the oral tradition of the Vedas was probably first written down during the Gupta age and it is easy to imagine the Brahminical Ram Lals of the period touching up the ancient texts to make them conform to the spirit of those reactionary days.

Though it is sheer speculation, it seems plausible to suggest that much of the mythological woolliness, the obliqueness, and the irrelevance of modern Hindu social and political thought stems from a tradition of apologetics founded by pundits of the Gupta age, who were faced with the hard problem of justifying retrograde social legislation to a society whose conscience had been awakened by the Buddhist-Jain revolution. Thus, if the hypothesis is correct, the hard realities of what modern left-wing jargon calls the class struggle were clothed in obscurantist religio-sexual symbols which assured the degradation of the lowest classes by assimilating any contact between them and members of the higher castes with sexual pollution.

Priestly logic, unwittingly duplicating one of the mechanisms of neurosis, pushed this curious dialectics to its ultimate absurdity of displacement in such rulings of Brahminical caste law as the one which allows a Brahmin to have sexual intercourse with a low-caste woman but punishes him with ostracism if he eats out of the same bowl with her. (In the American Southern states a white man would be subject to caste sanctions only if he ate with a Negro mistress in public, showing how much more rational than the Hindus we are.)

This priestly dialectic has so infected Indian thinking that even the modern Jains sometimes sink to grotesque parodies of Mahavira's teachings, as by allowing their wealthy money-lending members to collect 120 per cent interest from poverty-stricken farmers, while forbidding them so rigorously to take life in any form that orthodox Jains when troubled with bedbugs are sometimes reported to hire beggars to sleep in their beds the first part of the night in order to sate the appetite of the insects their religion does not allow them to destroy.

In the absence of sufficient historical evidence it seemed to me that the evidence of the living fossil, Ram Lal, illustrated at least one of the processes whereby the Hindu caste system had been elaborated over the centuries into the Jim Crow horror that it is today, without the Hindus themselves realizing how monstrous their society had become.

In every age of Indian history from Buddha to Nehru, it appeared that there had been reformers laboring to restore and to purify the true Vedic tradition, to develop and ennoble still further the noble ideals of Hindu culture, to broaden and sharpen the Hindu social consciousness. Likewise, every age had produced its Ram Lals, who distorted the thoughts of the reformers to combat reform, who used progress to promote regression, who considered themselves very modern in their day because they

dressed ancient superstition in current fashion, or piously traditional because they had managed to become more benighted than
their ancestors.

The outcome of this struggle between reform and regression in
Indian history was, it seemed to me, that the best features of
Hindu culture had become progressively better, the worse features progressively worse. The contrast between best and worst
in present-day Hindu society had produced many of the social
paradoxes of modern India, as it seemed to me that the contrast
between native reasonableness and imported or provoked delusion had produced some of the most striking political ones.

In any case, I felt sure — after listening to Ram Lal — that
the great cultural drama of modern India was not the struggle
between Western enlightenment and Eastern backwardness. It
was the struggle between the peculiar Indian forms of backwardness and enlightenment, both influenced to some degree by Western backwardness and enlightenment. Ram Lal used his knowledge of Western culture to darken the Indian heritage of darkness, an enlightened Indian like Nehru used his to brighten the
ancient tradition of light. Nehru and Ram Lal were both products of the West's impact on the East, their minds just happened
to be Western in different spots. One liked cocktails and motor-
cars, the other liked labor unions and printing presses. From
close contact with the British upper classes one had absorbed
British snobbishness and the other British love of freedom.

The meeting of East and West in modern India was the clash
and co-operation of two Easts and two Wests, for Western history
revealed the same struggle between progress and regression that
Indian history did, and the modern West was in some measure a
mixture of Western best and worst. On the whole, Western culture had seemed to move upward for the past two thousand years,
and Indian culture downward. The downward pattern of Indian
culture was particularly pronounced between the eleventh and
the twentieth centuries and the upward curve of Western culture
appeared to rise sharply between the fifteenth and the twentieth
centuries. On the other hand, India had been on the upgrade for

nearly fifty years — so much so that a Ram Lal appeared as an anachronism — whereas, since 1914 the Western best had been getting only slightly better, while the Western worst had become dramatically worse. (So much so that the equivocal enlighten-ment of half the West was then locked in a death struggle with the unequivocal darkness of the other half.)

Even the weird priestly logic which produced some of Ram Lal's strangest verbal effects, which has often been noted in Hindu thinking, which some Western students of India considered a specific, innate Vedic blight upon the Hindu mind, might be, in my view, merely the contagious influence of certain delusions arising from Indian social history — delusions appearing in the thinking of all peoples whenever their social conflicts resembled the Indian ones.

To test this view, toward the end of the evening I maneuvered Ram Lal around to the subject of untouchability — the greatest single cancer-spot in Indian social history — expecting some in-teresting results, and he did not disappoint.

His first approach implicitly annulled the socioeconomic reality that the Untouchables of India are a depressed, oppressed social class, as well as the human implications of their miserable status. Caste in general and untouchability in particular were — if one followed Ram Lal — purely ceremonial matters having no con-nection with living-standards, power-relationships, or human suffering.

'The basis of untouchability is really psychological, gentle-men,' our guest explained with bland persuasiveness. 'Let us take an example: When you go to your Christian church to pray on Sunday you put on your best clothes because that helps your religious mood. If you found yourself kneeling next to a filthy, stinking beggar that would disturb your mood and distract you from your worship. It is the same with us Hindus. When we go to our temples to worship, we exclude low people like sweepers and night-soil men and others whose occupations or way of life make them dirty. It isn't that we have any unkind feelings toward these poor people but we have to exclude them in order to maintain our temples as dignified places of worship. Also if we have any physical contact with people like that we feel we have to purify ourselves just as you wash your hands when you have touched a filthy, diseased beggar. This ancient Hindu practice helps prevent the spread of disease and shows that the importance of controlling epidemics was thoroughly understood in Vedic times.'

I doubted that the Gupta pundits had thought in precisely those terms, but I felt convinced that their dialectics had been designed to paralyze the Hindu social conscience by similarly divorcing the question of caste from such worldly considerations as living-standards. In the West the same psychological mechanism has made it possible for economists to discover healthgiving virtues in the periodic business depressions of capitalist societies, and for militarists to recommend war as a sovereign elixir of national rejuvenation, but such attitudes have become, at least temporarily, unfashionable in our day. They survive mainly in American apologies for American treatment of the Negro, particularly in the apologetics of those pseudoliberals who, while they admit that the Negro's low standard of living is a social injustice, deny that a form of racial segregation very close to the Hindu concept of untouchability implies any sentiment of racial superiority or inferiority. ('Negroes prefer not to mix with whites.')

When we pointed out to Ram Lal that his hygienic and esthetic arguments in favor of untouchability would disappear if the living conditions of the Untouchables were improved — as for instance by allowing them to draw water to wash themselves from communal wells — he showed his cultural versatility by passing up the Vedas and borrowing a stock weapon from the arsenal of Occidental antidemocracy.

'It wouldn't do any good to make it easier for the Untouchables to get water because they are so incurably dirty they would never use it to wash themselves,' he said. Then in a beautiful Indian afterthought he added: 'That may be why the people in some parts of the country where water is very scarce won't let the Untouchables use their wells — they know they would just waste the water.'

This argument which has often been invoked to justify the denial of sanitation and housing to Negroes in America, to the poorer classes everywhere in the Western world, is more than an expression of social backwardness. It is based upon a kind of animistic disbelief in the possibility of change, the superstition that everything which is, always has been and always will be, which contrasts so queerly with our constant technological progress, yet is characteristically Western.

Routed from this position by our indignant rebuttals, Ram Lal fell back upon the classic Indian defense of untouchability.

'I know that untouchability seems grossly unfair to the Western mind, but that is because you take too materialistic a point of view. According to our religion these unfortunate people have committed some sin in a previous life; through rebirth as Untouchables they have a chance to work out their evil *karma* [1] and improve their lot in their next incarnation. It is really a most fair and democratic system, you see.'

This argument has often been cited by Western writers as proof of the unbridgeable gap between the hazy, unrealistic Eastern mind and the rationalism of Western thought, but if one analyzes it carefully, it seems to me that it proves rather that there is an esperanto of illogic, an internationale of national anti-cultures, where human minds unable to fathom each other's meanings commune in unmeaning. The basic delusion in this favorite Brahminical apology for untouchability is that one class of men is morally inferior to other classes by accident of birth and the still more sinister corollary to this proposition that the members of the superior classes have superior rights as against those

---

[1] The Hindu and Buddhist doctrine of karma lays down a law of individual destiny in accordance with which the errors or sins which a man commits in one incarnation determine his fate in the next one. This soul-determinism is not viewed as a mere system of rewards and punishments. It is rather a question of being reborn to solve the problems of spiritual growth which were left unsolved in the previous existence. Thus a caste-Hindu who failed to acquire humility might be reborn as an Untouchable so that he would face the problem of humiliation in its most acute form. If he lived as an Untouchable without becoming bitter or losing hope, without building up new adverse karma, then he would have worked out his original karma and be reborn in better circumstances in his next life.

of the inferior classes. This is indeed irrational and monstrous, it is a typical delusion, but it is not typically Eastern and if the proposition is carried one step further — that those who have superior rights may legitimately persecute, oppress, and exploit their inferiors — it is just as antithetical to the moral code of the East as it is to that of the West.

Such delusions of superior moral value and superior moral rights are as common in the West as they are in the East. They provide the foundations for Western imperialism, for Western racism, for every form of class-exploitation within the Western societies, and for the invariably righteous wars which the different Western societies are constantly waging against one another.

It is true that, unlike the peoples of the East, we usually avoid founding our delusions of moral grandeur upon a metaphysical premise — at least that is the trend of the present age. We found them upon distorted readings of biology, history, law, economics, or some other relatively rational discipline. That does not make them less irrational. If on the whole, we think straighter than the Hindus do in regard to social problems, it seems to me it is less because of our vaunted rationalism and realism than because — within our own societies — we are not compelled to the tortured flights of logic that the Hindu resorts to in his attempt to justify such unjustifiable horrors within his society as untouchability.

Our worst crimes are external ones, crimes against the lesser breeds, and because our victims are strangers we feel so little compunction about the crimes that almost anything will serve as a pretext. Cynicism is the state-metaphysic of the West; there is no need for us to tire our minds by trying to prove that black is white when we are so convinced that white can do no wrong. The Hindu's crimes are against his own people. He knows they are crimes and must try to prove to himself that they are not.

In the days when our internal social conscience was stronger than our international social conscience is today, but still not strong enough to enforce social justice in our societies, we reasoned very much as the Hindu reasons. We still reason that way whenever conscience is strong, but not strong enough. The most justly famous of what Beverley Nichols calls 'the breathtaking convolutions of the Hindu mind' is the statement, cited in his own *Verdict on India* (Harcourt, Brace and Company, 1944), from *Father India*, by C. S. Ranga Iyer, a reply to Katherine Mayo's *Mother India* and a nice example of the Eastern pot talking back to the Western kettle. Mr. Iyer justifies the old Hindu institution of temple-prostitutes in the following words:

'The idea of allowing young girls of the prostitute class to grow up in the atmosphere of the temples is to instill into them some religion, some fear of God, so that when they come of age they may not indulge in promiscuity.'

This bit of Eastern antilogic has probably never been surpassed in the West but the hard-headed Lancashire mill owners in the early days of the industrial revolution surely did not fall far short of the mark with their favorite argument against reform — that any reduction in the sixteen- or fourteen-hour working day would expose the women or children employed in their mills to the temptations of idleness, thereby depraving their morals and ultimately undermining family life. In our day the writers of military communiqués — who sometimes have consciences — have used these same devices of annulment and inversion to transform disasters like the British-American-Chinese rout in Burma into brilliant defensive victories, proving that the Western mind, too, knows a good convolution when it sees one.

Ram Lal, with his bicultural background, certainly knew a good convolution when he saw one, and in his final effort of the evening matched his fellow-countryman's defense of temple-prostitution with the breathtaking statement that much of the opposition to lifting the taboos of untouchability came from the Untouchables themselves.

'You see, our so-called Untouchables are divided into numerous subcastes, many of which have rules just as strict as those of the higher castes. The individual Untouchable fears that if he violates the customs and rules of his own caste he will be declared a pariah, a man without caste. That is the worst thing that can happen to a Hindu, which explains why the Untouchables are so reluctant to accept reform.'

It was seldom, I realized, that one heard this kind of logic applied to domestic social problems in the modern West. Few employers, for instance, went around complaining that their workers refused to accept higher wages. (Though there were still some who could not understand why their motives were so misunderstood when they tried to protect their workers from labor unions.)

The Nazi institutions of protective arrest and protective invasion, however, depended for their propaganda-effect upon a similar reversal of reality through projection. The zeal of the defendants in Soviet political trials to convict themselves strongly suggested stage-managing to produce a similar effect. More than a trace of the same disingenuous mentality crept into Allied propaganda aimed at defending such wartime acts as our preventive occupations of Iceland, Greenland, the Azores — and Iran. The imperialist theme of the White Man's Burden, still used at times in colonial propaganda, almost implied that we had taken up this burden at the invitation of the lesser breeds, that it was they, not we, who would be wronged if we let it drop. The French, at least before 1940, seemed particularly addicted to thinking of their colonial activities as a sacred mission urged on them by the natives, rather than as the ruthless exploitation that they were.

As these examples flashed through my mind, it occurred to me that there were a great many more Hindus in the world than I had ever thought, at least a great many more Ram Lals. If I had been able on that night in Delhi to look into the future at the spectacle of Soviet Russia long protecting the Danubian states from imperialist exploitation by closing the Danube to free trade, at the spectacle of the American people — whose representatives castrated the United Nations with the shears of national sovereignty — believing that it was only the Soviet veto which blocked the attainment of one world, then I would have realized that everyone is a Ram Lal at some time in his life.

In the daze that followed Ram Lal's final assault upon our
reason, while the party was breaking up and my amazing guest
was magnanimously shaking hands with his intellectual tormen-
tors, a new thought came to me. There had been a kernel of truth
in Ram Lal's fantastic statement; it was true that even among
the depressed castes called Untouchables, caste taboos were sometimes rigorously observed. This was particularly true among the
castes which hoped to elevate themselves out of untouchability.
It was by no means uncommon in modern Hindu society for the
leaders of some Untouchable caste to persuade a liberal or venal
Brahmin pundit to promote them *en masse* to a higher station in
the Hindu hierarchy. Individuals born as Untouchables could
never rise above their birth-status but the whole caste sometimes
acquired a better social status in this way. In applying for such
group-promotions it was customary for the suppliant caste to
produce evidence that its members over a long period of years had
accepted the dietary, marriage, and other rules of respectable
castes, and that these rules had been enforced by rigid caste discipline.

Thinking of the caste councils and courts which in every region
and district of India enforced upon individual Hindus the most
direct, significant, and immediate social discipline in their personal lives — except possibly the discipline of joint-family life —
realization came to me that a good deal of the strangeness of
Hindu thought also arose from a fragmentation of the Hindu
conscience produced by the caste system. Hindu society as a
whole had its ideals and its moral code — lofty ideals and a noble
moral code — but there were no churchly or other organs for the
enforcement of total cultural discipline. Caste ideals and caste
ethics had a much narrower scope; in a sense they were only the
by-laws of social clubs, yet for the individual they were the most
important and the most real because his observance of them assured him of a respected place in a closeknit community, whereas
his rejection or disregard of them placed him beyond the pale of
society.

As a social authority, caste meant to the Indian almost what the nation means to us, yet this authority had no jurisdiction over, and paid little attention to, large spheres of the individual's life, both his private life and his life as a citizen. It was as if, in the West, our morality were derived from the municipal ordinances of the communities in which we live, as if we considered violating the traffic rules or leaving garbage upon the sidewalks graver offences than murder or treason, as if never failing to renew one's dog-license were the highest form of virtue.

Here was a real gulf between the Eastern and the Western way of life, yet as I pondered upon it, it seemed to me that nationalism had produced in the Western conscience the same fragmentation that caste had produced in the Hindu conscience. The pieces were bigger with us because the split came at a higher level of organization but the effect on our thinking was much the same. Our ideals were the ideals of humanity as a whole but our law was the law of nations or the law of race. We dreamed and even talked of a law of mankind but it existed only in our dreams and in our talk and therefore had no reality to us.

Within a much larger sector of life than the Hindu we had a genuine social conscience, upheld by numerous official and unofficial institutions, we had a vastly greater range of human brotherhood and a more inclusive sense of the dignity of man, and therefore we could think relatively straight about social and political problems. Outside the frontiers, whether national, racial, ideological, or religious, of our 'in-group' feeling we either glossed over our misconduct toward other humans with coarse cynicism or fattened our delusions on spiritual poisons akin to Hindu priestly logic. We used the holy words of our culture to cover at the same time our idealistic strivings toward a better world and our most unholy greeds and fears, and always gazed with bewilderment, with indignation, or with disillusionment, at the mixed crop of hate and co-operation, of progress and regression which we reaped.

Like Ram Lal, we considered ourselves, individually, as beacons of enlightment in a world of darkness. We — the Ram Lals of the West and of all nations and all times — had no superstitions and no prejudices, for we ate and drank anything. If all the world were like us then there would be peace and progress. No personal sacrifice for the common good would deter us, for we burned with a noble idealism. What was the use of our idealism, though, when others failed to respond to it, what was the use of our enlightenment when the rest of mankind was so backward, when the world was filled with millions of blighters so incorrigibly dedicated to darkness that they did not even know the difference between a good cocktail and a bad one?

The greatest single lesson of Ram Lal, I thought, is that both backwardness and enlightenment are sometimes very different from what we imagine them to be. Backwardness in all lands is not merely the failure of progress to achieve uniform cultural penetration, it is also the erosion of attained progress by myth and delusion. It is the result of de-education as well as of un-education. Being educated is no protection against becoming de-educated. For example, if the fractionalization of the Hindu conscience by the caste system is responsible for some of the weird illogic in Hindu thinking, then the fractionalization of the Western conscience by nationalism could possibly lead to the decay of rationalism in our society, if it has not already begun.

Therefore the problem of bringing enlightenment to backward peoples in some cases is both simpler and more complex than it seems. It is largely a matter of awakening them to the cultural myths and fallacies from which their current delusions spring, of convincing them that what they believe to be their culture is really an anticulture, a cancerous degeneration of what was once their culture.

I was grateful to Ram Lal for throwing light on certain aspects of the Hindu anticulture as the British sahib had helped throw light on some phases of our Western anticulture.

Meeting this strange figure had another consequence for me: It turned my interest more than ever to a subject I had already begun to study, the cultural significance of the Indian national revolution, which seemed to stand for the opposite of everything that Ram Lal stood for.

III

Resurrection in the East

In STUDYING the Indian nationalist movement I gradually became aware of a curious paradox which seemed to me to throw a new light upon the problem of cross-cultural understanding which is so closely related to the still greater problem of the unity of man and peace upon earth.

The paradox, as it appeared to me, could be put this way: For two centuries men of good will on both the Indian and the British sides had tried again and again to build a bridge between the East and the West, to learn to understand and respect each other's ideals and to develop a common purpose. Every attempt had seemingly failed; today the two races were farther apart than ever, the two cultures apparently more antithetical. The ideology of the Congress movement — unmistakably the intellectual pattern of the India of tomorrow — was, according to both its enemies and its adherents, a cultural as well as a political revolt against the West. Yet to me it seemed that this so-called Eastern revolt against Western culture was itself the very cultural synthesis of East and West, which the optimists of both races had finally given up trying to effect, which the pessimists, with increasingly triumphant conviction, had declared impossible. A true cultural mating had taken place and it had borne fruit but now the father disclaimed his offspring and the mother, as in a French bedroom farce, insisted he was right to disclaim it.

To me, as a relatively unprejudiced outsider in this family quarrel, it seemed certain both that the Congress movement was a genuine cultural revolution in Indian society and that it owed much more to Western influence than either the British or the Indians were willing to admit. By the end of my stay in Delhi I had met a good number of male and female supporters or sympathizers of the Congress movement, and little as I knew about India, I knew that they represented a completely new type of human being in Indian history. To these Indians the Congress program was not just a political ideology or cause but a new way of life — a way of life which I believed and hoped would become that of all India in the course of time. On the whole it seemed to me a noble and meaningful way of life and those who accepted it wholeheartedly and completely were ennobled by it and appeared to have a greater moral stature than other Indians — or most Occidentals for that matter.

The new Indian way of life differed from the traditional one in several essential respects. To me one of the most striking differences was that these new Indians possessed a highly developed social and civic conscience. In the early Hindu societies civic and social duties were regulated largely by the group-discipline of the joint family and the village commune; the point of view was a homely and parochial one, inadequate to cope with large-scale disasters such as famine, but essentially warm-hearted and human. British rule had broken up many of the basic Hindu social institutions, had stirred up group-antagonisms by the divide-and-rule system and had abruptly introduced the complications of modern urban and industrial life into a society which had evolved no cultural machinery for dealing with such problems.

The result — for several generations — was a kind of social anarchy reflected in private attitudes of greed, dishonesty, and callousness to human suffering in regard to public problems that was shocking by Western standards. During the great Bengal famine of 1942 whose horrors I saw at first-hand, the British sat in their Calcutta clubs passing house-rules against mentioning the unpleasant topic while starving men, women, and children literally died on the sidewalks in front of these clubs. Many of the Indians, both Hindu and Moslem, were even worse; they did not merely fail to do anything to relieve the famine but they exploited it by hoarding grain on a gigantic scale, and even more ghoulishly by organizing vast prostitution rackets, which according to one estimate, recruited thirty thousand starving women for the brothels of Calcutta.

Old-fashioned Indians shrugged their shoulders helplessly at such horrors — and at all the chronic evils of Indian society— but the new Indians by the thousands and the hundreds of thousands threw themselves selflessly, not merely into famine-relief, but into every form of social service as an integral part of the campaign for political independence.

Despite the exotic institution of nonviolence the political idealism of the new Indians, like their zeal for social reform, represented a break with the traditional East and a cultural rapprochement with the West. The basic pattern of Indian nationalism resembles that of any Western nationalism but Indian nationalists differ in their characters from Western nationalists, or any Western political idealists, by their simplicity, their instinctive as well as their ideological abhorrence of violence, and by the intense moral earnestness with which they pursue their goals. Quite consciously they are trying to effect a moral as well as a political revolution in India and contrary to the usual Western approach they have commenced by effecting a moral revolution within themselves. The attractive qualities of Indian nationalism emerge clearly in the characters and writings of their leaders, as clearly in the indigenous and sometimes incomprehensible Gandhi as in the westernized Nehru, surely one of the most human, noble-minded and generally engaging public figures of our day.

The women were particularly impressive, not so much because the genius of India is a feminine one, as because Indian culture, like most Oriental cultures, overvalues the social importance of the male, causing little boys to be spoiled by their parents and men to be mothered by their wives. This pattern of culture produces males tending to shallowness, egoism, and irresponsibility and sometimes crushes the females under too heavy burdens, but

those Indian women who are strong enough to survive the tensions of joint-family life arising from dependent males and domineering elder females of the household develop great emotional
depth, integrity, and dignity which, together with their outward
grace and their slightly asexual yet intensely feminine charm,
make them one of the most admirable as well as ornamental results of the human experiment upon our planet.

The female Congress sympathizers I met in Delhi exemplified
this ancient Hindu ideal of womanhood and even their passionate
political activism had a precedent in the Joan of Arc tradition
within the Hindu warrior caste which had produced such national
heroines as Lakshmi Bai, the Rani of Jhansi, who died fighting at
the head of her troops against the British in the Great Mutiny.
(The Japanese-sponsored Indian National Army had a feminine
combat contingent called the Rani of Jhansi Regiment.)   At the
same time the influence of Western feminism working through
such Indian reformist groups as the Brahmo Samaj was unmistakably traceable in the attitudes, opinions, and behavior of these
women.   In a civic sense they were as emancipated as any women
in the West; as part of their ideology they preached the doctrine
of the social emancipation of women and practiced it themselves
by claiming the right to choose their own husbands, by insisting
on monogamy, and in many other ways, but emotionally they
were not emancipated from the Hindu pattern of sexual and family relationships and they did not want to be emancipated.   Leading lives utterly different from those of their orthodox grandmothers and at the same time quite unlike any Western model,
these women, it seemed to me, had achieved a real reconciliation
between Eastern and Western ideals of womanhood and synthesized some of the most basic values of two antithetical cultures.

What was true of the new type of Indian woman produced by
the national independence movement seemed to me true of the
whole ethos of that movement.   Certain specific features of Indian nationalism appeared to have either a purely Indian or a
purely Occidental inspiration, but in the context of the whole they
took a meaning new both to the East and to the West.   Thus the

technique of passive resistance which Gandhi had elaborated into a major revolutionary arm was derived from a traditional Hindu form of individual or collective protest against injustice, but its elevation to a permanent political institution was without precedent in Indian history. The complex philosophy of nonviolence which Gandhi has built around this technique has its roots in an ancient Hindu tradition of metaphysical pacifism, its premises can be found in the teachings of the two greatest Hindu reformists, Mahavira and Buddha, but it was largely the impact of Christian pacificism via Tolstoy and some Quaker friends in Gandhi's South African period that turned his mind to these Asiatic sources.

The influence of the West is even clearer in the Gandhian — and Congress — attitude toward untouchability. Neither the Buddhist-Jain egalitarianism mentioned in the previous chapter nor the Buddhist doctrine of compassion (compassion for all human and even animal suffering is one of the laws of Buddha) suffice to explain the tremendous emphasis — almost equal to the emphasis on nonviolence and on national liberation — upon uplifting the Untouchable in Gandhi's philosophy. The symbolism of Gandhi's personal campaign against untouchability unmistakably expresses the Christian concepts of humility and redemption as well as the Buddhist concept of compassion. He has renamed the Untouchables 'Harijans' — Children of God — and has declared to his disciples that if he were reborn upon earth again he would like to be reborn as an Untouchable, 'so that I may share their sorrows, sufferings, and the affronts leveled at them in order that I may free myself and them from that miserable condition.' This quotation — from Ela Sen's admirable short biography entitled *Gandhi* — has a clear Christian ring to it, like much of Gandhi's teaching, but the implication of the 'myself' — that the caste Hindu partakes in the degradation of untouchability — reflects the mystic sense of total participation and collective responsibility derived from the Hindu form of pantheism (though it is by no means absent in Christian mysticism).

The reader who has not followed Indian affairs closely in recent

years may think of Gandhi primarily as a political leader with
eccentric personal habits, a sort of Oriental George Bernard Shaw,
but as I discovered when I began to document myself upon the
Indian nationalist movement, he is above all a cultural revolutionary, and his eccentricities are efforts to re-enforce his propaganda campaigns by personal example.

He is a vegetarian because he thinks of himself (somewhat
questionably) as an orthodox Hindu, and all Hindus — except
the forty million devotees of the death-goddess Kali — are forbidden to eat meat, chiefly because eating meat encourages the
slaughtering of animals. In the Hindu view, animals are perme-
ated with the same divine energy that man is, they are members
of a cosmic one world, therefore it is sinful to take even animal
life. The Jains, who have somewhat the relationship to Hinduism that the Quakers have to Catholicism, carry this view so far
— as I have already mentioned — that they cannot protect themselves against the attacks of bedbugs or other insect parasites,
and Buddhist monks in Southeast Asia, expressing a kind of
Hindu Calvinism or Methodism, always drink water through a
strainer, lest they inadvertently swallow some harmless insect.
Superorthodox Hindus even abstain from eggs and consider it
slightly indecent to drink the milk of the cow, a particularly sacred
animal. Gandhi now drinks cow's milk, but for a long time he
drank only goat's milk as a protest against the Indian peasant
practice called *phuka* — a cruel method of stimulating lactation
in cows for a brief period so as to wring the greatest possible income from them before selling them to a Moslem butcher.

The same Hindu reverence for life is at the basis of Gandhi's
lifelong campaign against Western medicine, which he considers
sinful because founded on animal experimentation, and in favor
of the traditional Hindu art of healing called Ayurveda — originally a complex mixture of homeopathy and magic which in recent years has been somewhat rationalized along the lines of
Western nature-therapy. Gandhi's struggle with Western medicine has produced two dramatic crises in his life. Once, when in
prison, he allowed a British surgeon to operate on him for acute

appendicitis, because he feared that if he died in jail it would provoke a nationwide outbreak of anti-British violence. When his eldest son lay near death with typhoid, Gandhi again compromised with his conscience by offering to bring in a Western physician, but was relieved when the son refused, and eventually cured him by applying mudpacks to his body (doubtless inadvertently destroying millions of micro-organisms contained in the mud).

Gandhi has also campaigned vigorously against birth-control, also on religious grounds, but, as the reader will shortly see, this campaign has led him to a curiously untraditional and even Western point of view, for he favors birth-control by the practice of chastity, while popular Hinduism has always attached a mystic, holy significance to the sexual act, and in all the Asiatic cultures children are held one of life's greatest blessings.

Though the symbol of the *charkha* (spinning wheel) which has played such a great role in Gandhi's political campaigns, is not a religious one, it is a cultural one, standing for the ancient Hindu way of peasant life. Like so many of Gandhi's eccentricities it was a shrewd political move for the Mahatma to urge his followers to spin their way to national freedom, since only a great production of cheap native cloth would make possible the boycott on British goods which he knew was one of India's strongest weapons against Britain. However, Gandhi, to the distress of many of the rich Indian industrialists who support the Congress movement, has urged home spinning not merely as a means of winning freedom but as one of the foundation-stones of a national peasant economy and as a discipline for elevating the national character.

All these doctrines and campaigns of Gandhi are rooted in India's cultural past, as he himself is, but they also reflect the struggle against foreign political and cultural domination — for example, the rejection of Western medicine clearly reflects nationalistic as well as religious prejudice — and most of them reflect a much greater degree of Occidental influence than Gandhi himself realizes. Just as Indians of the Ram Lal type consider themselves most modern when they are intellectually most backward, so do Indians of the Gandhi type sometimes consider themselves most traditional when they are most revolutionary, most indigenous when they are most responsive to foreign influence.

Even Gandhi's most famous apostasy — from the Western point of view — his denunciations of the machine as a symbol of Western materialism and his promulgation of the doctrine of the charkha as the panacea for India's economic ills is borrowed in part from the West.

Gandhi has acknowledged Ruskin as one of the great intellectual influences in his life and there is more than a touch of Ruskin in the philosophy of charkha. In its Indian context this backwash of an English protest against the industrial revolution is a great deal less nonsensical than it seems. Gandhi's basic economic premise that India is a poor country which must depend heavily upon a rural economy of self-sufficiency combining farming for home consumption with a huge labor-investment in cottage industries is probably sound, certainly nearer to being sound than the dreams of those enthusiasts who consider industrialization as the panacea. The error in the charkha theory is the failure to recognize the importance and urgency of limited industrialization as a means of increasing agricultural production and obtaining the greatest possible income from the limited natural resources of the country.

Though he may not draw all the right conclusions from it, Gandhi seems to be the only outstanding nationalist leader who has grasped the underlying economic reality of India: That Indians cannot hope to raise their living-standard to Western levels because no conceivable industrial and agricultural development of the country can keep up with the increase of population, at its present rate. Rapid industrialization and radical improvement of Indian agriculture could probably achieve a safe margin of production over famine for the present population of about four hundred million. This population has increased by at least fifty million — and probably much more, for all Indian vital statistics are merely approximate — in the past twenty years, and even the rate of increase seems to be mounting. Merely to prevent famine will be a tremendous task for India in the future, if the population continues to grow at present rates, and it is bound to grow unless Indians, by some means, restrict procreation. Gandhi might be criticized for not using his great influence to overcome the prejudice against birth-control instead of preaching chastity, but it is not unrealistic or retrograde of him to urge the Indian people to live within its means, which is the economic meaning of his doctrine of the simple life.

Gandhi has often been denounced by English critics for his intellectual gyrations, and despite his cult of the truth and his devastating honesty about his own mistakes and weaknesses, it is not difficult to find in his writings examples of intellectual dishonesty worthy of a Ram Lal. (It is not difficult to find similar examples in the writings of any Western politician.) This intellectual dishonesty which Gandhi has never ceased to combat even if he has sometimes succumbed to it himself is one of the few unadmirable attributes of the new Indian character which is being shaped in the Congress mold but even it has a bicultural ancestry. The pioneer nationalist leader Tilak, who was one of Gandhi's political masters, quite frankly and cynically preached the creed of intellectual dishonesty and though he dabbled — for political purposes — in some indigenous forms of superstition, his dialectics clearly proves that successive generations of Occidental cultural missionaries had not worked the Indian vineyard in vain. The Indian people, Tilak preached, were at war with the British Raj. Language — and thought — are weapons of war because they are instruments of propaganda. They should be used — like any weapons — to achieve victory. Any relation to the truth was purely coincidental and not important. Truth was what hurt the English. Readers with an extensive background in the Western literature of class warfare may detect something vaguely familiar in Tilak's doctrine.

Although Gandhi's rejection of Western medicine, based on the orthodox Hindu disapproval of vivisection, has probably done more to discredit him — and the whole Indian nationalist movement — in the eyes of progressive Westerners than anything else, and seems to prove that the Eastern and Western ways of life are indeed incompatible, another of his intellectual foibles (what I consider as a foible), his campaign in favor of *brahmacharya* — chastity even in marital relations — illustrates the manner in which Gandhi has subtly amalgamated Christian and Hindu concepts into a new religion that is the emotional fountainhead of a new national culture.

Brahmacharya really means the ascetic way of life, the discipline by which a sage attains the higher knowledge. It includes chastity, of course, and both the Vedic and Buddhist sages considered sexual passion as one of the main sources of man's bondage to illusion. The holy men of the East have always been expected to practice chastity and in ancient times in India it was fashionable for young men to practice it and other forms of asceticism for a year or so as a kind of spiritual conditioning. When Gandhi ceased having sexual relations with his wife, Kasturba, he followed a traditional Asiatic pattern as a spiritual leader. However, in declaring that sexual intercourse between man and wife was sinful for any purpose except procreation, and that even procreation was a rather low activity, the Mahatma turned his back on the Hinduism of all the ages, the gods of a thousand temple walls pausing in their riotous carven or painted loves to shout him heresy, and exceeded the most severe Buddhist moralists who have generally contented themselves with reminding the faithful from time to time that they could not hope to attain Buddhahood in one incarnation unless they stopped sleeping with their wives. Instead, under an Eastern name, Gandhi promulgated the teachings of the most rigorous Catholic ascetics.

Perhaps as Krisnalal Shridharani suggests, in his readable and well-documented if slightly propagandistic *The Mahatma and the World*, Gandhi's doctrine of chastity is largely the result of a personal conflict, but I suspect that, like so many other elements in his philosophy, it has political implications as well. Gandhi began practicing chastity in 1906, long before Katherine Mayo thought she had discovered that the decadence, lack of virility, and other evils which she found in India were ultimately trace-

able to the widespread custom of Hindu mothers quieting their
children by practicing masturbation upon them, thus prema-
turely stimulating their sexuality. (Since Miss Mayo wrote
Mother India long before Pearl Harbor she did not have to explain why the same custom had somehow failed to sap the virility
of the Japanese.) However, it had been popular in missionary
circles long before Miss Mayo was born to moan with despair
over Hindu sexual morals, and the nastiness of Hindu culture was
considered by many high-minded Englishmen as proving the unfitness of Indians for self-rule. Consequently the purification of
Indian morals has appeared to many Indian nationalists as one
means of increasing the West's respect for the Indian people and
Gandhi's doctrine of brahmacharya has the added merit in Indian
eyes of implying that ancient India was really much more chaste
than the West.

In reality, it is almost hopeless to speculate upon whether
Indians are more or less chaste than we are. They are as shocked
by many of our sexual institutions and attitudes as we are by
theirs. They consider the prevalence of divorce and adultery in
our society monstrous, for both are rare in Hindu society. They
are a great deal less shocked than we are by lascivious and even
perverse expressions of sexuality, they use the phallus as a religious symbol of the creative principle of the universe, and sometimes decorate their temples with pictorial matter equal on the
level of pornography to some of our water-closet art. On the
other hand, the tender embraces of movie stars, which seem perfectly respectable to Hollywood, are scandalously lascivious to
the Hindus, and their prostitutes cover themselves more adequately than our bathing beauties do. In general, it seemed to
me that the Hindus were franker and less inhibited in their thinking about sexuality than we are, but that their code of sexual
morality was stricter than ours in regard to marital fidelity and
premarital chastity, certainly for women, and possibly even for
men.

The pollinization of ancient cultural ideals by modern nationalistic and revolutionary fervor has produced in my opinion

Gandhi's unavowed new religion and the unrecognized new culture of India. Gandhi's interest in Christianity was stirred by friendly zealots who tried to convert him in South Africa, and shocked and disgusted him by their intolerance in the process. Mr. Shridharani relates how Gandhi was once excluded as a black man from a church in South Africa, where one of his Christian friends was preaching a sermon for his special benefit.

Such experiences caused him to read his Bible with particular care and then to turn to the ancient religious texts of his own culture. It is significant that — as Mrs. Sen points out — Gandhi discovered Buddhism and the higher Hindu philosophy through those Western protagonists of Eastern culture Mrs. Annie Besant, the Theosophist leader, and Sir Edwin Arnold. He had never read the *Bhagavad Gita,* the New Testament of the Hindu scriptures, until he read it in an English translation — as an antidote to the proselytizing techniques of the Plymouth Brethren, to which he was exposed in South Africa.

Because Gandhi is a genius — several kinds of a genius, including a moral genius — all these ancient and modern religious and secular influences coalesced in the heat of his own inner fire and emerged in his life and his teaching not as a hodgepodge of faiths, but as a new faith, not as a reshuffling, but as a revision of primary symbols. All that is noble and all that is petty in Gandhi's philosophy, all that is wise and all that is foolish, all that is serene and all that is delusive, has been shaped by the same forces, tempered in the same fire.

Gandhi's faith, from all that I could see, was in its broad lines the faith of the Indian revolution. His most westernized followers might scoff at the economics of charkha and deplore some of his health fads, his Moslem followers might refuse to give up meat, and his most orthodox Hindu followers think his attitude in regard to untouchability was too drastic — nearly all balked at integral celibacy and even at times at total non-violence — but their lives because of Gandhi were new lives.

Even without Gandhi the Indian nationalist movement would have been a cultural revolution. The concept of nationalism was

itself a Western importation (not altogether a happy one, I felt).
One foreign concept alone rarely suffices to produce a cultural
revolution, but there was something else more fundamental.
Compared with the political movements of the West, the nationalist movement in India seemed wholly alien and Eastern. Its
occidentalism lay in the fact that it existed at all.

Not only is the traditional Indian culture unpolitical but it is
also without social consciousness. Not only are its highest values
purely individual ones but they are also what we would be inclined to call escapist values. Whereas in the West idealism has
meant devoting one's life to the betterment of the world, in the
East idealism has usually meant renouncing the world. The most
perfect life to the man of the East has seemed the life of the holy
beggar or the hermit meditating in silence in a forest cave. It is
true that there is a strong case for thinking that apostolic Buddhism was a religion of social reform and even the *Bhagavad Gita*
can be read — probably should be read — as a defense of activism, but for nearly two thousand years the Buddhist and Hindu
scriptures have usually been read in Asia in a quietist spirit.

Because it is primarily a philosophic poem, the *Bhagavad Gita*
is not always thought of as a story, yet it contains a story in the
Western sense of the word, and the plot or theme of this story
provides a significant context for the metaphysical reflections
woven around it. The background of the story is the great civil
war among the early Aryan settlers in India which is the subject
of the epic *Mahabharata*, of which the *Gita* is a part.

The hero of the poem, the dispossessed prince, Arjuna, is called
upon to do battle with his kinsmen and friends for the recovery of
his rightful heritage. Like Hamlet, like many confused liberals of
modern times, Arjuna is torn between contradictory ideals and
duties, and falls into a state of neurotic depression upon the eve
of battle. The god, Krishna, appears and, somewhat in the manner of a modern psychiatrist, teaches Arjuna to reconcile his inner
conflicts, to accomplish his duty as a warrior without betraying
the more spiritual values of Hindu culture, including the ideal of
nonviolence. Depending upon what element of Krishna's teach-

ing one considers the most essential, the poem can be read as a tract in favor of integral nonviolence or as a dialectic for justifying violence in a righteous cause.

Today millions of Hindus are turning to the *Bhagavad Gita* to seek inspiration for a life of effort, struggle, and even conflict. Like the scripture's legendary hero, Arjuna, they are asking the gods how they can reconcile the modern idealism of combat in the worldly arena with the ascetic values of the Vedic sages, and the gods are replying to them — as, according to the text, they appear to have replied to Arjuna — that the reconciliation lies not in the rejection of worldly participation but in the renunciation of selfish gains, not in the avoidance of struggle but by preserving inner serenity while engaged in struggle, not in the refusal of combat but in refusing to hate the adversary one opposes. For many Indians political action and social reform have become a personal discipline of the spirit, a kind of social yoga, as well as a patriotic duty.

To me it seems that this new Indian attitude toward life obliterates the greatest single difference between the cultures of the West and those of the East. Many differences remain but no difference as great as that between the traditional activism of the West and the traditional quietism of the East. The unmeetable twain have met precisely at the point of widest divergence.

Why, then, do both East and West refuse to admit that this meeting has taken place? There is obviously a misunderstanding but it seems to me much more a political than a cultural misunderstanding. East and West have been at war for roughly some two hundred years. Perhaps this war is nearing its end but it is not over. Even the political independence of India will not abolish all worldly conflict between India and Britain. As long as the imperialist attitudes of the West survive in our economic, diplomatic, and social contacts with the peoples of the East a war-mentality will color the thinking of the East about the West and of the West about the East. As long as this war-mentality exists the Indians will refuse to admit to themselves — and to the world — the cultural debt they owe to the West.

On our side, our racial superiority complex, our desire to continue exploiting the East, and our slight sense of guilt about this
desire cause us to repudiate our own cultural victory. For this
victory is not a clear-cut one. In the case of India, at least, we
have not westernized the Indians — we have fertilized Indian
culture with Western concepts and thereby collaborated in producing a new culture. This is not enough for our egos. We are
not satisfied that the Indians have accepted our highest ideals;
we want them to accept our idiosyncrasies and even our vices.
Gandhi has accepted some of the most basic tenets of Christianity
but he rejects our cocktails, remaining an incorrigible drinker of
goat's milk, therefore a heathen.

Beneath these political and relatively superficial factors of misunderstanding, it seemed to me that the various misreadings of
the Indian revolution current in both East and West revealed a
complex illusion and a vast area of cloudiness in human thinking
— at least in the thinking of Western man — about cultural
phenomena in relation to international co-operation.

For one thing, this misunderstanding strongly suggests that
we — the human 'we' — not only fail to realize when our behavior conflicts with our ideals but fail to realize when one ideal
conflicts with another. The semanticists have shown what extraordinary variations of meaning, or absences of meaning, can
lurk in the mist-cloud of language and in so far as cultural patterns are transmitted or preserved in language it is easy to see
how vast cultural revolutions can occur without being recognized,
provided that the human group involved in the revolution expresses its new meanings by the very common device of reading
new meanings into old words. To some degree this explains why
the Indian revolution has not been recognized as a cultural one by
either Indians or British. Traditional words have been given
untraditional meanings and the Indians who have whole-heart-
edly accepted these new meanings have become new Indians
without realizing fully that they have changed.

It seemed to me, however, that in the changing pattern of
Indian life, nonverbal symbols as well as words were taking on

new meanings while preserving their traditional aspect. Thus, Gandhi sitting cross-legged on the ground in his loincloth, sunk in silent meditation, appears both to the adoring Asiatic crowds and to the skeptical Western onlooker as the perfect and timeless symbol of Hindu or Buddhist asceticism. Yet the message of this human statue is utterly different from that of the stone Buddhas of Ceylon and Southeast Asia. When Gandhi meditates in public he is propagandizing with a nonverbal symbol, and the meaning of this symbol as intended by Gandhi and understood by the crowd, can probably be most closely rendered in words by saying that it associates political and social action with the holiness-values which former generations of Indians ascribed to ascetic practices. The Congress follower who meditates with his leader gets up refreshed and inspired — not to spend the rest of his life meditating in a cave but to throw himself with renewed zeal into the worldly duties of organizing a political revolution and completing a social reform. The symbol of withdrawal has become the symbol of struggle, but nobody could be expected to grasp this without understanding the revolutionary context of Gandhi.

A little reflection reveals what we are always tempted to forget — that the meaning of any symbol is modified, sometimes reversed, by its context. In the interpretation of political and cultural symbols the difficulty lies in the remoteness or even the unlikeliness of the context. For example, the most effective American propaganda disseminated in Siam during the war was a short after-dinner speech delivered by a young army officer parachuted into Siam by OSS to train a group of Siamese guerillas. In halting Thai, this officer at the beginning of his mission delivered himself of the following remarks to an informal conference of Thai guerilla leaders:

'American officers hate Japanese, love Thai people. Otherwise no good, all time drink whisky, shoot craps, fornicate, masturbate.'

This extraordinary autocritique of the American army spread spontaneously throughout the entire kingdom in a remarkably short space of time and enormously enhanced American prestige.

Its author became the most popular American in Siam and despite his almost total ignorance of the language, customs, history and politics of the Thai people had an unsurpassed record in obtaining co-operation from them.

The reason why an apparent libel on the American army, and on American manhood generally, produced a favorable instead of an unfavorable propaganda effect was, in the first place, that the speaker actually meant something quite different from what he said and that everyone who heard the anecdote understood this, because it was unbelievable for a foreign officer to proclaim in earnest to his allies that his own people were no good. The Siamese, like the Kachins, have a convention of humorous boastfulness by self-deprecation sufficiently akin to the American humorous convention which had produced the statement to make it a comprehensible joke, and such a startling deviation from the normal language of military diplomacy was bound to attract attention, one of the conditions of any successful propaganda.

The decisive factor, however, was the remote and implicit context of the utterance. In so far as it is safe to apply the word 'all' to anything, it can be said that all Asiatics when they have any contact with men of the West or with any elements of Western culture worry about being considered inferior and bitterly resent any suggestion that they are in fact considered inferior. This is much less a preoccupation with the Siamese than with most Asiatic peoples, but it definitely exists even in Siam. The Siamese, like most Eastern peoples, often have had their morals criticized by Westerners and they are particularly sensitive to such criticism because their morals in some respects are not excessively puritanical. Therefore they were powerfully impressed by an American who did not seek to impress them with his superiority but instead went out of his way to deny it, without at the same time causing them the embarrassment of mentioning the subject at all. The cultural and political implications of the anecdote — to all Siamese who heard it — were that Americans were really different from other Westerners because they did not stand on their dignity and try to appear superior, therefore they must have some sincere affection and respect for the Siamese people and were possibly truthful in proclaiming that they had no motive except to help the Siamese drive out the Japanese.

This same preoccupation with the problem of racial superiority and inferiority is the hidden context of a great many Asiatic meanings. It is often more significant in the interpretation of many Asiatic symbols than their immediate referents. Not only the political and cultural utterances of the East must be analyzed in this context but many of the nonverbal symbols, the actions, even the emotions of Oriental groups must be regarded almost as propagandistic statements refuting or protesting against the myth of Asiatic inferiority. When an educated Indian hangs a bunch of flowers over his door to ward off cholera — an old Ayurvedic recipe — it tells us more about his feelings toward the British, and everything British, including medicine, than it does about his magical beliefs.

It is our failure to examine the deep contexts of cultural phenomena which causes us to overevaluate the importance of cultural conflicts and misunderstandings, to create in our minds unscalable walls and unbridgeable gulfs between ourselves and other peoples. We fasten our attention exclusively upon the symbol and forget the context. Group A is opposed to sin; Group B defiantly proclaims its approval of sin. Either we rack our brains trying to invent ingenious compromises between virtue and sin or we throw up our hands in despair, saying, virtue and sin can never be reconciled, therefore A can never co-operate with B.

Even if we take the trouble to make sure that A and B have the same sin in mind — something we rarely do — we do not ask ourselves whether sin has always meant the same thing to the members of these two groups and therefore whether the conflict of ideals between them is a permanent or temporary one. We usually assume it is a permanent one, because we fail to realize that throughout history our institutions have changed less frequently than the meaning of our institutions.

The deepest and ultimate context of any cultural institution is the psychological structure, the intimate personality, of the individuals who belong to the culture of which the institution is a part. If men were more clairvoyant and logical they would change their institutions whenever their personalities change, as they are constantly changing from age to age, often with the abruptness of biological mutations. Western man is not quite the same kind of man that his grandfather was; in regard to his psychological structure he is only remotely akin to Renaissance man and a tremendous psychological gulf separates him from Medieval man. Our institutions, however, reflect the history of our souls very inaccurately; sometimes, like a Ram Lal, because we drink cocktails, we believe that our personalities are more modern than they really are; probably more often, like the Indian nationalists, we fail to realize how much we differ from our ancestors — from those we believe to have been our ancestors — because we still go about partly clothed in their handed-down cultural garments.

Our natural tendency to consider our prejudices and our ideals as eternal values because, psychologically constituted as we are, we cannot imagine any others that would satisfy us, is re-enforced by our cultural myth that our ancestors have lived, and lived nobly, by these same values since the dawn of time. When history threatens to expose this myth we get around history by practicing the selective breeding of ancestors in reverse — by arbitrarily adopting or disowning them as the Nazis alternately adopted and disowned Charlemagne — or by reading current meanings into the texts of the past — as the Russians have uncovered the instinctive Leninism of Peter the Great and Saint Alexander Nevsky.

Even when we know better, we unconsciously think of a culture — our own or any other — as a single living organism growing from childhood to the adult state, and as it grows experiencing at the same time a hardening and a flowering of the innate traits which were present from the first. There is also in our minds the slightly contradictory image of a cultural family tree: Western culture started with the Hebrews, who married the Greeks and begot Rome; Rome had a clandestine affair with the Celts, producing Gaul and Britain, then all were raped by the savage Teutons and their Viking cousins, a terrible catastrophe but it worked out for the best in the end, because this somehow produced the Reformation which produced Science, and here we are today getting more Western all the time. By a similarly contradictory mixture of growth and reseeding, the Eastern cultures somehow got started and have kept on going, getting more Eastern all the time, just out of habit.

Once during one of my Sunday afternoon bicycle explorations of the countryside around New Delhi a naïve American friend supplied me with a particularly happy example of this curious blindness to inner change in our own or any other culture.

'Look at that old bird plowing his land with a crooked stick,' he said, pointing to a peasant laboring in a field near the roadside. 'I bet the Indian peasant hasn't changed in five thousand years — and he never will.'

My friend could hardly have picked a worse example to point his argument. It is true the Indian plow has not changed much in five thousand years, but the inner life and the very personality of the man who uses it has undergone a revolutionary change. In one decisive way the Indian peasant is closer to the American farmer with his tractors and combines than he is to his own ancestors. Like the American farmer he is a capitalist. He owns or rents his own land or works as a hired laborer for a man who does. He is paid in money for his work or produce, he pays interest — usually an exorbitant interest — to a money-lender, he is haunted by the economic anxiety arising from his indebtedness and spurred by it to produce competitively as against other farmers, so that he, too, can eventually become a money-lender and make his neighbors work for him.

None of this was true five thousand or even five hundred years ago. Capitalism and private ownership of the land were introduced into India by the British in the last two hundred years, when those who previously had been mere tax-collectors were proclaimed landlords. Before that, the basic rural economy was essentially a co-operative one, or at least a noncompetitive one, with the farmer cultivating fields which did not belong to him, in the sense that he could sell them to someone else, and owing fixed percentages of his crops to the state and to the village.

A static, noncompetitive society with a rigidly drawn system of social duties and privileges for the individual produces human personalities low in enterprise and ambition, in all the values of rugged individualism, very high in neighborliness, in social and civic co-operation, not so high in civic or humanitarian zeal, because since all the social duties of the individual are defined — and enforced upon him if need be — he is not spurred by conscience to exceed duty.

A capitalist society has almost antithetical values and produces a very different type of individual. The Indian peasant in accepting capitalist institutions has not yet adopted a capitalist personality-structure because the noncapitalist traditions of his ancestors still influence him but the conflict between these traditions and the economic realities of his life has produced a change in his character — probably a rather neurotic and unhappy change.

Capitalism — if it endures — is destined to produce still more drastic changes in the personality of the peasant and in that of all Hindus. It is slowly eating away the economic foundations of the joint family, which in the old days sometimes contained as many as forty or fifty human beings of varying degree of kinship, all pooling all their property and earnings, all living under the same roof, all subject to the parental authority of some grandfather or more often grandmother. The decline of the joint family has already begun to change Indian character and when it has disappeared entirely we can be sure that a completely new Indian personality will develop, for few things have such a determinant effect on the formation of a human personality as the kind of family in which its possessor was brought up.

The truth is that Indian culture and the types of personality it has produced have fluctuated widely throughout the ages, sometimes approaching the contemporary pattern of Western culture, sometimes evolving in the opposite direction.

A passage in the Hindu religious epic, the *Mahabharata*, says: 'Women were not formerly kept in the house. They used to have promiscuous intercourse from their maidenhood and were not faithful to their husbands. This was not regarded as sinful as it was the custom of the time.'

The remote racial ancestors referred to in the epic certainly did not have the same culture and the same type of personality as the modern Indians. The status of women in society has varied considerably throughout Indian history — and throughout parts of the country — from very high to rather low to rather high to very low to the present mixture of very high and very low. Each change in status must not only have reflected a cultural change but must have produced one, since the status of the mother has a very direct bearing on the way children are brought up in a home and the patterns of relationship with other human beings that they form. The prevalence of child marriage and polygamy — in some parts of India at various times polyandry also appears to have flourished — has similarly varied at different periods in Indian history and each variation has doubtless left a profound cultural mark.

Thus, it appeared to me, reflecting on all these things, that it was poor language to speak of Indian culture at all in an historical sense. There was — more or less — an Indian culture of today which had been influenced by the West and by a number of cultures — some of them quite dissimilar — which had flourished at different times in various parts of the Indian Peninsula. Among some but not all of these cultures there was a certain thread of continuity or at least accretion, but those institutions in the present culture which were most ancient had not all come from the same source and their meaning had changed more than once.

Whether even the current Indian culture could be considered as a national one, binding together all the ethnic and other groups of India, or whether Indian culture in our time really meant nothing more than the culture of the caste Hindu exposed to Western influence, was a question I never felt able to answer. I did not believe that a scientific answer was possible on the basis of data

available, even assuming that much of these data was unknown
to me. On the whole I felt more inclined toward the British view
that India was not a cultural unity than toward the Congress
view that some indefinable and almost mystic influence had created a basic unity in the souls of Hindus, Moslems, aborigines,
and all the other diverse inhabitants of the vast subcontinent.

Where I ceased to follow the British view was in failing to agree
that because India had not been — or even might not be — a
cultural unity she could never become one. If the Indian national
revolution — and the conditions of modern life generally — really
was a new way of life, as I believed, and if this way of life spread
throughout all India, as it seemed to be spreading, then a homeo-
genous Indian culture was being founded and under certain conditions it need be no less deeply rooted after one generation than
after a thousand. The oldest extant culture in the world is exactly the age of the world's oldest inhabitant, and the youngest is
the age of the last infant born since this was written, for the word
'culture' is only a symbol for the patterns we weave in our minds
to classify the behavior and works of other human beings.

If one took the long view of both Eastern and Western culture
it did not seem to me that the problem of reconciling them mattered very much. The important thing was to reconcile Eastern
and Western man to cultural reality, to lift the cultural myopia
which made them unable to see reconciliation when it had taken
place, to clear away the cultural superstitions which engendered
imaginary conflicts between them. Not only between East and
West, but wherever cultural or ideological factors play a major
role in human conflict, it is less because men's values clash than
because their delusions collide.

After I had been there less than a year I wrote my wife:

> Maybe I have been in the East too long because I find my whole
> viewpoint is changing. I am becoming much more cynical about
> ideals and much less cynical about human beings. Working with
> our Cousins has made me cynical about ideals — if we really
> believe our own propaganda we would have to declare war on the
> British, for they have set themselves up as the master-race in

India. British rule in India is fascism, there is no dodging that.

Does that leave us only the choice of the lesser fascism? To my mind it leaves us the problem of learning the contexts in which co-operation with the British produces fascist results and those in which it produces nonfascist results. Obviously this is not an easy thing to learn but it is a learnable thing. Sometimes we make mistakes but our most consistent mistake is to think that because the British are sometimes fascists they are always fascists and that because collaboration with them sometimes produces bad results the principle of collaboration itself is evil. At home you make the opposite mistake, you assume that because the British oppose German fascism they oppose all fascisms, and that any failure to co-operate with them is sabotage of antifascism.

The world will continue to be a mess as long as we think in rigid categories of good and evil, of hope and despair. There is nothing in the world worth fighting for except man himself, and we could not be sure that this is a war for man if our enemies had not revealed themselves — by their acts, not just their words — as blasphemers of man.

The most valuable lesson that I have learned in the East is that man is worth fighting for because there is nothing that dooms him to be less than himself. In a way it is even hopeful to see how the British in India have become so much less than Englishmen, because while downward movement is probably easier than upward movement, it suggests that when the British finally give up India they may become much more than Englishmen, which would be a very fine thing indeed.

But there is something still more important and convincing. That is the change which is coming over the Indian people. Because it is not complete yet, you can easily see how they are becoming much greater than themselves. What is to prevent us, too, and all men from becoming greater than ourselves? I didn't need to see fascism in the East to know that fascism can happen anywhere; now that I have seen resurrection in the East, I believe that resurrection can happen anywhere.

IV

The Parable of the Backward Deer

ONE of the most momentous things that happened to me in the East was a certain dinner party with some Indian friends in New Delhi in 1944. It was momentous for three reasons. First, it crystallized a trend in the development of my own ideas, produced over the course of several months by a kind of cultural osmosis, the unconscious absorption of Oriental influences through seemingly trivial contacts. Second, it shed new light for me on a chronic misunderstanding between West and East. Third, it produced what seemed to me the most valid and significant critique of the Western science-god that I had ever heard.

Momentousness began as table-talk. An intellectual and rather prim young Hindu woman sitting next to me said that she thought it was difficult for Indians to understand Americans, and *vice versa*, because India was the most idealistic nation in the world and America the most materialistic.

This contrast of some foreign speaker's national idealism with American materialism was an old friend. I had heard it often enough in Europe and had come to dislike it intensely, not on nationalistic but on semantic grounds. Idealism and materialism are not only treacherous but particularly woolly abstractions, so that arguments on this subject lack the value that some discussions of abstractions have — that of telling a good deal about the attitudes of the speakers toward what they believe they are discussing. Usually when a Frenchman disapproved of American materialism it meant that he resented the failure of most Americans to appreciate the idealism of French aperitifs instead of cocktails, to hide their money under the bed instead of investing it in sordid things like stocks, or to wax enthusiastic about the political ideology of the speaker. In England, American material-ism was our failure to appreciate the superiority of lichen-crusted piracies over fresh ones. In Germany it was not understanding the idealism of clubbing Jews, and so on in each country, until you got to the Russians, who refused to admit that America as a capitalist nation could achieve anything so idealistic as material-ism.

I pointed out all this to my adversary, who I suspected was a volunteer social worker in public life, and called upon her to de-fine her terms. This challenge aroused the interest of the whole table — Indians are very fond of defining terms, provided it is not required to define them concretely — and a lively general dis-cussion developed. All of the usual clichés emerged, from the Almighty Dollar to the Slave of the Machine, and one by one I dissected them, showing that they were meaningless in terms of anything tangible, or that they had no relation to anything that could reasonably be termed materialism and idealism, or that they could be turned around and applied with equal justification to both Indian and American culture.

It was clear after a few minutes' conversation that most of these Indians equated idealism with religion in their minds, and considered America materialistic because — in comparison with India — it was nonreligious. I finally got most of them to admit this, and even to admit that the orthodox Hindu brand of religion included a good many sordidly 'materialistic' elements. As the mist began to lift, the Indian side counterattacked and got in several telling shots. The most telling was scored by a young doctor who had studied medicine in an English school and had once made a brief visit to the United States.

'I share your dislike of vague abstractions,' he began, 'but I wonder if you realize some of the curious and almost paradoxical errors into which your countrymen frequently fall in their search for the concrete, the real, and the practical?

'Let me give you an example — I think it is an important and tragic example of the error in American thinking which causes American idealism to be misunderstood by the rest of the world and by Americans themselves: Mr. Henry Wallace once made a speech around the symbol of a quart of milk a day for everyone in the world. There was a very noble and idealistic and rational intent behind this speech — Mr. Wallace was reminding his countrymen that there were millions of human beings in the world who cannot afford to drink a quart of milk a day, who are undernourished because they are economically underprivileged. He was urging a world-program of economic reform aimed at attaining a minimal good-nutrition standard for the forgotten men of all nations.

'The symbol of the quart of milk seems at first glance a vivid and effective piece of shorthand, summarizing this program. Here, you say, is no empty abstraction, but something real, something tangible, something practical — a quart of milk. At the same time something noble and idealistic — the milk of human kindness.

'But wait. It is not a real quart of milk after all, not in the sense that Ghandiji's spinning-wheel is a real machine that the peasant can use. From the viewpoint of dietetics it is not at all sure that a quart of milk is the ideal supplement to the marginal or submarginal diet. Certainly, it would be no help to the Eskimos, nor to the tribes in Mongolia and Central Asia who already live on mare's milk. From an economic point of view I suspect that increasing the world's milk supply so as to provide a quart — or even a pint — for every human being on the globe would be one of the slowest and most expensive methods of raising standards of nutrition. Thus, Mr. Wallace's milk is only a loose metaphor, standing probably for whatever foods the poorest classes in each country need to raise them to the standard of health and well-being of an American whose food-budget is such that he can afford a quart of milk a day in addition to the other things he eats.

'Health and well-being, I said. Surely, I don't need to remind you how tricky and relative those terms are. Ghandiji, who does drink a good deal of milk but lives in general on what the average American would consider a starvation diet, is far healthier than most Americans of his age. If Mr. Wallace had meant that everyone in the world should have the same age-height-weight ratio as the average upper-class American, then his symbol would not have been noble at all, just stupid and chauvinistic.

'From what I remember of Mr. Wallace's speech he did not mean that. I believe that at the back of his mind was the image of the stunted man — the man who because of chronic undernourishment cannot be physically, emotionally, intellectually, or morally a man in the full sense of the word. The being whose human capacities are undeveloped, dwarfed, or distorted because of poverty experienced physiologically as undernourishment. I think Mr. Wallace was contrasting the abundant American man with the stunted man in the poorer countries of the world and, like a good farmer, expressing his horror at this miserable crop of humanity, calling for a reform of the economic causes of this poor growth of man, so that it might become a full growth.

'If I am right, then I agree with Mr. Wallace. I think there are other things besides undernourishment which are stunting the growth of man, but undernourishment is certainly one of them and I consider it a typical and very admirable expression of American idealism to work for the enrichment of man by trying to eliminate the economic causes of his poverty.

'The trouble is, Mr. Wallace did not say that was what he was trying to do. He implied it, but he did not say it. What he actually said was something about a quart of milk. What do I as a poor, ignorant Hindu conclude? I conclude that Mr. Wallace is an idol-worshiper. He worships a bottle of milk. That is not an evil idol, it is a rather kindly one, but it is still an idol. Who am I to condemn it, though? Enough Indians worship the cow.

'I think you are all idol-worshipers — except when you are devil-worshipers. Mr. Roosevelt is an idol-worshiper. He worships something called the Four Freedoms — among which I look in vain for the freedom of the Indian people from British rule. Wilson was an idol-worshiper. He worshiped plebiscites, thinking they were justice.

'It is because you are idol-worshipers that you are materialists. Your national idol is not Mammon. It is Anything. It is an abstraction like progress, a legal or political formula like democracy, or a concrete object like a machine or a bottle of milk, which dazzles you by its realness so that you are blinded to its unreality or inaccuracy as a metaphor. It is a symbol of your real beliefs and emotional goals which never quite expresses them, which leads toward meaning but falls slightly short, condemning you to the peculiar frustration of those whose clothes almost, but never quite, fit.'

'What you say is a new thought to me,' I replied, 'but I think I agree. Let me rephrase your idea to see if I have it right. You believe that there is an American materialism, something that may be called materialism, but that it is not a philosophy or a special attitude toward matter. You see it rather as a deficiency of meaning in American life, a consistent pattern of frustration in American society, so that we never achieve exactly what we hoped to achieve, or obtain what we hope to obtain. Our achievements and our possessions always seem a little empty and mechanical to us because they are only mechanical realizations of our dreams which fail to express the full meaning and implications of these dreams. Thus our young and still slightly inchoate society has the emotional atmosphere of one that is old and run-down, of one where form has stifled content and ritualism has dessicated faith. And this, you think, is the result of a semantic error sufficiently common to be considered one of the intellectual patterns of American culture: A tendency to flee from abstractions into false or inadequate metaphor. Our democracy, for example, is the political expression of a certain ideal of the ennoblement of man; it is difficult to define this ideal in terms which are significant both emotionally and semantically, therefore we use the political machinery designed to implement it as the symbol of the ideal; only we forget that it is a symbol and unconsciously attribute to it the values of the ideal it symbolizes; we pull the lever of the voting-machine expecting somehow that it will produce nobleness and we are disappointed when nothing but votes come out.

'Our materialism, therefore, is the habitual understatement of our ideals, the oversimplification of our goals; our slavery to the machine is our addiction to the verbal use of the machine as a symbol of the social purpose of the machine.'

The doctor agreed that I had correctly interpreted his thought. Throughout our long dialogue the rest of the company had listened attentively — Indians love fine talk — and although some of them looked a little blank at the more esoteric Americana, and several of the ladies had been shocked by the doctor's sneering reference to Hindu cow-worship, these were trivial flaws in the high delight of watching an Indian lasso a foreigner from the West with word-magic. I had no objection to being lassoed. I was ready for the rope-trick if necessary. I have always loved good talk, better than wine, and almost as much as women or adventure, have never encountered too much of it anywhere and seldom enough, except possibly in Paris, and beneath all this word-magic, beneath the fantasy and the sparkle of paradox and the quick sorties from verbal ambush which characterized the doctor's conversational style, it seemed to me that there lay something sober and important which would continue to ferment in my mind long after this dinner was over. As for the doctor, he obviously enjoyed hearing himself talk — I thought a little enviously that if I could talk so well I, too, would think it very fine entertainment to listen to myself — so there seemed no rudeness in converting this dinner party into a lecture by the doctor, with questions from the floor. I achieved this result, after our hostess had, with thoughtful foresight, seated us in comfortable chairs in the living room, by asking him how he explained the weakness in the thought-patterns of American culture which he had pointed out.

He sniffed for a few seconds at this conversational bait, finally accepted it, and gathered himself together for what I suspected he would remember afterwards as one of his best efforts.

'I don't know enough about America to attempt a direct answer to your question,' he said, 'but let me give you some of my views on science, which has a good deal of bearing on the matter we were discussing, since science is the chief tribal god of the Western peoples in our day, and nowhere is the cult of science so intense and at the same time so riddled with superstition as in America.

'I happen to have very strong views about Western science because I have been trained in one of its major disciplines — medicine — so that it is a life-problem as well as a mind-problem to me. My problem is that I am trying desperately to become a quack and I cannot, because of my Western training. It is the tragedy of my life.

'I see you smile. Yet it is not a light matter. It is a very serious thing — for me and for India. I have no right to be a doctor at all. India is too poor to afford doctors — too poor and, I suspect, too ill. Men who have had some medical training are critically needed, but they should be forbidden to practice medicine, just as in a military medical service the chief surgeon of a great hospital or a world-renowned specialist would never be allowed to serve in a field dressing station.

'What India needs is not doctors but public health officials, research workers, and, above all, instructors, who would train hundreds of thousands of nurses, midwives, vaccinators, dieticians, sanitary inspectors, and other types of medical technicians. Only these technicians would ever practice medicine, if I had my way. They would distribute atabrine, give smallpox vaccinations, possibly cholera-shots in serious epidemics. If we could afford penicillin and if there were no serious immunological risks — I am a little dubious on both counts — then these medical workers would be instructed to give certain standardized doses of penicillin to anyone who appeared to be seriously ill with symptoms suggesting an infectious origin or complications. Thousands would be killed, and millions probably not benefited, but hundreds of thousands would be saved annually.

'If the goal of medicine is to save lives then my system or something comparable to it is the best answer to India's medical problems. Considering the low national income, the high illiteracy, the difficulties of transportation, the time required to train qualified physicians, the small number of patients any doctor can treat directly, and the personnel available for the recruitment of physicians and medical technicians, then this system offers the greatest possible return in lives saved per rupee of national income invested in medicine.

'That is, it does if you must stay within the bounds of orthodox medicine. Personally, I think that the real hope of India is quackery. From the point of view of social medicine, the quacks of India — the Ayurvedic physicians, the nature-faddists, the tribal medicine-man and the village herb-healer — represent the greatest potential source of medical personnel immediately available. If some way could be found of indoctrinating these people in some of the rudiments of Western medicine without doing violence to their prejudices and superstitions, if for instance they could be persuaded to mix effective doses of atabrine or sulfaguanidine with their herb and cow-dung pellets — then, again, hundreds of thousands of lives might be saved.

'Research in quackery is perhaps even more important. Don't imagine that I am one of those Ayurvedic enthusiasts who try to treat syphilis with a pill, or cholera with an infusion of herbs — or typhoid with mudpacks like Ghandiji treated his son — but it is quite possible that some of the Ayurvedic or other traditional remedies have real and beneficial therapeutic effects even if none is an authentic cure for any serious disease. This possibility should be thoroughly explored, along with the possibilities of primitive dietary, physiotherapathic and similar treatments, if only as palliatives. A treatment that the Indian peasant can afford, understand, and believe in, even if it saves life or shortens illness in only one case out of a hundred, will accomplish more good than an effective Western remedy which cannot reach the Indian masses within less than two generations.

'Probably the greatest service I could render to India would be to engage in the kind of research I have mentioned. My duty is clearly to become a quack, but my Western training will not allow me to fulfill my duty. My mind recoils from duty. I go on treating my patients the way a strangler goes on strangling — because it seems the thing to do. I try to salve my conscience by telling myself that the kind of empirical quackery which I think India needs would not pay for itself in the end, because it would retard the development of scientific medicine. In my heart I fear that this is a lie, that I am simply an idol-worshiper like your Mr. Wallace, and that I am sacrificing my countrymen in the interests of an idol called Scientific Medicine.

'Excuse this long digression. But it isn't really a digression, you see. I am trying to show that Western medicine, which is assumed to be universal, does not fit the context of present-day India. It isn't that a Western drug will not kill an Indian germ or that an Indian symptom cannot be diagnosed by a Western technique. It is the Western concepts of the social role of the physician and the patient, even the concepts of disease and cure, which do not fit the Indian context.

'Perhaps that only proves that nothing, not even science, has any validity apart from its cultural and social context. I am too much a man of the West to admit that. I say that if medicine had a real context in any culture, it could easily be adapted to the conditions of any other. The trouble is that even in the societies of the West, medicine, like science and technology in general, does not know what is its context.

'Physicians, scientists of all kinds, inventors, engineers are not trying to solve the problems of man, they are trying to solve problems, period. They are trying to solve the problems conventionally assigned to their respective disciplines or specialties. They rarely ask themselves who assigned these problems or why. If they did, they would find the answer in most cases was: Historical accident.'

'What you say is not true of the social sciences,' I interjected.

'Let us say it is less true,' the doctor replied. 'Like all generalizations, mine has many exceptions to it. You may say for instance that the research carried on in the United States and other Western countries into the causes of cancer, arthritis, and heart disease, has a perfectly clear and reasonable context. So it has, but this context is an arbitrarily limited one. I consider it quite

likely that the same effort put into a comprehensive investigation
of the psychosomatic conditions and effects of modern life would
be more useful. Disease is an abstraction. In nature there is no
such thing as disease. There are merely successes and failures in
adaptation to environment, including chemical and bacteriological environment. The task of medicine, as I see it, should be to
facilitate the physiological adaptation of man to his environment.
Surgeons should spend less time perfecting the techniques of
operating on rare brain-tumors and help automotive engineers
design cars which would reduce the death toll from one of the
deadliest American diseases: Motor-accidents. Heart specialists
should go into commercial offices and try to discover what "over-
work" is. That is another American disease.

'I admit that Western science eventually gets around to such
problems and that the science of the adaptation of man to his
environment is, bit by bit,. beginning to take shape. Don't you
see, though, that there is always a terrible lag between a discovery
or an invention and the full realization of its social, biological,
cultural, and other implications? The discovery that any particular truth has a wider context than that within which it was made
is always the last discovery of Western science.

'The lag between discovery and full context is often catastrophic. Less in medicine, perhaps, than in most sciences, but
bad enough even here. It is perhaps most pronounced in agron-
omy and agricultural technology. You invent the plow and the
power-tractor and discover you are losing your topsoil through
erosion so you feverishly set to work to devise ways of checking
erosion and almost, but never quite, succeed. You reach a point
of equilibrium where the determinant factor may be a new and
ironic element in the balance of life — the struggle for survival
between present-day man and his descendants. You may find
that you will have to eat less so that your grandchildren may eat
at all.

'You invent chemical fertilizers to restore the fertility of the
soil, then you discover you are turning it acid and have to invent
the use of lime to restore the balance. You invent sprays to kill

insects which are damaging crops and find that sprays are also killing the bees which pollinize your crops, possibly the bacteria on which the growth of the soil depends.

'Probably you will get out of that particular hole somehow, but the means that gets you out will almost certainly put you in another. It is what your GI's would call a rat-race. And the stakes are mounting all the time as the population of the world increases on the assumption that science and industry can solve anything.

'All Western science and Western technology is a rat-race between discovery and disaster. This rat-race you call progress.

'Since we are now in the midst of the most terrible war the world has ever known, I shall not insult your intelligence by pointing out the consequences of the lag between progress in political organization among the Western nations and progress in the military applications of science and technology. Nor shall I waste much breath answering the puerile argument that science — meaning both individual scientists and the cult of science in Western societies — is not to blame because man misuses the discoveries of science. If I run over a child with my car while I am speeding to the bedside of another child, the judge doesn't pat me on the head and say it was noble of me to be in such a hurry to heal the sick.

'My real point is something else and I shall try to make it in reverse, so to speak. You in the West look down upon the backward nations of the Orient. You smile pityingly at our obsession with religion. You are amazed that we have made so little technological progress in the last three thousand years and you are impatient with us because even now we are so slow to accept the offerings of Western science and technology — all except the Japanese, as you may have noticed.

'You think you have nothing to learn from us because even our great specialty, religion, is obviously worm-eaten with superstition. As for politics, we were no closer to discovering democracy than we were to discovering the steam-engine, until you came to civilize us. Despite our traditions of nonviolence and respect for life we have probably had as many wars as you in the West have had. Oh, we are poor benighted heathen, no doubt about it.

'But look closer. Since we did not have sufficient intelligence
to devise ways of making peace permanent among all the peoples
of the Orient, wasn't it clever of us to be so stupid that we never
invented really effective ways of killing one another? Since our
political structures never evolved beyond the gunpowder-stage of
culture wasn't it brilliant of us to halt our military technology at
the gunpowder stage, too? You in the West — what is the level
of your foreign relations? The crossbow stage? No, you have
regressed below that. When your technology was at the crossbow stage you had the rules of the chivalry, you had the Truce of
God, you had the semipolitical concept of Christendom, you had
the Church, also as a semipolitical international authority, all
these institutions being more effective than your present international law and your League of Nations. Was it wise and progressive of you to develop your technological institutions when your
institutions of interstate pacification were decaying?

'Laugh, if you like. Call it accident that our backwardness has
preserved us from the horrors of modern war — or would have,
except for your kindly tutelage. Of course it is accident. The
same kind of accident, or a series of similar accidents throughout
thousands of years, has peopled our jungles with great herds of
deer, a most stupid and backward animal. Just think: Since the
dawn of time — of mammalian time — these benighted creatures
have been the prey of tiger, of leopard, and of panther. And they
have never done anything about it. Their survival is due to a
series of accidents: Their ability to live on the grass and shoots
which grow in abundance in the jungle, their keen hearing and
sense of smell, the swiftness of their legs, the speed with which
they reproduce compared with their enemies. A different series
of accidents caused the dinosaur to become extinct — because he
ceased to be adapted to his environment.

'Suppose the deer had possessed science and technology. Suppose the leading deer biologist of some past age had discovered
that the large cats were the chief cause of premature mortality
among deerkind and had called for a crusade against them, saying, "It is for our tigerologists, our leopardologists, and our

pantherologists to study the habits and vulnerabilities of these beasts; for our technicians to develop better means of defense and attack than those which Nature provided us."

'Suppose that after many years of research and many failures, a deer reptologist discovered by accident that young deer fed on a diet of shed snakeskins developed venom-glands in their heads, and a technician in the employ of a large antler-firm invented a method for causing the venom from these glands to run to the sharp tips of the antlers when the head was lowered in attack.

'If the deer had made such a discovery, within a few generations the race of large cats would have become extinct. In two or three generations more the deer would have become extinct, too, because their scientists in concentrating upon the problem of the carnivora would have neglected a social problem frequently denounced by the more high-minded deer moralists, but never eradicated: The quarrels among male deer induced by sexual competition. With their venom-tipped antlers the male deer would have exterminated all the breeding sires of the stock as effectively as they had exterminated the tigers and the leopards.

'Don't you see that there is a cultural balance in society as well as a biological balance in nature? That man is an essential part of the environment of man and that intertribal relationships are one of the keys of his biological adaptation?

'Then don't you see further that there must be an intimate relationship, a vital equilibrium between such phases of man's intellectual activity as science and technology and all the other phases of his life, his social, cultural, and personal emotional life? That the growth of any activity of life beyond the ability of the other activities to keep up with it is not progress, but merely disequilibrium?

'You know that no discovery, no invention ever occurs in a void. All science, all technology, all art, and all politics are part of a social heritage and related to the social, emotional, economic, or other needs or problems of a particular society at a given time. The trouble is that you think it suffices for science and technology to solve any problem, meet any need, deep or superficial, long-term or temporary, real or imaginary.

'You cannot bring yourselves to admit that a given scientific advance may raise more problems than it solves, though you have seen this happen often enough. Science is your god, it is always good — even when it is bad. It is the best thing of all, you think, because it can answer the problems of all other human activities. Therefore you concentrate more and more upon science and you neglect to develop the other aspects of your culture. In so doing you have upset the cultural balance and what you now have is not progress, but gigantism.

'Other societies in other ages have withered or disintegrated because of similar cultural disequilibria within them. It was not science they overdeveloped but militarism, or legalism, or religion, like us Hindus, or almost anything. The cause has always been the same: Some value, through historical accident, has acquired disproportionate weight, some human activity has been considered too noble or too useful, some class of men connected with it has been overvalued and become drunk on privilege.

'I don't know when this disequilibrium developed in your society but it was whenever the average man ceased questioning the results and aims of science and began to believe that science could do no wrong. I am sure it is growing on you now like a terrible malignancy.'

After allowing the doctor to pause in order to breathe, I spurred him on with a new question.

'I thought at first you were just making an argument for the social control of science,' I said, 'but it seems to me you have gone beyond that. If you are right, it would seem that even the subordination of science to the needs of a worldwide society — assuming one can be established — would hardly suffice. What remedy do you propose then, doctor — a moratorium on scientific research? The mass extermination of scientists?'

'Much as I sympathize with both of those proposals, I fear they are impractical,' he replied. 'The thing has gone too far for such methods. You can't survive without science, or even with less science. You need science to save you from the effects of science. As a matter of fact, the scientists themselves are no

longer the chief upholders of idolatrous science-worship. They
are at least getting confused and confusion is often the beginning
of wisdom. More and more of them are beginning to develop a
social conscience — perhaps even a biological conscience, which is
more surprising. A number of modern physicians and modern
agronomists seem to be tending toward a kind of agnostic humility
with regard to the processes òf nature which, at least in its results, is not far different from the superstitious nature-reverence
of the old-fashioned family physician and the old-fashioned gar-
dener. Your physicists are discovering mathematically the unity
of the cosmos which our philosophers discovered mystically.

'The real danger is not from the priests of science but from its
devotees among the masses — and above all from the temple
hangers-on, the capitalist masters of technology who need new
discoveries in order to create new needs, so they can sell new
gadgets, the soldiers and politicians, capitalist and otherwise, who
need science to provide them with the instruments of power.
These, if necessary, will imprison the scientists in their laborato-
ries and make slaves of them — as the feudal barons of Japan
enslaved the emperors — while continuing to prostrate themselves before science in public.'

'So you see no hope for the West whatsoever?'

'Oh, yes, I see a hope, but I was hoping that you would see it
yourself. It is right under your nose, though perhaps I should
not say that because I have noticed that, unlike many Westerners, you do not keep your nose tilted up in the presence of Asiatics.

'Look. We have agreed, haven't we, that the overdevelop-
ment of science has produced a cultural disequilibrium in the
West? You are suffering from an excess of the hormone, scientific
progress. What is the antithetical, the balancing hormone?
Backwardness. Where do you find backwardness? Answer: In
India, China, Asia generally. The disequilibrium of the East —
for I admit that our backwardness has ceased to be clever, that it
is also a disequilibrium — is the cure for the disequilibrium of the
West.'

This time I felt the doctor had finally overreached himself.

'It is a very pretty verbal formula, but how will it work?' I retorted.

'It will work — or it could work — by setting up for you a cultural opposition which functions like the political opposition within your parliamentary systems, acting as a check on the will of the majority and at the same time helping by its criticism to keep the dominant party faithful to its own ideology. If you believe in democracy, then you must believe in cultural as well as political democracy, and you will agree that there can no more be political democracy without the existence of an opposition than there can be cultural democracy without a cultural opposition. If my ideas prevailed, the new Asiatic cultures would owe so much to Western influence that our opposition would be a loyal one — His Cultural Majesty's Loyal Opposition. (Naturally we would expect to be paid for our loyalty.) If, however, the cultural extremes of some Asiatic nationalisms should prevail, that would still do you more good than harm.

'Let me give you an example, borrowed from the field of politics, of how such a cultural opposition would influence Western thought. You remember that at the outbreak of the war in Europe, India — over the protests of most of the Indian leaders — was declared at war with the enemies of His Majesty, the King-Emperor. We were not opposed to entering the war in support of Britain and France against the Axis. We were opposed to not being consulted in the matter, and we wanted assurances that the war-aims of the Allies were in accord with the ideals of the Indian people. You know what happened: We were disregarded, overruled, and overridden and our leaders in the end had no choice but to disassociate themselves from a war in whose justice most of them really believed.

'Suppose India in 1939 had been an independent nation, even a self-governing member of the British Commonwealth. We could not have been forced into war against our will. To gain our support, which was vitally needed, the British government would have been forced to formulate its war-aims and to formulate them in such a way as to appeal to the backward, nonscientific mind of

the Indian peasant, to the abstract, philosophical, deeply religious mind of the Indian Brahmin. The result would have been a
more just war, a more human war, a more religious war. In short,
the kind of war that is easier to fight because it lends itself so
marvelously to psychological warfare — surely a cause which
appealed equally to the cockney worker and the Indian peasant
could not have failed to stir something in the hearts of the German worker and the Japanese peasant — and the kind of war
that makes it possible to create a just and durable peace afterwards.

'It would be the same in cultural affairs if the nations of the
East were free. Some day — a near day, I think — we shall be
free. There will be cultural relations between the East and the
West — closer than at present, I hope — and there will be all
sorts of political and economic matters which have important
cultural implications in which you will need our co-operation.
Since you will no longer be able to win it by force, you will have to
make concessions to our point of view, our backward point of
view. You will be very impatient and annoyed with us, but you
will have to make the concessions anyway, and you will have to
waste a lot of breath explaining things to us that seem self-evident
to you. Sometimes in making these explanations you will be
forced to re-examine your own concepts and re-define your own
terms and you will make important discoveries about your own
culture. There may even be times when we will save you from
yourselves. Suppose some crackpot scientists — more likely
some chemical cartel — were to persuade you to seek an international agreement for spraying every square inch of the globe with
DDT, and suppose some chauvinist Indian demagogue, appealing
to the Hindu prejudice against taking life, even insect life, persuaded the people of India not to sign this agreement, and suppose that in the middle of your arguments to the Indians not to
hold up progress any longer you discovered that the areas where
DDT had already been used were turning into deserts? Wouldn't
you thank God for backwardness?

'Whether you like it or not, the coming political freedom of the

East is going to contribute to restoring the cultural equilibrium, not only between East and West, but within Western society itself. The process will be hastened if you consciously try to practice cultural democracy, if in your zeal to spread the Western gospel of scientific enlightenment throughout the East, you learn to adapt Western science to Eastern conditions, instead of trying to adapt Orientals to science. Science would learn a lot in the process, and not just about the East.'

That was the end of the evening and I thought it was a good end. The accidents of wartime service prevented me from ever seeing the doctor again, but in the next few weeks and months I found my mind repeatedly returning to our conversation. The more I thought about it, the more I felt willing to accept the whole of it, and the less I felt it necessary to discount the Hindu love of paradox and verbalism which — on the doctor's side at least — gave it such a picturesque flavor.

Regarding what I considered the doctor's basic point — the discrepancy between our power to control the forces of nature and our ability to control the social use of these powers — there could be no argument, and I thought it was helpful to think of this discrepancy as a cultural disequilibrium comparable to those biological disequilibria which had filled our dried ocean beds with the fossils of innumerable extinct species.

I agreed, too, with the idea that Asia could act as a 'cultural opposition' to the West and that the more this opposition was recognized by us as being just that, and the more we exploited it consciously, the more likely it was to redress the cultural balance in our society.

I recognized that the processes of cultural opposition in the doctor's bicultural mind had played an essential role in what seemed to me his fruitful approach to the problem of man's survival. In appearance, this was a criticism of the West in Western terms, an autocritique. He was attacking the culture which had produced Darwin for being insufficiently Darwinian, for lacking the humility and imagination to realize that sociology — and all the disciplines of man — had an ultimate biological context, that the final criterion for judging all the institutions of man was whether or not they contributed to the survival of man as an animal species.

In coining the phrase, biological conscience, as applied to a recent trend in Western scientific thought, it seemed to me, however, that the doctor had revealed the Indian and essentially religious background of his Occidental rationalism. Hinduism, without having biology, had a biological conscience, a keen sense of man's citizenship in nature, a zoological as well as a social ideal of fraternity, and a feeling for life as a civic mission accepted from, and discharged on behalf of, some total cosmic community.

It seemed to me that it was the submerged but never stifled opposition of this Hindu mysticism to the doctor's Western rationalism which had produced his sociobiological philosophy, and his awareness of this subjective process which had produced his concept of the East as a cultural opposition to the West. Both views seemed to me the fruit of a prolonged cultural debate within a single mind, and if this were so, it did indeed establish that such debate could be fruitful, and suggest that it might be still more fruitful if it took place between many minds.

In my own mind, I realized, exposure to Eastern influence had certainly operated as a cultural opposition. I could not think of a single Oriental institution, mental or otherwise, which I was prepared to adopt in place of those existing in our own culture. I had discovered many interesting and admirable things in the East; there were, unquestionably, departments of life in which the Eastern peoples surpassed us, but all these specialized achievements were realized at the price of neglecting values which I, as a Westerner, considered more important.

On the other hand, Eastern influence was constantly modifying my original Western view of the world, constantly causing me to question, and ultimately to alter or even reject, certain features of my own cultural heritage and to enrich it, for my personal usage, with new concepts or understandings which were neither Western nor Eastern. Thus, Gandhi's doctrine of nonviolence, perhaps the single most important cultural contribution which modern India had to offer, appeared to me an institution which could not in any way be adapted for transplantation into Western society, yet it had played a vital role in awakening me to the importance of institutional delusion in our lives and in leading me to the view that much, if not most, of Western violence was the clash of group-delusions rather than of group-ideals.

The great lesson from all this, I thought, was not so much that East was superior to West in some respects — and West superior to East in others — but that cultural exchange was superior to cultural monopoly, cultural debate to cultural monologue.

I remained too incorrigibly Western to attach great value to the backwardness of Asia as a brake on our ill-regulated progress, but the doctor had succeeded in making me take a more tolerant view of Asiatic backwardness. I was ready to admit that the technological backwardness of Asia might be intricately mixed up with values of great importance to us, and was thus inclined to excuse it, as one excuses the muscular flabbiness of a mental athlete. Before that talk I had been trying to prove to myself that the backwardness of the East was not incorrigible. Now I was ready to be shown that it did not in all ways require correction.

One result of this change was that I began at last to take a serious interest in the religions of the East, looking upon them not merely as supplying information about the Eastern mind but as something of possible intrinsic value.

PART V

A Quiet Visit with the Gods

I

The Syntax of the Soul

I DID NOT progress very fast with my attempts to study the values of Eastern religion — in fact, it was not until I was leaving India for Ceylon that I saw any light at all.

I read some books about Hinduism and Buddhism but they did not seem to tell me anything about religion that made sense to me. This was not surprising since I had read a number of books about Christianity and they had not made any sense to me, either. Like Stuart Chase, I had never been able to find any meaning in either theology or the higher philosophy, to me as to him they had always been a series of blabs.

Of course there were many intelligible and moving passages in all philosophical or religious books. Plato on the virtues of a good vintage hemlock was clear, if queer. The Sermon on The Mount was clear, the Book of Ecclesiastes was clear, and much of the Epistles of Saint Paul was at least as clear as *Finnegan's Wake*.

There were clear passages in the Buddhist and Hindu sacred writings, too. The Buddhist statement — perhaps the most important one — that 'hatred is not ceased by hatred at any time; hatred ceases by love' — is not only clear but verifiable. The *Upanishads*, the ultimate source of much later Hindu and Buddhist philosophy, seemed to contain many clear statements about man's awareness of the riddle of terrestrial existence and to suggest rather convincingly the possibility of facing this riddle in an affirmative mood, but there as far as I was concerned they stopped, there blab began.

Perhaps the furthest I could go was to achieve a sense of blab pregnant with meaning, but still undelivered, in the noble credo of Kabir, one of the fifteenth-century apostles of Hindu-Moslem brotherhood: 'The Hindu God lives at Benares; the Moslem God at Mecca. But He who made the world lives not in a city made by hands. There is one Father of Hindu and Moslem, one God in all matter.'

Kabir's God seemed an important blab, almost a piercing blab, but still blab. So did the God of our Christian fathers, so did the Moslem Allah, and the Hindu Brahma, whether called the Absolute, the Great Within, or what not; so for that matter did such terms as Heaven, Hell, Nirvana, soul, Atman, grace, original sin, predestination, free will, oversoul, transcendent ego, creative evolution, and dialectical materialism.

Though I had been brought up in the Roman Catholic faith, this, and all religious faith, had faded away in early adolescence without any particular storm and stress and I had never felt a sense of loss because of it. Neither did I feel any sense of inferiority about the failure of my mind to register meaning when confronted with metaphysical abstractions of any kind. Without having quite the same hearty conviction on this score that many of the professional semanticists seem to have, I was inclined to share their view that the metaphysical philosophers no more knew what they were talking about than I did.

The war had not changed me. Though I had not spent much time in foxholes, such time as I had spent in them had left me as much an atheist as ever, but my atheism was a very negative, undoctrinaire type, characteristic of our age, a vague no-religion differing only in vocabulary from the equally vague and negative belief of most nominal believers. My indifference to religion as a personal possession was so deep that I did not resent the belief of others; in comparison with some of the more modern intellectual fads, religion did not even seem to me a serious menace to rational thought.

I realized that even religious superstitions had some positive cultural value, especially, as the anthropologists have shown, in rather primitive societies. Religious myths might generate need-less anxieties among believers, but some psychiatrists believed that in our own society in earlier times they had released more anxiety than they had generated, and a reasonable case could be made for the argument that if we cannot relax our sexual morals, then it would make us healthier to tighten our religious beliefs.

As I stumbled around in the unfamiliar Eastern variety of re-ligious verbal fog, one new aspect of religion occurred to me, giv-ing to the subject the kind of distasteful utilitarian interest which a sophisticated churchman might discover in the Freudian soul-economics.

We, the unbelievers of this age, had been too hasty in crossing off religion as a preoccupation worthy of the adult mind, I felt forced to admit. In our deepest minds we were all, even the sturdiest atheists among us, much closer to religious myth than we liked to think. In discarding conscious myth we had neglected to readjust the attitudes which our culture had based upon myth.

For instance, we had discarded belief in soul — to the extent that we no longer understood even what the word meant — but we retained the contemptuous early Christian attitude toward dust, the dust which was all of man that remained when soul had departed. Perhaps we even retained some of the Christian con-tempt for the flesh compounded of dust, secretly despised our unique instrument for living, so that not only the end of life seemed mean and almost ignominous to us, but the whole experi-ence of living seemed a paltry one. The Christian, indeed, called it paltry, but it was not so to him, because it was a necessary prelude to the transcendent glory and transcendent meaning of the life to come. We dreaded the worm, and thinking of ourselves as worm-fodder lowered our sense of our own dignity.

The Hindus and the Buddhists, I noticed, were much less both-ered than we by the problem of Great Caesar's clay. That it should become a windbreak seemed no great irony to them, and not at all pathetic. Clay, as clay, was just as admirable, just as godlike as Caesar, and probably a great deal more useful to the cosmos; clay, like dust, was one of the mineral aspects of God.

Indian philosophy was not uniformly monist, as far as I could make out, but the popular pantheism or pluralism was even less inclined to sneer at dust, and even the dualist trend of some Buddhist thought did not contrast matter and spirit but illusion and reality. Neither the Hindu nor the Buddhist had ever possessed the Christian concepts of spirit and matter; soul — in so far as the fuzziness of language made comparison possible — was something quite different to them than what it was to us.

There were, I discovered, six orthodox schools of Hindu philosophy plus numerous heretical ones. One of these schools, known as the Mimamsa school, appeared to be mainly a rationalization of popular Hindu polytheism, which hinges around the worship of the Hindu trinity, Brahma, Vishnu, and Siva, and the lesser gods and goddesses like Kali. Another one, the yoga system, was a discipline of psychosomatic exercises and ethical training without any explicit metaphysical content. The other four schools included views that ranged from atheism to monotheism, from a clear-cut dualism of spirit and matter to the absolute monism of the Vedanta system which is usually identified with philosophic Hinduism in the Western mind. This system might be most concisely summarized by saying that there is one soul — the Atman — which pervades everything in the universe. The orthodoxy of these six philosophies arises from their claim to be based upon the *Vedas*, but it seemed to me that there were still deeper common denominators among them. All, as far as I could see, had influenced modern Hindu thought and their irreconcilable theoretical differences were somehow mystically reconciled in the Hindu mind.

Buddhism was slightly less complicated, I found. It had only two major divisions — the Hinayana philosophy of Southeast Asia, and the Mahayana philosophy of Japan, China, and Tibet — each composed of two minor schools. The Mahayana Buddhism was the more transcendent of the two and seemed to include at times the worship of the Buddha as a personal God. The Hinayana Buddhism in its popular forms closely resembled popular Hinduism and sometimes borrowed the Hindu deities as objects of reverence, but in its classic form it seemed to me merely a cautious, agnostic, and more realist Hinduism. It differed from Hinduism in its greater emphasis upon ethics, particularly its insistence upon nonviolence and selflessness, in its compassionate attitude toward human suffering and in its gloomy view that life is a sorrowful illusion from which the release is Nirvana, an indeterminate mixture of bliss and nothingness.

Many Hinayana Buddhists, like some Hindus, seemed to be almost materialists. It was impossible to tell whether they believe in soul or not. All one could say was that, in so far as Buddhists believed in soul, they thought of it in terms of the Hindu Atman, as something all-pervading and therefore a bridge between the personal within and the cosmic without. Both Hindus and Buddhists believed, with varying nuances of philosophic emphasis, in reincarnation governed by the law of karma and both considered that the spiritual goal of individual life was to work out one's karma completely so as to be freed from further reincarnation.

The Hindu or Buddhist of any school turned scientific materialist was quite different from the scientific materialist of the West (as my conversation with the doctor had revealed). To him we seemed both puerile and dejected materialists, just as even the most uncompromising Eastern materialism seemed refreshingly idealistic to me.

The really dominant philosophy of the West in our day, I concluded, was not materialism; it was 'nothingbutism' — the peculiar attitude of those, who having been taught that spirit is everything and matter nothing, later discover there is nothing but matter; of those who, having been taught that sex is the most base of human activities, later discover that it is really the most basic, so that the early Freudians could say religion itself was nothing but repressed sexuality.

Our nothingbutism was the inverted religion of those whose fathers believed that God had fashioned the universe in much the same manner that man fashions a clock, whereas they, the sons, could imagine no better explanation for the clock's existence than that its parts had somehow fallen together by accident (and they suspected the whole machine would some day run down, as all clocks do).

This clock-complex of ours, imprisoning our thoughts between the forbidding walls of accident and entropy, is always a gloom-spot in current Western philosophy, but Eastern minds throughout the ages have wandered freely over the same speculative field without bitterness or despair.

In the fresh vedic dawn of Hindu religious consciousness the authors of the much-admired *Song of Creation* looked out upon the universe, broodingly, as Nehru says, but more in awe than in despondency, and, referring the why and the how to an unnamed abstraction, contented themselves with the sober alternatives: He verily knows it, or perhaps He knows it not. Divine purpose and cosmic accident can hardly have seemed mutually exclusive to minds like these, one would seem as thrilling or awe-inspiring as the other, and though I never encountered the bald statement in my own readings, it would not surprise me to learn that some Eastern philosopher has proclaimed accident as the most divine feature of the universe.

As for the clock running down, that has always seemed quite the finest and most significant thing about it to the Buddhists. Nirvana is their goal, and while a number of Buddhists seemed almost as puzzled as I was by the meaning of Nirvana, unable to agree on how literal a nothingness it was, it seemed reasonably clear that in their philosophy this absolute-or-relative nothing-ness was a cosmic as well as a personal goal.

Buddhism, like Christianity, takes a gloomy view of the present and a bright view of the future, but for entirely different reasons. Tomorrow and tomorrow and tomorrow creeps into the Buddhist's petty pace as it does into our own, but his yesterdays have not lighted fools the way to dusty death, they have guided sages to bright Nirvana. Life is full of sound and fury, signifying nothing, but it is not just a tale told by an idiot, precisely because the rest is silence. That silence, to the Buddhist, is the most golden music.

I cannot recall having met in the East a former Buddhist converted to total nonreligiousness — since Buddhist belief can be
adjusted so easily to almost any hypothesis of science, there is
hardly any reason, except sheer contrariness, for a Buddhist to
become an unbeliever — but if such a creature exists his mentality must be very different from that of a Western materialist.
Doubtless the ex-Buddhist would carry over into materialism a
slightly contemptuous nothing-but attitude.

What is liberation from illusion? he would exclaim, why, it is
nothing but understood reality.   What is the extinction of consciousness? why, it is nothing but unconsciousness.   What is accident? why, it is nothing but happening.   What is a machine? why,
it is nothing but a creation.   What is dust? why, it is nothing but
life unassembled.

If Western scientists ever succeed in manufacturing life in a
test tube — a feat which would probably have the most disastrous
psychological repercussions at our present cultural level — the
Hindu and Buddhist East will take the affair quite calmly.

'What is so remarkable about that?', one Hindu sect will ask.
Life always starts somewhere, why not in a test tube?   Still, perhaps it is a progress — if these Westerners get sufficiently fascinated by their new game of making life they won't have so much
time left for killing.

It wasn't there yesterday and it won't be there tomorrow, the
Hinayana Buddhist of Southeast Asia will probably say.   One
illusion more or less . . . what does it matter?

The Mahayana Buddhist of the Far East, remembering the
words of the Japanese Enkaku-Sho, quoted by Lafcadio Hearn
(that never sufficiently marveled at ugly duckling of American
culture) — 'When every phase of our mind shall be in accord
with the mind of Buddha — then there will not be even one parti-
cle of dust that does not enter into Buddhahood' — will doubtless
exclaim: Nirvana is just around the corner.

And high up in the Himalayas some holy hermit, wandering
into a village to beg, will hear the news over the radio and fall into
a rapturous swoon.   Don't you see, he will explain to his disciples

when he recovers consciousness, these yogis of the West have made life-cells in a tube of glass. Tomorrow they will be able to make men, the day after, gods. The gods will make higher gods, the higher gods Brahma, Brahma a super-Brahma, and so on.

I cannot guarantee the plausibility of these imagined Asiatic reactions to an hypothetical event and perhaps I owe the reader, especially the Eastern reader, an apology for treating grave matters so irreverently, but it seems to me that both the fantasy and the irreverence are necessary to bring clearly to light the underlying puerility of the Western nothingbutist attitude, fatal alike to the cult of God and the cult of man.

Until I began to take an interest in Eastern religions I had never realized what deep roots the nothingbutist philosophy had in the culture of our age. I have always had an interest in living and a kind of inarticulate, embryonic reverence for the marvel of human aliveness, a reverence which has tended to grow as I grow older, but having a nonphilosophical mind and caring little for all these whys and whences and whatabouts, I had never realized how much it was unconsciously inhibited by vestigial theological attitudes, or rather by the conflict between these and the materialist credo to which I generally subscribed.

William James, I remembered, had exposed and vigorously combated the nothingbutist philosophy of his day — as had many others, before and since — but now James was relegated to the intellectual Nirvana of academic philosophy, and since his time the cultural battleground had shifted. It was no longer the conflict between religious myth and the objective results of science which was the main source of nothingbutism, but the attack launched by Freud on the subjective roots of religion, on what James had termed the religious experience.

Now Freud, too, was gone, condemned perhaps to a worse fate than James, to endless cycles of reincarnation as myth, and the great danger was not that his extravagances and crudities would go unrevised, but that the tools for man's deliverance forged by his mighty brain would eventually fall into bits of rust because someone had raised the hasty and implacable intellectual haro of our culture: Freud is out-of-date (as his disciples, among others, had raised it against religion).

Freud was not out-of-date, I reflected, any more than was James. What was out-of-date was the American society which had produced James and the Viennese society which had produced Freud. It was the Blu? Danube ideal of man's emotional life, the prewar bourgeois conception of the individual's role in society, the Dual-Monarchy pattern of personality-structure, which were out of date. Freud's discipline remained, but its implicit metaphysical goals have passed away with the Hapsburgs, as James's psychology had gone out with the Mauve Decade.

No doubt much the same thing can be said of religion itself. The impression many of us have that religious discipline, the religious experience, are anachronistic, may be due in part to the fact that the only religious idiom available to us is an archaic one, no longer suited to either our emotional or our intellectual requirements. Since in all other matters we usually believe what we want to believe, regardless of logic or evidence, the fact that we are so alert to religious superstition suggests that we have not so much repudiated religion as we have become bored with it, and to the extent that this is true it is the fault of religion itself. Nor can the modernizing of religious ritual help much if it is the basic emotional relationship between the Christian and his God which is archaic.

Again, it seemed to me that we had got ourselves tied up in a knot of our own making. Just as the East seemed immune to the psychic malady of nothingbutism, it seemed less concerned than we about the emotional archaicness of religion. Superstition, yes, that was even more of a religious problem in the East than in the West, but not emotional irrelevance. Though it is the kind of sweeping generalization of which one should beware, it seemed to me that on the whole the educated Hindu or the Buddhist — or even the Moslem — had less trouble in adjusting his religion to an expanding intellectual horizon and a critical sense sharpened by Western realism than we did in adjusting to cultural change within our own society.

Looking at modern Christianity with an outsider's eye, and with some Oriental perspective, it seemed to me that organized religion in the West tended to neglect certain vital elements in the religious frame of reference. Though every religion is implicitly or explicitly a brotherhood, this cardinal fact of brotherhood seems to receive little attention. The emphasis is upon the believer's relationship with God, either directly or through the authorities of the Church. The duty of loving the neighbor, of loving mankind in general, as a prerequisite to successful relationship with the Deity, is brought out, and a few elementary rules — mostly negative — of social duty and interpersonal relationships, are laid down. There is little conscious effort to use the church itself as a school for personal relations and the religious community as a gymnasium of social aptitude.

Consequently, religion contributes very little positive guidance to the believer in what are probably the major problems of his life, and fails to exploit the most significant personal sources of religious dynamism. The modern political religions such as communism, fascism, and nationalism, likewise neglect personal relationships, but the truly religious sense of social participation and purpose which they often give to their adherents shows strikingly the failure of formal religion to keep pace with all the emotional needs of man in our changing culture.

My contact with the followers of Gandhi, all deeply religious even when unbelieving, had awakened me to still another cultural significance of religion. These Indian revolutionaries had impressed me as human personalities, they seemed deeper, more significant, and possessed of a greater capacity for passion than we. The more I reflected upon this the more I was inclined to emphasize in my mind the 'bessemerizing' effect of religion — the way in which it tempered and hardened the individual personality in a given cultural mold — for it seemed to me that our own forefathers, living in an age when religion was an intense cultural reality, had differed from our present Western selves in much the same way that the new Indians do.

The decline of religion in the democratic societies of the West has produced an age of worthy pasteurized personalities, of amiable, meager passions and spiritual premature ejaculations. Our minds have become more adult, but our emotional natures have become childish and our moral values tend toward the infantilism of naughty and nice as polar limits of conduct. The mildly neurotic personality has become the norm and almost the ideal of our society.

The totalitarian societies produce a quite different personality, and however deficient or unpleasant it may seem to us, this personality unquestionably possesses dynamic qualities which ours lack. It is a kind of religious personality and has the power to make converts which we have lost. The emotional ore from which it has been forged seems to us a low-grade one but it does have a certain temper. Our democratic humanitarian ideals seem to us to be of much nobler alloy. The trouble is that we forget to put them in the furnace. There are a number of ways of putting ideals into the furnace, but it is doubtful that there is any way more effective than prayer, the ultimate and most intimate form of propaganda. Since to us prayer has always meant praying to God — or one of his saints — the moment we begin to lose God we cease praying and soon become pasteurized, never to look really vigorous again until the undertaker has gone to work on us with his beauty kit.

The case for considering religion as an intellectually respectable study, for treating religious problems as ones worth adult discussion in an age of scientific enlightenment, was clinched in my mind by a further discovery of such revolutionary simplicity that it seemed incredible I had never thought of it before.

Most of our ancestors were religious-minded men, I reminded myself, and so are nearly all of Asia's millions today. If you count in the Marxists and the nationalists as well as the Christians of the West, it is probably safe to say that nine-tenths of the inhabitants of this planet still believe in some kind of religion. That is not necessarily an argument for having a religion oneself, it is possible to be eccentric and still be right, but this is one of those situations in which it is very wrong to be too right. It is a great disaster to be right when that deprives you of the possibility of communicating with your neighbors and dispossesses you of one of the essential elements in your cultural heritage. It is not enough to be tolerant of people's religious foibles, it is necessary to try to understand them.

That does not mean that one has to accept at their face value all the grotesque and often sinister superstitions of the different creeds. It merely means that when a believer of any kind speaks one should assume that he is talking about something important — something important to the listener as well as the speaker. That goes for a Holy Roller or a Spiritualist or Father Divine. It is bigotry to dismiss Father Divine's religion as a paranoid delusion merely because its leader seems to have the delusion that he is God. There are few phases of man's mental activity into which delusion does not enter; Father Divine's delusion is merely the bad grammar which distorts whatever meaning he is trying to convey and the meaning may be nonetheless important for that.

Driven to the wall by my own logic, I had to admit that even nationalism — in the sense of having a religious feeling about one's country — was an important meaning distorted by the delusion of sovereignty. The hundred per cent American, for instance, can never be totally deluded, provided his nationalism is really based on love of country; at the worst he can be said to possess $\dfrac{130,000,000}{2,000,000,000}$ of the truth about man, and this is not just a mathematical pun. To create one world we must develop the fervor for humanity which the nationalist feels for country, and this fervor must arise from previous psychological experience, it cannot arise in a cultural vacuum. In one sense nationalism may play an indispensable psychological role in educating men for internationalism, and it is only because there is such an imminent danger of the schoolhouse burning down before we have mastered fractions that one is justified in exhibiting some impatience toward the superstitions and delusions of nationalism.

Probably the only total error in the world is the belief in total truth, and categorical attacks upon even this error are often self-defeating. Every pea of truth, including scientific truth, seems to be enclosed in a pod of superstition. Removing the pod without losing the pea has always been the Western mind's most difficult problem, but it hardly seems a problem to the East. The attitude of the Eastern sages toward it — the attitude which I found myself increasingly trying to make my own — seems to be expressible by saying that just as hatred is never ceased by hatred, so superstition is never ceased by unbelief, it ceases by right understanding.

In a few short weeks, I realized, my views about religion had undergone a profound change, yet so far as I could make out, there was one thing which had not changed: The words still had no meaning for me, they were still blabs.

During the trip from Delhi to our new headquarters in Kandy, Ceylon, in the summer of 1944, this problem of the meaning of religious terminology kept recurring to my mind. I had plenty of time to think about it, for I had volunteered to drive one of our detachment's jeeps the two thousand miles to Kandy, in order to broaden my picture of India. The trip, which I made with one friend, took ten days of continuous driving, averaging nearly twelve hours a day, and between turns at the wheel I gazed out wonderingly upon the slowly changing landscapes of India, hypnotically alike in some quality of emptiness more abstract than that of the desert, and let this emptiness fill my mind.

The emptiness of India is for the Westerner itself a kind of religion, a religion dappled with many dark superstitions. Though I knew a little about India by this time, I had forgotten that, had not realized when I set out with my friend that in India one does not just procure a road-map and some gasoline coupons and pile bedrolls and rations and arms into a jeep and start driving. We had planned the trip in a completely happy-go-lucky fashion, not at all as an expedition, pushing our heedlessness so far that when a final check of the car revealed that the tools for changing tires were missing, rather than waste time trying to draw them from the quartermaster in Delhi, we told ourselves cheerfully that no doubt we would be able to pick some up at the air-base in Agra, which was on our way.

By the end of the second day out, this carefree attitude had worn off, not because we had encountered any unforeseen mechanical difficulties, but because near the middle of Gwalior State, as night was falling, we entered a zone of dense delusion, centering around one of those incredibly sinister *dak*-bungalows portrayed in Kipling's horror-tales, the sort of place where you don't worry much about having your throat cut by the sullen-faced bearer because that seems a trivial fate in comparison to what may come to you out of the night.

The next night, at another dak-bungalow in a forlorn village set in the lunar, dry-forest landscape of the Vindhya mountains, it was still worse. Here there were no sinister presences, rather there were the most terrifying absences, concentrations of nothingness beyond imagination, crystallizations of despair unknown outside of insane asylums, and known there only to the most hopeless cases.

I am particularly sensitive to the moods of landscape and weather, quick to convert all somatic changes into psychic experiences, but my companion, a matter-of-fact and professionally rather spinal psychologist, admitted that he likewise felt the successive and varying enchantments which India seemed to lay upon us as we progressed from the rational Aryan north to the emotional, animistic, Dravidian south.

There were curious pockets of disputation where the psychologist and I quarreled fiercely over the choice of melons a peasant was selling by the roadside or over how far we should try to push before nightfall. There was a sort of gorge of mermaids skirting the mountain road leading to Poona that forced one to grip the steering-wheel tightly and constantly shake the hot, lulling wind out of one's eyes to avoid falling asleep on the hairpin turns. In the pass leading up to Bangalore the same awesome, basically antiforeign thunderstorm which had brought me Ram Lal was waiting for us, this time multiplied by mountains.

When real danger threatened or real disaster overtook us, when two punctures in rapid succession used up our one spare tire in the desolate heart of the Deccan between Belgaum and Bangalore, when the ancient and alien city of Madura had no lodging to offer us but a shed in the compound of a motion-picture theater, when the motor of our jeep drowned in the fording of a wide lagoon among the swamps and palm groves of the uttermost southern coast, it seemed a gay adventure. The dust, the heat, and the fatigue; the thirst, the cramping, and the jolting of the jeep over the worst roads in the world — these we hardly noticed after the first two days.

The real strain of the trip was the incessant battle against superstition and depression, both by-products of the loneliness and cultural isolation which grip the white man in India. For hundreds of miles at a stretch we never saw a white face or any visible sign of British occupation; sometimes in quite large towns we had difficulty in finding anyone who spoke a word of English. The thirty words or so of Hindustani we totaled between us were almost as useless as English beyond Gwalior. Despite the warnings which had been given us in Delhi of ambushes and mobs in remote villages, we never encountered a threatening or hostile gesture, hardly a sullen look, yet between us and every native that we saw on the roads or in the towns lay the invisible wall of which I had been so conscious when I first arrived in New Delhi. Faces looked at us curiously, often with kindness, but never quite the way one looks at a brother man. In the coconut villages of the south, where the soft-faced, ivory-yellow women normally expose one or both breasts in front of their own menfolk, I noticed that they always covered themselves as we passed and more than the sensual pleasure of seeing lovely feminine flesh was lost by the gesture.

The psychologist and I were two good friends sharing a good adventure, but we were traveling through a social vacuum, through a void of human presence horribly camouflaged with human appearance, and the worm of doubt gnawed constantly at our pleasure — the primitive and most terrifying of all human doubts, the doubt that any humans ever share anything.

Gradually, as one's eyes refocus in a dimly lighted room, we began to rediscover the comforting imprint of man upon the land-

scape, to adjust ourselves to our moving-jeep culture with its
fleeting but continuous relationship to the rooted cultures of the
Indian countryside, and the hours of our days began to fill, as
man's days should be filled, with gentle alternations of light and
shade.

There were times when the road seemed almost smooth and the
motor hummed a pantheist hymn, when we were filled with a
Whitmanesque sense of surge and cared not if around the next
bend we should be utterly quelled and defeated. There were
shady spots where we stopped to lie and stretch, to drink warm
chlorinated water from our canteens, to bury our faces in succulent breakings of melon, to smoke a windless cigarette, to unfold
our road-map, marveling at the intricate trailing roots of our
southward growth, and to be filled with a sense of purposeful
mission, of difficulties overcome and tasks well-done by good and
faithful servants.

We discovered increasingly the facile tepid charm of the south,
land of dark legend and dark practices to the Indians themselves,
but more accessible than Vedic India to the stranger because its
inhabitants share so readily, so unavoidably, their basic satisfactions: The shade of their enlacing banyan trees, the piercing
green of their rice-fields, their softly swaying coconuts, the communal bathing in tank or stream or canal, which, more than eating
or smoking or dancing, is the great social rite in all the cultures of
Southern Asia.

Above all, we discovered the dawn, perhaps the most blessed of
man's pleasures. We were always up by daybreak, or soon after,
in order to make headway, to enjoy two cool hours of driving and
because we had slept little during the night. Stiff and red-eyed
and cursing, we would pile our gear into the jeep, muttering and
wrangling about where we might hope to get a decent breakfast or
lunch. Then we would start off, the fresh, cool wind would rush
against our faces, the clear light would wash across the fields, we
would begin to pass peasant-carts drawn by patient bullocks, pa-
tiently urged on, and long files of women, swaying graciously beneath the heavy water-jars balanced on their heads, often carry-

ing flowers in their hands and singing the grave, simple, joyous morning hymns to creation with which Hindu religiousness reverences the creation of dawn.

Slowly the realization grew on me that these hymns — and many other experiences of the trip — carried the simple answer to my problem about the meaning of religion. The theologians of every creed piled abstraction upon abstraction, and system upon system, in trying to rationalize their beliefs, but the basic religious terms were not abstractions, were not blabs, they were explicit references to definite psychological realities, to perfectly intelligible, though curious human experiences, to terrible felt presences and absences like those which the spinal psychologist and I had felt in the dak-bungalows, to human sharing and isolation, to the feelings of surge and purposeful mission, to the experience of dawn.

The inaccessibility of religion to modern man lay, I decided, in a confusion about the nature of religious utterance. As far as I was concerned, it was very like the confusion about the nature of mathematical utterance which had made this study such a nightmare to me in my school-boy days, which had been dissipated by the brilliant elucidations of Lancelot Hogben, benefactor of the millions. Until I read Hogben's book, mathematics had meant to me a vocabulary of mathematical abstractions, meaningless in themselves. I had never grasped the idea that mathematics is a syntax rather than a vocabulary, a form of language, rather than an element of language.

And so it is with religion, I thought. Religion, like mathematics, is an operational syntax; religious symbols are meaningful when handled in accordance with the special rules of this syntax, otherwise not. Actually there is a double confusion in our minds about religion. The orthodox believers, themselves, frequently fall into the semantic error committed by the Pythagoreans with their number-magic, they forget that their symbols are symbols and treat them as mystic realities. We, the unbelievers, assume that this religious symbol-magic is religion. If we had lived in the days of Pythagoras we would have proclaimed arithmetic a study beneath the dignity of adult minds because it taught such nonsense as the sacredness of the number five. In our day, thinking that religion means believing in the existence of an all-powerful invisible old man with whiskers, we cry, 'Take it away.'

If the Western form of religion were the only form in existence it would be difficult for us to find a middle ground between accepting all religious statements, at least as symbolic truths, and rejecting them as either hallucinations or abstractions without any referents in the real world. Eastern religions, because they differed from the Western variety, not only in belief but in attitudes toward belief, furnished, I thought, a key to the interpretation of all religious utterance which abolished at least the language barrier between believers and unbelievers.

In all of the Hindu and Buddhist religious philosophies or disciplines, what James called the religious experience is emphasized much more than in Western religion and it even seemed to me that these various Eastern schools tended to found religious belief directly upon religious experience, almost invariably conceived as an awareness of something within. The various Oriental concepts of the Atman or Absolute as man's own soul — the idea that God, in some manner, is within man — are not so much attempts to answer the riddle of the universe as they are attempts to describe what sages and mystics have discovered by self-exploration. Before becoming rationalizations, these concepts are verbalizations of intense emotional experiences and they are often frankly presented as such. The Eastern mystic has no more doubts about the importance and validity of his experiences than the Western one has, but he often exhibits a diffidence that amounts almost to agnosticism with regard to the rational communication of them.

For this reason, the Eastern religions lead one to the view that religion as a cultural phenomenon is a peculiar kind of language that has been developed in most complex societies to describe certain types of psychic operations.

Since Freud, psychiatrists have been aware of the numerous analogies between religious symbolism and the symbolism of dreams, but whereas Freud established the existence of a relatively elaborate dream syntax, the possibility that religious symbolism is governed by a special syntax of its own seems to have been little explored.

In one important respect the syntax of religion has to differ from that of dream. Not only does 'secondary elaboration' — the Freudian term for the tidying up and rationalizing of dreams that occurs in remembering them — distort the symbolic expressions of religious experience more than it does the expression of dream-experience, but it is also a second-hand elaboration, the rationalization of other men's experiences. In every age and in every land it is the mystics, the saints, and the seers who make or remake religion for the masses, but the average man, who is not a saint or a mystic, interprets the experience of these exceptional beings in his own fashion.

For this reason it is impossible to give in psychiatric or any other terms the meaning of such religious statements as the Buddhist one that the phenomenal world is entirely illusion. It unquestionably refers to real and significant experience that many Buddhists have had — feeling the world as illusion. It may — sometimes probably has been — a banally accurate description of a bad schizoid state. It may equally refer to the discovery of an emotional reality so important that all else in consciousness seemed unreal — probably every lover has sometimes been a Buddhist in regard to all aspects of reality which did not concern love.

One peculiarity of religious syntax explained, I thought, some of my indifference to religion, and perhaps some of the prejudice of many modern Western minds. Religion had always seemed to me an egoistic preoccupation which implied for those who gave themselves to it intensely a withdrawal from the useful world of society. Religious values and religious problems seemed to me from my readings in Western religion to have exclusively a personal significance for the individual, though religion as a cultural institution obviously had great social importance. In the East this tendency toward social withdrawal through religion was even more pronounced than in the West. Both the Buddhist and the Hindu cultures of Asia had always appeared to consider that a narcissistic existence devoted to the most intense kind of introspection was the highest ideal of life. In India the number of hermits, religious beggars, monks, and others engaged in practicing this ideal of life to the exclusion of all social activity was so great that many experts considered it a serious drain on the country's economy.

Modern Christianity in the West frowned upon such extreme withdrawal but could not completely disavow its own earlier hermits and ascetics. Even the Christian ideal of social duty seemed to me without real social basis for it was a duty that one owed to God rather than to humanity; one served humanity in order to please God.

Why bring God into it? I asked myself. Why could not religious devotees of all creeds think of their ideals and experiences more directly? Why did they fail to realize that religious terror and religious despair are symptoms of psychological isolation from humanity, that the happy quietude or ecstatic joy which they experience through religious discipline are the fruits of human participations, that the appreciation of the benefaction of dawn is chiefly the perception of human gladness at the rebirth of day?

Puzzling over these questions I turned again for enlightenment to the contrast between Eastern and Western religious attitudes. The holy man of the West, I reflected, leads a socially useful existence in striving for a seemingly asocial goal. The holy man of the East seems completely asocial both in practice and in theory, yet in reality he is not. The successful Eastern mystic — the one who feels that he is making substantial progress toward his goal — usually follows the example of the Buddha, who, after years of solitary introspection, attained enlightenment, then devoted the rest of his life to intense social, cultural, and psychiatric labors. The life dedicated to withdrawal and introspection turns into one of social leadership, the hermit collects disciples and forms a school. The enlightened Eastern mystic may or may not engage in good works in the Christian sense, but his instruction of his disciples constitutes in itself a valid social activity, however asocial its content may seem to be.

The enlightenment of the Eastern mystic therefore turns out to be in final analysis a social enlightenment, a rearrangement of his social attitudes, and a reorganization of his personality which permits him to achieve a higher degree of social integration than was possible to him before. By becoming a *guru* — a religious teacher — he has achieved social success by Hindu standards as certainly as a millionaire has achieved social success by American standards. More than that, he has achieved emotional success by creating around himself a community whose members are all linked by emotional bonds closer, less troubled, and more satisfying than those of any lay community, even the family. The great religious leaders of both East and West have tried to refashion the whole of human society in the mold of the religious community in which they themselves have experienced the deepest sense of social participation.

East or West, the implicit goal of religion has always been a more perfect social integration, a more brotherly society. The pattern of the Eastern holy man who, more obviously than his Western colleague, perfects his sociability by introspection, suggests the explanation of the paradox in religious utterance which preaches brotherhood (for the most part) by talking about something else. What the mystic preaches is essentially a recipe for refashioning one's personality, as the mystic has refashioned his. It is a formula for attaining happiness or peace of mind such as the mystic himself has attained. Since he is not aware how much his happiness is simply the result of enhanced sociability — the psychic processes which have produced it being largely unconscious — he is forced to talk, and cloudily at that, in terms of intimate experience. Contemplating his navel or reciting his rosary have led him in ways he ignores himself to overcome anti-social attitudes in himself and develop positive social aptitudes which were latent in him, therefore, he advises his disciples to contemplate their navels or recite their rosaries.

To interpret any religious symbol it is necessary to spell out the implicit social context which influences and often determines its real meaning. The Western religious symbol, God, for instance, does not stand for a single entity of any kind. Its nonmystic referent is not a thing but a sentence, or group of sentences, one element of which is the statement: God is that which, when considered and felt as All-Father, causes one to feel toward all men as brothers. Since brothers in Western families do not always get along very well, the West has found it necessary to complement the God-symbol with the Christ-symbol, among other things a psychological device for making the older brother seem lovable.

Thus even if one adhered to the strictly atheist point of view that there is no objective reality in such religious concepts as God and Christ, it seemed to me that it was no longer possible to consider them as meaningless abstractions. They had at least the meaning that imaginary numbers have in mathematics — the meaning of furthering operations with real numbers — and the universality of religion strongly suggests that its projective and imaginary devices for enhancing sociability are useful. It is possible that they are indispensable, that social co-operation can flow only in channels laid down in childhood and that only the psychological devices developed by religion can funnel adult social relationships into these channels. It is possible — though of course not certain, or even probable — that the only way we can love our neighbors effectively is to construct in our imaginations transcendent entities of some kind which will say to us — in a voice our anatomical ears never hear — 'Love thy neighbor.' (It is also possible, since it cannot be disproved, that these transcendent entities, though constructed in imagination, are not imaginary but real.)

Having arrived at that point in my thinking, it seemed to me that I had gone a long way — in terms of my own personal usage — in converting religious terminologies from blab into meaning. Many things were still obscure to me: Why the religious mind was so addicted to the religious equivalent of imaginary numbers, why religious symbolism was always so hyperbolical, so overcharged, why the religious impulse flowed in such archaic, infantile channels.

Since the intellectual attitudes of the Eastern mind toward religion had already opened several previously locked doors for me, I decided that it was worthwhile to continue the study of Eastern religions, but from now on to forget as far as possible the conscious rationalized philosophies and concentrate my attention upon the simplest Hindu and Buddhist forms of religious experience, trying, as best I could, to feel rather than think them.

II

The Pantheist Mood

THE SOPHISTICATED PHILOSOPHIES of the East are even more abstract, subtle, and given to the splitting of unsubstantial hairs than those of the West, but the emotional basis of the oldest and richest Oriental religion — Hinduism — is perfectly accessible to the Western mind — more accessible, it sometimes seemed to me, than certain Christian moods.

Reduced to its crudest terms, the underlying mood of Hinduism is one of joyous acceptance of the universe — the mood exploited in American advertising by manufacturers of supervitaminized breakfast foods or nonirritant shaving creams, and in American literature by the worst and greatest of our poets, Walt Whitman. It is the mood which makes a man sing in his bathtub, thump his chest in front of an open window, remember to kiss his wife when he leaves for the office, and to say good morning to the office boy when he arrives there; the mood which turns the seedy tramp into a joyous adventurer, stomping lustily along the highroad of life and burbling uncouth ejaculations of comradeship in half a dozen languages as he goes.

There is nothing esoteric or incomprehensible about this mood. Nearly everyone has experienced it sometime during his life. For myself, I recognized that it was this which increasingly shed a morning light over my Asiatic adventure and the whole landscape of Asia to which I had hitherto been so chilly indifferent. Never before had these feelings been so intense, so prolonged, and so frequently recurrent, but I had experienced them from time to time since my childhood.

Moreover, once the connection between this euphoric state and the mystic ecstacies in which Indian religious history abounds is recognized, mysticism no longer seems something completely remote from normal human experience, at least not the kind of mysticism which may be described as the Whitmanesque mood at its highest pitch. Such mystic experiences, I suspect, are a great deal more common than they are thought to be. I have never considered myself, nor been considered by my friends, as a mystic type, yet several times during my life the feeling of the blessedness and perfection of creation has been so intense that any effort to express it verbally resulted in the kind of incoherent babble which is the official language of mysticism.

What is startling and at first incomprehensible to the Western mind is to find India, most tragic and horror-ridden of all lands under the sun, tainted with the curse of what James called 'healthy-mindedness.' It is a paradox but it is a fact. Despite cholera, communalism, caste, and colonialism; despite starvation, superstition, and delusion, the people of India have glad morning temperaments. They cannot, for the most part, be happy but their misery is interlit with flashes of pure joyousness. They cannot be optimistic but they are often blissfully acceptant.

The anxieties, the conflicts, and the inescapable sorrows of their lives are reflected in the dark spots of their religion — in Moloch traditions like suttee and in the tyranny of caste, in demons and ghosts, above all in the cruel goddess Kali, the projective image of man's sadist-masochist complex, in whose name Indians of bygone ages knotted the sacred noose around the throats of unsuspecting victims or discovered the delights of being eaten alive by sharks.

Yet, except to a small group of neurotic Kali-devotees, her worship as Goddess of Death fills only a small part of Hindu religious consciousness. Kali is loved and revered as the patron of one of the essential functions of life, the function of dying, but she is only part of a great whole, one which embraces both life and

death. More than any other religion, Hinduism hangs upon the
concept of wholeness, and the perception of wholeness to the
Hindu mind is the most joyous of all human experiences.

The conviction of the unity and orderliness of the universe is
so strong in the devout Hindu that nothing can shake it. He has
a kind of cheerful fatalism which the American GI, something of a
Hindu in his fashion, expressed in the popular epigram: What
must be, will be, whether it happens or not. Usually what is
going to happen to the Hindu is something dreadful and he knows
it, but the idea that it has to happen still seems joyous to him.

This euphoria of the Hindu seems almost unhealthy to us because we associate the state with high animal spirits, with the
abundant life and the gracious smiles of the goddess Success. The
undernourished, disease-ridden, and oppressed Hindu proves that
we are mistaken. In my own case I found that my mind was often
most joyously pantheistic when my body was depressed and miserable, when my nerves had been subjected to prolonged tension.
Fatigue, aching muscles, an empty stomach, a brief respite between air-raids or the buffetings of a monsoon thunderstorm flying in the mountains were propitious rather than adverse to the
mood, I discovered.

The Hindu acceptance, like a certain Christian resignation and
the systematic negation of the unpleasant in some of the extreme
Western forms of religious 'healthy-mindedness,' can be a serious
obstacle to social reform — in fact, it often has been. Yet it did
not seem to me that it should be considered as escapism in the
sense of escape into unreality.

Popular Hinduism, it is true, is more richly endowed with gods
and goddesses and all the trappings of mythology than even the
religion of ancient Greece, and this imaginative exuberance is
certainly connected with the pantheist emotional mood, but it
seemed to me more a by-product than an integral feature of it.
The higher Hindu sages have always dispensed with all this projective paraphernalia while retaining their pantheist hearts.

The emotional roots of the animism in Hindu village worship
seemed to me to lie in a heightened sense of reality rather than in

unreality, in the use of marvel to express the marvelousness of simple reality, in creating magical beings to explain the magic feel of normal experience. I could never help being an animist in the jungle because the jungle was always a magical place to me, full of quietudes beyond quietness, of wonders beyond wonder, of the mystery of wholeness. To walk along the banks of a jungle stream in the first dawn or at the hour of sunset, surrounded by a windless magic dusk, and to look up at the more transcendent miracle of light and wind in the high treetop world, the Olympus of the forest gods, only ceased being an animist experience when it became a religious one.

The great beasts of the jungle, which I hunted by passionate fits and starts, but rarely killed because I was too amazed by them to shoot straight, always seemed to me incredible materializations, and it was hard not to think of them as gods. No courtroom drama has ever been quite as tense or as solemn as that which confronted me one evening driving along a jungle road in Ceylon with three friends when we turned a sharp bend and were just able to pull up some ten feet short of a mighty bull elephant straddling the road. For several seconds while we sat chained by awe, hardly conscious of being afraid, the huge beast towered above us, brandishing his trunk over our heads, flapping his great ears, ruminating a judgment in his solemn dull brain. Then with the ponderous dignity of a high justice withdrawing, he backed away from us into the undergrowth, and all we could think was the fabulous thought: That was an elephant.

This is one way in which fable arises. The statement 'elephant' is too hyperbolical for the mind to accept, it requires the qualifying punctuation of miracle. Elephant? Well, very like one, if not an elephant at least a god, and gods are almost as wonderful.

Deer are a great deal more common than elephants, even the great elklike sambhur deer of Asia, but they are still more mythical. They have the strangest of all faculties, that of being on the tip of one's tongue like an almost remembered name, when one goes into the jungle looking for them. Steer, beer, fear . . . of course: Deer. There it is, the remembered name, the misplaced object, there all the time right in front of one's nose but just discovered, just perceived, like the mystic's vision; standing there in slenderness and majesty and the wonder of spreading antlers, and a stranger's hands aim the gun, a shot rings out from the mob of which one is an inadvertent member and a mob-panic breaks out as the vision crashes and flounders. Suddenly one is alone, alone, with an animal carcass crawling with vermin, a carcass that cannot be a sambhur, for no man has ever killed a sambhur, though many men have seen them.

Asiatics are somewhat less filled with awe than we at the larger wonders of the jungle (though I was once elephant-bound in a jungle rest-house in Ceylon for a whole night because the native chauffeur refused to drive me home after a heavy thunderstorm, on the grounds that the elephants liked to get out into the roads after a rain to cool their feet in the mud). Some young Kachins at our training camp in Assam playfully fired both barrels of a shotgun loaded with light birdshot at a tiger, annoying him keenly, and I have heard a Tamil guide say 'Sambhur, Sahib,' almost as casually as we would say 'There's a god.'

It is the grotesque, capering Brother Monkey and the sacred, felicitous Father Cobra which seem chiefly to captivate the Asiatic imagination. The cult of the cobra is particularly intense throughout Southern Asia. I had always assumed that this was a religious cult, in the Western sense of the word, and indeed the cobra is a holy symbol in popular Hinduism, but I discovered eventually that it was not so much a matter of doctrine as of warm and magical feeling toward snakes. The Ceylonese, in particular, seemed to feel that a dwelling was both homier and more interesting when there were snakes, preferably cobras, about.

I have read in a Ceylonese newspaper a long argument combating the popular prejudice against destroying termite-nests — a prejudice based on the fact that cobras are frequently found in them — by trying to prove that it was no serious hardship to a cobra to be driven out of his home since he would easily find another one. All the native help at our headquarters near Kandy once threatened to go on strike if we persisted in a project to establish a shooting range against a hillside near their quarters. They were blessed with a great abundance of cobras in the weeds around their huts and feared that the firing might make the snakes nervous.

Although I had outgrown my original Western snake-shyness by that time, and had even learned, Indian-fashion, to share my quarters equitably with several large wasps, this solicitude of the native help for the cobras' nerves seemed to me rather absurd — unless inspired by the practical hope that the detachment paymaster would raise their wages so they could afford to buy soothing syrup for their pets — and in general I found the Eastern snake-enthusiasm overdone, if not entirely misplaced.

One of my hunting experiences in Ceylon helped me to develop a more tolerant attitude toward the snake-cult. I was walking along a narrow jungle-trail at dawn, intent upon making a noiseless approach to the banks of a large river where I knew there were crocodiles, when a good-sized cobra reared itself menacingly almost under my feet.

I froze in my tracks, aimed the rifle at the snake's head, and was about to fire when I remembered I was so close to the river that a shot could hardly fail to alarm all the crocodiles in the vicinity and spoil my morning's chances. I was too close to try psychological warfare — which I had often practiced successfully upon the nationalist variety of Eastern water-buffalo — for the cobra might be frightened into attack rather than flight. I wanted, if possible, to avoid a noisy detour around the snake through underbrush. I hoped that eventually the cobra would slide away, leaving the path to me, so I stood still and waited, watching him closely and keeping the gun aimed at him.

He remained almost motionless, swaying slightly, waiting for me to slide away, and watching me closely.

This must have gone on for several minutes. I had plenty of time and the cobra seemingly had more. I felt stubborn, as well as frightened, and so, apparently, did he. I doubt that either of us looked frightened, or even stubborn; I think mainly we looked firm and courteous, I know the cobra did.

I did not personalize him in my mind as Father Cobra or feel
him directly as a message bearer. Rather it seemed to me I was
standing to one side watching both the man and the snake and
that there was a meaningful relationship between us as between
the figures in a ballet.

How wonderfully the snake-part is enacted, I thought, how
realistic the man is. What puzzlement and what understanding
in their postures. How innocently unsuspecting each is of his
dependence on the other, how admirable the unconscious partnership between them. When one moves a muscle a complementary
muscle moves in the other; the man's rifle arm rises slightly — the
snake becomes a fraction of an inch more erect; the man's body
sways to one side — the snake's head follows it. How curiously
alike the integrations of love and of hostility.

Now the tableau is changing. Slowly the man retreats, like a
dancer representing a snake withdrawing, slowly the cobra sub-
sides like a sentinel's vigilance relaxing when the countersign is
given. The man turns aside into the jungle given to snakes, the
cobra waits and broods on the smooth floor of the trail cut by
man. Identities are exchanged and recovered, the temporary
partnership founded on the confusion of enmity dissolves into the
general and permanent partnership of all living and nonliving
things, into the commonwealth of leaf and wind, of dawn and
clay, of man and reptile, of thought and electron.

So does the animist feeling of magic wonder at the uniqueness
of experience dissolve and merge into the greater pantheist wonder of wholeness perceived. The sacred animals, the holy rivers
and mountains, the anthropomorphic gods, are primitive mental
bridges between man and nature, between man and man, and
even between man and himself.

Monkeys and snakes are no more sacred than anything else,
just as elephants are no more awesome than gnats, and deer are
no more poignant than toads, but the emotional realities, awe-
someness, poignancy, and sacredness, exist, and the experiencing
of them is an essential element in man's adaptation to his environment. Man has several destinies, of which the primary one is

biological, and our psychological adjustment to this destiny depends upon the feelings that we have about our biological neighbors, the other animals, and the whole scheme of nature.

Perhaps, as the Hindus and Buddhists believe, man diminishes
himself when he takes the lives of other creatures. Certainly he
impoverishes himself by being unaware of them. I think that the
reason why the jungle was always a magical place for me, an
animist grove and at times a pantheist temple, was because I discovered in it, more vividly than I had in the Western countryside,
the biological background of the drama of human life, which our
present urban culture tends to push out of consciousness. This
discovery could not be a systematic one, it was a series of flashes
of awareness leading to irrational fixations of emotion upon a
particular symbol, to elephant-awe, to deer-wonderment, to
snake-partnership.

These creatures were as much mythological symbols to me as
the conventionally sacred monkeys and cobras were to the Hindus
and they served the same purpose, they were bits of emotional
shorthand summarizing my adjustment to my own role as a member of the biological cavalcade. The Hindu monkey-god, Hanu-
man, is a figment of man's imagination but he may be more useful
than Darwin — at least serve the same purpose — in aiding man
to understand his place in nature. As a language-device Hanu-
man is obviously unsatisfactory, he corresponds to the use of an
imaginary number where a real one should suffice, but after struggling with the problem of trying to express my jungle-experiences
in real numbers I came to the conclusion that no existing vocabulary or syntax was very satisfactory. Every word and every
idiom in the normal rules of syntax has a certain emotional pitch
as well as rational meaning. When the emotional awareness of a
given experience transcends the conventional evaluation of it,
meaning is lost unless one transposes into some form of magical
syntax. Failure to do so leads to absurdities of understatement
like a lover's saying to his mistress, 'I find the practice of oscula-
tion with you agreeable.' If elephants had been less exceptional
in my childhood it would have been equally absurd for me to say

that I found wild jungle-elephants awesome — or even elephants.

One element in man's biological destiny is his sexual mission and the popular Hindu pantheism has a rich magical and religious vocabulary to express the wonder and glory of sexual experience. Socially much more inhibited than we in the expression of sexuality, the Hindus seem much less so psychologically, so uninhibited in fact that the Western mind is a little shocked. Even a learned treatise on sexuality like the *Kama Sutra* seems to us puerile pornography with its emphasis upon the purely anatomic and mechanical, its crude and bizarre sensual recipes, involving the most implausible contortions and stage-props. Much Hindu sexual-religious art, from the naïvely realistic stone phalluses in the villages to the intricate mythological embraces depicted in temple carvings and paintings, seems to us on a level with the esthetic idiom of the public water-closet.

It is in the dance, the great Indian art-form and the one in which they surpass any other people in the world — that the pantheist attitude toward sexuality expresses itself most effectively. Here Krishna comes to life on the stage and frolics with the milkmaids; here enhanced, heavenly couples transform the stage into a connubial couch and upon it enact subtly, nobly, abstractly, almost chastely, more than poetically, the amazing psychosomatic drama which a depleted Frenchman once dismissed as the rubbing together of two epidermises. These are truly celestial loves, expressing a sense of sexual partnership, an elegant subtlety of appreciation, an awareness of harmony, and an acceptance of delight which only human faculties multiplied by godship could achieve.

Sexuality is not romanticized in the Hindu art of the dance as it is in all our arts, it is divinized. It is as if sexual experience were being recollected in a mutual postcoital tenderness, rather than anticipated in the fever of desire, and this displacement of artistic attention from the moment before consummation to the moment after — a theme which runs through many phases of Hindu culture — is responsible for a certain laxness of passion that sometimes makes Hindu art seem cold when it is merely replete. For the same reason the pantheist religious rapture — like all rapture and all religion intimately associated with sexuality — seems cold to hearts conditioned to the passionate anticipation of God, for it is a realization of God.

The direct — though by no means uncomplicated — Hindu attitude toward sex seems to me one of the fountainheads of pantheism, in the sense that the healthy-mindedness of Hindu religious sentiment is a reflection of minds sufficiently free from neurotic conflicts about sex at least to fill consciousness with an abstract sense of fulfillment which is very like sexual fulfillment — and to project upon the whole cosmos of experience a halo of satisfied sexuality. To the extent that this is true, it suggests that the sex-instinct is even more remarkable than it is generally recognized to be, and deserves some of the hyperbole characteristic of religious utterance.

Another fountainhead of Eastern pantheism is the sense of social participation developed by such institutions as the joint family and the co-operative village community. It is difficult not to see in the pluralist pantheism of village Hinduism a reflection of the Hindu child's feelings toward the older members of his large but closely knit family. The Hindu child does not have merely two parents but several — a collection of aunts and uncles that are almost mothers and fathers, a grandmother who is a supermother, cousins barely distinguishable from brothers and sisters.

This joint-family background can hardly fail to imprint a pluralist design upon the Hindu superego, leading to a multiplicity of projective images like the popular Hindu pantheon. What is even more significant is the strong family discipline and the close, generally harmonious, emotional relationships between the various members of the family, from which naturally arises the tendency of Hindu monism to conceive the universe as a unity of diversities, or simply as unity, ignoring the existence of any distinction between members of the family.

The concept of the Atman — the soul and at the same time the supreme God of the universe, the Absolute — probably has its emotional roots in a sense of family kinship and community participation. The pantheist rapture of wholeness possibly reflects such simple verbalizations of ecstasy as the thought: What a marvelous institution my family is, how full of protections, how rich in satisfactions, what a joy to be one of this group. The pantheist mood of joyous acceptance certainly arises, at least in part, from the feeling that the whole of earth is a home, the whole of creation a brotherhood, that wherever the head be laid the heart always has a roof over it, that wherever life is encountered a brother is found, be it brother man, brother monkey, brother shark, or even brother streptoccocus.

The social history of India, I suspect, is reflected in the history of Indian religions, but possibly the reflection is inverted. The impact of social upheavals caused by war, famine, and economic change upon family and village life is probably mirrored in recurrent waves of Hindu revivalism and epidemics of mysticism which were attempts to reconstruct psychologically the shattered unity of Indian life. The slow silting of the channels of brotherhood by superstitions reflecting class-tensions has led to explosions of religious reformism like Jainism, Buddhism, Sikhism, that probably should be considered as social revolutions in the individual unconscious mind, as escapes from the emotional isolation of a caste-ridden society.

Modern psychiatry and social science are always tempted to explain all religious phenomena in terms of catastrophism or conflict, personal or social, and I believe myself that such explanations are often plausible, when, as I have just suggested, they apply to religious change. It did not seem to me — we are here on the edge of a field where belief can have no foundation except emotion — that such explanations explained the whole of religion or accounted for all the peculiarities of religious utterance.

In my own case I recognized that the accessibility to me of some of the simpler forms of religious experience prevailing in the Eastern cultures was due to the need for combating the antisocial elements in my personality which participation in the war stimulated. Pantheism was a needed antidote to the paranoid atmosphere of cloak-and-dagger activity, the magic of the jungle was a tonic to nerves depressed by massive doses of military bureaucracy, the perception of wholeness a balm to a mind divided against itself by the neurosis of war.

At the same time it seemed to me that I could detect other and quite different roots of my religious sympathies. War was not just an education in hating and a trial by frustration. It was also an education in loving and an adventure in fulfillment. Caste-ridden and authoritarian though it be, the military society, which I was discovering for the first time, is a sort of brotherhood, akin in many ways to the religious brotherhoods. There is a distinct military culture and a military creed of which the members of the professional officer class are the carriers and priests. Being in uniform, I found, was an experiment in socialized living, and though I was often irritated or even exasperated by the military servitudes, and occasionally balked at the sacrifices of self which the military ideals of duty and obedience require, on the whole, I felt the military way of life an enrichment.

Thus, it seemed to me that my new religious sympathies and interests were not merely an escape, a compensation, or the resolution of a psychic conflict. They were also a projection upon the world at large of the well-being induced by my successful integration into the wartime military society, an overflow of the sense of participation, brotherhood and fulfillment resulting from this integration, and a search for still higher and more intense integrations.

In the same way, I thought, Hinduism expressed the integrations as well as the conflicts of Hindu social life, deepened the awareness of emotional satisfactions arising from participations in Hindu society. It was not based upon psychic famine and social catastrophe, but originally upon an emotional economy of abundance.

This conclusion brought me back to some of the questions which had been the point of departure of my inquiry into popular Hinduism. Why was the pantheist mood such a happy-child relationship with the universe? Why did my own satisfaction with my adult role as a member of a society express itself, among other ways, in a kind of small-boy wonder at the creatures of the jungle-zoo? Why this persistent infantilism in everything connected with religion?

The complete answers, I decided, would have to be left to the psychiatrists. As sheer speculation, the following possible explanations, not necessarily mutually exclusive, suggested themselves to me:

Religious experience always refers to infantile experience because it is emotionally intense and childhood is the period of most intense emotional experience. Consequently the adult mind can find only in childhood memory a frame of reference for its own most intense experience. According to this view, the Christian who discovers God conceives him as a father-image, not because his childish mind developed this conception of God, but because his memories of childish love and awe toward his real father are the nearest emotional equivalent he can find for adult experience of discovering God.

Modern psychiatry and anthropology have given a good deal of attention to these questions but attention has been focused primarily upon the intellectual content of religious belief, upon the childish mentality from which religious myth and religious utterance arise. The projective devices which most religions employ so lavishly are certainly characteristic of the childish mind.

It seemed to me, however, that religious mood as well as religious thinking was usually childlike in that it corresponded — both in character and intensity — to the emotional moods of childhood. Religious fear, an important element in all the brimstone varieties of religion, does not merely employ childish symbols of fearsomeness, but recaptures an intenseness and directness of fear, a kind of freshness of fear, more characteristic of infantile than of adult experience. It is the same with religious love, awe, reverence, and ecstasy.

In a sense it might be said that religious experience, like psychoanalytical experience, involves the reliving of infancy and the

reorientation of infantile attitudes, surviving in the adult unconscious, after these attitudes have been brought to consciousness.
Unlike psychoanalysis, religion accomplishes the resolution of
childhood neuroses only incidentally — when it does so at all —
and is primarily, though unconsciously, concerned with exploiting the memory of childish emotional experience. To the analyst,
the stratum of the mind where the remembrance of childhood experience is stored is important because the roots of adult maladjustments and conflicts are there. To the religious practitioner,
it is a treasure-house in itself, and though he does not realize it,
the heaven which is his goal is the same one that Wordsworth
declares lies around us in our infancy.

Whether religion should be condemned as being organized regression to childhood or whether it should be valued as a discipline of the personality which takes up where psychoanalysis leaves
off, depends upon the significance we attach to the emotional experiences of childhood. If, in any respect whatsoever, they are
more important than comparable adult experiences, then religion
in making infantile emotion accessible to the adult mind, and
available for use in adult living, performs a tremendously valuable
psychic service to the believer.

It is not impossible that childhood has a much greater importance than we realize, that, on the psychic plane, it is not just the
immaturity of man but a kind of preceding isotope of man in the
sense that a caterpillar might be called an isotopic butterfly rather
than an immature one. Physiologically there is no justification
for regarding children as larval men, but it seems to me that a case
could be made for considering the childish mind as the larval stage
of the adult mind — some child-psychologists seem to approximate this concept — and if so, we would have to concede that the
whole mission of childhood is not to grow up, but to fulfill childhood while preparing adulthood, in the same way that the mission
of the caterpillar is to fulfill its own caterpillar-life while preparing
the butterfly.

If this concept of childhood could be shown as valid, then we
should have to look upon children somewhat as the Hindus look

upon their gods, for though the gods have superhuman powers they actually belong to a lower spiritual order of creation than man, and can only attain the highest perfection by incarnating themselves in man. And doubtless we should have to look upon religion as the discipline which enables beings to retain the values of godship while fulfilling the destiny of man, religious utterance as the pidgin of the soul in which men converse with gods.

I do not know if I was a god in my childhood but I found that the adult recovery of childish emotion enriched experience to such a degree that normal language became inadequate, and it was necessary to construct a kind of religious pidgin to express what I felt.

Whether the basis of religious experience was the eruption into consciousness of childhood, the awareness of one's role as a member of a social and biological team, the conversion of sexual energy into conscious thought, or all of these at once, one thing is certain, I thought:

Religion has helped man to become aware of his own incredible potentialities, to appreciate some of the miracle of existence. It has distorted reality but enabled man to see a little more of it than he would have seen otherwise. It has demonstrated that the normal human field of consciousness is only an insignificant fraction of the reality that man is capable of perceiving, that no image of reality is whole which omits the concept of value.

All of the great religions of the world have contributed something to enriching human awareness. Each seems to have specialized in some particular phase of reality — as well as in some peculiar form of illusion. Christianity has made us aware of some of the most intense and important personal dramas — the drama of the individual's relationship to his own conscience, the drama of self as a mission, the drama of goals. Hinduism has emphasized the drama of integration, the attainment of relevance. More than any other religion, perhaps, it exalts and explains the values of social participation — which is the very reason that it seems so grotesque in modern India where its debased later forms have almost disintegrated the fabric of society.

III

The Magic Mango

THE IMPORTANCE of religion as a language-device permitting a
fuller description of the universe than any of the mechanistic
vocabularies struck me in a quaint manner one Sunday afternoon
as I was strolling in the beautiful jungle-park which climbs up the
hill above the Temple of the Tooth in Kandy, where a much-
revered relic of the Lord Buddha is enshrined.

It was a glorious pantheist day, with the southwest monsoon
blowing freshly, and the sun making bright mosaics upon the floor
of the jungle. Near the top of the hill I came upon a troop of wild
monkeys disporting themselves among the branches and I sat
down upon a stone to watch the antics of this biological brother,
so dear to the Asiatic heart. It was hard to see how anything in
the activity of these little beasts had caused them to be held
sacred, but I was ready to concede that Brother Monkey was a
grotesque, pointed, and even somewhat poignant caricature of
man, and that the problems of simian life had some sardonic relationship to those of human life.

The large male patriarch of the community upon which my
attention naturally focused, seemed to have many problems. He
had just finished having sexual intercourse with a female when I
began to observe him, but sexual satisfaction apparently did not
simplify life for him, for a few moments later he tried to grab an
infant female, who escaped from his clutch and fled chattering
through the treetops.

A grown female climbed to the branch on which he was sitting and seemed to offer consolation. The male made a few perfunctory overtures to her, then, profoundly fed up with the whole chimera of sex, with the tiresome skittishness and equally tiring exigencies of the females' always evading you when you wanted them and forcing themselves upon you when you did not, he broke off, plucked himself a ripening mango and began to munch it, at first morosely, then with increasing satisfaction.

Food was the thing. Women were only women, but a good mango was a chew, and a balm to the soul. This digestive approach to the problem of bliss, seemingly so promising, was rudely interrupted when I tossed away a cigarette with a sudden movement and some hysterical female in the troup, bedevilled by a confusion between the notions of suddenness and danger, set up the strident cry of doom.

Panic fused from monkey to monkey and finally exploded in a deflagration of sound and movement that was like a herd of invisible buffaloes crashing through the treetops, like a gale of shrillness in the leafy stratosphere of the forest.

Only the old male hesitated for a few seconds, reluctant to abandon the world of mangoid delight for the world of safety. Then the abstraction terror, the retarded impact of perhaps fifty cries of terror, multiplied by the repercussions of terror among the branches, overwhelmed him, the stern voice of biological duty bade him relinquish the fruits of gluttony for the nobleness of flight. He did so, with an incredible wild leap and an incredible wild cry, which expressed the basic anguish of every neurosis.

I had never before realized so clearly how much the monkey, in his uninhibited application of the pleasure principle, was plagued by frustration and haunted by anxiety. The real joys of the world, its acquiescent females and its succulent mangoes; its real terrors — the snakes and the leopards and the rare climbing-accidents, fear of which was apparently present from birth — these did not completely fill the simian life. Enveloping this world of immediate stimuli was another one of more elaborated and sometimes contradictory reflexes, of emotional reverberations.

The social life of the monkey filled his individual consciousness with the terrors and desires of other members of his tribe, from which he could not isolate himself if he desired. Total satisfaction and complete freedom from anxiety eluded him, as they elude man. To the emotional tyrannies and contagions of society were added the sediment of individual experience, the memory of the females that had sometimes eluded him, the mangoes he had dropped, the real or imaginary terrors which had never spent themselves wholly in flight.

Perhaps as with man, the monkey's adjustment to surplus reality was effected in sleep by means of dreams; failing this, or in spite of it, the state of monkeyhood, like the human state, should be considered as a biological neurosis. In monkeys, as in man, there seemed to be some accumulation of psychic energy based upon the disproportion between stimulus-reception and motor response. The monkey, even isolated from his community, probably possessed more appetites than his stomach and his sexual organs could satisfy, and more fears than he could run away from.

Perhaps this accumulation of psychic energy in the nervous systems of the higher animals mirrors a broader kinetic process in the universe. Perhaps the mystery of life is that it is an accumulation as well as a conversion of charges, a chain of augmenting integrations, causing the whole to exceed the sum of its parts in our understanding.

In any case, if we are correct in assuming that thought and feeling are potentialities of matter — realized when matter is organized in the pattern of living tissues — then meaning is one of the attributes of matter, and the meaning of anything can be no less than the sum of all the meanings it can have for all possible minds, including the greatest meaning it can have for any mind. Not only Descartes, but whatever has been or can be thought exists, including God, but God, like Descartes, may only be the echo of something which once was thought.

Monkeys are generally assumed to belong to the Behaviorist school, because in the West their closest human contacts have been with the members of this school, but, sitting on the stone in

the jungle-garden above the Temple of the Tooth, listening to the
fleeing simian commotion in the treetops, it seemed to me that
monkeys would really be better off if they had a religion. Their
apprehensiveness would probably be diminished if part of it could
be discharged in ceremonial propitiations of the principles of
terror, and they would understand certain significant aspects of
reality which now escape them. They would discover, for instance, that in addition to the pleasure-principle which they
exemplify by eating mangoes when they are hungry, the universe
also contains a joy-principle which a monkey might discover by
eating mystically more mangoes than his physical stomach had
ever been able to hold, by eating in imagination all the mangoes
that all the monkeys in the world have ever wanted to eat, or ever
will want to eat.

No doubt if monkeys did have a religion, I reflected, it would
include among other symbols, the symbol of the magic mango,
the mango of the gods. Though imaginary, this would not be an
unreal mango, but a mango of augmented reality, a fulfillment of
one of the possibilities of the fruit, mango, as significant as its
chemical composition or the Latin name of the plant that bears
it: Namely, the possibility of quickening monkeys to delight.

The monkey-god would be an augmented reality, too, a real
god-monkey incarnate in the mind of his worshiper, become an
augmented consciousness, a being more aware of mango, and
therefore of delight, than the normal, noncelestial, nonreligious
monkey.

Monkeys or men, we need gods to become them, we need dreams
to perceive reality. Probably there is no dream of man which
cannot be realized in some way, except the dream of the individual
that he can possess the group, the dream of the part that it can be
the whole.

IV

The Neurosis of Self

SOME MONTHS after I had left India I had a remarkable conversation with an OSS colleague who in civilian life is a distinguished anthropologist, one of the numerous practitioners of this discipline attached to our headquarters, lending an incongruous scientific luster to our dark practices. It was on the verandah of our bungalow in Kandy, after dinner, the hour of vegetal awakening from the heavy-lidded day, the vesperal dawn of the tropics when the spirits of men and animals float like fishes taking their ease upon the surface of a tepid sea. We had put out the lamps and were sitting motionless in a revolving firmament of fireflies, looking out across the valley at the dark folds of the Kandy mountain, aware, in the pauses of our relaxed conversation, of the palms rustling in the dying monsoon.

It was not an hour for shop-talking but we began by talking shop. I had asked my friend to come and talk shop upon the verandah with me because I was considering a project on which I wanted his professional opinion. This project had several military merits, one of which was that if it were successful it would cause the death of quite a few Japanese soldiers.

It had the possible drawback that it might arouse Japanese suspicions against the innocent civilian population in the area to which it was applied, leading to a frenzy of torture and killing in a remote Asiatic jungle-region where the harmless people of the villages had always shared their rice, their bananas, their courtesies and the casual favors of their women with the Japanese as they would with any other guests.

This might prove a liability when the time came for the remote jungle-folk to play a military role. Normally we could count on them for some help. They might not feel any crusading zeal against the Japanese but they would be pleased to change guests for awhile, and at the very least, they would give concealment to agents of their own race, trained by us and parachuted back into their jungles. If, however, the tortures and killings they might suffer as a by-product of my project drove them into abject terror, then they would be afraid to give shelter to our agents, they might even denounce them to the Japanese to save their own lives, and our small profit from the death of a few enemy soldiers would be wiped out by the loss of several highly expensive, though expendable, agents.

Of course, it might work the other way. The Japanese terror unleashed by the project might turn the villagers into flaming guerillas; instead of breaking their spirit, it might furnish us a ready-made jungle underground as fanatical as any in Europe. That would be a great military advantage.

Altogether it was a very interesting intellectual problem. Everything depended upon how torture and killing would alter the souls of these natives, whether it would cow them or infuriate them, and that is where the anthropologist came in. Eventually he gave me his opinion, a very plausible and well-reasoned opinion, a most cool and scientific one, I thought, and the matter was closed as far as we two were concerned.

We stopped talking shop and let our minds drift with the incoming flood of tropic night to other things that interested us. Hinduism was one of these things, and I described to my friend my attempts to analyze Indian religious attitudes and my understanding of the basic pantheist experience, as it seemed to me from my own experience.

It is like floating upon a very sure current, I said, not a swift one but magically certain — implacable with a friendly purpose.

The world parts into a fluvial landscape. You are not lifted above phenomenon, you glide between its banks. Every object stands out sharply, with lucidity rather than clarity.

All of life is stretched out before you along those two banks. You see every bit of it and everything you see you feel, you feel much more strongly than in any normal state of consciousness. You feel every leaf, every blade of grass, every hill, every house, every animal, and every human. You are not detached from them but you are sped by them.

You are intensely quiet. You hear no music but it is as when music stops. You are happy because nothing can hurt you, not because you cannot feel, but because you have no enemies. Fire would not hurt you because fire is a friendly element. The current cannot bring you to harm because it is implacable, and implacability is a friendly principle.

It is, of course, a kind of dream or trance-state, I continued, but it is not merely a lucid dream, it is a perception of reality in which all real objects retain their logical relationships while taking on completely new emotional meanings. It is a spiritual planet whose central order is the law of harmony as the law of gravity is the central order of our planet, Earth. On this planet of which I speak ugliness and strife and fear are excluded, not by excluding the objects which are associated in our minds with these emotions, but by abolishing paradox: A skeleton on this planet looks exactly like a skeleton upon the Earth, but here it is a symbol of friendliness, as perhaps it is intended to be, without succeeding in being, in some surrealist paintings.

I went on in this vein for some time and as I tried to communicate to my friend the psychological atmosphere of this curious state of consciousness which I had reached from time to time, apparently accidentally, walking by myself on the Plain of Delhi, drowsing between the earth and the stars in a darkened plane at night, or simply sitting in some quiet place at the hour of twilight, the memory of these experiences became more and more vivid, the words in which I spoke of them more heavily charged with emotion.

Quite literally, I said, it is being in love with the universe, for

the object of your love is the whole universe and as such it bene-
fits from the classic overevaluation of the love-object which is one
of the clinical symptoms of the disease of being in love. You do
not deny that the universe has a large nose or even pretend to
yourself that a large nose is beautiful; you love the universe for its
large and not beautiful nose. Even a lover does not necessarily
convince himself that a sadistic mistress is kind, and the lover of
the universe when he thinks of cruelty, thinks: Cruelty is the
tenderness of the universe.

'And of course, death is the consummation of union with the
universal love-object. That is what you have been leading up to.'

My friend had been muttering like thunder behind the hills for
some time and now we began to wrangle, but with unnatural gentleness, for he was so really horrified at me that he tried to keep
his disapproval guarded and gentle. He spoke of the fey-state of
the ancient Druids, he touched very guardedly upon those incomprehensible Hindu orgies of self-immolation which so shocked
the earliest Western travelers in India — the entranced throngs
hurling themselves under the wheels of the Juggernaut-chariot,
the pilgrims wading out to the waiting sharks, the grotesque,
masochistic disciplines of the *saddhus* — and I think he had even
got to the Japanese Kamikaze pilots, who illustrate so beautifully
how a paranoid nationalism can make a military asset even out of
the cult of suicide, normally the most asocial of all religions, when
I counterattacked.

'I do not deny that these trances or dreams or reveries of mine
may contain suicidal or masochistic elements,' I said, 'and for this
reason they can unquestionably be dangerous. However, I don't
think they are essentially suicidal in character. They embrace
death because they embrace everything. Somewhere in the
depths of the soul there is an invisible source of light — we have
already had an allegorical river and a new planet, so we might as
well have some invisible radiations now — and whatever idea or
object this invisible beam is focused upon it causes to glow and
seem beautiful in glowing. If you fix your attention while in this
state upon the idea of death, then death will glow for you with a

beautiful and beckoning light; if you fix it upon God then God will glow for you. He has never glowed for me, because I have never understood the idea of God well enough to know where to focus my attention. Perhaps God is himself the invisible light and can never be seen, not even as a reflection, but only as an induced radiation. I don't know if that is Hinduism as Hindus feel their religion but I feel confident that a Hindu would understand easily what I am talking about, that if he disapproved of these experiences of mine it would only be because they are too shallow, not because they are too dangerous.'

We argued about my treason to the West, more gently than friends usually argue because it seemed such a great treason, until late into the night. When we parted we both had an impression that the moon must have risen while we were talking and gone down behind the hills unnoticed. I cannot remember whether it really had or not, though I should be able to remember such a thing, because we were very interested in the moon in those days. We had a moon-chart in our planning room and we lived in a military sense by the lunar calendar; the moon is as propitious to parachutists as to lovers, more propitious to them than to philosophers, and most of our operations took place during the moon-period of the months.

I am not sure, either, that I noticed at the time the contrast between my friend's horror at what he took to be my schizoid mysticism and his cool, detached consideration of the paranoid fantasy, disguised as a military plan, which was the first topic of our long conversation. Perhaps it was because the latter was a professional topic and men engaged in war delegate to suffering humanity as a whole the function of feeling for them, as they delegate to some undefined authority, probably a general somewhere, the function of conscience, leaving them free to think, and even to act like beasts, without feeling like beasts, and perhaps without being beasts.

I suspect, however, that the paradox has a deeper explanation. Our modern culture, compared with most Asiatic cultures, seems to me a rather paranoid one in that it tolerates highly paranoid behavior on the part of individuals and only locks them up or even disapproves of them when they go to great extremes. The cult of self is so important to us that we can easily forgive small excesses of self-worship — at the expense of others — while excesses of self-abnegation, even if of some benefit to others, make us uneasy, they seem slightly unclean even if socially useful, and self-immolation fills us with horror and loathing. We can discuss coolly a proposal for condemning several hundred harmless Asiatics to torture and death on the vague chance that there might be some military benefit in it, but a philosophy which seeks bliss — or even excuses the seeking of bliss — in the contemplation of death, perhaps in the rite of suicide, fills us with indignation. While most of us are not any kind of monster, we are on the whole closer spiritually to the sadistic monsters of Belsen than to the masochistic monsters who threw themselves under the wheels of Juggernaut. If Juggernaut really must have victims we tend to step back — or even push — and let someone else be crushed.

The way we misuse the symbol Juggernaut is in itself highly suggestive. In our minds Juggernaut is very like our own Moloch — a merciless abstraction to which the individual is sacrificed. War is a Juggernaut to us, and I have heard the word applied to the totalitarian philosophies of government which insist upon a complete sacrifice of the individual to the state.

The historical Juggernaut is the symbol of an excitement like sexual excitement leading to outbreaks of mass-suicide, to voluntary consummations of excitement in self-destruction. Perhaps our confusion about the word is due solely to ignorance, but it is possible that we know better, that Juggernaut is a protective mechanism in our minds warning us of the perils of any selfless enthusiasm, that it is an echo of one of the numerous governess-voices in our culture, which, from infancy, remind us of our sacred duty to put our rubbers on, to buy bewarily and to look out for number one.

It would probably be going too far to say that our Western feeling about the sacredness of life is mainly a feeling about the sacredness of our individual lives, but it is undeniable that most

of us look with deep suspicion upon any philosophy which mini-
mizes death, and it seems probable to me that this attitude is one
of the important barriers to cross-cultural understanding between
East and West, possibly, even, between the Western democracies
and Soviet Russia.

In my own case, I found that a cultural prejudice toward what
I conceived to be the Buddhist philosophy of death had rendered
the values of this religion much more inaccessible to me than
those of Hinduism. The death-motif in Hinduism which had so
shocked my friend when we talked on the verandah, seemed to
me only an excess of Pantheist healthy-mindedness, an acceptance of life so joyous, so exuberant, that it paid tribute to death
the way a millionaire might toss a bill at a beggar. The suicidal
and masochistic extravagances of some Hindu cults I considered
as mere errors in syntax, cases of mixed tense.

Buddhism, on the contrary, seemed to me to wear the dour face
of an Oriental Calvinism, to be morbidly dedicated to the negation of life. In James's terminology it was one of the sick-minded
religions.

Outwardly it was hard to distinguish between them. Popular
Buddhism, at least in Ceylon, borrowed lavishly from Hindu
ritual — even from the Hindu Pantheon — while the higher Hinduism was often as abstract and rationalist as Buddhism. Both
were religions of the Atman, the Great Within. Both professed
the doctrines of Maya — Illusion — and Karma — soul-destiny
through reincarnation. To the degree that the individual soul in
a given incarnation allowed itself to become enmeshed in the
illusion of life it was doomed to rebirth, and each new existence
confronted it anew with the unsolved spiritual problems of the
preceding one.

No man could escape the karma he had accumulated in a previous life, that had to be worked out in living, but if no new illusory
attachments were formed, then at the end of life the spirit was
liberated from the cycle of births and deaths, it entered into the
Buddhist Nirvana or merged with the Hindu Absolute.

The Buddhist doctrine of illusion, as interpreted in most modern Buddhist literature, seems to be a metaphysical one. All matter, all phenomena, all experience, all thought, and even all spiritual values appear to be dismissed as illusion. Hunger is illusion, pain is illusion, life and death are both illusions, beauty and ugliness are illusions, fear is illusion — as are all the possible objective causes of fear — and even, according to some Buddhist philosophers, compassion is illusion. This last point is extremely interesting, for compassion toward human suffering is one of the cardinal tenets of the Buddhist faith, and is intricately wound up with the doctrine of right living embodied in the so called Middle Way — a recipe for freeing the individual from illusion which avoids the extremes of ascetism and preaches the holding of sound, sober religious belief, the practice of honesty, nonviolence, abandonment of the more carnal and egoistic pleasures, compassion and service to others.

As Lafcadio Hearn has pointed out, in Japanese Buddhism the sentiment of compassion is the last attribute of personal consciousness to disappear as the soul penetrates into Nirvana. In fact, some of the more transcendent Mahayana philosophers hold that even the spirit which has attained Buddhahood and thereby entered into total Nirvana retains its compassion for suffering humanity.

This view that the most generous and least egoistic elements of consciousness are at least the noblest forms of illusion, combined with the emphasis on ethics rather than metaphysics in all the Buddhist schools, strongly suggests that the more abstract doctrine of illusion which Buddhism has elaborated in the course of centuries was originally an intense awareness of individual maladjustment to social and emotional reality.

The real differences between Hinduism and Buddhism, like those between Protestantism and Catholicism, are differences of emphasis rather than of belief, but in each case these differences are highly significant. The Hindu searches for reality; the Buddhist struggles against Illusion. The Hindu seeks fulfillment in everythingness; the Buddhist seeks release in nothingness. The Hindu attitude implies that personal life is a good thing because it leads to the greater bliss of impersonal existence. The Buddhist attitude implies that life is a sorry business, and the finalization of death a blessing.

This, at least, is the impression created in the Western mind by comparing some representative Hindu and Buddhist utterances and the impression almost inevitably leads to distaste for Buddhism. As illustrated by Whitman, Christian Science, and Pollyanna, it is very easy for the American mind to slip into a pantheist attitude akin to the emotional mood of Hinduism. All we have to do is to cease boosting local real estate and start boosting the universe.

Buddhism is a much harder nut to crack. The mere fact that advertising plays such an enormous role in our culture renders us emotionally allergic to the doctrine of illusion and if the doctrine of reincarnation ever became popular in the West it is probable that the cemetery and baby-buggy lobbies would combine forces to make propaganda against the concept of Nirvana.

Paradoxically, it was a grotesque parody of the Buddhist attitude which I witnessed once in Ceylon that first awakened me to the possibility that Buddhism might have a more pertinent and affirmative message for Western man than it appeared to have. A local Sinhalese (Ceylonese Buddhist) personage of some prominence had died and his elaborate funeral services were held in a paddy-field near our camp. A towering pyre of expensive coconut logs had been erected for the cremation, and near it a microphone hooked up to a public-address system mounted on a truck had been set upon a platform. Some of the greatest Buddhist preachers on the island, I was told, had come to deliver the funeral sermons. The microphone was for them and for the political associates of the deceased, who could deliver the lay eulogies when the clergy had finished.

A large and enthusiastic crowd, including little children and infants in arms, had gathered to see the fun. This did not shock or surprise me, because it went without saying that the deceased must have been worthy since he was important, and in the Buddhist societies when a worthy man dies that is an occasion for re-

joicing, for it means that he has one more incarnation to his credit
and presumes that he has therefore one less to go before he attains
Nirvana.

Somehow, though, it did not seem quite in keeping with the
Buddhist mood for small boys to express their rejoicing on behalf
of the released one by exploding firecrackers throughout the ceremony, and still less for them to squabble among themselves for
possession of the printed eulogies which were passed around by
the friends of the dead man and to circulate among the crowd
hawking these leaflets at a stiff price as souvenirs.

Thanks to my experience as a reporter interviewing celebrities,
and as a writer putting down immortal thoughts on paper, I had
no trouble interpreting the expressions on the faces of the yellow-
robed shaven-headed Buddhist clergy whenever the public-address system broke down in the middle of a sonorous period.
There was at least one illusion which these followers of the Middle
Way had not learned to conquer — the illusion that when one's
words are lost it is a disaster for humanity.

The final incongruity, invalidating my belief that advertising
and the doctrine of illusion are enemies, occurred at the end of the
speeches, when a little man in European clothes jumped up onto
the platform and after an unctuous beginning in the clerical manner, launched into an impassioned harangue. A kindly, English-
speaking neighbor in the crowd translated for me:

'That is salesman for radio company in Colombo. He is saying
that dead man was very fine man, and he is having great honor to
put up radio for such a man's funeral. Then he is telling people,
when they have funerals, always call up his company in Colombo.
That way they will hear holy word of monks, and they will not be
cheat, because his Company very honest company, not rascals
like all others.'

The contrast between sick-minded religious belief and a kind of
native healthy-mindedness which enjoys all the good things of
life, including funerals, and overlooks few opportunities for turning an honest, effortless penny, was, I learned later, not peculiar
to Sinhalese Buddhism. Much the same attitude prevailed in

Burma and in Siam, where wealthy men can make religious merit by such worldly gestures as offering the public a free water carnival.

My personal feeling toward this kind of religion was the opposite of scornful but it did seem to me that there was a discrepancy between practical and theoretical religious attitudes in the Buddhist lands of Southeast Asia. The popular religion which had grown up in these countries admirably suited the emotional requirements of the people, but the pure, classic Buddhist doctrine was completely out of place. The people of these happy lands did not have enough problems for a religion like Buddhism. Poverty was almost meaningless, intense social co-operation unnecessary, while the great sexual freedom which has always prevailed in most of these Southeastern Asiatic societies resulted in such an exuberance of procreation that it was impossible to take death very seriously. The Buddhist doctrine of compassion, spiritually akin to Christian charity and pity, was wasted in a country like Siam where, in order to exercise it, the priesthood had to think up such ingenious devices as advising the faithful during electoral campaigns to vote for the stupidest candidate, on the grounds that the clever ones could make money in other ways and did not need a political job.

When one only knew Buddhism from books, the real Buddhism of Southeast Asia inevitably seemed incongruous and, at times, grotesque. This was not the fault of Buddhist doctrine; it just happened to be out of context in this part of the world. Buddhism belonged in the land of its birth, back in modern India. Hinduism was too healthy-minded for a society as sick as the current Indian one. It had once expressed the surplus sociability of a well-balanced, highly co-operative society. In the disintegrating transitional society of modern India, Hinduism with its inevitable pantheist deficiency in selectivity, with its acceptance of evil as well as good, was a barrier to social progress. When one world has been achieved — and a socialist world at that — we can all become Hindus.

To the extent that man's sufferings arise from social conflict

and isolation, the sick-minded religions like Buddhism and certain Protestant Christianities have an important message. When
Buddhism tells a Siamese peasant who eats a good curry every
day, has a cheerful wife and a compliant serving maid and lots of
children by each, that the joys of curry-bowl and sleeping mat are
illusion, then the message does not carry much meaning. When
it speaks of the blessedness of Nirvana to an old man dying of a
painful cancer or to a hopeless cripple, the message is more significant, though no more so than that of Christianity. Probably the
Buddhist message is less significant than the Christian, particularly the Protestant one, when it is addressed to an arrogant and
vainglorious aggressor.

It is when — as in the Indian society of its origin — Buddhism
speaks to minds imprisoned in self-imposed frustration, condemned to self-inflicted penalties — to the self-righteous Brahmin whose ritual purity somehow fails to produce enlightenment,
to the jealous lover who kills what he loves, to the miser starving
so that he can hoard, to the crusader for peace who finds himself
perpetuating war, to the antifascist unconsciously turned counter-
fascist — that the Buddhist utterance has a penetrating and
unique ring. It is when Buddhism exposes the emotional roots of
superstition and prejudice and cant that it produces a special enlightenment.

Whereas Christianity is par excellence the religion of the out-
cast and the defeated, Buddhism is the religion of the self-exiling
and the self-defeating. John Donne's sermon on the tolling of the
bells is almost a Buddhist utterance, and Hemingway's book is
quite clearly one, for it is above all a study of one of the most
basic and stubborn human illusions — the illusion of security, the
illusion that we can escape death.

The legend of how the Lord Buddha came to seek enlightenment, as related in Buddhist folklore, began to take on a new and
much deeper meaning for me once I realized that Buddhism, like
any religious doctrine, has to be studied in the light of its historical and potential social context. Most Western readers are
familiar with this legend, which is the story of an adolescent

traumatism, the story of a wealthy child sheltered from reality by its parents, confined within a palace from which all symbols of human misery have been banished, who, all at once in a late cataclysmic awakening, wanders beyond the gates, sees some beggars, and thus discovers poverty, discovers social oppression, discovers pain, discovers death.

The shock of this discovery, according to legend, caused the young Buddha to renounce his luxurious home and become an ascetic. Up to a certain point the story of Buddha is the story of every one of us, of all men in all ages, but most particularly of men in those ages when social ideals are in bitter opposition to social practices, when social goals are a sardonic commentary upon social achievements, when peace is a breathing spell to prepare for war. The divergence is that most of us remain mildly neurotic about the whole problem of social reality, whereas the sick mind of the Indian princeling, after a period of introspection, eventually healed itself. The formula of this self-healing became Buddhism, became the doctrine that all personal paradises are illusion, all protections from reality a vulnerability, all attempts to escape the common fate of mankind an aggravated death.

Never hold to anything, said in effect the healed Buddha, remembering how his parents had tried to hold to his own childhood, all holding is illusion.

Never guard against anything, all guarding is illusion.

Welcome whatever comes, welcome death, which comes.

Never own anything, all owning is illusion.

If one considers the Buddhist doctrine of illusion as an explicit reference to the psychic experience recounted in the legend, and keeps in mind the social background of the experience, then it becomes perfectly comprehensible. The addition of a parenthetical clause here and there in Buddhist religious utterance reveals the rules of Buddhist syntax, and makes Buddhist statements more easily translatable into normal language than those of any other religion.

The world is illusion . . . (Our emotional relationship to) the world is (based upon the) illusion (that we can escape from all the

unpleasant realities of life by locking ourselves up in some sheltered palace of the mind).

In other words, illusion in the Buddhist sense is merely a philosophical rationalization of a concept which at first may have applied literally, and even exclusively, to the mental phenomena
described by modern psychiatrists as fixations, unconscious fantasies, and delusions, and the Buddhist doctrines of nonattachment and renunciation, as interpreted by the noblest Buddhist
teaching, may mean nonattachment to delusion and renunciation
of fantasy, rather than withdrawal from the real world. Judging
from his behavior, they seemed to have meant that to the Buddha
himself, and to early Buddhists like the great Indian monarch and
social reformer, Asoka.

To the extent that Buddhist illusion and psychiatric illusion
are identical, psychiatry has superseded Buddhism, but in certain
respects the doctrine of illusion is a social prolongation of psychiatry. Psychiatry teaches that any withdrawal from social
reality is unhealthy, and condemns personal worlds like Buddha's
childhood palace, among other reasons, because they collapse so
traumatically when one discovers the beggars at the gate. Buddhism teaches that it is an illusion even to seek private enrichment
as long as there are beggars anywhere in the world. Psychiatry
declares that it is paranoid to feel persecuted when nobody is persecuting you. Buddhism teaches that it is illusion to feel persecuted even when someone is persecuting you. Psychiatry calls
groundless fears neurotic. Buddhism considers all fear the consequence of attachment to illusion.

Psychiatry views the overevaluation of self as a disease. Buddhism thinks it is part of the disease, illusion, to consider the individual self as any kind of a value.

Many Western psychiatrists consider that the intense fear of
death which exists in our culture is neurotic, and anthropology has
supplied considerable corroboration for this view by discovering
societies in which the neurosis of death seems absent. Beyond
giving some comfort to the dying — when they are wealthy
enough to afford death-bed psychiatry — and some rather vague

hints about raising children, our psychiatrists have done little to realize the implications of their hypothesis.

Buddhism has made a much more intensive, if less scientific, study of the neurosis of death and has elaborated its findings both in the doctrines of illusion and in the doctrine of Nirvana. The realization that Nirvana may be much more than an attempt to cheat death by renouncing life came to me very vividly one night in the course of a maritime expedition along an enemy-held section of the Arakan coast of Burma.

It was in January, 1945, during the brief brilliant campaign of the British XV Corps under Lieutenant General Christison to liberate the Arakan coast. A sizable OSS group had been attached to this corps for the campaign, and I had flown from Kandy to our new advance base at Akyab to study some of the problems involved in co-ordinating secret intelligence activities with combat operations by regular forces. I had accompanied the British assault forces which made a virtually bloodless landing on the northern part of Ramree Island, near the little town of Kyaukpu, and when we were asked a few days later to make a night reconnaissance of Sagu Island, farther down the coast, which the British planned to occupy in the near future, I managed to have myself included in this expedition in the dual roles of headquarters observer and radio-telephone operator.

Our flotilla, consisting of two Royal Indian Navy motor launches and two smaller, speedier OSS craft, carrying a scouting party of ranger-type OSS troops and a team of our underwater swimmers, left Kyaukpu in the late afternoon. As the sun sank into the purple waters of the Bay of Bengal we were nearing the southern tip of Ramree Island, still in Japanese hands, and holding a course and speed calculated to give enemy lookouts on the island the impression that our objective was Bassein, far down the coast.

The plan developed by the leader of the scouting force, Major Lloyd Peddicord, in conjunction with the skippers of the four motor craft, was simple, bold, and ingenious. The moon rose late that night, and in the interval of darkness between last light and the rising of the moon, we would change course, swing back in a wide arc toward Sagu, and lie a few miles off the tiny island until the moon was high. Then, with engines throttled, we would slip noiselessly into a little bay indenting the coastline of the island, a pair of men from my craft would be paddled in a rubber boat to the main beach, which they would scan for any evidence of an enemy guard. They would then return to my craft, report their findings to me, I would communicate to the other boats by means of a portable, walkie-talkie type telephone, and if no enemy had been sighted, the scouting party would go ashore, also in rubber boats, and the swimmers would set out on a nautical mission of their own, studying currents and looking for mines in the narrow channel between Sagu and Ramree Islands.

The whole plan was based upon a paradox, the fact that the moon, shining in a clear winter sky upon the unruffled water of the bay, would create such an excess of brilliance that it would conceal us almost as effectively as fog, envelop us in a mist of radiance.

Except for a slight delay in entering Sagu bay, the plan went off without hitch. No enemy guards were found on the beach, the scouting-party landed without incident and headed into the jungle leaving at the beach an automatic rifleman and a telephone operator with whom I carried on a desultory conversation for a while, the swimmers set out for the entrance of the channel, and the crew of my boat turned into their bunks to rest, leaving me alone on deck with the moon.

The light was so brilliant that I could read easily the non-luminous second hand of my watch, but as Peddicord had predicted, the range of effective visibility was only a few score yards. I could not see the shore line of the island, less than a half mile away, and though I knew our sister craft lay within four hundred yards of us I could not pick up her silhouette. A more highly trained eye, if it knew exactly where to look, might have been able to do so; our safety depended on a psychological as well as an optical principle, upon the enemy's illusion of visibility. An enemy watcher, looking out over the bay, would think he saw everything clearly, his visual alertness would be lulled by the clarity of the night, and he would fall below his own capabilities as a looker.

My own mind was a battlefield of illusion, and my senses were locked in the struggle with hallucination which besets all inexperienced guardians of other men's sleep when they feel themselves alone with the enemy. Once I was sure I heard the throb of an engine which could not be one of ours, and another time I reported to my invisible neighbor and fellow guardian of the night on the nearest craft an erroneous mystical attainment: I had not seen a light, but, over where reason proclaimed the tip of the island to lie, it was as if I had seen a light. He, too, had noticed something which was not a light, but as if he had seen a light, only it was in another spot. This exchange of spookeries between disembodied voices annoyed the operator on the shore, who had been listening in and was apparently prey to the materialist illusion that the high-frequency radiations which carried our thoughts through space were audible to human ears. In a hoarse hastened, dodging whisper he identified himself as Charlie, and asked Abel and Baker for Christ's sake to please keep off the air when they didn't have to, and then was over and out before we could acknowledge.

The illusions which battled within my mind were first, and rather feebly, an illusion of safety, the belief that all things on earth or the sea shared the cool friendliness of moonlight. The luminous dial of the moon, sliding down the curving walls of night, marked no change, the scene by its very nature was changeless and immutable, the absence of enemy seemed an established permanency. Indeed, it was fairly clear by now that the Japanese garrison had evacuated Sagu, and that we would have some welcome news to report to XV Corps headquarters, but there was as yet no certainty that we would survive to make the report in the flesh, for the enemy might have left a couple of watches behind on some height, or a native agent might signal our presence with a fire, and in that case we were certainly in for some kind of unpleasantness, at the very least, long-range shelling of our gasoline-filled cockleshells as we ran out through the channel.

The other illusion, the stronger one, was an illusion, not of danger, but of the dangerousness of danger. It pivoted around an intense feeling of nakedness and a neurotic apprehensiveness of modesty, threatened in imagination with exploding flares that would sear the moon-veiled flesh with exposure.

I felt a close bond of sympathy with the swimmers, paddling around on the still bright waters in their absurd little rubber cushion, diving, breasting currents, but the tightened part of me felt a little envious toward the members of the shore party. Wrapped in the night cloak of jungle as they were, what could happen to them? Death, of course, menaced them much more immediately than it did those of us out upon the water, but not danger. Danger was not in hidden machine guns and shadowed bayonets and undetectable land-mines; danger was the capacity of darkened emptiness to become lit emptiness; the precariously repressed tendency of gasoline-power boats to become incendiary bombs at the touch of a tracer bullet. Danger was what menaced self, illusion was other men's sense of peril.

A small bodily sensation interrupted this train of thought. I had been sitting on the deck in the same position for a long time, resting my back against a machine-gun mount, and I was beginning to feel uncomfortable. My life-jacket made a disagreeable bulge between my shoulders, and my pistol-belt was cutting into my ribs. Why am I wearing these things, anyway? I asked myself.

The pistol served no conceivable purpose, would contribute nothing to my safety in any emergency that might arise. The life-jacket seemed somewhat less nonsensical. As the skipper had explained when he handed it to me before turning in, if an incendiary bullet hit the fuel tanks I might be blown into the water in one piece — I had seen that very thing happen to several British sailors when a small sweeper went up on a mine during the Kyaukpu landing — and the crew sleeping below decks would not have time to develop any hard feelings about my being a survivor, so why not wear the jacket?

This logic had seemed sound, so I wore it. The fallacy in the reasoning, of course, was the assumption that it was desirable to be a survivor in these waters. In my case, since I was a staff officer familiar with many secrets of Allied clandestine activity in the theater, it was clearly undesirable from a personal as well as from a military point of view. I had no right to be a survivor in any situation which involved a serious risk of falling alive into enemy hands. Therefore, I should take off the jacket.

Well, I thought, I would take it off if anything started, but it gave me a feeling of security to wear it, so why not leave it on as long as everything remained quiet?

This debate went on for a little while, and then I took off the jacket and the pistol belt, and put the jacket behind my head and leaned back looking up at the moon, and it was as if I had been looking at her before through a veil, and now the veil was removed.

I remained in this position for a long time, perhaps an hour, but there is no way of telling, just as there is no way of telling what passed through my mind, because in reality nothing passed through it. There was simply a great feeling of freedom, of freedom from life-jackets and pistols, from the mathematics of survival, from the neurosis of death and the illusion of security, from the barrier of identity which lay between me and the men sleeping below decks, from the veil which normally lies between all men and all sources of light, from the sense of self, from the sense of time, from the tyranny of comfort and discomfort, from everything, in fact, except the feeling of being free.

My mind did not even formulate the thought that this absolute sense of freedom provided the emotional radiations within the conceptual vacuum of Nirvana, which had made it for more than two thousand years the light of Asia. This realization only came later, when the moon went down and the gray mist of dawn lay over the bay, when the swimmers had returned reporting no mines, and the shore party had presented me with a live Arkanese farmer for questioning, and the positive assurance of no Japs; when I had composed a signal for headquarters and eaten a hearty

American breakfast and come up again on deck to find the sun
shining, the coastline of Ramree Island invisible beyond the horizon and all four craft skimming northward upon the surface of a
sapphire sea, apparently at top speed.

'We're just keeping up with cousins,' the skipper explained.
'The British have the wind up because there's another landing on
down the coast this morning and they don't want to be caught
anywhere near when the RAF shows up. These guys don't give a
damn for the Japs, but they're sure scared to death of their own
air force.'

Here, I thought, was a new variant of the illusion of danger.
These intrepid little mongooses of the sea, these inveterate pokers-
into-snakeholes, these prodders of nocturnal hornets, feared no
traps that night could set for them; no land-locked fjord was ever
too narrow for them, no reef and mine-strewn channel too peril-
ous. Danger for them dwelt in the free open seas and the clear
morning sky, it was a brother's delusion, encased in metal, sped
by zeal and folly and youthful carelessness, banded with the colors
of fraternity, diving upon them out of the sun.

Taking off my shirt and stretching on the deliciously warm,
deliciously spray-cooled deck, I looked at my brother Buddhist,
the Sagu agriculturalist, squatting in serenity near the rail, weigh-
ing in his mind the relative absurdities of the illusion of warm tea
and the illusion of seasickness, and I thought:

If Buddhism were what we imagine it to be, Buddhism could
no more have survived in southern and eastern Asia than it did
in India. If it were nothing but a religion of negation and withdrawal from reality, it would be of no use except to men too sick
to use it. If the Buddhist doctrine of illusion were only a metaphysical abstraction like Bishop Berkeley's which Samuel John-
son refuted by stubbing his toe on a rock — as my friend, the
prisoner, here, is shortly going to refute the illusion of seasickness
by throwing up his tea — then no sane man — and this quiet
little Arakanese is as sane as any farmer — could ever remain a
Buddhist after his hangover had cleared up. If Nirvana were
merely the worship of nothingness, it would not have the millions
of worshipers that it has.

Beneath all the rationalizations and confusions and the conventionalized bad grammar, Buddhism, I feel sure, is a religion of important affirmation. Doubtless many Buddhists, themselves, do not know quite what they mean by illusion, but I think the Buddhist sages have known. I think that to these sages Maya has not meant the illusion of perception but the false conclusions which we base upon perception — the superstitions of permanency we develop about impermanent things, the illusion of immutability that we have about changing things, the illusion of possession we develop about things we use.

The illusion of life to these sages has meant the private delusions of immortality which make it so difficult for us to accept the reality of death. The illusion of death is the psychological defenses which we build up against the idea of death, the absurd life-jackets we put on in order to become survivors when we know survival is impossible, the pistols we wear so that we can shoot death when he comes for us — pistols with which we sometimes shoot our neighbors, thinking they may be death in disguise.

The illusion of self is not a denial of the sense of identity, it is the superstition that one identity is more important than another, that we are not cut off when we cut ourselves off from our brothers, that we can be blown free of the wreckage in one piece when they are turned to cinders in their bunks.

Nirvana is not void, it is consciousness void of illusion, it is the sense of peace and freedom which fills the mind when it is emptied of all attachment to illusion; it is the subjective realization of resolved conflicts, of attained integrations; it is totality felt by the whole, not a light that one sees, but the light by which one sees.

Because of this, Buddhism is not so much a religion for those seeking a light, like Christianity, as for those trying to bring light to others who are frustrated by the darkness within themselves. Unlike Christianity it is incapable of giving a sense of purpose until the purpose is almost achieved, its goal becomes a motive only when it is nearly attained. It is a technique of orientation rather than a statement of mission.

It is a good religion for people close enough to civilization to imagine themselves civilized, for those who are full of aim but always missing, for those whose love of truth becomes the delusion of rightness, for those who seek unity so passionately that they shatter into fragments, for those whose ideal of brotherhood causes them to crack their brothers' skulls, whose ideal of freedom turns them into defenders of slavery, whose progress becomes regression; for those whose illusion of danger dwells on the open sea and in the clear morning sky, whose peace is troubled by their brothers' delusions — and by their own delusions of their brothers' delusions.

It is the religion of not quite one world. A great deal of it would do the West, as well as modern India, a great deal of good, just as a little Christianity would doubtless do the Burmese and the Siamese no harm.

V

Mission Into Morning

THE DOCTRINES of reincarnation and karma, common to both Hinduism and Buddhism, for a long time seemed to me the most incomprehensible feature of these religions. As a purely metaphysical concept, I could grasp the theory that every human soul lives through a cycle of terrestial lives, instead of just one, and that the pattern of each of these lives is determined by what happened to the soul in the previous ones, the degree to which it mastered or succumbed to worldly illusions.

I could not see, however, how this concept related to any normal human experience, or expressed in religious syntax any emotional reality. The pantheist raptures of Hinduism, the intense Buddhist awareness of illusion and of freedom from illusion, seemed to me merely enhanced elaborations of psychic states with which most of us are familiar from personal experience. Even Western man is capable of fleeting Hinduisms and Buddhisms in the sense just mentioned, and for this reason it helps us both to develop our own capabilities and to recognize Eastern man as a brother if we can understand what the specialists in these moods are trying to say about them.

I simply could not make out what the Eastern masters were trying to say when they said reincarnation and karma.

If I had ever experienced the feeling some people in the West say they have had (usually when falling in love or on arriving in a strange land) — that of having known all this in some previous existence — then I might have been able to understand the East-

319

ern meaning of reincarnation. I have never had this feeling, and suspect that it is a highly literary one, something imagined rather than really felt.

There was one experience, accessible to normal consciousness, to which it seemed to me the doctrines of reincarnation and karma might refer, but it hardly appeared adequate to explain the importance of these concepts in Eastern religious thought. This is the awareness of adult experience as a reliving of childhood experiences, of adult destiny as a pattern determined by the emotional adjustments or maladjustments of childhood. Reincarnation and karma would be handy utensils of communication for an analyst trying to explain the Freudian theory of neurosis to a Hindu patient.

It is possible, of course, that these doctrines do refer to experiences of something like autopsychoanalysis on the part of the Hindu sages who first enunciated them, but this hypothesis did not satisfy my mind somehow, and my failure to find a broader emotional frame of reference for them bothered me, since it was implicit in my whole approach to the study of religions that most major religious utterances contained a message of importance to nonbelievers as well as to believers. I did not believe in the literal reincarnation of soul (if soul be understood to include the individual personality), but I felt almost sure that those who did believe in soul-reincarnation must have elaborated their belief out of something that I, too, believed — or at least felt — and that, because they evidently attached greater importance than I to the whole subject, might have discovered some useful things about our common basic belief, or feeling, which I had overlooked.

That this was, in fact, the case, first occurred to me flying over the Burma-Siam border country on a night between peace and war. It was during the long military hiatus between the first Japanese offer of surrender and the formal ceremony of surrender which took place on the battleship *Missouri* in Tokyo bay, and I was on my way to Bangkok to lay the groundwork for the evacuation of American prisoners of war, once hostilities were officially at an end.

Kandy was already having a victory celebration when I left, but when I reached Rangoon I found that Allied planes were still being fired upon when they crossed the Japanese lines, Allied bombing missions were still being flown against the Japanese remnants in eastern Burma, and our underground headquarters in Bangkok had warned me to observe strictly all the usual conditions of a clandestine arrival, since the Japanese commander there refused to consider the war over until he had formal instructions from Tokyo.

Consequently my immediate destination on this night was the secret jungle airfield which we had used for many months to fly in supplies and liaison officers for the Siamese underground. With an OSS colleague, Dr. Dillon Ripley, and several Siamese officers returning from missions to our headquarters or training camps, I had driven late at night through a tropical downpour to the blacked-out, deserted, waterlogged Rangoon airfield, piled a full panoply of warlike equipment into the plane and watched the faint scattered lights of shattered Rangoon dim to nothingness beneath me as we swung eastward into a dense bank of raincloud, that was like the delusion of war shutting in again after a moment of peace.

This was probably the last clandestine mission of the war in our theater — if it could still be called war — and something of the superstitious dread that pilots have of final missions before the return home gripped me, along with a more complete sense of strain. There was an intense loneliness in the darkened, nearly empty plane; the noise of the motors made conversation difficult, and none of us felt much like talking. This was neither war nor peace, so there was between us in the plane neither the bond of common peril and common mission which unites the members of operational parties in combat; nor the casual fraternity of peacetime passengers, sharing the human heritage of victory over the normal perils of the sky. Each of us had an emotional adjustment to make which had to be made in loneliness, an adjustment to the borderland between war and peace which was like some complex problem of human relations. We had to separate from war without bitterness, to reknit the severed integrations of peace. It was a very anxious and rather poignant moment in time.

Looking back on it, I realized that participation in the war had been for me an absorbing and fulfilling experience. Never had I felt so reconciled to war, but the reconciliation was retrospective — to continue or resume my wartime existence after this foretaste of peace seemed unendurable. The present hiatus between war and peace filled me with uneasiness. It was a perfectly natural consequence of the military situation in the Eastern theaters, but, as a symbol, it fitted too aptly into the pattern set by the equivocal success of the United Nations Conference at San Francisco and by the ambivalent triumph of Hiroshima, still too fresh for the mind to digest. Like everyone else who heard the news, even those who had no idea what atomic energy was, I realized instantly that Hiroshima, which ended the war, had not ended war.

Now, as we flew eastward through the rain-filled night, protected by cloud, and possibly by indifference, from the Japanese gunners on the ground below, a deep sense of futility, and almost despair, filled my mind. Had all the toils and sacrifices of war resulted only in deepening the world's insecurity, and thus aggravating the delusions which had given rise to global war? Was every human effort ultimately in vain, was man forever and in all circumstances the self-defeating animal? Was man's mission — if he had one at all — that of a biological cancer cell?

I was so wrapped in these gloomy thoughts that it was some time before I noticed that we had risen above the clouds and were now flying in still clear air between the impersonal stars and a pearly floor of mist, faintly illumined by the last rays of an invisible moon. The other occupants of the plane seemed to be asleep, and as I looked out the window upon the soulless beauty of the upper night sky I had the illusion of being completely alone in outer space. Gradually an asteroid, Nirvana-like feeling of tranquillity came over me. I ceased to despair over man's desperate mission and even futility was swallowed up by nothingness.

Then the mist began to break up into patches, and I looked

down, far down, through these rents in the stratosphere of illusion and saw row upon row of jagged, jungle-clad ridges, separated by sheer crevices of night and knew we were flying over the wild mountain country that divides Burma from Siam, one of the loneliest landscapes that man can look upon.

Suddenly, in the heart of this desolation, near the top of one of the saw-toothed ridges which seemed calculated gestures of hostility on the part of Nature toward man flying over, I saw an almost unbelievably poignant thing — a fire lit by man. It was a fire lit by man, not an ember of the mountain, for it was surrounded by smaller, scattered fires that unmistakably outlined a human encampment.

Perhaps it was a Karen hill-village, perhaps a camp of woodcutters, perhaps a Japanese outpost of some kind. It did not matter to me in the slightest whose fire it was, for it was my fire, a signal to me from some brother on the ground that I was not flying alone in outer space, because he was there, that the world of man was still accessible, and that I was not doomed to eternal life among the asteroids. If our plane crashed against one of those savage ridges we would be killed but not unfound, some human eye would mark our passing and some human tongue would pronounce our epitaph, even if it was only an enemy's exclaimed sardonic triumph or a woodcutter's loutish amazement. Whatever survived of our equipment, perhaps the most personal thing about men in war, would be used by those who found us, used perhaps strangely or perversely, but that did not greatly matter, whereas it seemed to me that it would be unbearably tragic if my forty-five became a handful of scrap-iron, if my canteen-bottle turned to white dust, if the intricate escape-kit attached to my belt, my special pride which I wanted willed to humanity, should disintegrate in the jungle without finding a legatee. Nothing in life is so essential as having heirs, I thought.

That fire in the mountains reminded me of Antoine de Saint-Exupéry, the talented French writer, whom I had met in Bordeaux, when France was crumbling, and again as a refugee in the United States, whose body, according to reports from friends at home, now lay unfound, somewhere in the Mediterranean theater, amid the disintegrating wreckage of his plane, and as far as anyone knew, without heirs for whatever equipment had been his special pride. In one of his books Saint-Exupéry describes such a fire, a light seen when lost in the desert night, and my fire certainly owed much to his, he had taught me to see that fire through his eyes, as he had taught me to understand many of the experiences of flying with his understanding.

Then a very curious memory came back to me. The last time I had thought of Saint-Exupéry in this way had been several months earlier, one evening as I was driving back to Calcutta from the base of the American Twentieth Bomber Command at Karagpur in western Bengal. I had gone to Karagpur to see if there were not some way the OSS chain of clandestine bases in enemy territory could be used to facilitate the activities of the B–29's over enemy territory and had run into an exciting bit of drama. The Twentieth was flying its last mission — before moving out of the Pacific — to Singapore that very night. Casualties over the target were seldom very heavy on these raids but nearly every one resulted in particularly tragic losses from planes being shot up and forced to ditch in the Bay of Bengal on the way home. By the time rescue planes and naval craft reached the scene of the ditching the survivors were often impossible to find, especially in thick weather, and the poor prospects of rescue for the crew of a damaged plane weighed more heavily on the morale of the Twentieth than the danger of being shot down once and for all by fighters or ack-ack over the target.

'Give me a safe ditching-area that our boys can head for when they get into trouble, a place where we can find them without losing any time in searches, and that will be the greatest thing you can do for us,' the intelligence officer of the group had told me. 'You may save the lives of a crew or even two crews on tonight's mission if you can give me that information. What's equally important, you have no idea what a difference it will make to the morale of those boys flying up there at thirty thousand feet, fifteen hundred miles or more from their base, to know that there's some place where they can come down and be found.'

The intelligence officer had spoken so earnestly, with such deep human feeling, that I was strongly moved by his appeal. I knew the perfect safe haven for his fliers — a small island off the Malayan coast, less than half the way back from Singapore, and in sight of a larger island where OSS maintained a ship-watching party equipped with radio. Moved though I was, I was reluctant to let the airmen know about that island because their knowledge — and above all their use of it — would compromise the security of our important and terribly exposed ship-watchers. It was contrary to all cloak-and-dagger traditions to reveal the exact locations of clandestine parties to fliers constantly exposed to capture by the enemy, and apart from this tradition, it was clearly gambling with the lives of one group for the sake of another. If I gave the Twentieth that information it meant that we would have to evacuate our party as fast as we could — hoping that we would be fast enough — and it seemed a heavy sacrifice for just one bombing raid. These thoughts raced through my mind as I weighed the intelligence officer's plea, and I was about to say I was sorry, when some dim memory rose almost to the surface of consciousness and then sank, but its rising had been enough to make me take a deep breath and say, 'All right, here are the co-ordinates ——,' and the intelligence officer had thanked me over his shoulder as he raced off to get the fliers briefed before they left.

On the way back to Calcutta there had been a great roar and I had stopped the car and stepped out in time to see the great B-29's fade into the darkening eastern sky, heading for Singapore. That was when I had thought of Saint-Exupéry. I had thought — and wondered at the time why that name should have occurred to me — 'Perhaps Saint-Exupéry would have been able to put down on paper what I feel at this moment.'

Now I was flying myself through night and loneliness, not at thirty thousand feet but high enough to feel close to outer space, not fifteen hundred miles from my base but far enough so that one unknown fire on the ground seemed to me more beautiful and more important than all the stars in the sky, more poignant than any human contact in life, and it was as if I had foreseen all this that afternoon at Karagpur, and out of a sympathy born from an experience which had not yet taken place, had given away our precious secret to the fliers.

I knew, though, it was not I who had given the secret to the fliers, it was not I who had saved the lives of eleven men by a reckless sentimental impulse — for one of the B–29's had been shot up over Singapore and had been able to limp back as far as our island, but no farther, and had been ditched in the Bay within easy swimming distance of it, and all the crew had been saved by rescue planes. It was Saint-Exupéry — already dead, as far as I could make out from my friends' letters — who had done this. It was the memory of the strangely moving images of the loneliness and comradeship of fliers, so vividly conjured up in his writings, which had risen almost to consciousness when I was talking to the intelligence officer of the Twentieth Bomber Command. If Saint-Exupéry had never written *Flight to Arras* or *Wind, Sand and Stars*, I would not have been moved enough by the intelligence officer's plea. I would have said, 'I am sorry.' The rescue of that B–29 crew had been part of Saint-Exupéry's testament, they were his legatees, and I, unwittingly, had been his executor.

What strange heirs men have, I thought, and even what strange executors of their unfulfilled purposes. If I were any kind of a disciple of Saint-Exupéry the heritage would seem less extraordinary, but I hardly knew him as a man, the few times that I did meet him I rather disliked him because I thought him conceited and surly, and though his writings always seemed to have some special personal relevance, I never considered him as one of the important French writers. Also, what curious chains of conversion link our inner purposes with their ultimate results, what remarkable transformations take place in our thoughts when they become the actions of other men, what unexpected metamorphoses when our experiences are reincarnated in other men's destinies. Surely the doctrines of reincarnation and karma reflect this same intense, awesome awareness of past and future social context to all one's thoughts, to all one's feelings, to all one's acts, this feeling of being executor and legatee to accumulated human testaments reaching back to the dawn of man, of projecting one-self as testator to the end of time, of being a link between all men who lived and all who shall live.

It was not only because Saint-Exupéry had been a writer and I a reader that I had become his executor, I reflected. That was only one of the more direct lines of transmittal, but there were many others. Here another curious personal experience came back to my mind and in reliving it a wholly new awareness of its significance occurred to me.

Nearly a year before I had narrowly escaped death, when a passenger plane in which I was riding had a critical mechanical breakdown on take-off. A bare fifty yards above the ground one of its two engines failed, and since we were fairly heavily loaded, we should have crashed. Thanks to the quick reflexes of the pilot, the perfect balancing of the load, and the ruggedness of the other engine, which was instantly stepped up to its maximum speed, we were able to maintain ourselves in the air without per-ceptibly losing or gaining altitude. For five extremely tense moments, the pilot jockeyed the ship around trees and houses and smokestacks in a long, flat turn which ended in a perfect landing. During that time there had been very little in my mind except the determination to look reasonably composed and a mental picture of the plane as a great heaving beast struggling to keep its head above water in a roaring flood. Once the ordeal was over, I forgot about it quickly and it had lain dormant in my mind all these months.

Now, as the experience came back to me, I realized how re-markable and complex it had been, how much it was a part of everything that had ever happened or ever would happen in the world of man. The engine-failure which had provoked this crisis in flight was an accident from the point of view of myself as an individual consciousness, but as an element in the continuum of human experience I was working out — by being a passenger in the plane — the karma of other lives. My fright was the end-

result of a chain of human errors reaching back not only to the
ground-crew that had last serviced the plane, the inspectors who
had passed the engine, the workers who had created it with a
flaw, but to the men and women whose illusions and delusions
engendered their errors.

The engine, as it came out of the factory, was the result of some
workman's sloppy work; perhaps it was the end result of a neglected childhood. The inspector might simply have been tired
and overworked, but it was quite possible that he had once been
an honest man who had married a whore, greedy for money he
could not afford to give her out of honest earnings. The mechanics at the air base who should have detected the defective equipment — however many others had missed it — suggested strongly
the kind of soldiers whose officers do not realize it is their duty to
set an example as well as to give orders.

Perhaps the chain of casualties which had produced the accident was something quite different, but it was more than likely
that it involved somewhere along the line at least one individual
deficiency in social conscience, and therefore at least one inade-
quacy or trouble in social background.

A similar chain of positive karma had saved our lives, but the
social context of this fortunate chance was even more clearly
apparent, for the airmen among the passengers agreed that we
owed our survival chiefly to the pilot's instantaneous appreciation of impending catastrophe when the engine failed, and to the
unhesitating, automatic way he had instantly acted to avert it,
by accelerating the remaining engine.

In the idiom of sport, the pilot had staged a championship performance. In addition to good training and good judgment, this
performance indicated an unusually good biological inheritance,
plus a superbly healthy mind. No neurotic dread of death possessed this mind, or the pilot would have lost his head at the
moment of crisis, but neither did it contain, like the minds of
many men, strong, unconscious longings for death. Above all, it
was a mind admirably adjusted to reality, quick to adjust to
changing realities. Had there been any clinging to the dead past,

any animistic hope that wishing would start the stalled engine turning over again, the pilot would not have acted quickly enough, and I would not that night have been on my way to Bangkok, thinking these thoughts.

Doubtless there were plenty of healthy beasts, blonde or otherwise, in the world, capable of an equally good performance in similar circumstances. In our American culture, however, with its rigorous idealistic imperatives constantly goading the individual onward and upward, with its harsh taboos on infantile sexuality, with its complex and nearly incomprehensible devices for stimulating, and at the same time curbing, aggressiveness, for fostering and combating delusion, with its tense but meager emotional relationships between the sexes, the kind of psychic health which the pilot had expressed by his behavior at a moment of crisis almost necessitated the co-operation of a large number of individuals. It implied that the pilot, as a champion, descended from a long line of champions, by the heritage of influence as well as that of blood. It established his piloting-performance as the culmination of a series of superior performances in various fields by men and women, each as outstanding in some way as he was in his professional capacity.

Good parental care in childhood, loving but not spoiling, had been needed to nurture him into a healthy pilot. That meant a mother who had been a good mother, a father who was a good lover because his own childhood had not turned him into a hater or a fearer. The technical skill, without which his untroubled reflexes would have been useless, could not have been acquired if the pilot had not possessed a strong sense of duty and purpose, an attitude toward learning that made instruction fruitful, the requisite mixture of self-confidence and humility. In addition to the good instructors at his flying school, childhood teachers, scoutmasters, coaches, uncles, godfathers, older brothers or other trainers and personality-models had all helped to make him a good pilot.

Since the performance was on the championship level, even recent, slight, or superficial influences may have been significant.

Perhaps at the time of the crisis the pilot's psychic tonus had been above his own normal level. Perhaps a strict but thoughtful commanding officer, weary of his administrative burdens, but never too weary to remember duty, had taken time from a dozen more urgent tasks to call in the pilot and praise him for his work, or to reprimand him — in a way that made him glad to be reprimanded — for once not having been equal to himself. Perhaps the pilot's wife or sweetheart had written him a warming letter, reflecting the minute, innumerable victories of a lonely woman over personal illusion and delusion, the kind of letter which can only be written by a woman whose mind, shaped in a school of love and reality, contains no self-impoverishing mechanisms to aggravate the impoverishment of absence. Even a cheerful room-mate or a loyal crew might have made an indispensable psychological contribution to the feat of skill which had saved my life.

There was no telling, in fact, who had contributed to the pilot's performance, or exactly what they had contributed. There was no tracing the intricate channels of conversion whereby the wisdoms of others had become the pilot's coolness, their tendernesses his skill, their idealisms his muscular co-ordination, their generosities his courage, their sense of duty his will to live.

All one could say of the incident as a whole was that a long chain of human fears, hates, greeds, and self-indulgences had somehow culminated in the failure of an airplane engine while I happened to be riding in the plane, and that a chain of contrary values, of personal victories over the negative emotions, had somehow neutralized the effects of the first karma-system, leaving me the frightened but living legatee to the good and bad purposes, to the private victories and defeats, of many human beings I had never known.

As social legatee, I was also a historic testator, ancestor as well as descendant of many fragmentary lives. Since I had not been killed in that plane, my experience of survival had certainly added a new link to the chain of causation of which the near-accident was a part. Both my fright and any wisdom I had learned from it would eventually and in some form be reborn in other lives. How they would be reborn would depend on my personal assimilation of the experience, on whether it finally represented a victory or defeat for me.

I could look upon the experience with the eye of illusion. I could, for instance, retain out of it only my fright and use this to strengthen the neurosis of death within me, thereby creating a cowardice which would eventually become some other human's frigidity or hate. I could weave out of the survival some delusion of personal grandeur, some myth of invulnerability or divine selection, thereby adding my bit to all the other delusions of grandeur in the world.

Equally, I could drain out of the experience its accumulated negative charge and transmit to other men, my future selves, the earlier victories, with my own added. For example, in my relations with my own military subordinates I could use it as an aid in thinking of them as if they were pilots who might be confronted at any moment with a crisis requiring them to surpass themselves, and so conduct myself toward them, so praise or reprimand them as occasion required, that I would add to their ability to surpass themselves.

Up to the present, I reflected, my experience of survival had borne very little fruit of any kind. For nearly a year it had lain unassimilated in my mind, unrelated to the rest of my experience, enclosed in a light envelope of shock. It had to be relived before it could be fully assimilated and a curious assortment of factors had just caused me to relive it. Among these were the fire on the mountain lit by unknown brothers, Saint-Exupéry, Hiroshima, and the peculiar Japanese technique of surrender.

Now the stream of consciousness washed up a new bit of un-assimilated experience. Long ago, early in the war I think, someone had shown me the transcription of a Japanese broadcast, which I had contemptuously dismissed as an example of the enemy's delusive mentality, yet had not been able to forget. The broadcast had been a speech by some Japanese official intended to stimulate war production. In it, the official told his listeners that victory would be certain if they built a great number of bombing planes, for every Japanese bomber carried the spirits of ten thousand Japanese workers, who protected it against enemy fire, and assured its success on every mission. Apparently the official had meant this as a literal statement of fact, not as a patriotic metaphor.

This Shinto delusion had been only a slight distortion of a Buddhist truth, I thought. What was not delusive in it was actually an understatement. Neither Japanese nor any other spirits could protect a plane from enemy fire, but the spirits of Japanese workers had literally been converted into bombers. The bomber did not carry the workers' spirits, it was their spirits in metallic form.

Whatever is made by man is the incarnation of human experience, and the reincarnation of earlier human experience. Because a man is gentle with a woman or a woman kind to a man, a child may be born who will be lighted by a glow of gentleness and kindness, and this light will be transmitted to other children, to many children, for children are made in many ways, and may be many things — a song may be a child, or a gentle law, or a kindly treaty, or a mathematical formula expressing the tenderness of figures, an idea that will become a machine, expressing the tenderness of cogs and levers, before it becomes again an idea and then an emotion, again a child of someone's flesh, expressing the love of man and woman.

There can be, my thought continued, no absolute separation between thoughts and feelings and things, and there is no valid distinction between public and private acts, for history is not a play put on by a professional cast, it is the interaction of all men upon all men. Men are not islands, as Donne said, but man is a continent in time as well as in space. Every continental convulsion is a private neurosis, and every private delusion is a secession from social history, just as every personal discovery of social reality is a diplomatic victory.

Some Hindu sage's meditations on nothingness produced the mathematical symbol, zero, which by a chain of cultural conversions became, as Lancelot Hogben and others have pointed out, one of the foundations of Western science and technology. By another chain of conversion, I reflected, this strange converted gift of nothingness became Hogben's book, which, by providing me with the analogy of a religious syntax, helped to break down the barriers of understanding that made the Oriental concepts of Nirvana, of karma, and of reincarnation meaningless to me.

My own private doctrine of reincarnation and karma was not exactly what the Hindus and Buddhists meant, I realized. Reincarnation as I visualized it was not a transmigration of souls but a transmission and conversion of human influences. Yet, if I understood the higher Eastern philosophy correctly, the gap between my view and it was not so great as it seemed. Soul, especially to the most abstract Buddhist thinkers, had never meant what it means in the West. What we call soul — the spiritualized conscious personality — has always seemed an illusion to the East, for in Eastern religion as in Western materialism, the conscious personality is considered as an accidental and ephemeral assemblage or equilibrium of influences, automatically destroyed by the death of the individual.

The soul which the thinkers of the East believe is reincarnated in successive existences is merely some form of cosmic energy in some way patterned or affected by the beings through which it passes, by their personal lives and experience. To me this concept seemed dubious and I could think of no way in which a man's personality lives after his death save as he has transmitted it through some release of energy during his lifetime.

Yet the great theoretical difference between the mystic Oriental concepts of reincarnation and karma and my literal, mechanistic one, seemed to me unimportant. Either concept, if one followed out all its implications, led to the same sense of total participation in mankind, to the same sense of social solidarity and responsibility, to the same feeling of being a link between the past and the future, to the same realization of one world, to the same continent of man.

Even the Christian concept of personal inheritance in heaven, though it sometimes involved believers so deeply in the problem

of their own salvation that they forgot their fellows, could lead —
as Donne proved — to the same goal.

It seemed to me unimportant whether one regarded oneself as
one's own heir in heaven, like the Christian, as one's own heirs on
earth, like the Hindu and the Buddhist, or whether, as I did, one
considered all future men as one's heirs. Each of these views,
rightly held, caused one to feel like a testator and to be assured of
heirs.

This feeling was the important thing. It was an intense personal and social reality which made one's slightest experiences,
one's smallest acts, seem extremely significant, while preventing
the greatest ones from seeming excessively, tragically significant.
It made one a soldier in the ranks of men, lending to the individual
self the dignity and importance which derives from belonging to
something greater than self — from being a volunteer in a great
cause.

At least some of the emotional roots, and most of the social
significance of religion lay in this feeling, it seemed to me. All the
religious myths, and even the religious delusions, that I had so
far examined appeared to refer in some way — however obscurely or twistedly — to this basic religious experience. All
religious roads traced back to man, though they sometimes led
away from him.

The weakness in religious utterance, especially Western religious utterance, as I saw it, was that in telling men about the
peaks of human experience, it neglected the values of the plain.
In forging the indispensable verbal device of miracle, it often
overlooked the miraculousness of the commonplace. In empha-
sizing the emotional significance of certain aspects of life by the
punctuation of spirit, it sometimes dimmed realization of the
spirituality of all life, and even of the implicit spirituality of all
matter. In speculating upon the transmigration or ascension of
the individual soul after death it distracted attention from the
daily apotheosis of its transmission throughout life, from the millions of testamentary acts by which a personality perpetuates
itself, from the myriads of accepted legacies which constitute a

consciousness. In promising us the mystic return of bread cast upon the water, it omitted to remind us that, if we cast our bread upon the waters, after many days we become able to cast more bread farther.

The danger in mechanistic utterance — at least in an idealistic context — was that it tended to create myth by understatement. It tended to make us milk-worshipers, as my friend, the doctor, thought it had made Henry Wallace one. By insisting, however, accurately, that peaks were nothing but elevated plains, it made them seem less high than they are, thereby quite literally creating an illusion. To say — which is all that mechanistic utterance normally says — that it is pleasant and healthful for the individual to participate as extensively as possible in the social life of humanity, is to formulate an under-myth, to create an implicit illusion, as one might by declaring that it is unhealthy to stop breathing.

Hiroshima, it seemed to me, had made this tendency to think of the world in terms of under-myth particularly harmful. In those days — on this night between war and peace — I did not yet know that the 1945 atomic bomb was considered by the best authorities unlikely to start a chain reaction, that the man-encompassed disintegration of our planet must await the next advance of science, that the most we can hope to achieve with present weapons is to wipe out organized human society everywhere on earth.

In my ignorance, I believed that the consummation of a planetary suicide-pact of all animate and inanimate things lay within our immediate attainment, and was likely sometime to be attained, for whatever man can do, he generally ends by doing.

If one used religious syntax it was not too difficult to verbalize this possibility after a fashion. A Christian could say that it was the final victory of Satan, the triumph of chaos o'er creation, uncreating. A Buddhist could say that it was a false Nirvana, a total regression into illusion. I could say that it was a voiding of the testament of man. All of these were powerful utterances to anyone who accepted the basic symbols employed in them, all expressed the deep half-conscious, possibly irrational, sense of mission, the instinctive man-reverence and even nature-reverence which most healthy beings feel, the creative and cohesive emotions which I felt must be mobilized if the possibility of disintegration were to be averted. Yet none of these statements seemed wholly satisfactory.

In mechanistic terms — for I no longer considered my own purely mechanistic — one was forced into one of two extremities. One had to combat under-myth by deliberate understatement, or raise the voice, crying shrilly: It is the end of everything. The second alternative seemed particularly unsatisfactory. It is necessary to love our planet if we are to preserve it, but if we love it as some mothers love an only child, we may be so paralyzed by the dread of losing it that, in the moment of emergency, we cannot act effectively to save it.

It is a grave defect in all the languages and all the cultures of man, I concluded, that we really have no adequate means for verbalizing the main social problem of our time, the problem of the end of the world. What used to be a religious fantasy or a cosmic speculation has almost become a political issue. What used to be the most impersonal of all man's worries has now become one of his most intimate ones. What formerly seemed the final judgment of God or the ultimate fulfillment of a primal curse now appears to hinge upon the possibility of an individual error in arithmetic, or a false move in diplomacy.

How can we hope to verbalize such an incredible revolution in our thought-channels? Yet how can we think straight about it, and therefore act effectively, if we do not? We must do the best we can. We must borrow every possible tool of tongue and thought that man has ever applied to the problem of the end of the world and use them all at once, hoping that understanding will arise. We must use lyric pathos and mechanistic understatement and religious hyperbole or paradox. All are equally bad and equally good.

My own view of man's survival, I suddenly realized, was just such a mixture of pathos, understatement, and paradox. Belief in heirs is necessary to inspire the testamentary act, I thought, but the validity of man's testament is not contingent upon his heirs being found. Though man cease to be his own heir, the testament will not be voided. It is because of this, not despite it, that we must struggle to uphold the testator's act. The legacy itself cannot be lost because I know that — in ways unknown to me, but not necessarily unknowable — nothing is ever lost, or can be lost. It is because of this, not despite it, that we must work to save the legacy.

That, I decided, was probably as much religious belief as I would ever possess, and I had never before realized that I possessed so much.

Unrealizing that my wrestlings with the problem of no-world still anticipated progress by a few years, unrealizing, too, that more than four hours had gone by since I left Rangoon — four hours and only a few lives — I looked out of the window and saw that the unfulfilled glory of dawn had begun to tarnish the enamel of night, that the sawtoothed mountains had become low jumbled hills and the velvet purple jungle a muddied palette of off-green and browns.

At this moment the co-pilot beckoned me and I went forward to witness the naïve miracle of reason validated by navigation, to hear the pilot say 'There she is,' to look down upon a tiny patch of bare earth on which some antlike figures were swarming. We went into a steep dive but not steep enough. Seeing that we were going to overshoot the minuscule strip just as the wheels were about to touch, the pilot pulled up sharply and for a minute we were locked in a desperate struggle with the landscape, which kept trying to throw tenacles of forest and hillside around us, then we were clear and approaching again, and as the wheels touched the bumpy sod, the antlike figures came again into focus, this time waving and grinning little yellow men, my Siamese brothers, the unconscious heirs of many of my thoughts and executors of some of my wartime purposes.

PART VI

Back to Man

I

A Time for Gathering

IN MANY WAYS the period of my Asiatic existence which began
with the Japanese surrender was the most crowded, the most varied, the most absorbing — and even the most interesting — part
of my stay in the East. In a purely geographical sense, it was the
period of most extended travel. In a political sense, it was the
period of most extended documentation.

Yet it was only rarely a period of new experience. It was a
period of clarified and sometimes extended meanings, of expanded
applications. It was the season of mental harvest, the gathering
of understandings planted much earlier in my travels and slowly
ripening in the fields of my mind.

In a sense my pilgrimage in search of private understanding
reached its goal in the plane flying me into Siam when I .com-
pleted the adventure of discovering what — for lack of a better
and less pretentious term — might be called a personal faith or
fragmentary religion, an individual one-world, a faith developed
out of a kind of reverse cultural opposition to the great religious
philosophies of the East. For a Western mind trained as I have
indicated to the reader that mine was, this represents a long
journey, a final exoticism of adventure, a successful, or at least
concluded, pilgrimage.

My geographical travels, of course, continued. I eventually
reached Bangkok and accomplished the missions which I had to
accomplish, remaining there until after the Japanese surrender

341

had been formalized; then I returned to Kandy toward the middle of September, 1945, then accompanied the movement of our headquarters to liberated Singapore, and, after various travels, to Saigon and Batavia, where a new colonial war had broken out, and back to Bangkok, finally taking a plane home from Calcutta at the end of January, 1946.

It hardly seems worthwhile, however, to recount these travels, even in the loose manner that I have recounted my earlier ones. Instead these concluding chapters largely repeat for the reader the process which was going on in my own mind during the last few months of my stay in the East — the process of recapitulating, assembling, digesting, and applying the discoveries and conclusions deriving from my earlier travels.

Some of these discoveries and conclusions, it seemed to me, had simply been aids to immediate understanding which had lost their importance as soon as they had fulfilled their purpose. Others were so banal or self-evident that there was no need to do anything but recall them. They were personal realizations of importances rather than new ideas.

Thus, living in the East had made me realize how much cultural, racial, or other prejudice prevents the psychological attainment of one world by the individual, even when he considers himself unprejudiced. I had also learned what a valuable discipline for the mind and spirit it is to attempt to put aside cultural prejudice and learn the values of another people. I had no illusions about how little I had learned of the Orient, and wished I had a much deeper knowledge of it, but I had proved to my own satisfaction that it is not necessary to know a subject thoroughly to derive enrichment from trying to understand it.

I had further learned the immense importance that institutional delusion plays in our lives, as a barrier to understanding, and in many other ways.

These discoveries — in fact, all my discoveries — I owed in some way to the East, to my exposure to its cultural influences. As they arose in my mind they did not represent Eastern thought in all cases, but they always reflected it somehow, if only through the mechanism of cultural opposition. None of these discoveries would have been made by me if I had not traveled in the East and been exposed to Eastern influence. Since I considered them valuable I could not consider Eastern influence worthless, which was a far cry indeed from my prewar attitude toward the Orient.

The very concept of cultural opposition which an Eastern mind had given me seemed a most useful one, avoiding sterile comparisons between ultimate values (thus sparing me the effort of trying to determine whether there is more truth in hamburger than there is in curry), one which eliminated the necessity of trying to defend indefensible things in either Western or Eastern culture, which made possible a broad and constructive approach to the whole problem of cultural relations between peoples.

The dawn of the atomic age had dispelled for me any lingering doubts as to the soundness of the cultural philosophy expressed by my friend, the young Indian doctor: The view that there is an ideal balance between social institutions and social needs, with the resultant corollary that progress beyond real need may be as disastrous as when institution lags behind need — in the context of biological survival for the human species as a whole, even more disastrous. I failed to see how anyone can deny today that such a disequilibrium exists in our society, and that man is very likely to become extinct unless we can restore the equilibrium quickly.

It was in developing the implications of this diagnosis of the world's disorder, and in suggesting remedies, that it seemed to me I was most likely to deviate from the normal trend of Western thinking.

A number of sound Western thinkers, I knew, consider that the remedy for the world's critical disorder lies simply in raising our political institutions to the cultural level of science in the atomic age by establishing effective world government, whereas in my view the trouble was more profound, it was a whole revolution in human thought that must be effected.

This difference of opinion, I decided, was more apparent than real. It is true that I would like to place the problem of cultural equilibrium in a broader context than that of merely controlling atomic energy, but I am convinced that establishing effective world government will produce such a profound revolution in all human thought that many of the deeper social problems I have pointed out will tend to disappear. There is no doubt in my mind that world government is the solution to many problems besides the basic problem of peace, and that if it can be achieved man will be close to realizing the most audacious dreams that have ever been dreamed for him, the personal ones as well as the collective ones, the religious ones as well as the economic ones.

Nor do I believe that the political foundations of this revolution of unity are beyond achievement in our time. The analogy that I have drawn between the political conflicts of India and those of the world as a whole reflects this optimism. The thesis that humanity, in its present divided form, is essentially a curable disease, crops up in some manner throughout the whole account of my travels. Have we not seen through the clouds of group delusion that hang over India a glint of hope — at least enough to prove that hope is possible, for India and for man? Have we not seen the imperialist abscess which has poisoned British political thought for more than two centuries begin to drain, and noticed an almost instantaneous awakening in dormant British faculties of statesmanship, at least as applied to India? Have we not even seen the morbid modern Hinduism, in my view the cumulative result of two thousand years of regression, rapidly giving way to a promising new Indian culture which synthesizes some of the noblest ideals of East and West? And does not this Indian example of cultural change, on top of the examples of the United States and Soviet Russia — to say nothing of the examples of rapid de-culturation furnished by scores of primitive societies, including our own Red Indians — convincingly suggest, that, of all the barriers to man's unity, the barrier of so-called national character is one of the least insurmountable? (If national character were as unchangeable as we think, the Indian personality could not be changing as it is.)

Probably some of my friends, especially in America, will feel that I have built up needless complications around a very simple problem. Abolish the veto in the United Nations, and you have one world, these friends will say. That is all there is to the problem.

Those who hold this view are almost bound to disagree with some of my conclusions, because my stay in the East convinced me that as long as our Western attitudes toward certain problems remain what they are, the veto is not likely to be abolished in the United Nations, and we are not going to have one world. I believe that one world is attainable but I do not believe that our present approach to the problem will attain it for us. I believe that the disorder of man is curable, but I do not believe that the doctors who are trying to treat it have found the right cure. A tubercular physician may be able to heal a tubercular patient, but a sadistic psychiatrist would not be helpful to a patient suffering from delusions of persecution. While our physicians of one world are not sadists, it seems to me that they are as neurotic in many ways as the world they are trying to treat, as lacking in total vision as those whose national myopias they denounce. Unaware that they are preaching globalism with the bias of a cultural particularism, our world-federalists unconsciously create one world in the image of Western society — in the image of democratic-capitalist Western society — for I consider the Slavic Communist societies as also belonging to the cultural West.

Neither the Slavic Eastern half of the West nor the true Orient is likely to feel any great enthusiasm for our concept of a united world. We would feel less enthusiasm for one world if we had first heard of it from Gandhi and in the same frame of reference as vegetarianism, marital chastity, total nonviolence, and nonvivisectional medicine. We had very little enthusiasm for it when we heard of it from Lenin in the context of world revolution. No matter how much we repudiate any desire to force our cultural institutions upon the rest of the world, the communist and the Oriental societies can hardly fail to associate it in their minds with capitalism, our peculiar Western form of democracy, the philosophy of individualism, birth-control, color-prejudice, and imperialism. This is not merely a cross-cultural misunderstanding, or at least it is not wholly one. It is the inevitable result of trying to realize one world politically without first, or at least simultaneously, trying to realize it in our own minds, that is to say, without attempting to use other peoples' ideals of humanity to enlarge our own.

This need for the enlargement of Western cultural ideals, which is the lesson I derived from many of the mental adventures I have related, seems to me particularly great if one includes among them the ideals of what I have called the Western anticulture. Even if the reader does not follow me in thinking of the contradictions, the ethical anomalies, the hypocrisies in our Western way of life, as having an institutional pattern so definite that it deserves to be called an anticulture, he will doubtless agree that in our society there is far too wide a gap between ideal and performance and that many of us much of the time fail to realize how wide the gap is, that we are much less civilized, less Western, than we imagine ourselves to be.

Many of my conclusions go beyond that, however. It is not only our adherence to an unavowed anticulture which frustrates our efforts to attain one world. I believe that some of the true values or respectable patterns of Western culture are psychological barriers to the attainment of human unity.

For example, what I have called our delusion of rightness — our feeling of holiness about the rightness of our opinions — is not one of our secret cultural heresies. This attitude, implicit in our doctrine of national sovereignty, is one of the foundation-stones of our characters. Whether we are democrats or communists, Christians or atheists, we are sure that we are right and fear that we will somehow be damned if we do not fight to the last gasp for our beliefs. So we fight to the last gasp — which is not a good method for realizing one world, even if our belief happens to be one world.

We have a keen sense of reality, which is a very valuable possession, but it is allied with a tendency to see reality where it is not, that is, to fall into delusion. We are particularly blind to institutional delusion, and this is a highly dangerous defect.

We — in the western part of the West — are fairly rugged individualists and we think of ourselves as being even more individualistic than we are. This makes for considerable needless confusion in our own societies and causes the nonindividualistic philosophies of the East to seem repellent.

We have a myth of progress which takes little or no account of the social context of progress, and therefore often leads us, like Ram Lal, to put backwardness in modern dress and call it progress.

Our ideas are deficient in relevance generally, perhaps because we tend to think in terms of such rigid categories that the relationships between things escape us.

Our minds are rational as human minds go, but in trying to avoid the irrational we have fallen into the habit of mechanistic understatement which often leads to under-myth. The result is that we lack an adequate vocabulary for discussing the greatest problems of man and for propagandizing our ideals, in fact, we lack the verbal tools for developing our personalities by impressing our ideals upon our own minds.

These seem to me among the major weaknesses of Western culture from the one-world point of view. The fact that it has them does not mean that Western culture is worthless but in my opinion it does mean that Western culture inevitably must develop, among those who belong to it, attitudes which render effective action to attain one world difficult, if not impossible. Therefore, if we really want to cure the world's disorder, we must begin by treating ourselves so as to correct the disorders or deficiencies which our culture has produced in us.

This conviction that the first problem of realizing one world is to modify the attitudes of those of us who believe in it in such a way that our belief can become fruitful instead of self-defeating, is one of the major conclusions I developed out of my Eastern travels. It is linked in a number of ways with my more personal concept of individual contribution to the legacy of man as the goal and meaning of life. Both ideas are outgrowths of a modification and development of my own attitudes, brought about by my stay in the East, and are therefore to some degree the acceptance of an Eastern legacy.

Closely linked as the two ideas are, there is an important difference between them. The second one depends for its value upon a subjective criterion: It is true if it feels true. The first one, however, must be objectively validated. It is only useful if it can lead to some positive point of view toward the problem of human unity which can be accepted by the Western mind, yet does not contain the vices inherent in our culture.

During my last months in Asia I made an effort to elaborate out of my personal discoveries and conclusions an affirmative, coherent doctrine of right attitude toward the problems of the modern world — a general approach to the specific social or political problems of our day, which would not contain some implicit self-defeating premise.

The problem seemed simple enough, yet even attempting to define its terms proved arduous. I was not looking for a new philosophy of history or a new social theory — we have too many of them already. I was trying to find rules for personal conduct and attitude toward public questions, which, if followed by the individual, would enable him to escape the fate that has often befallen me — that of betraying his ideals in trying to implement them by participating in group action. Whenever I sought to express my quest in a general and impersonal statement it eluded me. The mental situation which I envisaged was one which apparently our culture — and perhaps all the cultures of man — fail to take into account. The right approach to public questions seems to us either a matter of having the right public ideology or a matter of private integrity. In my view a man could have noble, rational ideals, try honestly, sincerely, thoughtfully to implement them — and still end by doing as much harm as good, or be ineffectual in terms of his own ideals.

Puzzling over this problem, I stumbled over what seemed to me an important discovery. Most of our humanitarian ideologies omit a vital element — the element of conflict. We are told what our goal should be, and often precisely what means we should use to attain it, but we are given little or no guidance as to how we should behave when our efforts to realize our ideals bring us into conflict — as inevitably they must — with men of opposing ideals.

The early Christians had something to say on this score and so do the modern pacifists, but it is largely negative. We must turn the other cheek, not hate the enemy who hates us.

For some, this philosophy of conflict was adequate, but I did not feel it was adequate for me, and as I had noticed in India, even many of Gandhi's followers did not feel that the doctrine of nonviolence solves the whole problem of how to behave when one's ideals lead one into violent conflict with other men. Not only did pure nonviolence seem to me beyond the West's attainment, but I thought that there were a number of problems, beside the problem of violence, which arise out of social conflict — for instance, problems of morale, problems of strategic perspective, problems of delusion.

The problem of attitude toward one world — or toward any better world — therefore seemed to me to boil down to such specific questions as the attitudes of believers in one world toward nonbelievers in various situations, the attitudes of believers in democracy toward believers in some kind of totalitarianism, the attitudes of believers in progress toward practitioners of backwardness.

The answers to these and similar questions would constitute the doctrine of right attitude for which I was searching, I decided. I thought that my contact with Asia had already supplied me with many of the answers but during my last few months in the East I attempted to test and clarify my views by applying them to new and broader contexts.

II

The Nature of the Enemy

THE ATTITUDE that one should take toward groups, such as nations, which commit aggressions, has long been one of the most difficult problems of private relationship to public reality in the Western societies. The problem has never been solved and it has almost endless ramifications.

Are aggressor nations incurable? Do peace-loving peoples ever turn to aggression? Is appeasement always evil, and what constitutes appeasement anyway? How does one tell an aggressor-nation from one that is merely frightened? When a nation commits aggression, who is guilty, its leaders or its people as a whole?

These are only a few of the anguished questions which our confusion in regard to the whole problem of aggression generates in our minds. We usually have some sort of answer, but the answers even within a single society for a given moment in time are frequently far from unanimous, and they differ widely between the several Western societies and at different periods.

Thus, at the beginning of the war recently finished there was a widespread tendency in the democracies of the West to consider the Axis peoples as the innocent victims of their evil leaders. This changed as the war progressed to a fairly general view of the Japanese and German peoples as monsters of darkness. Since the end of the war the pendulum of our attitudes seems to me to have swung back and forth without as yet reaching an equilibrium.

All these uncertainties, these confusions, these contradictions in our thinking, appear to me to have been expressed in the Nuremberg trials of German war-leaders, resulting in a verdict which, though it seemed monstrous to very few, really satisfied nobody and provided no clear lesson for history, except that it is unwise to lose wars.

The conscience of man as revealed at Nuremberg seems to exist but has not yet learned to express itself in a manner that can be distinguished from the *vae victis* of all the ages.

The problem of aggression first began to seem a really puzzling one when Soviet Russia, which long had figured in my mind as an outstanding champion of peace, entered into a temporary partnership with the Axis powers in 1939, committed what clearly seemed an aggression against Finland, and then again emerged as a champion of peace, thanks to an aggression committed against her by her partners. I was spared the strain of changing my mind about our Soviet allies for the third time in the course of the war by being so engrossed in the problems of the East that the acts which presumably caused a number of people in the West to do so somehow escaped my notice.

On the other hand, during this period I had to undergo the trying experience of discovering that our British allies, whom I had always considered even more reliable champions of peace than the Russians, were regarded by my Indian friends as predatory and ruthless oppressors — nor could I deny the validity of their accusations, as far as British behavior toward them was concerned. These same Indian friends shocked me still more by pointing out that my own country — whose addiction to the ways of peace had once seemed to me almost a vice — had quite a dubious international record. Without counting our systematic extermination of the Redskins, surely one of the great crimes of modern history, we had fought the British in 1812 out of sheer bad temper, had fought the Mexicans in 1846 out of undisguised lust for land and power, had fought the Spaniards in 1898 out of feebly disguised imperialism, and had blundered somewhat questionably into World War I, even if we had blundered in on the right side.

In addition to that, we had seized the Panama Canal zone from Colombia by gangster methods and had practiced armed intervention in the affairs of our Latin-American neighbors up to 1928.

Much of this, of course, was ancient history by our standards, but, as my Indian friends pointed out, our present pacific ideology had not been flourishing long enough to validate our claim to being a peace-loving nation. All that could be said of us was that we were no worse than the other great powers, and better than some.

Viewed through Asiatic eyes, American history likewise offered an equivocal answer to the question of whether it is always and in all circumstances self-defeating to appease the nationalist greeds or fears of a sovereign power.

All the great colonial and maritime powers of Europe had appeased us by accepting the Monroe Doctrine, our hemispheric iron curtain, but we had not, because of this, inordinately expanded the strategic frontiers of the New World — at least we had not yet done so. England had practiced appeasement upon us at numerous times, notably by a generous offer of compromise in reply to the grotesque American territorial claims upon Canada expressed in the jingo slogan, 'Fifty-four Forty or Fight.' This appeasement had proved highly successful from the viewpoint of both parties.

Appeasement had proved rather costly to Colombia and Mexico, but had ultimately contributed to our new Good Neighbor policy, which in terms of their national security, was probably worth all that it had cost them.

China had appeased us, as she had appeased all the Western powers, by granting us rich commercial bases and accepting our arrogant colonial doctrine of extraterritoriality, but this appeasement had seemingly awakened our conscience rather than increased our appetite.

For many decades, until she passed from appeasement to aggression, Japan had also appeased us. In response to Perry's gentle persuasions, she had opened up her ports to American and world trade. In response to Anglo-American economic pressure,

backed up by naval power, she had set a foreign exchange rate for
her yen so disproportionate to its real value that it amounted to
paying tribute to the commercial powers of the West.

She had ended her first victorious war with Russia on what
were closer to being American than to being Japanese terms.   In
1922, after we had reversed our own policy of violent intervention
in the Russian civil war and ordered Japan to follow our example
in withdrawing from Siberia, she complied.   With a deep sense of
national humiliation she signed the Washington Naval Treaty of
1923, limiting the size of her navy to a figure that seemed emi-
nently reasonable to the Western powers because it theoretically
assured continued Anglo-American naval domination of the
Pacific with a reduced burden on the American and British tax-
payer.

Like her signing of the Washington Treaty, many of the Japanese appeasements were mere duplicities.   One could argue
either that Japan's policy of appeasement only led to war when it
was discontinued — or because it had never been sincere — or
that it had been self-defeating from the first.   In any case it was
not necessary to view the Japanese mind as notably more addicted
to delusion than the human mind generally to understand why
the Japanese people came to regard their relations with the West
as an endless series of unilateral appeasements, why they overlooked, or misinterpreted, the concessions which· increasingly
were being made to their point of view, why they failed to notice
— or dismissed as mere hypocrisy — the evolution away from
imperialism which occurred in the American mind between the
time of Perry and the time of Franklin Roosevelt.

Furthermore, the Japanese would have had to be keen cultural
anthropologists to disentangle hypocrisy from reality in the
strange subtle body of unwritten international law which slightly
tempers the lawlessness of Western power politics, which makes
the neighbor's foxes fair game for all, but holds it crime against
humanity to shoot a sitting fox.   As newcomers into the world
arena, the Japanese could hardly be expected to understand that
imperialism is not the right of unlimited oppression, but merely

the right to oppress defenseless peoples up to the point where they start hitting back, that exploitation ceases to be licit when it comes too close to enslavement, that bullying is aggression whenever the victim is strong enough to resist, that every power makes its own rules to suit its convenience but thereafter must abide by them, even against convenience, that fomenting revolution in other lands, like drinking absinthe, is a vice whenever it threatens to become habitual, that the power of veto, like other attributes of sovereignty, is unlimited but intended for use only in emergencies, that there are some contexts in which it is dishonorable to repudiate one's pledges and others in which it is not cricket to hold one's partners to theirs.

Whether or not it would have made any difference to them, the rulers of Japan can hardly have realized the distinction between their actions in China and Britain's actions in India, or for that matter, the actions of all the Western powers, including the United States, in China up to the foundation of the Chinese Republic. They could not be expected to understand that not only had Western political morality changed, but that China had changed, that to treat the China of Sun Yat-sen and of Chiang Kai-shek as the West had treated the China of the Opium War and the Boxer Rebellion was not merely an injustice but a disorder, not merely a crime but a mistake.

The Japanese, unused to our ways, failed to perceive that between the Sunday morality reflected in the covenant of the League of Nations or the Kellogg-Briand Pact and sheer international anarchy, the older nations of the West had developed a loose, elastic code of workday behavior, rooted in moral cynicism but recognizing the futility of war. The Japanese were not the only ones who had failed to see this. In all the countries where revolution had brought new social classes to power — in Germany, in Italy, and in Russia — these new men, unmellowed in the tradition of mitigated fascism which the age of princes had handed down to the chancelleries of modern Europe, tended to shock us by the naïve directness of their cynicism, which we hated the more because we unconsciously recognized in it our own, writ

large. The American Government, it seemed to me, tried harder
than most others to found policy upon the Sunday morality, but
was not always successful, particularly in judging the acts of
other governments. The criterion for determining aggression
with us seemed to be partly ethical, partly geographical, while
the color of the victims and the table-manners of the aggressors
were not considered wholly irrelevant. This American inconsistency had something to do with the origins of World War II,
I thought, and in some future circumstances might be an even
graver menace to the world's peace than the consistent cynicism
of other powers.

All this helped to make Japanese foreign policy prior to Pearl
Harbor seem comprehensible to me, that is, to say, merely stupid
and wicked instead of mad and monstrous. It did not, however,
explain the Japanese paradox, perhaps a more extreme one than
the German paradox. Just as I had often wondered how the people of Goethe and Beethoven had become the people of Lidîce and
Belsen, I wondered still more how the sons of Lafcadio Hearn's
friends had come to accept — perhaps to join — the Kempei Tai,
the brutal prison-guards, military police, counterespionage service
and sometimes flatfooted cloak-and-dagger men of Japan.

I wondered how the people who had invented the tale of the
One Perfect Morning Glory and the Legend of the Quarrelsome
Sword had succumbed to the shoddy myths of modern Japanese
nationalism, how those whose sense of the artistry of living begot
the arts of flower arrangement and the tea-ceremony had learned
to practice the arts of cannibalism and mass-rape upon their
enemies, how the land of the most transcendent Buddhism had
become the land of synthetic Shinto, producing the neo-samurai
madness which expressed itself in the half-superhuman, half-
bestial heroism of Okinawa, in the wholly bestial atrocities of
Nanking and Manila.

I was confronted with this Japanese paradox in a dramatic
form during my stay in Bangkok. My instructions had been to
remain under cover at our secret headquarters in Bangkok and
not to contact the Japanese authorities in regard to the release of

prisoners until I heard from SEAC Headquarters in Kandy, which itself could take no initiative until informed by General MacArthur that the surrender had been completed.

As the days went by I became increasingly impatient. Many of the prisoners were in bad physical condition and it was unsatisfactory to try to make arrangements for them without direct contact. Furthermore, the Japanese had set up in town an Allied prisoners' headquarters, staffed by the senior Allied officers from the various camps, and had given these officers complete liberty to roam about the city. I had even met some of them clandestinely, and it seemed utterly absurd for me to remain in hiding while they came and went as they pleased. The absurdity reached its climax when our Siamese friends staged in our honor what was probably the first underground ball in history, complete with caterers and orchestra, and seemingly invited most of Bangkok to attend.

This final Graustarkian touch was too much for me. The next morning, two days before the ceremony in Tokio Bay, after consulting with Captain Howard Palmer, the permanent OSS representative in Bangkok, who through long dangerous months had lived in the midst of the enemy, I decided to surface without waiting for instructions from Kandy. Even if the Japanese wondered about the presence in Bangkok of an unknown American naval officer, they were not going to make any unpleasantness at this late date. This reasoning seemed irrefutable to Palmer and to me and it finally convinced the directors of the Siamese underground movement, who that afternoon sent a military car with two Siamese staff officers as escorts, to take me to the prisoners' headquarters.

It seemed less self-evident a few minutes later when, turning into a narrow street, we became entangled with a long column of Japanese cavalry and had to crawl along with it at slow speed for nearly ten minutes. I had put on my best uniform and had strapped on my pistol as a symbol to any who noticed it that I considered myself as a representative of Allied victory, but, as I sat stiffly in the car, looking neither to right nor left, while the squat little horsemen with the strange sinister caps milled all around, sometimes accidentally clanking their sabers against the car, I did not feel like a representative of victory, but rather like a helpless hostage in the hands of a savage enemy.

These blank-faced soldiers who looked at me with unseeing eyes, devoid of hate or curiosity, recognition or nonrecognition, were the samurai fanatics who had fought to the death on a hundred battlefields, never giving or asking quarter, whose inhuman fury recalled the Mongol madness of Genghis Khan. It seemed incredible that I, an enemy openly flaunting his identity, could move among them and still live. Surely one of them would seize this chance to join the Shinto pantheon by sacrificing an enemy to the Sun Goddess and dying himself a fanatic's death. Surely among these hundreds of warriors there must be one fool who would not understand what grave consequences such an act would have for his people, or one dervish of honor who did not care.

There was not one, however, not even one who stared at the implausible spectacle which met his eyes, and by this studious avoidance of attention I knew that they knew I was an enemy and understood that this was an ununderstandable situation which called for no reaction whatsoever because it corresponded to no category in which minds had been trained to think. Enemies to them were something that one met on a battlefield, officers were a type of Japanese uniform that one saluted, human beings were brown or yellow men and women in ships, in houses, on streetcars, with whom one joked or bargained, to whom one was polite or bullying, according to one's mood. I was none of these things, therefore to the Japanese soldier who saw me it was as if I did not exist.

Realization came to me that this ride through the streets of enemy-held Bangkok was providing me with one of the rarest human experiences — that of meeting the enemy face to face. Normally, I reflected, the enemy always wears a mask which hides his true face from us. We can never see him as he is because we always look at him through a double lens of delusion — his own

and ours. Perhaps the most basic delusion of war is to think of
the enemy as a presence. In reality he is an absence, a void of
human contexts, a removal of most categories of experience from
any personal frame of reference, an accumulation of lost meanings, a blank look on a stranger's face.

The stories which the prisoners told me of their treatment at
the enemy's hands fitted into this same pattern of lost meaning.
Prison life had really been a hellish nightmare for them, but the
most nightmarish feature of it had been its utter senselessness.
The enemy had always been harsh to them, often sadistic, but
usually capriciously so. The lack of proper food and medical care
suggested a deliberate policy of extermination, but the prisoners
themselves doubted that their captors had thought things out so
completely. The strict discipline, the constant petty humiliations to which the prisoners were subjected, reflected the Japanese racial inferiority complex, the need to refute their inferiority by bullying the helpless white man. Mainly the Japanese
seemed obsessed with the idea of enforcing perfection upon the
captives in their official roles as prisoners-of-war, without having
a definite ideal of prisonerhood and jailerhood in their minds, and
without any clear concept of the correct relationships between
these two categories. The whole business was a kind of perverted
and improvised tea ceremony in which thousands of prisoners
were starved, beaten, or executed for infractions of rules which
the captors kept changing and never succeeded in properly interpreting themselves, for failing to make the right gestures when
the Japanese were not sure what the right gestures were.

There was a kind of brutal logic in putting the prisoners to
work upon the Burma-Siam railway, where they died by the tens
of thousands in the malarial jungles, but the manner in which this
policy had been carried out was utterly senseless and often self-
defeating.   For example, the prisoners remembered vividly —
because he symbolized so perfectly the whole Japanese attitude
— a prisoner guard who had once read out to them the list of their
members detailed that day for work on the railroad.   One of the
men designated was dying of malaria and could not even stand

on his feet. The senior officer among the prisoners asked to have this invalid excused, promising to furnish a substitute, but the guard got furious and threatened to bayonet him if he did not obey the order without further argument. The sick man was therefore carried in a litter to the railroad and lay all day on the ground while the members of the working party accomplished their tasks. At night they carried him back to the camp with them. The guard seemed perfectly satisfied with the arrangement. He had given the prisoners their orders and they had obeyed; from his point of view the amount of work accomplished on the strategically vital railroad was as irrelevant as the comfort of the dying man.

This unreflecting mechanical obedience was characteristic of the super-Prussian discipline in the Japanese army, as the preoccupation with conventionalized social relationships was characteristic of Japanese culture generally. Perhaps more than any other soldier in the world, the Japanese soldier was brutal or kindly, reasonable or fanatical, by order, and more than most humans he felt in a given situation what he was traditionally supposed to think.

He was no mere robot, however, and the Japanese paradox was more than a clash of directives at the highest cultural levels. The Japanese had a peace-personality and a war-personality. He was an entirely different being according to whether he saw things in a war frame of reference or in a peace frame of reference.

Thus, when surrender was recognized as inevitable, orders were issued for the Allied prisoners of war to be given good treatment, and these orders were as scrupulously obeyed as the earlier ones to be harsh. In accordance with these orders, the gravely ill prisoners had been turned over to the Siamese government and placed in Siamese hospitals where they were being both lovingly and skillfully tended. That may have been mere good sense. However, it was something beside good sense which had caused an anonymous Japanese officer to send flowers to several of the ill Americans.

The prisoners, commenting on this extraordinary occurrence,

did not think it was merely an example of enemy craft or duplicity, still less did they see it as a gesture of repentance. They thought it was just like the Nips to do such a thing, meaning that the officer who had sent the flowers had simply taken off his war personality and put on his peace personality, which happened to be a kindly one. He had heard that these particular Americans were ill in a Siamese hospital and he thought that it is always a kindly thing to send flowers to the sick, so he had sent them. Not being at war with the Americans any longer — for all practical purposes — he did not look upon these sick men as enemies, and would doubtless have been quite pained to discover that the recipients of his kindness found it somewhat incongruous.

In the days that followed the surrender, all the Japanese in Bangkok put on their peace personalities and seemingly forgot that we had ever been their enemies or they ours. Very quickly, we, the victors, put them to work driving our cars, hauling our supplies, cleaning or repairing buildings for us. They performed these tasks conscientiously and cheerfully. They were deferential, almost obsequious, toward their conquerors, but somehow they always seemed to retain their self-respect, and inevitably won ours. Their cheerfulness was infectious, and despite all the ghastly horrors of the prison camps, it was difficult to be exposed to them and not like and in some ways admire them. As soldiers they had nearly always failed to meet the test of victory, but probably no army in history had ever met the test of defeat so admirably.

The truth was that, like the Japanese, we were taking off our war-personalities. It took us several days or weeks, whereas the Japanese apparently had done it overnight. They were apparently completely untroubled by the inconsistency in their two attitudes. We had to rationalize ours. We had to invent myths to explain to ourselves why we really liked the Japanese when we felt we should hate them. We had to separate them into sheep and goats in our minds, discover some who were unquestionably bad so we could consider the rest as basically good, but somehow misled.

It proved a very tricky business. Some of the liberated prisoners who were in fair physical condition volunteered to remain in
Bangkok and help us with the task of preparing lists of Japanese
war criminals in the area. Up to a point it was easy. Specific
Japanese officers or prison-guards were known to have committed
specific atrocities. There were general policies contrary to the
rules of war or to humanity, which could be traced to the high
officials who had laid them down. When one had done all this,
however, only a small part of the horrors in the prison camps was
accounted for. The prisoners, though they seemed without hate
or bitterness or desire for revenge, were not satisfied with the
result. They wanted to see justice done, neither more nor less
than justice, but the enemy who had been responsible for most of
their suffering could not be brought to justice. He was unfind-
able, and finally in sheer weariness we all gave up looking for him.

In a sense he was the whole Japanese people, but he was what
the Japanese people had become and then ceased to be, what they
might conceivably become again in the future, but certainly were
not at the moment. He was not one Japanese social class though
he seemed more present in certain classes than in others. He was
not just the Japanese Army, though he was mostly there. He
was not merely the emperor-principle or the totalitarian-principle
or the militarist principle or the principle of national sovereignty.
He was certainly not Japanese culture as a whole, because that
would include Buddhism and Western rationalism as well as
Shinto. Shinto was the ideology of the enemy but Shinto had
long been a submerged element in Japanese culture and in its
modern form seemed more of a propaganda device than anything
else.

What then is the enemy? What is any enemy? It seems to
me there is only one way of identifying the enemy that is not too
narrow or too broad, too cynical or too unrealistic, too implacable
or too soft. My attempts to understand the Indian paradox suggested this definition of the enemy to me, but it applies as well to
the Japanese paradox, the German paradox, the Russian paradox,
or the American paradox — for there is an American paradox,

too, the contrast between our peacetime personalities, expressed in war by the speeches of President Roosevelt, and our wartime personalities expressed in peace by lynchings and every form of racial persecution.

The enemy, it seems to me, is always a kind of morbid group personality, an *ad hoc* paranoia, which develops under certain conditions of cultural upheaval. It expresses itself in systematic ideologies of delusion like those which have grown up around the communal conflicts of India, in mythologies of hate and persecution and divine mission. As in the mind of Ram Lal, these delusions are elaborated partly out of national anticultures, the survivals of savagery, which exist in every civilized people, partly out of current propaganda. They represent delusive approaches to group problems, particularly the problem of relationships with other groups, and ultimately lead to aggression — either preventive aggressions corresponding to the delusion of persecution, or aggressions of divine right, corresponding to a national delusion of grandeur.

The Germans and the Japanese were not the first great peoples to succumb to such seizures. In modern history and among civilized nations the other outstanding example is the Napoleonic madness which possessed the French people at the end of the eighteenth century, arising out of the vast cultural upheaval of the French Revolution.

Judging by the French and German examples, the chief factor likely to turn a civilized people into beasts of prey is insecurity — national insecurity, arising from external attack or menace, social insecurity arising from revolutionary conflict, and perhaps most important of all, emotional insecurity, arising from the sudden changing of old cultural values or institutions. In addition, the existence of a deep-rooted military tradition, the loss of territory considered as a rightful part of the national patrimony, and the confidence arising from initial success in aggression or intimidation, all seem to be important secondary factors. All these factors are easily detectable in the rise of Napoleon and in that of Hitler — to say nothing of Mussolini's rise.

In the case of Japan, the cultural revolution produced by sudden westernization is sufficient to explain a deep sense of emotional insecurity in the modern Japanese personality. The manner in which the blessings of Western progress were forced upon Japan is enough to explain a deep sense of national insecurity. Class struggle seems to have played less of a role in Japan than it did in either France or Germany, but it existed, notably the conflict between wealthy industrialist families and the younger officer-class. No Japanese territory was taken, but the attempts of the Western powers to exploit Japan commercially, the contemptuous Western attitude toward the Japanese as a yellow people, the humiliating political or military pressures put upon various Japanese governments, all created a sort of emotional irredentism in the Japanese soul. Japan, of course, did possess a military tradition and her first aggressions or intimidations were successful.

It can, of course, be argued that the aggressiveness of Japan and Germany is not a temporary and accidental paranoia, as it seems to me to be, but a true collective paranoia analogous to the private disease in every way. One American psychiatrist, Dr. Richard M. Brickner, has indeed advanced the argument that the German people has been suffering for many years from such a paranoia.

Nothing as far as I can see proves that defeat has cured the Japanese and the German paranoias, but nothing proves that it has not. In any case, from our point of view, the lesson seems to be that the enemy is a disease, a disease that can happen to anyone. Whether or not it is a curable disease, it is something which cannot be found apart from its symptoms, which does not exist outside of its historical context.

Hence, many of the questions which worry us about aggression are needless questions. The important thing is to remove the obstacles which prevent the realization of one world, to establish the rule of law. It is no use erecting barriers against the enemy — except in the sense of creating conditions which make it unlikely that anyone will become an enemy — because we do not know who the enemy is, or even who he is likely to be. There is no use trying to punish him, because he cannot be found.

Thus, the real error of Nuremberg was not that ten men were hanged for a crime that had not existed until they were convicted of it, but that nobody thought to say, as they were led to the gallows, 'There, but for the grace of God, go we.'

III

Talking Sense to a Dutchman

THE PROBLEM of controlling and dispelling institutional delusion seems as difficult to us as the problem of aggression, and right attitude toward this problem is even more important than right attitude toward aggression. The paranoid transformation which seems to take place in the national character of various peoples under certain conditions, leading them to programs of aggression, is after all, merely a crystallization of institutional delusions, and even without this pathological change in group-character, delusion may lead two groups of sane and civilized human beings into violent conflict.

The problem of delusion is an intensely personal one, for delusion, even institutional or group delusion, can only exist in the individual mind — its collective manifestations are but the sum of many individual delusions about public questions. Yet because institutional delusion expresses itself in attitudes toward group-relationships or other public questions, it is also an intensely public problem. In this day when the consequences of delusion may be a war that would virtually extinguish human civilization upon this planet, it is the problem of man as a whole, perhaps his most urgent problem.

One world is needed to remove the most dangerous sources of collective delusion, but seemingly it cannot be realized unless they are removed. Indeed, any step toward a better world, any kind of social reform or progress, necessitates removing the bar-

riers of group delusion which block progress, and this almost
inevitably implies struggle — perhaps violent conflict — between
the groups working for progress and the backward ones still bound
by delusion.

How can we convince those in our own country and in other
countries who still cling to the delusion of absolute national sovereignty that this doctrine, from the patriot's point of view, is a
self-defeating one, leading not to the preservation but to the
destruction of his fatherland?

How can we convince the American racist in our Southern
states or on the Pacific coast that his doctrine of the white man's
superiority over the black or yellow man leads him, by exhibiting
his own moral inferiority, to disgrace the biological heritage of
which he is so proud?

How can we persuade Soviet Russia, our only equal in the
world as a military power, that her quest for national security is a
delusive, not a realistic one?

Above all, how can we — we, in general, and the individual
idealist in particular — go about trying to alter the delusive attitudes in others that I have just listed, without exasperating them,
without inspiring by our actions new delusions graver than those
we seek to remove?

This is the problem of delusion in our time and it, too, is an
anguishing one — or would be, if we ever paused before rushing
into action to look back upon the lessons of history. For history
tells us that the struggle against group delusion is often self-
defeating — so often, in fact, that one can legitimately raise the
question as to whether it is ever anything else. My own view is
that group-struggle against group-delusion is not, and need not
always be, self-defeating, but there are many discouraging in-
stances to the contrary.

The Abolitionist struggles against the delusion of slavery finally
abolished slavery — but they also produced the Ku Klux Klan
and lynching in the modern South. The war to end war ended
the delusion of kaiserism in Germany — but it begot Hitler. The
pacifist campaigns in the Anglo-Saxon countries after World War

I against the delusions of militarism converted America and Great Britain into the most peace-loving of the great powers — but they produced appeasement in Ethiopia, in Spain, and at Munich. Lenin's lifelong struggle to free the Russian *muzjik* from darkness has enlighted the steppes — but how bright are the reading-lamps in the Kremlin today? Antifascism has rid the world of the fascist nightmare — but is the end of the world less near than it was ten years ago? Even too-rapid technological advance, as we have seen, can produce grave cultural regressions; excessive progress, instead of removing, merely modernizes — and sometimes aggravates — the delusions of backwardness.

The East has given much thought throughout the ages to this problem of self-darkening enlightenment, and has developed very definite views about it. Much Buddhist philosophy is really an attempt to solve the problem. What we call delusion is only one element in the broader Buddhist doctrine of illusion, so it is difficult to summarize concisely the Buddhist solution to the specific problem of delusion, but the general trend of Buddhist thinking on this subject is unmistakable. Delusion may be denounced, but not the deluded one. He must not be punished or reproached for his delusion or told that he is evil. Many Buddhist thinkers, indeed, warn against preaching at the sinner or deluded one at all. He must be left to find his own way to truth. The salt of reproof must not be rubbed into the wound of his error. Any victory, even victory over the standard-bearers of delusion, is really a defeat, for it breeds hatred.

Gandhi, though influenced by Buddhist thought, goes less far than the Buddhists. Like the early Christians, he has no qualms about using the most intense moral pressure against those whom he considers deluded. Regarding the use of material force, however, he is in complete agreement with the Buddhists. He considers that any victory won by violence, even victory in a righteous cause, even victory against the forces of delusion, is really a defeat. The delusions of the sword may not be opposed by the sword.

These seem extreme and unrealistic views to us, acceptable

only if one accepts the mystic, and therefore unverifiable, premises on which they are based. Looking back upon recent history, it is difficult for us to imagine any way in which the German and Japanese madnesses could have been prevented from engulfing the whole world except by mobilizing a greater violence against them, as we did. Unquestionably there is as much delusion in the world today as there was before we took up arms against the fascist crystallizations of delusion. Perhaps there is more. Yet, had we not taken up arms, it seems to us that there would have been nothing but delusion in the world, and no weapons left to combat it, not even spiritual ones.

On the other hand, it seems undeniable to me that we have achieved victory at the cost of grave defeats. In destroying fascism we have all to some degree become infected with it. We have saved the world, but not the world we wanted to save. The very best we can say for ourselves is that, as between two defeats, we have chosen the lesser one; in perpetuating delusion by converting it from fascism into counterfascism we may have effected a loss of destructive energy. In final balance, these statements are all arguments against the Eastern solution to the problem of delusion, but they are at the same time eloquent admissions of its near-rightness.

Paradoxically, the strongest evidence for the near-rightness, if not rightness, of the Eastern view that the most vigorous methods of combating delusion are self-defeating — particularly the extreme Buddhist prejudice against any strong pressure rather than the Gandhian prejudice against violent pressures — appears to me to be supplied by some of the pacifist campaigns in the West between 1918 and 1939. Though it cannot be scientifically established, my own belief is that certain pacifist propagandas aggravated the fascist or nationalist delusions of Europe and undermined the morale of peace-loving men throughout the world. This was my view in 1939, as I developed it in *The Strategy of Terror*, and it is one of the few public opinions which participation in the late war and exposure to Eastern influence did not drastically modify.

On the contrary, first-hand experience with psychological warfare in the early days of the war made me understand much more clearly how and why the pacifist campaigns against the delusions of nationalism and militarism had been self-defeating. The campaigns which I have in mind were chiefly the activity of left-wing groups — social democrats, anarchists, sometimes communists — and they bore an extraordinary resemblance to some of the wartime techniques of mental subversion which both the Allies and the enemy practiced lavishly. They were campaigns of innuendo, of derision and division. Instead of attacking the fallacy of war, they sought to discredit the ideals in the name of which men usually go to war, but by which they also live in peace. Instead of combating the delusions of security which flourish particularly in the military mind, they tried to smear the military uniform with dishonor, instead of warning against the dangers of fanaticism, they exalted cowardice. Instead of attacking the mythologies of nationalism, they defamed the ideal of patriotism. Few single individuals did more to encourage the growth of French fascism than Jean Zay, a fairly prominent prewar Radical Socialist politician, who, carried away by a burst of pacifist and literary enthusiasm, in his younger days once wrote a little poem in which he referred to the tricolor of France as a dirty scrap of rag. This is an object-lesson in how not to combat delusion. The flag of any country is sometimes a sinister symbol, but it is never an ignoble one, and it is always sacred to millions of human beings, including many who do not realize that they hold it sacred.

Though my European experience had suggested to me a resemblance between pacifist propaganda and the Nazi techniques of subversion which I saw at work in France, full realization that they were the same, that their unconscious object was not conversion but undermining the morale of an opposing social group and thereby disintegrating it, did not come to me until I became, myself, a psychological warrior.

My close connection with American psychological warfare ceased when I went to the East, but the two years it lasted gave me a training which enabled me to recognize subversive psycho-

logical warfare in a multitude of human activities where I had
never noticed it before.

When I got home from the East I discovered many of my Jewish friends conducting frantic and vicious psychological warfare
against Britain — not to mention their poison-pen campaigns
against the Arabs, and all defenders of Arab rights, including
some of their own people. They were poisoning the American
mind with hatred of Britain as Hitler's agents had long striven to
poison it with anti-Semitism. In retaliation, certain of my British
friends in this country seemed to be trying to stimulate the anti-
Semitism of American groups already inclined in that direction —
doubtless in the hope of frightening the Zionists out of their psychological warfare activities. It was a reckless and suicidal duel
from the viewpoint of both parties, to say nothing of the viewpoint of American peace of mind.

The British-Zionist poison-propaganda duel seemed to me a
fairly professional affair on both sides, but some of the unofficial,
amateur or semiprofessional psychological warfare campaigns
which I noticed on my return were no less dangerous. There was
no mistaking the existence of an organized campaign against the
United States Navy — a campaign which at one time had a no-
ticeable effect on Navy morale — being conducted by certain
partisans of the unification of the armed services. These partisans — mostly army officers or reservists — had a patriotic and
sound goal, but they were using the same methods of inspired
tendentious press articles and deliberately circulated rumor all
official psychological warfare services used against the enemy in
war — and with much the same disintegrative result.

It did not shock or surprise me to find Army officers resorting
to these methods to combat the autonomist delusions of the
Navy. In the course of the war I had seen the same thing happen
too many times. I had repeatedly seen highly secret information
concerning the activities of OSS appear in the American press —
sometimes with real risk to the security of our operations against
the enemy — in circumstances which left little doubt that the
information had been communicated by highly placed officers or

officials of the government. Only some highly placed enemy of
an independent cloak-and-dagger agency could have had access
to the ammunition necessary to launch these cloak-and-dagger
attacks upon us.

We ourselves were sometimes guilty of using psychological warfare practices in our institutional feuds with other American gov-
ernmental agencies — notably with the Office of War Information, the official Psychological Warfare service — and we did not
always abstain from them in our organizational battles within
OSS.

What did shock and alarm me was to find in the spring of 1946
a group of officers and civilian officials, some with very high connections, who not only were preaching the necessity of a preventive war against Soviet Russia but were seemingly trying to bring
it about by launching rumors of an impending Pearl Harbor style
attack upon us. Having some friends who were apparently along
the channels of dissemination of these rumors, I was often able to
follow them from close to the source to their publication in the
gossip columns of the press a few days later, whence they passed
into the editorial columns and headlines of the papers and into
the speeches of congressmen or other public figures.

Other friends were attempting to counteract this campaign by
some extraordinary psychological warfare of their own. Some
were spreading rumors of a British plot to involve the United
States in war with Russia, partly because they believed it but
mainly, I think, because they believed the anti-British element in
their propaganda would give it greater weight with isolationists,
Jews, and Middle-Western conservatives. Another group had a
still more tortuous and, in some ways, more dangerous approach
to the problem of combating anti-Russian and militarist delusions. These friends were naming no names, launching no attacks, but they were industriously inventing and launching by
word of mouth the most hair-raising stories they could think up
about the atomic bomb, and they gravely debated among themselves such psychological niceties as whether you could give the
public a greater shock by quoting a physicist on the likelihood of

a chain-reaction, or by reporting that all the male workers at Oak Ridge had been rendered sexually sterile by exposure to the insidious radiations. The object of this propaganda was to shock the American public into a realization of the horrors of atomic warfare — and the self-defeating effect was to contribute to the public apathy over the sinister and untimely Bikini tests.

In reality there is hardly any social group in the West that does not indulge in psychological warfare at some time or other and certain groups are habitually addicted to it. The foremost of these is unquestionably the Communist Party, closely linked with the Soviet government, which since the Russian revolution has conducted an almost unremitting psychological warfare campaign — as distinguished from the open, legitimate dissemination of propaganda in favor of Marxism or Russia — against the capitalist societies. Though its goals are very different, the psychological warfare activities of the Society of Jesus are comparable in method to these of the Communists, and from the viewpoint of world-peace, may at a given moment be equally pernicious.

Within the United States, the Democratic and Republican Parties constantly wage psychological warfare against each other, which means that they do not confine themselves to open, avowed propaganda, but resort to the whispering campaign and other subversive techniques of morale-disintegration. The National Association of Manufacturers and the labor unions frequently utilize the same methods.

Even in personal relations psychological warfare is not unknown. Many husbands practice it upon wives or *vice versa*, and parents practice it upon children.

The truth is that we are all addicted to psychological warfare, because it is sometimes an effective means of gaining victory. What we forget is that whenever the goal of victory implies some progress of human enlightenment, the use of psychological warfare is self-defeating, for it darkens the minds both of those against whom it is used and of those who use it. Because delusion is socially disintegrating and the goal of psychological warfare is social disintegration, psychological warfare usually consists of trying to implant delusions in the minds of one's adversaries. Thus, when it is directed against organized delusion it can at best lead only to substituting one delusion for another, and more often leads to two delusions growing in place of one, for, as exposure to Eastern thought and my own experience taught me, it is almost impossible to delude others without developing delusions oneself.

All this was clearly understood by the Buddha more than two thousand years ago, even though the term psychological warfare had not been invented. Without adopting all the extreme Buddhist views, it seems to me that we can safely lay down one rule in regard to the problem of delusion: Never attempt to combat delusion by using the subversive, disintegrative, and delusive techniques of psychological warfare against those who are afflicted with it. General adoption of this rule would, I believe, greatly reduce the amount of delusion in the world.

Another safe approach to the problem seems to me to look for institutional traditions which tend to foster or generate specific delusions. Attacks aimed at the roots of the weed frequently meet with less resistance than those aimed directly at its nettles, and they have more permanent if slower-acting effects.

There is one institutional tradition, existing in nearly every country of the world, which seems to me even more of a threat to peace than the delusions of nationalism and militarism, and yet is much easier to combat. This is the Machiavelli tradition, or Machiavelli myth, of relationship with foreign colleagues, in which every professional soldier and every professional diplomat of the world has been brought up. Peacetime diplomacy, wartime relationships with allies, are seen in terms of this myth as a contest, as a kind of ritualized game in which the object is to outwit the adversary while respecting the rules. Whether the field of contact is an allied staff in war, an international conference, an organization like the United Nations, or a bilateral negotiation of some kind, the assumption is that every power represented in the contact is in litigation with some other, or with all the other powers, therefore, that the primary duty of the representatives is to best the other representatives in whatever way the rules allow. Secret psychological warfare is one of the 'ways that the rules allow, and some of the most sinister delusions in the world were originally nothing but tactical weapons in a minor diplomatic contest.

Because of his conception of his own proper relationship toward foreign colleagues, the professional soldier or diplomat almost invariably conceives relationships between nations in the same light. Peace, co-operation, progress — yes, he believes in all these things, but they are distant goals to him, the immediate reality is winning the litigation which he assumes must exist, and to make sure of winning, he must plan for all the litigations which might arise, an infallible recipe for making them arise.

As long as the delusive Prince, absolute sovereignty, reigns over the world, the Machiavelli myth will remain in some measure a Machiavellian reality, but even in a world of sovereign nations, there are many contexts where it does not apply. Little disagreement will be encountered in pointing this out, and only mild resistance will meet public pressure's insisting that international co-operation be effective in the fields where even the general staffs and the chancelleries agree it is desirable. The lesson of the sordid inter-Allied squabbles, costly in treasure, in time, and in blood, revealed by books like Ralph Ingersoll's *Top Secret* or Fred Eldredge's *Wrath in Burma*, to say nothing of the present volume, is plain to read — as plain as the lesson of the sordid squabbles between the American Army and Navy which had much to do with our early disasters in the Pacific. It is that intergroup co-operation of any kind, but particularly international co-operation, is a complex art or science, as well as an ideal, and that soldiers and diplomats seldom understand this art or science, not because they are unusually deluded men, but because nobody has ever thought to teach them.

To insist that our technicians of power be indoctrinated in the ideal of intergroup co-operation as well as in the ideals of patriotism or service-loyalty, and that they be scientifically trained, as an essential part of their professional formation, in the arts of co-operation, especially the basic art of recognizing and combating institutional delusion — this is not very subversive. It is no more subversive than to insist that undercover psychological warfare be outlawed in the normal peacetime intercourse of nations and in the legitimate contest for the favor of public opinion between opposed ideological groups. To campaign for these objectives effectively, it is only necessary to realize that undercover psychological warfare exists and that international co-operation virtually does not, yet one can wage these useful and potentially effective campaigns without shocking or infuriating any large body of opinion. Any victories won in such campaigns will not seem self-defeating ones, even to the strictest Buddhist, but in the long run they will be extremely important, for delusion springs from delusion, and the fewer delusions a mind contains, the fewer it is likely to develop; the more it succeeds in dispelling, the more it will be able to dispel.

Global wars are only the ultimate chain-reaction of institutional delusion, and in the mental field — as, possibly, in the biochemical field — integration, like disintegration, can seemingly be progressive, so that dispelling delusion may culminate at some point in the reversed chain-reaction of enlightenment. For this reason, even within the narrow limits of national security, it is possible to contribute to world peace by combating the delusions which render an army or a nation unready for war. Brotherhood and social justice, racial equality and equality of economic opportunity, all promote national morale, increasing ability to withstand shock and resistance to enemy penetration or psychological warfare, therefore they are potentials of war, like bases and rocket-bombs.

The truth is that all men in every country and in every sphere of activity who are trying to combat delusion are partners, whether they realize it or not, in building one world. The internationalist and the true patriot, the realistically minded pacifist and the clear-minded soldier, are brothers, not only in humanity but in progress. To realize this, to exploit it for the common goal, to refrain from criticizing needlessly the narrowness of the partners' context, is one of the requirements of a sound attitude toward the problem of delusion.

The main dilemma seemingly remains. Either we refrain from direct attack on the most violent and immediately dangerous forms of delusion, as Buddhism recommends, or we necessarily enter into conflict with the groups who hold these delusions, thereby aggravating them and almost inevitably developing delusions ourselves. Either we disarm ourselves and make no effort to oppose aggression, as Gandhi recommends, thus leaving armed delusion triumphant, or we arm and inevitably tend to become deluded because we are armed, to fear attack because we are capable of attacking others.

After much puzzling over this problem, it finally seemed to me that I could see a solution, one which leaned more to the Western than to the Eastern side, yet was derived by analogy from the Buddhist doctrine of the Middle Way, the golden mean between the extremes of asceticism and self-indulgence, and from the Buddhist-Hindu doctrine of karma.

The law of karma, as propounded in the Oriental philosophies, establishes an important distinction between attachment to illusion and the effects of attachment to illusion. Within some undefined limits, the individual is free to accept or reject illusion as, in the usual Christian view, he is free to sin or to avoid sin. But there is a strong element of predestination in the doctrine of karma. The effects of previous attachment to illusion cannot be removed, they are fate. Enlightenment does not eliminate the consequences of previous illusion, as repentance in some Christian philosophies assures forgiveness of sin. The individual must work out the evil karma determined by past actions, his problem being to avoid building up new karma in the process.

It seems to me that a somewhat analogous law operates in the public affairs of men. The consequences of past mistakes and delusions can never be eliminated. Cause must spend itself in effect. Every group-conflict leaves a heritage of bitterness, every victor is hated by the vanquished, every threat provokes a counterthreat. It is no use saying to ourselves, let us forget the past and start anew, let us wipe the slate clean. The slate cannot be

wiped clean. All that we can do is avoid putting new marks on it
while we wait for the old ones to fade.

This may seem a negative and defeatist doctrine, but if it is
sound, it is far better to accept it than to blunt our idealisms and
shatter our morale by trying to accomplish the impossible and
then falling into despair when we fail. Even more important, if
we accept it, we become alert to what I consider our greatest psychological hazard, that of adding new delusion to old, of hating or
fearing those whom our past actions have caused to hate us. Instead of attempting the hopeless task of removing irremovable
delusions in others, we concentrate on the difficult but possible
task of preventing them from begetting new delusions in us.

Thus, the national hates and fears generated by the delusion of
absolute sovereignty cannot be dispelled by pointing out that
world government will assure safety and justice for everyone.
We know that world government will bring safety and justice for
all if adopted by all, and it is our duty to point this out as strongly
as possible, but we must not expect to be believed immediately,
and above all we must not assume that those who refuse to believe
us are irrevocable enemies. They will believe when they cease to
hate or fear us, as they will eventually, if we do not give them
new grounds for hate or fear.

Pending the establishment of one world it is our duty to try
persuading other nations to join us in extensive disarmament,
particularly in outlawing the two weapons which represent a real
threat to the whole of human society — the nuclear and the
bacterial ones. Again we must not expect to be trusted or
followed immediately, for too much suspicion has been sown for
too many years in the world. We must resign ourselves to seeing
other nations insist on retaining some war-making potentialities,
and be pleased if they accept any limitations at all.

This same principle of regarding the consequences of delusion
as ineluctable and concentrating on preventing them from creating
new delusions in us, can be applied in many other contexts. For
example, it seems to me that all civilized Americans should try to
use every pressure, including the pressure of the law, against the

practice of race discrimination arising out of the racist delusions
of many Americans. In doing so we shall inevitably stir up bitter
hatred, but if we accept this as an inevitability and refuse to
meet it with counterhatred, then it will eventually die down. It
was because the North after Lincoln's death tried to punish the
South for having upheld slavery — and opposed the Abolition-
ists — that emancipation is not complete to this day.

This doctrine of a middle way between absolute pacifism and
the normal Western philosophy of legitimate violence is based
partly on conclusions developed out of following at a distance the
debates of the United Nations and the Paris Peace Conference
after my return to America, and partly out of personal observa-
tions of the colonial wars in French Indo-China and in Java.
These latter conflicts in particular suggested the concept of political karma to me, for there was a striking, almost Grecian, inevitability about them.

It was inevitable that, in the long interregnum between the end
of Japanese resistance and the formal surrender, while Admiral
Mountbatten's troops were held back by General MacArthur's
orders, native nationalist leaders in Indo-China and Indonesia
should seize power and establish themselves as independent governments. It was inevitable that, having done so, they should be
unwilling thereafter to accept anything less than complete independence, and that the sleeping fires of Asiatic nationalism should
have blazed up in the hearts of the entire Annamese and Javanese
peoples upon seeing an almost impossible dream seemingly come
true.

It was equally inevitable that the French and Dutch authorities in Southeast Asia should have failed to foresee this situation
and consequently should have neglected to forestall it by offering
in concrete terms limited home rule and colonial reform while their
colonies were still under Japanese occupation. It was virtually
inevitable that, cut off as they were from their colonies, the
French and Dutch should have failed to realize how much the
peculiar Japanese mixture of persecution and liberation propaganda, plus the decline of the white man's prestige, had awakened

Annamese and Javanese political consciousness. It was delusion,
but almost inevitable delusion, that caused the French and
Dutch, after their humiliating initial defeats at the hands of the
Japanese, to be fanatically obsessed with the idea of recovering
their prestige in the eyes of their subjects.

It was equally inevitable that the British occupation forces,
which went in to disarm the Japanese, should have felt obliged to
uphold the rights of their allies, therefore, ineluctably to come
into conflict with the native authorities who were prepared to
welcome them.

When I reached Saigon toward the end of October, 1945, the
conflict had reached its climax. By force of circumstances the
British had been drawn into the war of extermination, marked by
appalling atrocities on both sides, which the French and the
Annamese were waging against one another. In retaliation for
the murderous Annamese guerilla tactics, the British had deliberately burned down great sections of the native quarter of Saigon.
This further inflamed the anti-British sentiments of the Annamese, whose fanatical if clumsy attacks became such a menace to
the inadequate British occupation forces that for a long time they
had to cease disarming the Japanese and to use their late enemies
as auxiliaries in fighting the newer ones — a chore the Japanese
performed quite conscientiously, although they had armed the
Annamese in the first place and still had many instructors and
secret agents in the Annamese ranks.

Thanks to the recent arrival of some trained French forces
under General Leclerc, Saigon was reasonably safe by day, but
even in the bright sunlight the atmosphere was that of a town
newly occupied by Franco's forces in the Spanish Civil War. At
night delusion ruled the darkened streets and heavy firing —
mostly French and British patrols shooting at each other or at
shadows — went on until dawn. Annamese terrorists were kid-
naping French women and children, usually killing them and
mutilating their bodies, while the French were torturing and
shooting the rebels they captured.

In Batavia, where I flew from Saigon, the atmosphere was bet-

ter but only slightly better. General Christison, the victor of
the Arakan, was in command of the Allied forces and had established realistic and reasonable relations with the Indonesian republican government of Dr. Soekarno and Premier Sjahrir. He
was doing his best to keep the peace, and the Indonesian authorities were meeting him more than half way, but the native extremists in the hinterland, and Dutch newly liberated from Japanese
prison camps or arrived from overseas, were frustrating his efforts.

Nearly every night Javanese and Dutch battled it out in the
streets of Batavia, and I slept with a submachine gun and hand-
grenades under my bed, ready to jump up at any moment and
help repel the massed Indonesian attack on Allied billets which
the Dutch intelligence officers were daily predicting. By day the
Dutch filled the town with stories of native atrocities against
white women, many of them true; with angry criticism of America
for not sending help, with bitter tirades against British duplicity
and dark hints of sinister British designs on Holland's colonies,
with scornful or violent denunciations of Dr. van Mook, the official Netherlands representative, for appeasing the natives by
negotiating with them, and with paranoid fantasies of uninhibited
Dutch troops scattering the cowardly native rabble with a few
well-placed bursts from their machine guns.

Serious fighting between the British and the Indonesian forces
had not yet broken out. It broke out while I was in Batavia as
the result of a brave but deluded Dutch naval officer's action.
This officer, without consulting the British, had flown to the
naval base at Surabaya and ordered the Japanese commander to
lay down his arms. The Japanese had accordingly ordered his
men to stack arms on the airfield, had presented the Dutch officer
with his own samurai sword, had bowed and hissed and marched
off with his men — and then the Indonesians had walked in and
picked up the arms, also the Dutchman, who was never heard
from again.

There were a number of Dutch women and children in camps
at Surabaya who had been perfectly safe under Japanese protection until then, but were safe no longer, and General Christison

had no choice but to send a force to rescue them. This force, under Brigadier A. W. S. Mallaby, a highly regarded Indian Army officer, landed at Surabaya without opposition and began negotiations for the evacuation of the Dutch civilians with the local Indonesian leaders. These, reassured by Mallaby's promise that he would not attempt to disarm their militia, agreed to co-operate with the British, when an airplane, which as far as I know was never traced, dropped leaflets, not authorized by General Christison, ordering the natives to give up their weapons by a certain hour.

Furious at what they believed was Mallaby's duplicity, the Indonesians broke off negotiations and began to fight. In the fighting Mallaby was killed and his forces badly cut up. The British, to avoid a fatal impression of weakness and to save what was left of the Dutch civilians, then sent a large force to Surabaya and a stubborn, protracted battle began.

Future historians may regard the battle of Surabaya as one of the decisive colonial engagements of our day, for the fierce resistance of the poorly trained, summarily armed Indonesians removed the last doubts in the minds of most British, Dutch, and French colonial soldiers that the old imperialist way was gone forever. If empire meant fighting full-scale battles with modern weapons, then imperialism was no longer profitable.

A number of thoughtful British, foremost among them Christison himself, had apparently reached this conclusion even before the battle of Surabaya. This remarkable soldier had once during the Arakan campaign revealed the wide range of his interests by requesting the clandestine parties operating in the jungle behind the enemy lines in his sector to report to him the location of any rhinoceroses, as well as of any Japanese encountered by them, for he was a keen zoologist and had developed some theory about the migrations of these beasts which he wanted to verify. The mind that was able to remember rhinoceroses while planning a major campaign against the enemy proved itself able to remember reality while engaged in a two-front war against delusion.

Despite Surabaya, despite many other battles and ambushes

and cold-blooded assassinations, Christison never allowed the war between the Dutch and the Indonesians in which he was involved to become an all-out war between the British and the Indonesians. When the latter would talk he would talk to them and when they shot at him he shot back at them, and he stopped shooting when they did. In the same patient, clear-minded way, he would talk to the Dutch whenever they would listen to him, and when they would not listen, he would simply wait for them to recover their senses. It is chiefly owing to Christison that after many months, some glimmerings of reason began to penetrate the fog of delusion which lay between the Indonesians and the Dutch, and the political karma which their joint errors had engendered appeared to be spending itself.

One evening while I was in Batavia, a British friend, one of Christison's staff officers, came into my room, flung himself wearily into a chair, poured out a stiff drink, and began a long tale of woe about the mulishness of the Dutch, with whom he had been dealing all afternoon.

'I give up,' he said, 'this situation is utterly hopeless. You just can't talk sense to a Dutchman.'

History has proved him wrong, as it proved me wrong, for I wholeheartedly shared his opinion about the ineradicability of Dutch delusions. History always proves those wrong who, after struggling to overcome the delusions of others, throw up their hands and yield themselves to the delusion of despair.

In reality, it is our inability to free our own minds from delusions, our tendency to build up new karma while fighting the old, to give up trying to talk to the Dutchmen of all nationalities with whom we have to deal, that blinds us to the tremendous power for dispelling delusion exercised by a mind which is itself free from delusion. The key to the problem of combating delusion therefore appears to be mainly a question of trying to acquire this power.

IV

The Problem of Backwardness

THE BRITISH FRIEND in Batavia, who sometimes felt it was no use trying to talk sense to a Dutchman, also had his troubles with the Indonesians. One day while I was still in Java he had such a big trouble with them that for nearly thirty-six hours he was convinced that the Dutch were right, even if you could not talk sense to them.

The trouble was that an official of the Indonesian republican government, a reasonable and willing little Javanese whom the British had always found most co-operative, had lost a locomotive which was badly needed for hauling military supplies from the port into town. There was no suspicion of sabotage or duplicity on the part of the Indonesian authorities, and the missing locomotive could not have been captured by native extremists in the interior, for there was only one line between Batavia and the port, and it was heavily guarded along its whole length. Apparently the Indonesians had some extraordinarily unsound idea of the way to run a railroad, and left the locomotives lying around where they could not find them.

My friend had tried to explain this to the Indonesian transport official.

'The locomotive must be lying around somewhere,' he had said. 'Just look for it — but quickly, please.'

'But we have looked, sir, and we cannot find,' the Indonesian had replied. 'The locomotive is lost.'

'Man, that is impossible! You can lose your pocketbook. You can lose your watch. You can lose your automobile. You can even lose your wife. But man, you cannot lose a locomotive. That is something which just can't happen.'

'I know it can't happen — but it has happened.'

That was the conversation between the Indonesian railway official and my friend, as reported by him. Doubtless there were some elements missing from his account which would have made the whole incident seem slightly less implausible, but this very implausibility was psychologically significant. In the Britisher's mind the incident was implausible — so far beyond the limits of tolerable human muddle that the Indonesians seemed to him monsters of ineptitude. It had converted him temporarily from an extraordinarily liberal, sympathetic, and broad-minded man into an Old Colonial Tie imperialist of the worst sort.

'All natives are hopeless,' he spluttered. 'They'll never learn to manage themselves. What can you do with people like that? Nothing that I can see except turn them back to the Dutch — God have mercy on the poor little beggars.'

My friend had an exceptionally clear, undeluded mind. It had withstood everything except the supreme and almost superhuman test of trying for days on end to talk sense to the Dutch in Batavia. Now a trivial incident had seemingly laid it open to invasion by the crudest sort of delusion. Many worse provocations had failed to achieve this result. When defenseless Dutch women and children were massacred by infuriated mobs of native extremists, when unarmed British soldiers were stabbed in the back or crashed British fliers were captured and chopped into small pieces by villagers, my friend merely shrugged his shoulders fatalistically. You had to expect that sort of thing in a colonial war. The tribesmen on the Indian northwest frontier had equally rough ideas of sport, yet the British were quite fond of them. Atrocities one could forgive. But losing locomotives — no, that was too much.

Railroads are a particularly sensitive area in the Western psyche — was not Mussolini's boast that he had made the Italian railroads run on time sufficient to justify fascism in the minds of many otherwise civilized and intelligent people? — and apparently technological prejudice is the most stubborn of all. We can forgive the Eastern peoples everything except their technological backwardness. When we are asked to swallow backwardness, to treat as equals peoples whose mechanical aptitude seems inferior to that of our children, to accept as civilized men who wantonly mangle machinery, to admit as profound philosophers men whose scientific notions are more superstitious than those of our cooks — then we rebel, even the most liberal of us. Indeed, the only difference between a Western liberal and a Western reactionary in the East is that the former believes backwardness is curable, while the latter does not. Both have the same definition of backwardness and the same contempt for it.

There is no doubt that, properly trained, any of the Asiatic peoples can produce as good mechanics, engineers, physicians, or research workers as we can. Stillwell proved that by making first-class modern soldiers out of the Chinese troops under his command. Stillwell's experiment, however, was not as conclusive as it sounds. For example, in order to stimulate the combativity of his division commanders, he had to make arrangements, unprecedented in the Chinese army itself, to supply them with replacements so that their rank would not decrease as the number of effectives under their command dwindled in battle. Also he had to employ American paymasters to make sure that the Chinese soldier collected his rightful pay. To Stillwellize the whole Chinese army would have implied a drastic reform of Chinese society. Many features of Asiatic backwardness are the result of basic cultural institutions which the Asiatic peoples are loath to change. Thus the problem of backwardness in Asia is deeper than one of mere technical training. It is always curable when the patient is willing to take the cure, but he is not always willing. This creates a serious problem of attitude for the Westerner who believes in co-operation between East and West and in human progress generally.

The problem of attitude toward Eastern backwardness came

up frequently in our wartime dealings with various Asiatic peoples, especially the Siamese. The Siamese had a strong and willing underground movement, but accustomed as we were to the
scientific cloak-and-dagger techniques and the elaborate security
measures practiced in Europe, we sometimes felt that the Siamese
form of underground warfare was exceedingly backward. We
were particularly appalled at what seemed to us the sloppy and
primitive security methods used by our Siamese friends, and the
temptation was always strong to demand that they adopt our
procedures and principles of organization, since we were risking
the lives of American officers by sending them into Siam.

We resisted this temptation to the end, and it seemed to me the
only sound policy, but there were moments when I had doubts
about it myself. The most intense of these moments occurred
upon my clandestine arrival at the Bangkok airfield before the
cessation of hostilities. There was no great problem about remaining in the plane until we were rolled into the Siamese air-force
hanger without being seen by any of the Japanese who were strolling around the field, but the hangar could not be closed and an
enemy pilot or mechanic might wander in at any time to chat
with the Siamese guards — in fact, one did, while my colleague
Ripley and I made ourselves as inconspicuous as possible behind a
plane at the end of the hangar. To protect us against such
eventualities a closed car was supposed to be waiting in the
hangar to take us into the city, but there had been a slipup and
it was not there. After an hour of uncomfortable waiting one of
the Siamese officers with us telephoned an important figure in the
air force and asked for a car to be sent urgently to get the Americans into town. This required some rather lengthy explanations.
The air-force officer did not know that any Americans were expected in Bangkok, in fact, he did not know that there was an
underground movement co-operating with the Allies. He joined
the movement then and there — surely the first member of an
underground ever recruited by telephone — and sent the car.
This is not quite the way things were done in Europe, but it
seemed to work all right in Siam, and the Siamese casualness in

regard to security may actually have been more effective in disarming Japanese suspicions than the most rigorous cloak-and-
dagger techniques.

In any case we operated for more than a year in Siam without
losing a single American — except those shot down or killed in
air accidents on the way in and out of the country — and by plac-
ing the lives of our men unreservedly in the hands of our Siamese
hosts we gained for them loyal if not always elaborate protections.

We would have had a much more efficient-seeming organization
in Siam if we had been able to run it along American rather than
Siamese lines, but I doubt that its results would have been more
satisfactory, and, above all, we would not have had it. The
Siamese had much to learn from us about modern warfare, and
they were eager to learn, but they were determined to learn in
their own way. They wanted to be advised on how to run certain
of their affairs, but they did not intend that Siamese affairs should
be run by any foreigners. This was a basic question of dignity
with them, and the condition for obtaining their co-operation was
to respect it — which inevitably implied accepting at times what
we considered military backwardness.

The basic condition for obtaining any Asiatic co-operation today is to respect Asiatic dignity. The failure of the Dutch to
realize this was largely responsible for the bitter Indonesian
hatred of them, and the Indonesian national revolution was primarily a revolution for dignity as was revealed by the revolutionary slogans which I saw plastered all over the walls of Batavia.
The two most popular of these slogans had a very familiar ring:
'All men are created free and equal,' and 'Give us liberty or give
us death.'

If we consider that the Asiatic peoples are not entitled to liberty because they lose locomotives or are backward in other ways,
we have no choice but to fight them, and that inevitably means
᠂uniting all of Asia against us.

If we want the co-operation of the Asiatics, we must grant them
political freedom and social equality of status with us. That
means giving up all attempts to force or bully them out of back-

wardness. It means even accepting their backwardness in certain respects and for a long time to come. Very often we can say to them, 'This is how we do it in the West,' and they will follow us, because the West still has a great cultural prestige in the Orient. There will be other times, though, quite a few times, when they will simply answer, 'We do it differently in the East.'

Many Western students of the Orient have suspected for some time that our cultural domination of the East is waning. These students are several years behind the times. Our cultural domination of the East has set, it is no more, and it is unlikely ever to rise again. There are several reasons why this is so, but there is one which is decisive: Since the Russian revolution the West has ceased to be a cultural unity. Today there are two cultural Wests, the Communist West and the capitalist-democratic West. These two cultural groups have many affinities and common denominators but it cannot be denied that there are important differences between them.

Both cultural blocs are trying to project their influence upon the East, and though it is a strange thought to us, the East is free to choose between them or to take what it wishes from each and reject the rest. Neither cultural influence can be enforced upon any large part of Asia except by military conquest, which would mean automatically a new world war. Even without the rivalry between ourselves and the Soviet bloc, our cultural monopoly, and therefore domination, in the East would be ended. A new Asiatic culture, owing much to the West but a great deal more indigenous than the dominant Chinese or Japanese cultures, has arisen in India. Much will be heard from this new culture in the near future, I think, and we are going to see some developments in the world which we would not have believed possible a few years ago.

Since all the Asiatic cultures contain a good deal of what we consider backwardness, the problem of backwardness stares us squarely in the face. Western believers in the principle of federal union have given some thought to the problem of Eastern backwardness in relation to one world. To enlist the support of the

Asiatic peoples, particularly the Indians and the Chinese, for the ideal of world government would be a powerful means of hastening its realization. On the other hand, under a normal system of proportionate representation, India and China would dominate the world-parliament, and hundreds of millions of illiterate, backward Asiatic peasants would have a decisive voice in the affairs of the planet. To avoid this situation, some world federalists have proposed a weighted system of representation which would take into account literacy and industrial potential in determining the voting power of any nation.

In my opinion it is hopeless to expect any independent Asiatic people to recognize Asiatic cultural inferiority by accepting such a scheme. Merely talking about it is likely to prejudice the Asiatic mind against the one world ideal.

Most of us want one world but we conceive it as a hegemony of the bourgeois democracies. We want a one world uniformly dedicated to the cults of parliamentary democracy, free enterprise, and science. I think myself that this might be a pleasant world to live in but I consider it unattainable. By striving too hard for it I believe that we are likely to encompass the destruction of the world.

If we really want to realize one world in our generation — the only way to be sure that it will be realized at all — then, in my opinion, we must resign ourselves to including in it what we consider the political backwardness of Russia and the technological backwardness of Asia. Not only must we accept the Communists and the Asiatics as cultural equals, though the former do not seem to care about a free press and most of the latter can read no press at all, but wherever our way of life impinges on other peoples we must modify our institutions to avoid giving offense to backwardness. I can see no other solution.

It is fortunate that, in certain ways, Asia lies between us and Russia, while, in other ways, Russia lies between us and Asia. On the whole, I think we are closer to the Russians than we are to the Orientals, but the ethical values of the East, perhaps the most important in any culture, are generally closer to ours than the Russian ones.

Sooner or later India is going to demand a permanent seat on the security council of the United Nations, and there is no valid reason why what was granted to China should be denied her. Personally, I think it would be a realistic and statesmanlike move for the democratic powers of the West to add India to the world's Big Five without waiting for her to claim her rightful place.

Whether or not India is formally recognized as a great power, we are going to have to treat her as a great power, and that is going to involve some extraordinary compromises with backwardness. The problem of attitude toward backwardness is therefore really a very simple one in the present circumstances: It is largely a question of accepting the inevitable.

I think it is important, however, that we should learn to accept the inevitable gracefully and derive the greatest possible benefit from the mechanisms of cultural opposition which will automatically come into operation when we begin to treat the peoples of the East as equals. There is some danger that for a long time the lesser and more backward peoples of Asia will disappoint us by the tameness of their behavior in the council rooms of the world. Like many Chinese and Japanese, they may try to earn our respect by leaving all their backwardnesses at home, and being wholly Western abroad.

There is little danger that India, once she is firmly established as an independent nation, will falsify the machinery of cultural opposition in this manner. I doubt that the extreme Gandhian views in regard to nonviolence, the evils of industrialization, chastity, birth-control, prohibition, and Western medicine will prevail in the new Indian culture, but I shall be surprised if their influence is not noticeably reflected in many Indian views on world problems.

The philosophy of nonviolence is certainly going to color official Indian thinking in regard to the problems of disarmament and security and it will help give the Indians a perspective on the Soviet-Western Bloc power struggle which both parties will find disconcerting at times. Both we and the Russians will learn to our great surprise that many of the policies and attitudes which

seem so reasonable — or even generous — to us appear aggressive or deluded to Eastern eyes.

At every level of the United Nations and in every international gathering we are going to see our hypocrisies denounced and our cultural insularity exposed and some of our questionable idealisms criticized. We are not going to be able to use backwardness as an excuse for oppression. It will not be enough for us to say, 'They have lost a locomotive,' when we want to send the Marines or the world-police into some disturbed Asiatic area. It will not even be enough to say, 'They can't keep order,' or 'They are oppressing minorities,' for the same argument could be used against us to demand an international mandate over Mississippi.*

* The accuracy of my crystal ball clearly needs no apologies in this particular instance, but the very thoroughness and rapidity with which my prediction has been fulfilled may raise the question as to whether I have not over-estimated the usefulness of "cultural opposition." As it functions in the United Nations, at least, there are undoubtedly times when the phenomenon appears harmful as well as ludicrous. The demagoguery of anti-colonialism today threatens to replace the *mystique* of imperialism, if it has not already done so. Nothing has done more to foster this unhealthy tendency, however, than the demagogic attempts of the great powers to outbid one another for the favor of the newly emergent nations in former colonial areas. In some cases these nations themselves are artificial creations of colonialism without any real sense of nationhood, and in a sensibly organized world would have been prepared for self-government under an impartial international authority for at least a generation before acquiring the attributes of unlimited sovereignty and a voting membership in the United Nations. Though the evils of the present situation are self-evident, I fail to see in them any retrospective justification for the policies of those Western groups or leaders who attempted to maintain the colonial system where it plainly could be maintained by naked force alone. Nor can I see that the fact that certain members of the United Nations may for the moment have nothing to contribute to world civilization, except possibly the gastronomy of cannibalism, invalidates my thesis that formerly dependent peoples with an ancient if nontechnological civilization, like the Indian people, do have an important contribution to make.

We did not feel — even those of us who strongly disapproved of the Bikini tests — that we were committing a really serious offense against peace, therefore the deep feeling of guilt we had seemed slightly superstitious to us, and we brushed it out of our minds, falling into an unnatural apathy. The Indians could have explained to us why our guilt was real and not superstitious, why Bikini, though it lacked the element of sadism, constituted the same basic blasphemy which is what really shocked us the most in the showerbaths, the gas-chambers and the crematoriums of Belsen, in Goering's grotesque experiments with frozen prisoners and naked gypsies, in the researches of Nazi medicine aimed at discovering the ideal poisons for injecting through the eardrums of children. The Indians would have told us that our blasphemy, like the Nazi ones, arose from an idolatrous worship of the techniques of science divorced from any ethical goals, that the man-made cataclysm of Bikini was a black mass of physics as the German experiments were a black mass of medicine, that it was a mob-insurrection against the pantheist sense of citizenship in nature, which we share with the Hindus in our hearts, but consider a childish foible.

Moreover, the Indians, whom history has rendered sensitive to all the nuances of imperialism, would have pointed out to us that in uprooting the Bikini natives from their homes in a kindly manner to make these tests, we were not abiding by the laws of humanity but only following the code of the Society for the Prevention of Cruelty to Animals, that instead of treating a backward people as cattle for the slaughterhouse, as the Nazis did, we were treating them like the members of a valuable milch-herd, but without the reverence for the dignity of manhood which the Hindus feel for the dignity of cowhood.

The Russians could not talk to us in this way, for they share our science-idolatry and the lacunae in our sense of human dignity. The Indians could have so talked — had they possessed the means of expression available to an independent nation — and our guilt was so close to the threshold of consciousness, we were so near to admitting to ourselves what the Indians would

have pointed out, that I think their words might have been dramatically effective. An ounce of political expediency added to
the heavy burden of conscience might have tipped the scales of
opinion. We could think of no realistic answer to the arguments:
'Who cares what happens to the fish?' or 'What difference does it
make to the natives if they change one coconut tree for another?'
If we had been able to tell ourselves, perhaps we are causing
four hundred million Indians to lean to the side of Russia, then it
would have been different, then conscience would have been freed.

Had India, the real India, been psychologically integrated into
the victorious wartime coalition, had she been really an ally instead of the prisoner of an ally, we would have heard an ally's
voice tell us in August, 1945, what we knew but could not compre-
hend: That in dropping the atomic bombs on Hiroshima and
Nagasaki we had committed a crime against all nations, comparable to the crimes for which the surviving leaders of Nazi Germany were hanged at Nuremberg. We could not rationally justify our guilt to ourselves because it was an *ex post facto* guilt,
remorse for something that we did not know was a crime because
it had never until then been committed by man. What we had
done, of course, was mass-murder, but seemingly the conventionalized mass-murder called war, and therefore legitimate. Because we had apparently only done on a larger scale the things
that all nations do to gain victory in war, we could not understand
why we felt like the Biblical Cain, like the inventor of murder.
We have killed more human beings than have ever been killed
before in a single air-raid, we told ourselves, but really we have
saved lives, even Japanese lives, by so doing. A landing would
have been much worse.

That should have made us feel all right but it did not. It did
not make us feel all right because our guilt was not for the hundred thousand or more Japanese that we had killed — though
that was grounds for guilt in itself — but for having invented
biological and even chemical crime, as the Nazis had perfected
social crime. It was for having made ourselves the ancestors of
the end of the world, as Cain, the first murderer, made himself the

ancestor of all the murders which will ever be committed.

That guilt still lies buried in American conscience as a neurotic guilt, because it is unrecognized, unavowed, and unatoned. That guilt is making us sick. If anyone could have made us understand our guilt, we would have suffered but we would not be sick. I think the Indians might have made us understand it, not because they had any clear idea themselves of what Hiroshima and Nagasaki meant, but because their mystic pantheist philosophy instinctively made them react as to an irreverence, a blasphemy, a horror, rather than as to merely another inhumanity of war. The Indian comments which I heard or read on Hiroshima did not seem to me particularly profound, but they had a different ring from any protests uttered in the West, and in my mind they lit a slow fuse, which exploded at last in realization.

It seems to me that this is a good example of the services which Asia can and will render us through the mechanism of cultural opposition. If we admit that these services are valuable, then we must also admit that we owe them to Asiatic backwardness as well as to Asiatic enlightenment. Only a culture which has despised technology and given highest place to soul-values can produce in its members the awareness of blasphemy needed to shock us into a realization of what is happening to us because of our failure to develop our soul-values as fast as we have developed our technology. Only a culture which has such a horror of taking life that its members will die in a diabetic coma rather than use the pancreas of slaughtered animals to save their own lives can develop the protests necessary to awaken us to the impiety of nuclear warfare.

Specialization is required to develop any talent or capability and it is impossible to specialize in certain ones without neglecting others. It is impossible to compose the *Bhagavad Gita* and at the same time devise foolproof methods for keeping track of locomotives. The same men who discovered the law of karma could not be expected to discover how the atom can be split, or *vice versa*. The backwardness of any people is merely the field of activity in which it has not specialized. The strength of one cul-

tural group is always the weakness of another. No single man, community, or culture can realize all the human capabilities or formulate all the possible human values.

The possibilities of man are so limitless that there is probably no culture which does not surpass all others in some useful field, just as the needs of man are so complex and so great that there is probably no human culture so well-rounded that it does not suffer from some grave disequilibrium. Man has never discovered the full measure of his capabilities because there has never yet been created a machinery which fills the deficiencies of every human society with the abundances of every other society, which corrects the backwardnesses of every group with the sum of all human progress. Only a world of free, equal, but united societies, free from cultural as well as political domination, from intellectual as well as economic or military barriers, can create such machinery, and until it is created we shall all remain tied to backwardness, all tend to lose locomotives or planets when we get careless, to intoxicate ourselves with too much or too little progress.

V

The Problem of Personality

THOUGH it is not strictly a problem of attitude — except in its
implications for individual morale — the problem of personality
seems to me one of the deepest connected with one world, and I
cannot see how one can have a rational faith in the attainability
of this ideal without having faced and somehow answered it.
Until I went to the East, I had never faced the problem. In fact,
I did not realize that it existed. One world, it seemed to me, was
a matter of opinion. When enough men believed in it we would
have it.

My travels in the East — chiefly because they opened my eyes
to the distortions and deficiencies in Western character — convinced me that the slow progress which we are making toward the
creation of a unified world is due to attitudes and beliefs so deeply
rooted, so strong, so habitual that they must be considered as
essential ingredients of the modern Western personality. It is not
merely a question of specific delusions, fallacies, myths, and
blanks in understanding. It is not enough to expose the suicidal
significance of the doctrine of absolute sovereignty and the de-
monstrable consequences of our fogginess about the social context
of science. We say:

'Absolute sovereignty? What an absurd, sinister delusion.
How backward of our ancestors to have believed in it. World
government is clearly the thing — of course we must have
weighted representation, to keep it from being dominated by the

backward peoples, and we can't have any iron curtains impeding the free circulation of patented laxatives, birth-control propaganda, or the *Wall Street Journal*. (Or, of course, we must have the dictatorship of the proletariat, to keep the capitalists from disuniting us again, and world government by the Communist Party while the state is gradually withering away.)

'Social context of science? An absolute must. We must harness atomic energy to the peaceful service of humanity without delay. Then our scientists will be free to continue exploring the great secrets of the universe. Who knows? Perhaps in a few years they will find some way of harnessing the energy in cosmic rays so that we can melt the polar icecaps by pushing a button or disintegrate Mars by pulling down a lever. Just think — perhaps in our grandchildren's time we may be able to grow oranges in Greenland, assuring a quart of juice a day for everyone, and send space-ships throughout the solar system, looking for backward peoples we can civilize.'

Delusion and aggression seem to be hydra-headed monsters in all the Western cultures, and the holes of relevance in the social flooring of our ideal of progress apparently give into a bottomless pit. Our vices seem almost inseparable from our virtues, and our anticulture is intimately interwoven with our true culture.

All this is grave enough, but it is not hopeless. We are not totally deficient in the sense of reality, and the reality-pressures forcing us toward one world are so enormous, so inexorable, that we would have to be a great deal worse than we are to resist them indefinitely. Furthermore, I believe that the present division of power in the world favors the diffusion of Eastern influence through the mind of the West by the processes of cultural opposition I have already described, and since the Eastern virtues and faults are nearly the opposites of our own, this should lead, in time, to a reorientation of our personalities. When the political unity of the world is achieved, character-modification by cultural interaction and reaction will be greatly accelerated, and the mere fact of participating in a united world will automatically revolutionize many of our viewpoints.

It is in relation to the time-factor that the problem of Western personality seems to me most significant. There is almost certainly some deadline on the realization of effective world government. There is some point at which the present trend toward a new global war will become irreversible, owing to the operations of the law of political karma, and it seems uncertain — if not unlikely — that organized human society on earth could survive such a war. Hence political unity must be achieved before the point is reached at which the chain-reaction of fear, hate, and delusion leading to war begins. That may give us only a few months or five years or fifty — I doubt that we have much longer. It depends upon whether, in our political relations, we are generally moving toward peace or toward war, toward unity or greater disunity. If there is steady progress toward peace and unity, the rate of progress will not be so crucially important. It seems unlikely, however, that we can count upon any steady progress. Our hopes for one world — or any world at all — seem to rest upon a tremendous release of idealistic energy, realistically and intelligently directed, upon a sudden blazing of enlightenment, a surge of leadership, almost without precedent in our societies, a moral lifting of ourselves by our own bootstraps. In its immediate context the problem of one world seems one of conversion — in the religious sense — and we have to convert, almost simultaneously, ourselves, our nearest neighbors, and our most stubborn foes.

This is not a small task, and in face of it, the inadequacies of Western personality show up most glaringly. We are not lacking in force, but moral force is not our forte. We possess qualities of leadership, but they always shine most brightly on the battlefield. We have some passionate idealisms but they are always our most sanguinary ones. We have a strong sense of purpose but our purpose has never before implied unity with the enemy. If one world could be won by arms against some enemy of man, if society could be saved by defending human civilization against an insurrection of the apes or by repelling an invasion from Mars, then we would today be very close to our goal. We have defended civilization before, and victoriously fought the enemies of man — but the enemies of man, in the past, have always meant some group of men to us, and civilization has meant the civilization of one human tribe or of a collection of tribes. One world cannot be realized by an offensive or even a defensive crusade of arms. Organized opposition to the doctrine of one world might be vanquished — if it were localized in one nation — by military victory, but there would be too few survivors left to celebrate it. As *Hamlet* and many subsequent works of literature prove, this type of problem, involving the reconciliation of contradictory ideals, is not one which brings out the strongest elements in our character.

No movement progresses without propaganda and it is hard to make stirring propaganda for one world — or for anything — if we do not realize precisely what we are propagandizing for, and if our addiction to materialistic understatement inhibits us from raising our voices. If we use mixed and inadequate metaphor, we elicit incoherent and feeble response.

If we do not try to clear our own minds of delusion we cannot expect to dispel the delusions of others.

If we want wide success we must appeal to the mass, and the mass includes Asia, which cannot be appealed to unless we abandon cultural imperialism.

There is also a little matter of aiming. We must not forget to convert representatives of governments on the assumption that because they are official they are not human, nor must we give up trying to reach peoples because we imagine their governments pay no attention to their wishes.

Our failure to remember these things helps to explain the feeble influence, the low power of emotional penetration which idealism in the modern West, especially the idealism of one world, seems to have. It does not explain it entirely. There is some deeper factor — some deficiency in our characters, or at least some blind spot in our cultural view of the world.

Again it was Asia which revealed this deficiency to me, though the same evidence can be found in the West. The revelation came on the eve of my departure home as I was awaiting transportation

in Calcutta. Gandhi, during a tour of the eastern provinces, had
stopped in Calcutta and established a temporary *ashram* — religious and cultural center — on the outskirts of the city. According to his custom he led evening prayers in public every day
and the attendance at these meetings, together with the extraordinary demonstrations of mass adoration which had greeted
him wherever he stopped, proved that though he had retired as
an active political leader he was still the most popular, the most
revered, and the most influential man in India, if not in all Indian
history.

It was my first and my last chance to see the non-violent,
vegetarian, chastity-practicing George Washington of India, and
I took advantage of it. I felt somewhat self-conscious, squatting
outdoors in the dust in my blue uniform, the symbol of Western
violence which the newly acquired braid on my cap seemed
somehow to aggravate, but no one in the large native crowd paid
the slightest bit of attention to me. Judging by the variety of
dress, every social group, every caste, every faith, every opinion
in India was somewhere represented in the crowd. The slanting
winter sun, the long shadows, the warm still air on which the
evening smells floated, made it a pleasant spot, and there was
a pleasant, peaceful and relaxed atmosphere about the gathering
— no fanaticism, not even an air of hushed reverence. When the
familiar, bent, spectacled figure in the loincloth, with a white
homespun shawl thrown over his shoulder, appeared, surrounded
by his close disciples, there was no demonstration of any kind.
Gandhi mounted a sort of dais decked with flowers, sat cross-
legged on a cushion, and began silent meditation, while one of his
disciples led the crowd in the singing of pleasantly monotonous
hymns, not unlike Christian ones, which were accompanied by the
slow rhythmic clapping of palms raised above the head.

After about half an hour of this, the hymns stopped, Gandhi
looked up from his meditation, a microphone was placed in front
of him and he began to speak. He spoke softly, casually, intimately, like a grandfather speaking to his children, in an earnest,
reasonable voice, marvelously controlled, full of self-discipline

and inner harmony. The text of his sermon, which I read next day in the Indian press, was typically Gandhian. It was neither wholly religious nor purely political. It was the application of a religious point of view to a political problem and the use of attitude toward a political situation as a religious exercise.

The political content of his sermon referred to some riots and outrages in eastern Bengal which were greatly agitating opinion in Calcutta at the time, though nobody seemed quite certain whether they had resulted from intercommunal or from British-Indian friction. The Mahatma did not enlighten his listeners on this point or discuss the political implications of the situation. He simply told them how he thought they as believers in non-violence and workers for national freedom should react to the reports about the riots: Namely, that they should retain their serenity, not allow themselves to get excited by rumors nor excite others by spreading them. Then he launched into a more general homily on the philosophy of nonviolence, explaining, as he has explained thousands of times, that it applies to mental as well as to physical violence, that it means avoiding hate and uncharitable thoughts about others, that it was not merely a political technique and an ethical doctrine but a way of life. He then gave other examples of the nonviolent way, linking the theme, as he usually does, with a wide variety of things, with Indian independence, social reform, and even with spinning.

In strict logic, Gandhi, on the occasion that I listened to him — without knowing exactly what he was saying — was apparently misusing the term 'nonviolence' abominably. There is no logical reason why a belief in the harmfulness of violence should automatically be reflected in one's attitudes toward such subjects as spinning and social reform, but Gandhi went out of his way to tie them together. He used the symbol *satyagraha*, among others, to do this. Satyagraha is an untranslatable term. It stood for the organized use of nonviolence ·in passive resistance to gain not only freedom but regeneration for India, and passive resistance, as understood by Gandhi, was not just passively resisting the civil authority but generating soul-force for the accomplishment of collective ends. It all seems very confused when put down on paper but it has proved extremely effective in Indian history. A poor semanticist, Gandhi was a great manipulator of the human psyche.

The secret of Gandhi's technique of influence, if not of his doctrine, seemed to me a little clearer after I had actually seen him practicing it at his prayer meeting. Not being able to understand his words was probably a help because the meaning of the nonverbal symbols was more apparent to me.

Gandhi was not merely trying to convert others to his opinions, in the normal Western way. He was obsessed with the notion of soul-force and tried both to use it himself to win over others to his beliefs and to generate it in them so that they could convert and activate still others. He had always preached that in the end this soul-force would take effect even upon his British enemies, and certainly now nobody is going to be able to prove that he was wrong.

The Gandhian concept of soul-force is a mystic one and seems to me basically unscientific. Yet the techniques based upon it proved as effective as any techniques of mass influence that have been developed in our day. They not only won converts to a political cause, they not only generated enthusiasm and lasting morale, they not only produced zealous workers and volunteers for martyrdom, but they developed followers into dynamic leaders capable of attracting new followers — and they totally refashioned the personalities of millions of Indians. This is no slight result and the man who achieved it, the man who perfected these techniques, was surely more than an exhibit in the sideshow of history.

It seems to me that without being able to describe in scientific terms what he was doing, Gandhi operated in a most scientific manner. His leadership was aimed at refashioning the personalities of those upon whom it was exercised by modifying their central attitudes. It was not enough that they believe in Indian independence. The attainment of Indian independence had to become their dominant interest in life and all their lesser interests and attitudes had to be rearranged to conform to the psychic pattern of one who lives for Indian freedom. It was not enough for them to feel that violence is evil. Their whole mental field had to be colored by this intense central feeling about violence. They not merely had to support social reform but be dedicated to it as they were to independence. They had to breathe with a social reformer's lungs, see with a social reformer's eyes, eat a social reformer's food.

How did Gandhi succeed in imposing this pattern on the minds of Indians? First of all, by becoming Gandhi, by adopting these central attitudes himself. The Gandhi that the world knows today is not the uxorious schoolboy husband who was once obsessed with his adolescent bride's body, the timid, awkward student in London, the sensitive, bewildered young lawyer in South Africa wrestling with the problem of religious belief. The ultimate Gandhi was the result of years of rigorous concentration on a few simple, emotionally significant ideas, of strict self-discipline and intensive self-training.

This produced the Gandhian personality, a combination of inner peace, arising from a more total integration of all the elements in the personality than most men achieve, with a tremendous, controlled release of energy. One could not talk to Gandhi or listen to him or even see him from a distance without becoming aware both of the peace that was in him and of the energy he radiated. They expressed themselves as well — though necessarily less forcibly — in his literary style and even in the structure of his thought. Because he was a poor semanticist and in many ways a confused thinker, they expressed themselves best in certain nonverbal symbols, chiefly in exemplary acts that were like propaganda and sermons in action.

More than any other great leader of modern times, Gandhi followed the sound rule of military leadership, that the best way to get men to do anything is to show them by doing it yourself, to make them follow by leading. At the first All-India Congress meeting that he attended as a young man he was appalled by the filthy condition of the latrines and suggested that this detracted from the dignity of the meeting. Everyone agreed with him but said nothing could be done because the Untouchable latrine-cleaners were staging a protest strike. Gandhi, thereupon, cleaned out the latrines himself, an unprecedented violation of caste rules as well as a gesture of religious humility and of leadership by example. He was never able to define his views on Untouchability in words as clearly as he did by this gesture.

All his later life he had been startling, shocking, and ultimately capturing the imaginations of his compatriots by equally extraordinary exemplary acts, of which his symbolic gestures of passive resistance — like panning salt in violation of the excise laws — and his fasts in protest against the treatment of the Untouchable or the violation of his nonviolent teachings by his own followers were the most famous.

Training by action, by deeds, another military principle, was also part of his secret. The convert to Gandhian ideas was immediately put to work developing a Gandhian personality by carrying on Gandhi-like activities. It was not enough for him to hold the right views and even to labor in the party cause. He had to spin in his spare moments, because spinning was a personal act of satyagraha, which the individual can perform, while at the same time it helped the anti-British boycott. Direct, personal action, rather than mere participation in the general Congress campaign was one of the keynotes of Gandhi's teachings to his disciples. Help all you can on the big things but do some little thing yourself. Show that you are a real revolutionary not just by risking your life and going to jail, but by giving up tobacco, especially British tobacco, and alcohol. Learn Hindustani, your national tongue. Sit down to table with an Untouchable. Above all, spin, spin, until your hands become as nationalist as your heart or your mind.

This was the discipline, supported by propaganda, by personal example, by encouragement and scolding, which the active Congress member was expected to follow. It was this discipline, and not the teacher's precepts alone, which refashioned his personality in a Gandhian pattern, which produced in him something of the inner peace, accompanied by release of normally pent-up energy, that turned him into a minor Gandhi himself, capable of influencing others, of winning new converts, as the Mahatma did. This is the manner in which the Gandhian soul-force operated. It is the manner in which soul-force has operated throughout the ages.

Like most great leaders, Gandhi probably owed much of his success to historical accident, to being forced into greatness by having great handicaps to overcome. He had to develop the technique of nonviolent noncooperation which proved so brilliantly successful in its Indian context, because it was the only form of revolt that he could have persuaded a demoralized, unarmed people to adopt — as it was perhaps the only kind of attack to which British rule was vulnerable. He had to strike at the weak point of his enemies — their consciences and their pocketbooks — and minimize the weaknesses of his followers — their dread of violence, their unworldliness, their technological backwardness. He had to specialize in soul-force because it was the only kind of force that India possessed.

Likewise he had to use the methods of deep and slow-building influence because they were the only ones that could reach the Indian masses. He could not buy time on the Indian radio, like a maker of soapflakes, because the British would not have sold him the time, and not enough Indians had radios to make it worthwhile. It was no use persuading the leading hostesses of India to tell the nation that they put national independence on their faces every night before going to bed, thus making their dreams lovely to the touch, because the Indian peasant would never have heard about it. It was no use asking Indian movie stars to endorse nonviolence, as American ones endorse shaving-lotions, breakfast foods, and the democratic way of life, because the message would not have carried. Thus the Indian public was spared the fate which has overtaken the American public — that of having most of the right ideals, but having them in the same mental frame of reference as the right shaving lotions and the right breakfast foods.

From Gandhi's point of view it was no use persuading the political, professional, or intellectual leaders of Indian society to let their names be used on the letterheads of committees favoring independence, as the names — without the personalities — of our leaders appear on the rosters of committees favoring world government or other worthy causes. The names of these people meant very little to the Indian countryside — as the names of our leaders probably mean little to the American countryside — but it did mean something to the Indian peasant when he heard that a government official, who was a great sahib in New Delhi, almost as great as an Englishman, had given up his appointment to wear homespun cloth and work among the Untouchables, when a lawyer who earned thousands of rupees winning cases for foreign companies went to jail like a bazaar-thief for refusing to pay his taxes, when a great surgeon who opened up all the maharajahs of India and even the white sahibs when they were sick, had his own head split open standing unarmed against a police charge.

In all his campaigns Gandhi seldom used a favorite Western technique of public influence — that of collecting millions of signatures in favor of some public cause. There were not enough Indians who could sign their names to get up an impressive resolution. Millions of Indians were thereby deprived of the satisfaction which going on record against war has afforded millions of worthy men and women in the West — and were saved from feeling as we do, that going on record against war is like going on record against sin, that fighting war is as hopeless as fighting sin.

For all these reasons, some of Gandhi's greatness was undoubtedly the by-product of Indian backwardness. It was his own genius, however, which enabled him to choose so infallibly the significant gesture — the small literal act which has a great symbolic meaning, the one which generates soul-force in the person who makes it at the same time that it contributes to achieving a tangible result. It was his own keen sense of public reality and his shrewd common sense, so queerly allied with his mystic idealism, which enabled him to maintain his followers' morale by always assigning immediately attainable objectives in furtherance of more distant goals, by recommending procedures which were always feasible in the context of the moment. When he knew that few Indians really believed independence was attainable, he contented himself with campaigning for home rule, when he realized that mass-resistance was not feasible, he told his followers to keep on spinning for the cause and wait for the moment when more effective action was possible.*

* Gandhi's moral grandeur and his political realism were both revealed most impressively in the last months of his life. Though the partition of India deeply wounded his nationalist sentiments, he publicly accepted the creation of Pakistan and devoted himself more than ever to promoting reconciliation between Hindus and Moslems. He died a martyr to this cause; he was shot and killed at one of his public prayer meetings in New Delhi in 1948 by a Hindu fanatic. His death was a cruel blow to the young Indian nation he had labored to bring into existence but the shock it inflicted on moderate nationalist opinion, reinforcing his teaching and the example of his life, helped to save India from the paranoid nationalism that partition might otherwise have brought forth.

VI

The Philosophy of Integration

BECAUSE, in writing this book, I have been primarily concerned with the development of my own thought during the two and a half wartime years I spent in the East, I have not as yet been able to give the reader a coherent and comprehensive summary of what that thought is. By selection, by emphasis, by approach, by the inevitable inability to present earlier experience except in terms of later understanding, I have revealed a rather sharply patterned series of attitudes and beliefs, but I have not been able to indicate clearly or completely the interrelationships among them. Since in any mental experience or view of the world it is the wholeness of the experience or view which is most interesting or important, the time has come to try to present the final impact of Asia and military service upon my Western and civilian mind as a wholeness.

I feel very really and deeply that the lessons of my wartime experience in Asia constitute a wholeness in my mind. For me, it is not just a question of feeling that I have learned this or discovered that, or come to see certain things in certain ways. All these learnings and discoveries and seeings are generalized in my consciousness and have systematic interrelationships. They constitute a wholeness.

It is, perhaps, ambitious to call this wholeness a philosophy. I am too untrained as a philosopher even to know whether this description of my wholeness is technically accurate, but it seems to me that in my own life — when I think or behave consistently with its teachings — it fulfills the pragmatic purpose of any philosophy: That of contributing peace of mind and coherence of action to the individual who holds it.

My philosophy does not attempt to embrace the whole field of personal consciousness, or the whole cosmos of experience. Neither does it pretend to be one of eternal and universal validity. It is a philosophy of individual life, since it is developed from the viewpoint of the individual, but one primarily concerned with the individual's role in social history.

Like Marxism, like the implicit philosophy of the Indian revolution, it is a positional and functional one, constructed around the individual as a social unit in time and space, as a participant in a great historic drama. Its basic premise is the banal one — perhaps most eloquently formulated in America by Walter Lippman — that the drama, the value, the meaning, the subjective reality of our personal lives lies in the individual contribution we make to the outcome of the world's drama — whether we contribute, by having lived, to the unification of man or to his disappearance from this planet. Whatever the meaning of individual life may have been in times past, whatever it may be in times to come, in our day it is this. Other things in life may matter to us, but nothing so much as this. We may have other duties besides the duty of founding the society and the commonwealth of man, but this one overrides them all. We may have been shaped for other ends besides the biological one of perpetuating our species, but the goal of preserving it dominates all the rest.

We are all living in a corridor of history, leading from everything that has been on earth to something much greater than the sum of it all, or to something less than the least part of it. Within this corridor no truths of the past or the future can fully apply, for the corridor-lives that we have to lead are unlike any that men have lived before or are likely to live again. The moment is unique, the issue without parallel, the experience without precedent. We must guide our steps and find our way by analogy. We must call probably true whatever seems to indicate to us the exit of construction, probably good whatever impels us toward it, probably significant whatever is connected with the determination of exits. There may be other truths, other virtues, other significances, but for us it is as if there were only these.

I need not have gone to the East to discover this, but in going I discovered why it was so, I learned that all these public imperatives are private compulsions, that all these social meanings are personal awarenesses, that the collective fate of man is important because it is important to me and thee.

Many particular experiences contributed to this general understanding. For instance, watching the old-fashioned psychological drama of the Indian revolution coming to its close was a kind of education by understatement. It awakened me to the meaning of participation in history the way that watching the stage-burglars or the stage-Hessians in an old melodrama awakens one to the modern meanings of crime and war. It was easy to realize how, for an Indian, the drama of national independence must seem like the drama of life itself, how standing aloof from it would seem like standing aloof from life, and working against it like revolting against life. On the circumscribed Indian stage this drama was indeed an intense one, and in its emotional essence it repeated all the great creative crises of history, when public destiny was so transcendent that it engulfed private experience. Meeting the Indians who were taking part in it made me envious of the fulfillment they had found by giving themselves to history.

If it was impossible to live meaningfully and fruitfully in the time of the early Christians without following the cross, if it was impossible to live fruitfully and meaningfully in the Russia of the last Czars without somehow preparing the Russian revolution, if it was impossible to live in Gandhi's India and have one's life mean anything without joining the Congress movement, what are we to say of the present time when the drama of man himself is being played out upon the stage of history? What can any man mean, if man himself means nothing? What works can a man leave behind him if all the works of man perish? Conversely, what greater meaning can a life have than to perpetuate meaning?

It is not a question of social duty, it is a question of healthy instinct. It is a choice between emotional richness and emotional poverty, between breathing or not breathing.

Historical integration is only the highest and most complete form of social integration, it is integration into the societies of the past and the future as well as of the present, and living in the East taught me in a deep and personal way what many Western psychologists and psychiatrists have long maintained: That social integration is the key to personal integration, which in turn is the key to inner peace, to outer effectiveness, to every kind of fruitfulness. To be isolated from one's brothers is to suffer from the sahib-sickness, to lower one's spiritual metabolism, to contract one's emotional horizons, to atrophy one's muscles of achievement, to impoverish one's estate of meaning. To be at war with one's brothers is to be at war with oneself, to disinherit oneself by cutting off one's heirs. To participate most fully in the society of which one is a member is to perfect one's own inner wholeness, to enhance to oneself one's personal meaning, to multiply all one's possibilities.

This, I think, has been true at all times and among all tribes. The greatest personal problem of individual man has always been to integrate himself most effectively into the tribe of which he is a member. The reward for success in solving this problem has always been peace and fulfillment, the penalty for failing has always been neurosis and frustration.

The problem is much greater today than it ever has been before, and so are the rewards and the penalties. In a world where societies are as close as individuals are in many primitive communities, where the actions of any large group of individuals in one nation directly affect the lives of individuals in other nations, the drama of integration is no longer played out exclusively on the tribal stage between the individual and the community. The individual can find peace and fulfillment in tribal participations only if the tribe itself is at peace with other tribes. If he is forced to participate as a warrior in tribal wars, he may be less torn than if he rises against his own tribe, but he cannot be whole.

It is probably impossible to prove this statement, but I think that during the late war many of us verified it by personal experience, as I did, and that we feel it now, during the uneasy peace. There is also an objective reason why it should be so. Tribal war always causes tribal delusions to flourish, and these seemingly tend to stimulate private delusion, which is the greatest enemy of inner peace. Very possibly, as the Buddhists and some Hindus believe, the mere fact of hating an institutional enemy causes one to be intimately diseased.

In times like ours, therefore, the problem of the individual is to achieve personal integration within the framework of a group of societies which are themselves confronted with the problem of integration within the commonwealth of man. The collective solution, one world, is the only conceivable one to the personal as well as to the tribal problem. We cannot achieve total unity within ourselves without effecting the unity of man, we cannot hope for maximum personal fulfillment except by integration into the tribe of man.

The phrase, 'in times like ours,' renders this an understatement. There have never been times like ours before and there are not likely to be again. The immensity of the historic issue, from one point of view, makes the drama of personal integration seem utterly insignificant, but from another point of view, it intensifies it almost beyond the limits of comprehension. In the biological field the decision as between one world and the end of the world means that the individual living and breeding today becomes the ancestor of beings who will seem like gods compared with any men who have lived before, or that he will be the last of his line. In the psychological field it will mean that the generality of mankind will easily attain to what the Eastern mystics considered the highest enlightenment; either that or — assuming that there are any individual survivals from ruins of global atomic war — the survivors will have the mentality of those whom today we consider the most tragic cases in our insane asylums.

Most of us would like to father gods and to attain enlightenment, or have our sons attain it. Most of us would feel depressed to think of ourselves as the last of our line, to die without issue or heirs, and the possibility of surviving as lunatics is not calculated to cheer us. Since these are in fact the alternatives confronting us, it is not an exaggeration to call our situation dramatic. It is no exceptional feat of historic acumen to recognize this personal drama as being one, and it implies no unusual amount of public spirit to feel impelled — even quite desperately and imperiously impelled — to work for the happy ending and to feel that the days of our life and the sum of our acts possess important meaning only in so far as they have contributed toward this goal.

Here it is necessary to introduce a second premise. This, that in working toward the objective goal, one world, we attain it in some degree psychologically, we realize by anticipation its subjective rewards. In striving for the unification of the world we promote unity in our own personalities, even if the world remains disunited despite our efforts. The inner unity can never be total so long as the outer one is not, and there is certainly some relation between the objective validity or importance of our contribution to building one world and the subjective reward we reap from it. The relationship, however, is not a direct one. A very small contribution to world unity may produce a great progress toward personal unity on the part of the individual who makes it. The criterion is probably one of individual potentiality. The soldier in battle who feels most victorious is not necessarily the one whose side is clearly winning — indeed, in modern battle it is difficult for the individual soldier to know whether his side is winning or losing — but the one who knows that he is making the most effective possible contribution to the victory of his side which he as an individual is capable of making. We are close to paradox here: One world can only be realized in the individual mind when it is attained for the world at large, yet when realization of this fact impels the individual to make his maximum contribution to the general attainment, it is almost as if his personal goal were already attained.

To this fairly complex view of the relationships between the individual and one world, a new factor of complexity must be added. Every individual act toward public unity is a private unification, but so is every personal unification an act of public unity, indeed, the very perception of wholeness is an act of wholeness, both public and private. Effort and awareness, thought and emotion, individual and group, are all part of the same chain of happening and being, of the same continuum of action and reaction, transmission and conversion of influence. Though the study of Eastern philosophies and mysticisms awakened me to this view of the social world, it is one which can be validated by objective reasoning and is corroborated if not confirmed by much objective data.

It hardly requires much demonstration to show that in the modern world group-morale and group-delusion affect the psyches of the individuals composing the group. The converse is equally true, as everyone who has been in military service or participated in political campaigns knows. In any small military unit a soldier whose morale is high for purely private reasons contributes to the good military morale of the whole unit. One whose morale is low depresses the morale of his platoon and thereby that of his company. A mind free from delusion has a quieting and liberating effect upon all minds that are exposed to its influence, while the deluded mind engenders or aggravates delusion in others. The relationship between private and group delusion is complicated and somewhat obscure, but it undeniably exists as a reciprocal one. Therefore, any victory over delusion in a single mind is a blow struck at the accumulation of group delusions which is the main cause of the world's disunity; any thought, action, or feeling which raises the morale of those who are striving to attain one world is a step toward its attainment.

The distinction between active and passive, as well as between public and private, tends to dissolve if we look at the world in this way, as do the distinctions between moral and material, conscience and interest, subordination and responsibility. Not only are all our experiences, even our dreams at night, public experiences but they are also political acts. During the war we were all war-heroes and war-criminals because we created heroism by applauding it and inspired crime by hating the enemy. Today, in what we have to call peace because it is not yet war, we are all of us, consciously or unconsciously, waking or sleeping, building the unity of man or plotting the end of the world. Almost inevitably, most of us are doing both these things at once and we are not even sure to which scale we are adding the heaviest personal contribution. Obviously there are hierarchies of influence and effect, as there are degrees of leadership and responsibility and scales of directness, but there are no bulkheads of category.

The complexity of this approach to the problem of man, necessitating as it does a constant switching of viewpoint from objective to subjective and back again, from the projecting of influence to the realization of influence, from the historical to the personal, is sometimes bewildering, but I can see no escape from it without distortion of perspective. Whatever has been true of individual man before, in the corridor of history through which we are now passing no view of personal life can be sound which does not reflect the complexity of personal relationships to society and history, which does not simultaneously elucidate the meaning of the current situation for the individual and the meaning of the individual as a factor in the situation. Not only are we as individuals both historical products and historical factors, actors and spectators, architects and clients, subject and predicate, warriors and battlefield, but we are to some degree aware of these polarities of role. We are not merely static grains in a fixed continent of man, but marching soldiers in a marching army of man, and we know it.

If this symbolic army were a true one, commanded by some cosmic Captain, ordered and bound together by divine regulations, maneuvering in accordance with plans drawn up by some celestial general staff, then our problem would be simple: Merely that of being good soldiers, and fighting the good fight. Being good soldiers, fighting the good fight, is, in fact, part of our problem, but it is not the whole problem or even the greatest part of it. Few persons in the modern West, even among religious believers, think that the principles of the Salvation Army can solve all of the complex political, social, economic, cultural and other problems involved in realizing one world. Yet, for our own personal salvations, we must have one world, or at least contribute to having it, and it is not enough for our effort to be earnest and our contributions to be sincere — they must also be at least slightly efficacious, in our own estimation, and even in reality, for the problem is an objective as well as a subjective one.

Thus, in our own realization as well as in reality, the army of man is a loose guerilla band of volunteers, and each of us must be his own staff and his own infantry. Furthermore, the enemy is not only among us, he is within each of us, therefore he must be combated by personal counterespionage and propaganda. For these reasons we must apply the staff-approach as well as the line-approach to the problems of personal life in relation to one world. The individual mind must look upon the total self — as well as upon other men it seeks to influence — as combat effectives, for whose training, equipment, morale, and employment in accordance with sound strategic and tactical doctrines it is responsible.

This may seem a most curious metaphor, for though the symbol of the individual militant in a cause as a soldier is common in Western religious and philosophical thought, the element of generalship is usually omitted as irrelevant to personal life. It is, however, intensely pertinent in our day, at least to all those who possess the slightest glimmering of political consciousness and the least sense of responsibility for promoting the welfare of man. By the very nature of the problem confronting us, a new duty is laid upon us, that of being effective in action, and our ethical code must include principles of strategy and tactics. Even though we be already enrolled in some disciplined social formation, and content to leave the major decisions of our lives to some earthly or unearthly captain, there is no party line and no golden rule which can direct toward the proper goal every one of the thousands of acts of influence we accomplish in a single day, consequently there is always some level at which we cannot evade the responsibility of generalship over ourselves.

This doctrine, which I owe to the curiously diverse experiences of my wartime service in Asia — my military indoctrination, my exposure to the mystic collectivisms of the East, my study of Gandhi as a revolutionary leader, all reacting upon a mind shaped by the basic Christian activism of our culture — cannot lead to detailed rules for sound decision in all circumstances, and we cannot hope to avoid being sometimes mistaken or ineffectual. Much of the time we cannot even tell whether our decisions — in terms of the one world objective — are sound or not. We can, however, follow certain principles without which, or against which, no sound decisions are ever likely to be reached or effective acts committed.

We must have sound intelligence of the enemy situation and of our own. This means that it is our duty to keep ourselves informed of what is happening in the world, and to reflect upon the information available to us with a sober, objective, even skeptical mind.

We must keep up our own morale — and the morale of others. It is in regard to this vital problem of morale, the condition of all effective effort, that the East taught me the most lessons, I think. Negatively, it revealed to me some of the pathology of social disunity, the mechanisms of cultural heresy, of social regression, of accumulating delusion creating irreversible but self-consuming karma, the inherent but correctible personality-deficiencies of both East and West, all of which concepts developed in my mind the general conviction that the world's maladies seem incurable to us only because we fail to apply the right remedies.

Positively, the East, especially my attempts to understand its cultural values, broke down the language barriers and threw bridges between the thought-gaps in mind which had previously divided it into wholly separate compartments labeled Science, Politics, Religion, Social Ideals, Private Emotions. In the plane flying into Siam, this process of intellectual unification was carried even further. The compartments labeled Past, Present, and Future, merged into one, as did the ones labeled Self, and Others and finally the ones labeled Life and Matter. Upon this merger of Western physics and Hindu monism was grafted in my mind the unverifiable but not unreasonable concept that influence is transformed but never lost, and the mystic conviction — derived perhaps from the *credo quia absurdum* of my Catholic background — that precisely because of this there is an imperative mission to preserve, by transmitting, the influences of our human world until they are ripened for whatever unimaginable cosmic conversions may take place in the fullness of planetary time. Thus, there were released in my mind mechanisms of reciprocal enrichment between categories of experience which are normally isolated sovereignties, and I have found my morale greatly fortified thereby.

This personal metaphysic is a demountable one, which can be replaced in a given mind by whatever serves better to promote the sense of unity and mission, and I have listed it merely as a factor of morale because this seems to me the correct perspective to apply to any broader view of the world in attempting to fit it into the corridor-philosophy which must be ours at this moment in time. Whatever helps us to be effective artisans of one world is good, whatever hinders us is bad. I can see, however, no real problem of reconciliation between the one world ideal and such religious ideals as Catholicism, Protestantism, or Hinduism, or between it and such secular ideals or goals as nonviolence, national security, patriotism, socialism, democracy, and science. Neither church nor country nor social co-operation nor freedom nor science can survive if man perishes, all suffer by his divisions, all will be strengthened by his unity. Neither God nor science nor man can be served by blasphemy.

Though there is no conflict between one world and the other ideals in which we believe, there is a problem of emphasis and perspective, and the determination of it is the strategic basis of our problem of personal generalship. Emphasis is the core of strategy and if we do not in all circumstances emphasize the goal of promoting unity above any other goal our effort will never be most effective. It must be a matter of individual appreciation at a given moment to determine what is likely to promote or retard

the cause of human unity, but we can be sure that we shall fail to
determine correctly if we are thinking primarily of something else.
Even peace is not an infallible guide to unity — though it is more
reliable than most. Too much emphasis on peace can lead in certain circumstances to war, whereas in different ones, peace at any
price may be the only alternative to the end of the world. What
is true of peace is true of violence. I believe there are contexts
where a small violence may avert a great one. The same depend-
ency on context applies to the principles of democracy. To uphold them in one context, even if one arouses fierce resentments,
sometimes promotes pacification and unity in the end. To insist
on them in other circumstances may be mere counterfascism,
leading to war. One never knows, but if one thinks unity day and
night, one is less likely to go wrong than otherwise for unity is
the key to man's survival.

Besides the primacy of the goal, human survival, over all others
there is another basic principle of one-world strategy which I
think should be reflected in our personal generalship. This is to
see the problem of building one world as one of conversion in the
religious sense — conversion of hearts and minds, transformations
of personality. To be completely effective, this moral conversion
of individuals must be reflected in workable international political
institutions, but the institutions themselves will only be workable
in so far as they reflect the changed personalities of the individuals who support them, and it is not likely that they will even be
adopted unless the change has already taken place on a large
scale. To devise practical, feasible plans for world government —
a useful activity which has become highly developed in the United
States in recent years, thanks largely to the pioneering efforts of
Clarence Streit — and to try to arouse public opinion to adopt
them, is an effective method of preparing minds for conversion,
but it does not convert. To transform believers in the principle
of world government into followers of the cause of man, it is necessary that this cause become for them something by which they
live, something for which they are willing to die. When large
numbers of them acquire this feeling, then the cause advances,

by the processes of conversion, through the operation of what the army called leadership and Gandhi called soul-force.

Once the principle of conversion is understood and accepted, the problem of individual tactics in working for one world is simplified. The tactics of direct conversion will always be effective, and sometimes the most effective. There always remains for all of us the hazard of self-defeating tactics, arising principally from our tendency to fall into delusion and from the fixed delusions which our culture breeds into us. I think for this reason that to understand and value the mechanisms of cultural opposition — not only those operating between West and East but those operating between all nations that have cultural contacts — is important, for these mechanisms, if we allow them, will expose to us our own delusions, fallacies, and inadequacies, thus making it possible for us to overcome them.

The tactical problem which dominates all others, is the problem of delusion while combating delusion, and it seems to me that the intense awareness of it which my peculiar wartime experience and my exposure to Buddhism developed in me, is the indispensable condition of any effective action, as well as being itself effective action, for here again — as at many other points in this doctrine of integration — conclusion leads back to premise, negative merges with positive, the subjective with the objective, the line point of view with the staff point of view. By freeing ourselves from delusion we acquire personal peace and growth, which fortifies our morale, sharpens our strategic faculties, and augments our powers of conversion, thereby making us more effective warriors for peace.

The same spiral of enhancement sets in when we consciously try to develop our potential for influence by influencing, by practicing conversion through converting ourselves, and fortifying our own conversion by projecting it upon others. The faculties of influence and leadership, like all others, develop by use. The difficult is achieved, making the impossible of yesterday the feasible of tomorrow, and darkness overcome lights the flame of hope within us, pushing back the darknesses that remain, until they, too, become light, enlightening the world.

RICHER BY ASIA

Second Edition, Revised

EDMOND TAYLOR

The truth which Edmond Taylor tells in his classic study, *Richer by Asia,* is not a new truth. It is the core of the religious and philosophical thought of mankind throughout history. It is the simple fact that in the hearts and minds of men lies the solution of the world's disease, and not in pacts and armaments. *Richer by Asia* was first published in 1947. This new edition has been extensively revised and brought up to date.

As many of us are coming to see each day, our future depends on building a bridge between East and West. The first step, Mr. Taylor points out, is a recognition of the fact that the Asiatic is a man, even as we are men; that in an understanding of the ways of thought, in an appreciation of the principles which govern his life, lies the only hope of avoiding a final World War or of preparing men for a true World Government.

While stationed in India for the Office of Strategic Services during World War II, Mr. Taylor studied the people with whom he lived and worked — both Asiatics and Europeans — not as a representative of a ruling race, afflicted with "the disease of being a Sahib," but as an intelligent man, trained in the methods of psychological warfare, whose mission is the understanding of his fellow man. Those who waged psychological warfare had to look beneath the sur-

continued on back flap